FROM GROUP DYNAMICS TO GROUP PSYCHOANALYSIS

THE SERIES IN CLINICAL AND COMMUNITY PSYCHOLOGY

CONSULTING EDITORS:

CHARLES D. SPIELBERGER and IRWIN G. SARASON

Averill	• Patterns of Psychological Thought: Readings in Historical and Contemporary Texts
Becker	• Depression: Theory and Research
Brehm	• The Application of Social Psychology to Clinical Practice
Endler and Magnusson	• Interactional Psychology and Personality
Friedman and Katz	• The Psychology of Depression: Contemporary Theory and Research
Kissen	• From Group Dynamics to Group Psychoanalysis: Therapeutic Applications of Group Dynamic Understanding
Klopfer and Reed	• Problems in Psychotherapy: An Eclectic Approach
Reitan and Davison	• Clinical Neuropsychology: Current Status and Applications
Spielberger and Sarason	• Stress and Anxiety, volume 1
Sarason and Spielberger	• Stress and Anxiety, volume 2
Sarason and Spielberger	• Stress and Anxiety, volume 3
Ulmer	• On the Development of a Token Economy Mental Hospital Treatment Program

IN PREPARATION

Bermant, Kelman, and Warwick	• The Ethics of Social Intervention
Cattell and Dreger	• Handbook of Modern Personality Theory
Cohen and Mirsky	• Biology and Psychopathology
Iscoe, Bloom, and Spielberger	• Community Psychology in Transition
Janisse	• A Psychological Survey of Pupillometry
London	• Strategies of Personality Research
Manschreck and Kleinman	• Feet of Clay: Quests and Inquiries in Critical Rationality in the Fields of Psychiatry
Olweus	• Aggression in the Schools
Spielberger and Diaz-Guerrero	• Cross-Cultural Anxiety
Spielberger and Sarason	• Stress and Anxiety, volume 4

FROM GROUP DYNAMICS TO GROUP PSYCHOANALYSIS

Therapeutic Applications of Group Dynamic Understanding

EDITED BY

MORTON KISSEN
Institute of Advanced Psychological Studies
Adelphi University

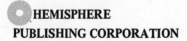**HEMISPHERE**
PUBLISHING CORPORATION

Washington   London

A HALSTED PRESS BOOK

JOHN WILEY & SONS

New York   London   Sydney   Toronto

Hemisphere Publishing Corporation
1025 Vermont Ave., N.W., Washington, D.C. 20005

Distributed solely by Halsted Press, a Division of John Wiley & Sons, Inc., New York.

1 2 3 4 5 6 7 8 9 0 D O D O 7 8 4 3 2 1 0 9 8 7 6

Library of Congress Cataloging in Publication Data

Main entry under title:

From group dynamics to group psychoanalysis.

(The Series in clinical and community psychology)
Bibliography: p.
Includes indexes.
1. Group psychoanalysis.   2. Small groups.
I. Kissen, Morton. [DNLM: 1. Group processes.
2. Psychoanalysis. 3. Psychotherapy, Group. WM430
F931]
RC510.F76   616.8'915   76-14844
ISBN 0-470-15132-3

Printed in the United States of America

To MARSHA, JENNIFER, and DEBRA
three important women in my life

Contents

III PHASES OF GROUP DEVELOPMENT

IV FREUDIAN CONCEPTS RELATED TO GROUP DYNAMICS

V GROUP PSYCHOTHERAPY AND PSYCHOANALYSIS

VI SPECIAL DYNAMICS OF THERAPY GROUPS

VII CONCLUSION AND INTEGRATION

Preface

In attempting to assemble conceptual and clinical reading material for a graduate course entitled *Group Process,* I became aware of a major gap in the literature. Although a plentiful supply of books devoted to the social psychological issue of group dynamics[1] and an equally plentiful supply devoted to group psychotherapy[2] were available, no single text could be found containing integrated group dynamics source materials relevant to the psychoanalytic group treatment modality.

A good group dynamics course offers the best opportunity for a therapeutically useful conceptual integration of associative connections between group dynamic processes and the group psychoanalytic approach to the treatment of various emotional disturbances. After a rather careful, comprehensive, and rigorous review of the literature, a number of exemplary articles were selected for incorporation in a doctoral-level course at the Institute of Advanced Psychological Studies, Adelphi University. The final series of articles was adapted from a reading list successfully used previously in a group dynamics course taught in the Brooklyn College graduate psychology program.

Although the readings chosen come from disparate sources, they were selected predominantly from articles published in the *International Journal of Group Psychotherapy.* A lesser number were obtained from *Group Process* and the *British Journal of Medical Psychology.* A very few were selected from other journal sources and unpublished manuscripts.

---

[1] (*a*) Bonner, H. *Group dynamics.* New York: Ronald Press, 1959. (*b*) Cartwright, D., & Zander, A. (Eds.). *Group dynamics: Research and theory* (3rd ed.). New York: Harper & Row, 1968.
[2] (*a*) Foulkes, S. H., & Anthony, E. J. *Group psychotherapy.* London: Penguin, 1954. (*b*) Wolf, A., & Schwartz, E. K. *Psychoanalysis in groups.* New York: Grune & Stratton, 1962. (*c*) Yalom, I. D. *Theory and practice of group psychotherapy.* New York: Basic Books, 1970.

The organizational scheme connecting the articles internally is based on their essential relationship to the development of a group psychoanalytic model of psychotherapy. Thus, the initial focus of attention is on the concept of group dynamics viewed from both a social psychological and a psychotherapeutic perspective. Carefully chosen articles from the t-group literature are explored next in terms of the concrete clinical examples they offer of dynamic processes occurring in "unstructured" but nontherapeutic groups and in terms of their attempts to conceptually integrate the clinically discernible dynamic phenomena observed in countless groups.

A series of articles exploring the typical thematic and conflictual concerns naturally occurring in the specific "developmental" phases of nontherapeutic t-groups are next. The fact that t-groups go through relatively discrete stages of development has had important ramifications for the methodology of group psychotherapy. Essentially, it has pointed up the need for group therapists to take into account group dynamics phenomena during treatment interventions. More specifically, an awareness of the fact that groups "develop" has led therapists to attempt to make their interpretations mesh with the particular thematic preoccupation of the groups they are leading. Thus, a group intensely conflicted over feelings of dependency must be dealt with differently from a group struggling with the conflict between the gradually increasing sense of cohesiveness among the members and their need to protect and maintain a sense of self and ego boundaries via frantic individuation strivings. Although therapists continue to be sensitive to *vertical* processes of individual dynamics, they have now the task of scanning the *horizontal* sphere of group interaction—searching for the group-as-a-whole dynamics implicit in the particular developmental phase present in their groups.

Perhaps no theorist has been able to conceptualize the complex but definitely discernible developmental processes inherent in groups better than Bion. His elucidation of the *dependency, pairing, fight–flight,* and *work* aspects of group phenomena has radically changed the understanding of what happens in therapy groups.[3] The shift from an almost totally individual-within-the-group (vertical) treatment orientation[4] to one combining this vertical treatment with a sensitivity to group-as-a-whole processes (vertical-horizontal) has in many ways resulted from Bion's pioneering conceptual investigations. His impact on the group psychotherapy field is similar to Freud's importance in the field of individual psychotherapy; hence, it is fitting that an article comprehensively summarizing Bion's theories be included in this volume.

Freudian theory, too, has had a tremendous impact on the understanding

---

[3] Bion, W. R. *Experiences in groups.* New York: Basic Books, 1959.
[4] Wolf, A., & Schwartz, E. K. *Psychoanalysis in groups.* New York: Grune & Stratton, 1962.

of dynamic processes in both nontherapeutic and therapeutic groups, and a series of articles relating to select aspects of Freud's theory has been included. The metapsychological aspects of concepts such as regression, identification, and the "Pleasure and Reality Principles"—all of which have both group dynamic and ego psychological significance—were particularly chosen for analysis and study. The ego psychological ramifications of these concepts, largely neglected by the Bion theoretical model, are essential to this study. Ultimately, a more systematic group metapsychology will probably be derived from a synthesis of the group dynamic concepts of Bion and the more ego psychological theoretical notions of Freud.

Finally, and perhaps most importantly, a selection of articles is included on clinical and theoretical issues involved in the utilization of group psychoanalysis as a treatment technique. Since the essential focus of the book is on the significance and importance of various group-as-a-whole and subgroup phenomena discernible in therapeutic and nontherapeutic groups, it is natural that the book culminate in an exploration of essential aspects of the psychoanalytic group therapy model. This treatment paradigm follows directly and logically from the basic assumptions implicit in the group dynamics literature and relies heavily on the discovery and interpretation of dynamic processes inherent in the total gestalt configuration of an interacting group of individuals. Concepts such as "common group tension," "group-specific factors," "group resistance," and the "therapeutic contract," important in the group psychoanalytic movement, can ultimately be derived from the earlier clinical and theoretical findings of the psychoanalytically oriented group dynamicists. Indeed, the group processes inherent in both t-groups and group psychoanalytic groups have contributed to the discovery of a number of special group dynamics that can be both replicated in subsequent groups and utilized, once observed and understood, to maximize the therapeutic gain derivable from any form of unstructured group experience.

The therapeutic potential of group dynamic experiences (in which the leader's interventions are largely delivered as group-as-a-whole interpretations) is quite evident. Therapeutic experiences occur both in psychoanalytic groups whose goals are manifestly therapeutic and in unstructured t-groups and group workshops whose goals are—at least outwardly—educational. The group workshops conducted during the annual meeting of the American Group Psychotherapy Association[5] are alluded to several times in this volume because they reflect the frequently powerful therapeutic impact of the group dynamic experience, even when it occurs within the context of a learning laboratory for highly sophisticated group professionals.

---

[5] The American Group Psychotherapy Association, 1865 Broadway, New York, N.Y. 10023, conducts a large number of intensive group laboratories during its annual institute and conference. Members attending these meetings are generally well-trained group psychotherapists from the disciplines of social work, clinical psychology, and psychiatry.

   The carefully selected articles in this volume fall along a continuum stemming from nontherapeutic t-groups at the one end to psychoanalytic psychotherapy groups at the other. The common denominator unifying all these articles is their relevance for a sophisticated and clinically useful integration of group dynamic processes within the essential framework of a group psychoanalytic model of psychotherapy.

Acknowledgments

Much of the organizational spirit and thematic consistency of this volume stems from an appreciation of the intrinsic interrelatedness of group dynamic and group psychoanalytic phenomena that was initially fostered during my involvement in a group dynamics seminar at the Menninger Foundation in 1966. That the present volume contains articles by Leonard Horwitz and Stephen Appelbaum is, in part, an expression of the significant impact of that experience on my conceptual development in this area.

My membership in the American Group Psychotherapy Association and involvement in numerous institutes and workshops during the course of the annual conferences of that organization have also significantly enriched my sensitivity to and understanding of group process phenomena.

In more practical terms, I am deeply indebted to the Institute of Advanced Psychological Studies, Adelphi University, for the secretarial services so kindly and generously offered. I am particularly grateful to Audrey Cunningham for allowing me to avail myself of these services and to Valerie Behrens for her expert secretarial assistance during the preparation of the manuscript.

I

THE
CONCEPT
OF
GROUP
DYNAMICS

1

Group Dynamics
and the Individual

Dorwin Cartwright
and
Ronald Lippitt
Research Center for Group Dynamics
University of Michigan, Ann Arbor

[In this chapter, the complex relationships between the issue of individuality and certain ubiquitous group phenomena are explored by Cartwright and Lippitt from a largely social psychological perspective. They present five propositions of a generalized nature with regard to the effect of group dynamics upon the individual and utilize them as a springboard for a discussion of the positive and negative consequences of group pressures toward consensus. Finally, they make an important distinction between the concepts of *conformity* and *uniformity*.]

How should we think of the relation between individuals and groups? Few questions have stirred up so many issues of metaphysics, epistemology, and ethics. Do groups have the same reality as individuals? If so, what are the properties of groups? Can groups learn, have goals, be frustrated, develop, regress, begin and end? Or are these characteristics strictly attributable only to individuals? If groups exist, are they good or bad? How *should* an individual behave with respect to groups? How *should* groups treat their individual members? Such questions have puzzled man from the earliest days of recorded history.

In our present era of "behavioral science" we like to think that we can be "scientific" and proceed to study human behavior without having to take

From "Group Dynamics and the Individual" by D. Cartwright and R. Lippitt, *International Journal of Group Psychotherapy*, 1957, 7, 86–102. Copyright 1957 by the International Journal of Group Psychotherapy. Reprinted by permission.

sides on these problems of speculative philosophy. Invariably, however, we are guided by certain assumptions, stated explicitly or not, about the reality or irreality of groups, about their observability, and about their good or bad value.

Usually these preconceptions are integral parts of one's personal and scientific philosophy, and it is often hard to tell how much they derive from emotionally toned personal experiences with other people and how much from coldly rational and "scientific" considerations. In view of the fervor with which they are usually defended, one might suspect that most have a small basis at least in personally significant experiences. These preconceptions, moreover, have a tendency to assume a homogeneous polarization—either positive or negative.

Consider first the completely negative view. It consists of two major assertions: first, groups don't really exist. They are a product of distorted thought processes (often called "abstractions"). In fact, social prejudice consists precisely in acting as if groups, rather than individuals, were real. Second, groups are bad. They demand blind loyalty, they make individuals regress, they reduce man to the lowest common denominator, and they produce what *Fortune* magazine has immortalized as "groupthink."

In contrast to this completely negative conception of groups, there is the completely positive one. This syndrome, too, consists of two major assertions: first, groups really do exist. Their reality is demonstrated by the difference it makes to an individual whether he is accepted or rejected by a group and whether he is part of a healthy or sick group. Second, groups are good. They satisfy deep-seated needs of individuals for affiliation, affection, recognition, and self-esteem; they stimulate individuals to moral heights of altruism, loyalty, and self-sacrifice; they provide a means, through cooperative interaction, by which man can accomplish things unattainable through individual enterprise.

This completely positive preconception is the one attributed most commonly, it seems, to the so-called "group dynamics movement." Group dynamicists, it is said, have not only *reified* the group but also *idealized* it. They believe that everything should be done by and in groups—individual responsibility is bad, man-to-man supervision is bad, individual problem-solving is bad, and even individual therapy is bad. The only good things are committee meetings, group decisions, group problem-solving, and group therapy. "If you don't hold the group in such high affection," we were once asked, "why do you call your research organization the Research Center FOR Group Dynamics? And, if you are *for* groups and group dynamics, mustn't you therefore be *against* individuality, individual responsibility, and self-determination?"

FIVE PROPOSITIONS ABOUT GROUPS

This assumption that individuals and groups must necessarily have incompatible interests is made so frequently in one guise or another that it requires closer examination. Toward this end we propose five related assertions about individuals, groups, and group dynamics, which are intended to challenge the belief that individuals and groups must necessarily have incompatible, or for that matter, compatible interests.

1. Groups do exist; they must be dealt with by any man of practical affairs, or indeed by any child, and they must enter into any adequate account of human behavior. Most infants are born into a specific group. Little Johnny may be a welcome or unwelcome addition to the group. His presence may produce profound changes in the structure of the group and consequently in the feelings, attitudes, and behavior of various group members. He may create a triangle where none existed before or he may break up one which has existed. His development and adjustment for years to come may be deeply influenced by the nature of the group he enters and by his particular position in it—whether, for example he is a first or second child (a personal property which has no meaning apart from its reference to a specific group).

There is a wealth of research whose findings can be satisfactorily interpreted only by assuming the reality of groups. Recall the experiment of Lewin, Lippitt, and White (15) in which the level of aggression of an individual was shown to depend upon the social atmosphere and structure of the group he is in and not merely upon such personal traits as aggressiveness. By now there can be little question about the kinds of results reported from the Western Electric study (18) which makes it clear that groups develop norms for the behavior of their members with the result that "good" group members adopt these norms as their *personal* values. Nor can one ignore the dramatic evidence of Lewin, Bavelas, and others (14) which shows that group decisions may produce changes in individual behavior much larger than those customarily found to result from attempts to modify the behavior of individuals *as* isolated individuals.

2. Groups are inevitable and ubiquitous. The biological nature of man, his capacity to use language, and the nature of his environment which has been built into its present form over thousands of years require that man exist in groups. This is not to say that groups must maintain the properties they now display, but we cannot conceive of a collection of human beings living in geographical proximity under conditions where it would be correct to assert that no groups exist and that there is no such thing as group membership.

3. Groups mobilize powerful forces which produce effects of the utmost importance to individuals. Consider two examples from rather different research settings. Seashore (22) has recently published an analysis of data from 5,871 employees of a large manufacturing company. An index of group cohesiveness, developed for each of 228 work groups, permitted a comparison of members working in high and in low cohesive groups. Here

is one of his major findings: "Members of high cohesive groups exhibit less anxiety than members of low cohesive groups, using as measures of anxiety: (a) feeling 'jumpy' or 'nervous', (b) feeling under pressure to achieve higher productivity (with actual productivity held constant), and (c) feeling a lack of support from the company" (p. 98). Seashore suggests two reasons for the relation between group cohesiveness and individual anxiety: "(1) that the cohesive group provides effective support for the individual in his encounters with anxiety-provoking aspects of his environment, thus allaying anxiety, and (2) that group membership offers direct satisfaction, and this satisfaction in membership has a generalized effect of anxiety-reduction" (p. 13).

Perhaps a more dramatic account of the powerful forces generated in groups can be derived from the publication by Stanton and Schwartz (24) of their studies of a mental hospital. They report, for example, how a patient may be thrown into an extreme state of excitement by disagreements between two staff members over the patient's care. Thus, two doctors may disagree about whether a female patient should be moved to another ward. As the disagreement progresses, the doctors may stop communicating relevant information to one another and start lining up allies in the medical and nursing staff. The patient, meanwhile, becomes increasingly restless until, at the height of the doctors' disagreement, she is in an acute state of excitement and must be secluded, put under sedation, and given special supervision. Presumably, successful efforts to improve the interpersonal relations and communications among members of the staff would improve the mental condition of such a patient.

In general, it is clear that events occurring in a group may have repercussions on members who are not directly involved in these events. A person's position in a group, moreover, may affect the way others behave toward him and such personal qualities as his levels of aspiration and self-esteem. Group membership itself may be a prized possession or an oppressive burden; tragedies of major proportions have resulted from the exclusion of individuals from groups, and equally profound consequences have stemmed from enforced membership in groups.

4. Groups may produce both good and bad consequences. The view that groups are completely good and the view that they are completely bad are both based on convincing evidence. *The only fault with either is its one-sidedness.* Research motivated by one or the other is likely to focus on different phenomena. As an antidote to such one-sidedness it is a good practice to ask research questions in pairs, one stressing positive aspects and one negative: What are the factors producing conformity? *and* what are the factors producing nonconformity? What brings about a breakdown in communication? *and* what stimulates or maintains effective communications? An exclusive focus on pathologies or upon positive criteria leads to a seriously incomplete picture.

5. A correct understanding of group dynamics permits the possibility that desirable consequences from groups can be deliberately enhanced. Through a knowledge of group dynamics, groups can be made to serve better ends, for knowledge gives power to modify human beings and human behavior. At the same time, recognition of this fact produces some of the deepest conflicts within the behavioral scientist, for it raises the whole problem of social manipulation. Society must not close its eyes to Orwell's horrible picture of life in 1984, but it cannot accept the alternative that in ignorance there is safety.

To recapitulate our argument: groups exist; they are inevitable and ubiquitous; they mobilize powerful forces having profound effects upon individuals; these effects may be good or bad; and through a knowledge of group dynamics there lies the possibility of maximizing their good value.

A DILEMMA

Many thoughtful people today are alarmed over one feature of groups: the pressure toward conformity experienced by group members. Indeed, this single "bad" aspect is often taken as evidence that groups are bad in general. Let us examine the specific problem of conformity, then in order to attain a better understanding of the general issue. Although contemporary concern is great, it is not new. More than one hundred years ago Alexis de Tocqueville wrote: "I know of no country in which there is so little independence of mind and real freedom of discussion as in America.... In America the majority raises formidable barriers around the liberty of opinion.... The master (majority) no longer says: 'You shall think as I do or you shall die'; but he says: 'You are free to think differently from me and to retain your life, your property, and all that you possess, but they will be useless to you, for you will never be chosen by your fellow citizens if you solicit their votes; and they will affect to scorn you if you ask for their esteem. You will remain among men, but you will be deprived of the rights of mankind. Your fellow creatures will shun you like an impure being; and even those who believe in your innocence will abandon you, lest they should be shunned in their turn' " (25, pp. 273-275).

Before too readily accepting such a view of groups as the whole story, let us invoke our dictum that research questions should be asked in pairs. Nearly everyone is convinced that individuals should not be blind conformers to group norms, that each group member should not be a carbon copy of every other member, but what is the other side of the coin? In considering why members of groups conform, perhaps we should also think of the consequences of the removal of individuals from group membership or the plight of the person who really does not belong to any group with clear-cut norms and values. The state of anomie, described by Durkheim, is also common today. It seems as if people who have no effective participation in groups with clear and strong value systems either crack up (as in alcoholism or suicide) or they seek out groups which will demand conformity. In discussing this process, Talcott Parsons writes: "In such a situation it is not surprising that large numbers of people should . . . be attracted to movements which can offer them membership in a group with a vigorous esprit de corps with submission to some strong authority and rigid system of belief, the individual thus finding a measure of escape from painful perplexities or from a situation of anomie" (17, pp. 128–129).

The British anthropologist, Adam Curle, has stressed the same problem when he suggested that in our society we need not four, but five freedoms, the fifth being freedom from that neurotic anxiety which springs from a man's isolation from his fellows, and which, in turn, isolates him still further from them.

We seem, then, to face a dilemma: the individual needs social support for his values and social beliefs; he needs to be accepted as a valued member of some group which *he* values; failure to maintain such group membership produces anxiety and personal disorganization. But, on the other hand, group membership and group participation tend to cost the individual his individuality. If he is to receive support from others and, in turn, give support to others, he and they must hold in common some values and beliefs. Deviation from these undermines any possibility of group support and acceptance.

Is there an avenue of escape from this dilemma? Certainly, the issue is not as simple as we have described it. The need for social support for some values does not require conformity with respect to all values, beliefs, and behavior. Any individual is a member of several groups, and he may be a successful deviate in one while conforming to another (think of the visitor in a foreign country or of the psychologist at a convention of psychiatrists). Nor should the time dimension be ignored; a person may sustain his deviancy through a conviction that his fate is only temporary. These refinements of the issue are important and should be examined in great detail, but before we turn our attention to them, we must assert that we do *not* believe that the basic dilemma can be escaped. To avoid complete personal disorganization man must conform to at least a minimal set of values required for participation in the groups to which he belongs.

PRESSURES TO UNIFORMITY

Some better light may be cast on this problem if we refer to the findings of research on conformity. What we do know about the way it operates?

Cognitive Processes

Modern psychological research on conformity reflects the many different currents of contemporary psychology, but the major direction has been largely determined by the classic experiment of Sherif (23) on the development of social norms in perceiving autokinetic movement and by the more recent study of Asch (1) of pressures to conformity in perceiving unambiguous visual stimuli.

What does this line of investigation tell us about conformity? What has it revealed, for instance, about the conditions that set up pressures to conformity? Answers to this question have taken several forms, but nearly all point out that social interaction would be impossible if some beliefs and perceptions were not commonly shared by the participants. Speaking of the origin of such cognitive pressures to uniformity among group members, Asch says: "The individual comes to experience a world that he shares with others. He perceives that the surroundings include him, as well as others, and that he is in the same relation to the surroundings as others. He notes that he, as well as others, is converging upon the same object and responding to its identical properties. Joint action and mutual understanding require this relation of intelligibility and structural simplicity. In these terms the 'pull' toward the group becomes understandable" (1, p. 484).

Consistent with this interpretation of the origin of pressures to uniformity in a perceptual or judgmental situation are the findings that the major variables influencing tendencies to uniformity are (a) the quality of the social evidence (particularly the degree of unanimity of announced perceptions and the subject's evaluation of the trustworthiness of the other's judgments), (b) the quality of the direct perceptual evidence (particularly the clarity or ambiguity of the stimuli), (c) the magnitude of the discrepancy between the social and the perceptual evidence, and (d) the indiviudal's self-confidence in the situation (as indicated either by experimental manipulations designed to affect self-confidence or by personality measurements).

The research in this tradition has been productive, but it has emphasized the individual and his cognitive problems and has considered the individual apart from any concrete and meaningful group membership. Presumably any trustworthy people adequately equipped with eyes and ears could serve to generate pressures to conformity in the subject, regardless of his specific relations to them. The result of this emphasis has been to ignore certain essential aspects of the conformity problem. Let us document this assertion with two examples.

First, the origin of pressures to uniformity has been made to reside in the person whose conformity is being studied. Through eliminating experimentally any possibility that pressures might be exerted by others, it has been possible to study the conformity of people as if they existed in a world where they can see or hear others but not be reacted to by others. It is significant, indeed, that conformity does arise in the absence of direct attempts to bring it about. But this approach does not raise certain questions about the conditions which lead to *social* pressures to conformity. What makes some people try to get others to conform? What conditions lead to what forms of pressure on others to get them to conform? The concentration of attention on the conformer has diverted attention away from the others in the situation who may insist on conformity and make vigorous efforts to bring it about or who may not exert any pressure at all on deviates.

A second consequence of this emphasis has been to ignore the broader social meaning of conformity. Is the individual's personal need for a social validation of his beliefs the only reason for conforming? What does deviation do to a person's acceptance by others? What does it do to his ability to influence others? Or, from the group's point of view, are there reasons to insist on certain common values, beliefs, and behavior? These questions are not asked nor answered by an approach which limits itself to the cognitive problems of the individual.

Group Processes

The group dynamics orientation toward conformity emphasizes a broader range of determinants. Not denying the importance of the cognitive situation, we want to look more closely at the nature of the individual's relation to particular groups with particular properties. In formulating hypotheses about the origin of pressures to uniformity, two basic sources have been stressed. These have been stated most clearly by Festinger and his co-workers (5), who propose that when differences of opinion arise within a group, pressures to uniformity will arise (a) if the validity or "reality" of the opinion depends upon agreement with the group (essentially the same point as Asch's), or (b) if locomotion toward a group goal will be facilitaed by uniformity within the group.

This emphasis upon the group, rather than simply upon the individual, leads one to expect a broader set of consequences from pressures to uniformity. Pressures to uniformity are seen as establishing: (a) a tendency on the part of each group member to change his own opinion to conform to that of the other group members, (b) a tendency to try to change the opinions of others, and (c) a tendency to redefine the boundaries of the group so as to exclude those holding deviate opinions. The relative magnitudes of these tendencies will depend on other conditions which need to be specified.

This general conception of the nature of the processes that produce conformity emerged from two early field studies conducted at the Research Center for Group Dynamics. It was also influenced to a considerable extent by the previous work of Newcomb (16) in which he studied the formation and change of social attitudes in a college community. The first field study, reported by Festinger, Schachter, and Back (7), traced the formation of social groups in a new student housing project. As each group developed, it displayed its own standards for its members. The extent of conformity to the standards of a particular group was found to be related directly to the degree of cohesiveness of that group as measured by sociometric choices. Moreover, those individuals who deviated from their own group's norms received fewer sociometric choices than those who conformed. A process of rejection for nonconformity had apparently set in. The second field study, reported by Coch and French (3), observed similar processes. This study was conducted in a textile factory and was concerned with conformity to production standards set by groups of workers. Here an individual worker's reaction to new work methods was found to depend upon the standards of his group and, here too, rejection for deviation was observed.

The next phase of this research consisted of a series of experiments with groups created in the laboratory. It was hoped thereby to be able to disentangle the complexity of variables that might exist in any field setting in order to understand better the operation of each. These experiments have been reported in various publications by Festinger, Back, Gerard, Hymovitch, Kelley, Raven, Schachter, and Thibaut (2, 6, 8, 9, 11, 20). We shall not attempt to describe these studies in detail, but draw upon them and other research in an effort to summarize the major conclusions.

First, a great deal of evidence has been accumulated to support the hypothesis that pressures to uniformity will be greater the more members want to remain in the group In more attractive or cohesive groups, members attempt more to influence others and are more willing to accept influence from others. Note that here pressures to conformity are high in the very conditions where satisfaction from group membership is also high.

Second, there is a close relation between attempts to change the deviate and tendencies to reject him. If persistent attempts to change the deviate fail to produce conformity, then communication appears to cease between the majority and the deviate, and rejection of the deviate sets in. These two processes, moreover, are more intense the more cohesive the group. One of the early studies which documented the process of rejection was conducted by Schachter (20) on college students. It has recently been replicated by Emerson (4) on high school students, who found essentially the same process at work, but he discovered that among his high school students efforts to influence others continued longer, there was a greater readiness on the part of the majority to change, and there was a lower level of rejection within a limited period of time. Yet another study, conducted in Holland, Sweden, France, Norway, Belgium, Germany, and England, found the same tendency to reject deviates in all of these countries. This study, reported by Schachter, et al. (21), is a landmark in cross-cultural research.

Third, there is the question of what determines whether or not pressures to uniformity will arise with respect to any particular opinion, attitude, and behavior. In most groups there are no pressures to uniformity concerning the color of necktie worn by the members. Differences of opinion about the age of the earth probably would not lead to rejection in a poker club, but they might do so in certain fundamentalist church groups. The concept of *relevance* seems to be required to account for such variations in pressures to uniformity.

And, if we ask, "relevance for what?" we are forced again to look at the group and especially at the goals of the group.

Schachter (20) has demonstrated, for example, that deviation on a given issue will result much more readily in rejection when that issue is relevant to the group's goals than when it is irrelevant. And the principle of relevance seems to be necessary to account for the findings of a field study reported by Ross (19). Here attitudes of fraternity men toward restrictive admission policies were studied. Despite the fact that there was a consistent policy of exclusion in these fraternities, there was, surprisingly, little evidence for the existence of pressures toward uniformity of attitudes. When, however, a field experiment was conducted in which the distribution of actual opinions for each fraternity house was reported to a meeting of house members together with a discussion of the relevance of these opinions for fraternity policy, attitudes then tended to change to conform to the particular modal position of each house. Presumably the experimental treatment made uniformity of attitude instrumental to group locomotion where it had not been so before.

SOURCES OF HETEROGENEITY

We have seen that pressures to uniformity are stronger the more cohesive the group. Shall we conclude from this that strong, need-satisfying, cohesive groups must always produce uniformity on matters that are important to the group? We believe not. We cannot, however, cite much convincing evidence since research has focused to date primarily upon the sources of pressures to uniformity and has ignored the conditions which produce heterogeneity. Without suggesting, then, that we can give final answers, let us indicate some of the possible sources of heterogeneity.

Group Standards about Uniformity

It is important, first, to make a distinction between conformity and uniformity. A group might have a value that everyone should be as different from everyone else as possible. Conformity to this value, then, would result not in uniformity of behavior but in nonuniformity. Such a situation often arises in therapy groups or training groups where it is possible to establish norms which place a high value upon "being different" and upon tolerating deviant behavior. Conformity to this value is presumably greater the more cohesive the group and the more it is seen as relevant to the group's objectives. Unfortunately, very little is known about the origin and operation of group standards about conformity itself. We doubt that the pressure to uniformity which arises from the need for "social reality" and for group locomotion can simply be obliterated by invoking a group standard of tolerance, but a closer look at such processes as those of group decision-making will be required before a deep understanding of this problem can be achieved.

Freedom to Deviate

A rather different source of heterogeneity has been suggested by Kelley and Shapiro (12). They reason that the more an individual feels accepted by the other members of the group, the more ready he should be to deviate from the beliefs of the majority under conditions where objectively correct deviation would be in the group's best interest. They designed an experiment to test this hypothesis. The results, while not entirely clear because acceptance led to greater cohesiveness, tend to support this line of reasoning.

It has been suggested by some that those in positions of leadership are freer to deviate from group standards than are those of lesser status. Just the opposite conclusion has been drawn by others. Clearly, further research into group properties which generate freedom to deviate from majority pressures is needed.

Subgroup Formation

Festinger and Thibaut (8) have shown that lower group-wide pressures to uniformity of opinion result when members of a group perceive that the group is composed of persons differing in interest and knowledge. Under these conditions subgroups may easily develop with a resulting heterogeneity with the group as a whole though with uniformity within each subgroup. This conclusion is consistent with Asch's (1) finding that the presence of a partner for a deviate greatly strengthens his tendency to be independent. One might suspect that such processes, though achieving temporarily a greater heterogeneity, would result in a schismatic subgroup conflict.

Positions and Roles

A more integrative achievement of heterogeneity seems to arise through the process of role differentiation. Established groups are usually differentiated according to "positions" with special functions attached to each. The occupant of the position has certain behaviors prescribed for him by the others in the group. These role prescriptions differ, moreover, from one position to another, with the result that conformity to them produces heterogeneity within the group. A group function, which might otherwise be suppressed by pressures to uniformity, may be preserved by the establishment of a position whose responsibility is to perform the function.

Hall (10) has recently shown that social roles can be profitably conceived in the context of conformity to group pressures. He reasoned that pressures to uniformity of prescriptions concerning the behavior of the occupant of a position and pressures on the occupant to conform to these prescriptions should be greater the more cohesive the group. A study of the role of aircraft commander in bomber crews lends strong support to this conception.

In summary, it should be noted that in all but one of these suggested sources of heterogeneity we have assumed the process of conformity—to the norms of a subgroup, to a role, or to a group standard favoring heterogeneity. Even if the price of membership in a strong group be conformity, it need not follow that strong groups will suppress differences.

MORE THAN ONE GROUP

Thus far our analysis has proceeded as though the individual were a member of only one group. Actually we recognize that he is, and has been, a member of many groups. In one of our current research projects we are finding that older adolescents can name from twenty to forty "important groups and persons that influence my opinions and behavior in decision situations." Indeed, some personality theorists hold that personality should be viewed as an "internal society" made up of representation of the diverse group relationships which the individual now has and has had. According to this view, each individual has a unique internal society and makes his own personal synthesis of the values and behavior preferences generated by these affiliations.

The various memberships of an indiviudal may relate to one another in various ways and produce various consequences for the individual. A past group may exert internal pressures toward conformity which are in conflict with a present group. Two contemporaneous groups may have expectations for the person which are incompatible. Or an individual may hold a temporary membership (the situation of a foreign student, for example) and be faced with current conformity pressures which if accepted will make it difficult to readjust when returning to his more permanent memberships.

This constant source of influence from other memberships toward deviancy of every member of every group requires that each group take measures to preserve its integrity. It should be noted, however, that particular deviancy pressures associated with a given member may be creative or destructive when evaluated in terms of the integrity and productivity of the group, and conformity pressures from the group may be supportive or disruptive of the integrity of the individual.

Unfortunately there has been little systematic research on these aspects of multiple group membership. We can only indicate two sets of observations concerning (a) the intrapersonal processes resulting from multiple membership demands, and (b) the effects on group processes of the deviancy pressures which arise from the multiple membership status of individual members.

Marginal Membership

Lewin (13), in his discussion of adolescence and of minority group membership, has analyzed some of the psychological effects on the person of being "between two groups" without a firm anchorage in either one. He says: "The transition from childhood to adulthood may be a rather sudden shift (for instance, in some of the primitive societies), or it may occur gradually in a setting where children and adults are not sharply separated groups. In the case of the so-called 'adolescent difficulties,' however, a third state of affairs is often prevalent: children and adults constitute two clearly defined groups; the adolescent does not wish any longer to belong to the children's group and, at the same time, knows that he is not really accepted in the adult group. He has a position similar to what is called in sociology the 'marginal man' . . . a person who stands on the boundary between two groups. He does not belong to either of them, or at least he is not sure of his belongingness in either of them" (p. 143). Lewin goes on to point out that there are characteristic maladjustive behavior patterns resulting from this unstable membership situation: high tension, shifts between extremes of behavior, high sensitivity, and rejection of low status members of both groups. This situation, rather than fostering strong individuality, makes belonging to closely knit, loyalty-demanding groups very attractive. Dependency and acceptance are a welcome relief. Probably most therapy groups have a number of members who are seeking relief from marginality.

Overlapping Membership

There is quite a different type of situation where the person does have a firm anchorage in two or more groups but where the group standards are not fully compatible. Usually the actual conflict arises when the person is physically present in one group but realizes that he also belongs to other groups to which he will return in the near or distant future. In this sense, the child moves between his family group and his school group every day. The member of a therapy group has some sort of time perspective of "going back" to a variety of other groups between each meeting of the therapy group.

In their study of the adjustment of foreign students both in this country and after returning home, Watson and Lippitt (26) observed four different ways in which individuals cope with this problem of overlapping membership.

1. Some students solved the problem by "living in the present" at all times. When they were in the American culture all of their energy and attention was directed to being an acceptable member of this group. They avoided conflict within themselves by minimizing thought about and contact with the other group "back home." When they returned to the other group they used the same type of solution, quickly shifting behavior and ideas to fit back into the new present group. Their behavior appeared quite inconsistent, but it was a consistent approach to solving their problem of multiple membership.
2. Other individuals chose to keep their other membership the dominant one while in this country. They were defensive and rejective every time the present group seemed to promote values and to expect behavior which

they felt might not be acceptable to the other group "back home." The strain of maintaining this orientation was relieved by turning every situation into a "black and white" comparison and adopting a consistently rejective posture toward the present, inferior group. This way of adjusting required a considerable amount of distorting of present and past realities, but the return to the other group was relatively easy.

3. Others reacted in a sharply contrasting way by identifying wholeheartedly with the present group and by rejecting the standards of the other group as incorrect or inferior at the points of conflict. They were, of course, accepted by the present group, but when they returned home they met rejection or felt alienated from the standards of the group (even when they felt accepted).

4. Some few individuals seemed to achieve a more difficult but also more creative solution. They attempted to regard membership in both groups as desirable. In order to succeed in this effort, they had to be more realistic about perceiving the inconsistencies between the group expectations and to struggle to make balanced judgments about the strong and weak points of each group. Besides taking this more objective approach to evaluation, these persons worked on problems of how the strengths of one group might be interpreted and utilized by the other group. They were taking roles of creative deviancy in both groups, but attempting to make their contributions in such a way as to be accepted as loyal and productive members. They found ways of using each group membership as a resource for contributing to the welfare of the other group. Some members of each group were of course threatened by this readiness and ability to question the present modal ways of doing things in the group.

Thus it seems that the existence of multiple group memberships creates difficult problems both for the person and for the group. But there are also potentialities and supports for the development of creative individuality in this situation, and there are potentialities for group growth and achievement in the fact that the members of any group are also members of other groups with different standards.

SOME CONCLUSIONS

Let us return now to the question raised at the beginning of this paper. How should we think of the relation between individuals and groups? If we accept the assumption that individuals and groups are both important social realities, we can then ask a pair of important questions. What kinds of effects do groups have on the emotional security and creative productivity of the individual? What kinds of effects do individuals have on the morale and creative productivity of the group? In answering these questions it is important to be alerted to both good and bad effects. Although the systematic evidence from research does not begin to provide full answers to these questions, we have found evidence which tends to support the following general statements.

Strong groups do exert strong influences on members toward conformity. These conformity pressures, however, may be directed toward uniformity of thinking and behavior, or they may foster heterogeneity.

Acceptance of these conformity pressures, toward uniformity or heterogeneity, may satisfy the emotional needs of some members and frustrate others. Similarly, it may support the potential creativity of some members and inhibit that of others.

From their experiences of multiple membership and their personal synthesis of these experiences, individuals do have opportunities to achieve significant bases of individuality.

Because each group is made up of members who are loyal members of other groups and who have unique individual interests, each group must continuously cope with deviancy tendencies of the members. These tendencies may represent a source of creative improvement in the life of the group or a source of destructive disruption.

The resolution of these conflicting interests does not seem to be the strengthening of individuals and the weakening of groups, or the strengthening of groups and the weakening of individuals, but rather a strengthening of both by qualitative improvements in the nature of interdependence between integrated individuals and cohesive groups.

BIBLIOGRAPHY

1. Asch, S. E.: *Social Psychology.* New York: Prentice Hall, 1952.
2. Back, K. W.: Influence Through Social Communication. *J. Abn. & Soc. Psychol., 46*:9-23, 1951.
3. Coch, L. and French, J. R. P.: Overcoming Resistance to Change. *Hum. Relat., 1*:512-32, 1948.
4. Emerson, R. M.: Deviation and Rejection: An Experimental Replication. *Am. Sociol. Rev., 19*:688-93, 1954.
5. Festinger, L.: Informal Social Communication. *Psychol. Rev., 57*:271-292, 1950.
6. Festinger, L., Gerard, H. B., Hymovitch, B., Kelley, H. H., and Raven, B.: The Influence Process in the Presence of Extreme Deviates. *Hum. Relat., 5*:327-346, 1952.
7. Festinger, L., Schachter, S., and Back, K.: *Social Pressures in Informal Groups.* New York: Harper, 1950.
8. Festinger, L. and Thibaut, J.: Interpersonal Communication in Small Groups. *J. Abn. & Soc. Psychol., 46*:92-99, 1951.
9. Gerard, H. B.: The Effect of Different Dimensions of Disagreement on the Communication Process in Small Groups. *Hum. Relat., 6*:249-271, 1953.
10. Hall, R. L.: Social Influence on the Aircraft Commander's Role. *Am. Sociol. Rev., 20*:292-99, 1955.
11. Kelley, H. H.: Communication in Experimentally Created Hierarchies. *Hum. Relat., 4*:39-56, 1951.

12. Kelley, H. H. and Shapiro, M. M.: An Experiment on Conformity to Group Norms Where Conformity is Detrimental to Group Achievement. *Am. Sociol. Rev., 19*:667-677, 1954.
13. Lewin, K.: *Field Theory in Social Science.* New York: Harper, 1951.
14. Lewin, K.: Studies in Group Decision. In: *Group Dynamics: Research and Theory,* ed. D. Cartwright and A. Zander. Evanston: Row, Peterson, 1953.
15. Lewin, K., Lippitt, R., and White, R.: Patterns of Aggressive Behavior in Experimentally Created "Social Climates." *J. Soc. Psychol. 10*:271-99, 1939.
16. Newcomb, T. M.: *Personality and Social Change.* New York: Dryden, 1943.
17. Parsons, T.: *Essays in Sociological Theory.* (Rev. ed.) Glencoe: Free Press, 1954.
18. Roethlisberger, F. J. and Dickson, W. J.: *Management and the Worker.* Cambridge: Harvard University Press, 1939.
19. Ross, I.: Group Standards Concerning the Admission of Jews. *Soc. Prob., 2*:133-140, 1955.
20. Schachter, S.: Deviation, Rejection, and Communication. *J. Abn. & Soc. Psychol., 46*:190-207, 1951.
21. Schachter, S., et al.: Cross-cultural Experiments on Threat and Rejection. *Hum. Relat., 7*:403-39, 1954.
22. Seashore, S. E.: *Group Cohesiveness in the Industrial Group.* Ann Arbor: Institute for Social Research, 1954.
23. Sherif, M.: *The Psychology of Social Norms.* New York: Harper, 1936.
24. Stanton, A. H. and Schwartz, M. S.: *The Mental Hospital.* New York: Basic Books, 1954.
25. Tocqueville, A.: *Democracy in America,* Vol. 1. New York: Alfred A. Knopf, 1945 (original publication, 1835).
26. Watson, J. and Lippitt, R.: *Learning Across Cultures.* Ann Arbor: Institute for Social Research, 1955.

2

Toward a Common Basis for Group Dynamics: Group and Therapeutic Processes in Group Therapy[1]

Helen E. Durkin
Postgraduate Institute for Psychotherapy
New York, New York

[The complex relationships between the group processes often noted in largely social psychological work group settings and those typically observed in more clinical and psychotherapeutic settings are explored by Durkin. She concludes that despite a number of important structural differences between these two types of group interaction, certain distinct areas of overlap can be noted. An effort is made to integrate the two spheres of study via the concepts of *group goal specificity* and *ego interaction*. Significantly, Durkin states that an awareness of the dynamic processes occurring in psychotherapy groups can both enhance the overall sophistication of the group therapist and increase his or her capacity to move the group toward therapeutic goals.]

Extensive material has been produced in recent years by a large number of sociologists, social psychologists, and group psychotherapists who are interested in the nature of groups. A review of the literature presents an impression of confusion if not chaos because of the widely diverse methods and the contradictory results described. But a closer scrutiny reveals two

From "Toward a Common Basis for Group Dynamics" by H. E. Durkin, *International Journal of Group Psychotherapy*, 1957, 7, 115–130. Copyright 1957 by the International Journal of Group Psychotherapy. Reprinted by permission.

[1] See Durkin, H. E.; Group Dynamics and Group Psychotherapy. *Int. J. Group Psychotherapy*, 4:359, 1954.

general trends consisting of the clinical presentations of the group therapists, and the experimental findings of the social scientists. Until recently little has been done by either side to understand its relationship to the other. The proverbial visitor from Mars would have thought it very peculiar indeed that two groups of scientists interested in the same subject had seemed to be working as if there were an invisible barricade between them. The truth is that a serious problem of communication must be solved before mutual under-standing and integration between the two approaches are possible. And it is of paramount scientific importance that such an integration be made of their findings and their theoretical implications.

Since 1950 a beginning has been made in this direction. The work of Bach (1) is an example. He attempts to fuse the group dynamics viewpoint with analytic group therapy in his clinical work and theoretical papers. However, he does not attempt to clarify the taxonomic foundations of the subject before he proceeds to use the sociological findings as if they were of established clinical value on a par with known therapeutic process. My own view is that mixing these findings on a clinical level is less important than a more discriminating integration on the level of knowledge, and that it leaves the danger of clinical misapplication. At the Postgraduate Institute for Psychotherapy, Deutsch, Kadis, and Durkin gave a course (1955-56) which attempted to integrate these approaches in a meaningful and more systematic way for students of group psychotherapy.

When I made my first attempt to review the literature in the middle of the 1940's, I came up against one very puzzling situation which forced me to recognize the lack in communication I speak of and to search for its causes. I found that the social scientists had not only used different terms than the group therapists but seemed to be operating on a different wave length altogether. (Quite apart from the fact that they used different kinds of groups—a subject which I shall discuss in detail later.) To illustrate, the word "dynamics" conjures up concepts to the analytically oriented group therapist which are connected with the motivating forces of individual human inter-action—emotions, drives, conflicts, defenses, etc. Such concepts, however, are conspicuously absent in the writings of the social scientists. Instead, they use terms referring to group behavioral phenomena such as leadership, status, role, structure, climate, standards, pressure, communication, contagion, and so on. Conversely, these terms are rare in the writings of the group therapists, although few, if any of them, would deny their validity as part of group process. This verbal "by-pass" highlights the gap between the two approaches. What does it signify?

The easy and obvious answer is that they were studying different types of groups.[2] The clue to the deeper understanding of these disparities and to

[2] They could have worked with different types of groups and come up with the same findings if they used the same methods and had the same goal.

making any sort of integration possible lies, it seems to me, in comprehending the goals and the "mental set" of the researchers, for their differences grow out of their "mental set" and their omissions occur as the result of their respective professional lacunae. This hypothesis leads inevitably to certain pertinent observations. Psychotherapists in working with groups were primarily interested in therapeusis and only secondarily in knowledge about groups. From a research point of view, however, they were interested in whether or not the basic principles of group psychology are the same as, or different from, those of individual psychology. They worked clinically, continuing to use the same research tool they had found so productive in individual psychoanalysis. They analyzed transference and resistance. The only difference was that now they were studying many transferences in process of interaction. Social scientists, on the other hand, were interested only in the nature of groups as such, not at first in their clinical value, nor in comparing group with individual functioning. They too applied their traditional tools of experimentation. Out of these disparate purposes and methodologies came another factor that made the findings of one side almost incomprehensible in terms of the other. Group therapists focused on the latent meanings of the interaction among the members, while the social scientists dealt only with their overt manifestations. The latter were not interested in or trained to observe or deal with the latent content behind the overt behavior. As Robert Bales (2) puts it, "all our relevant empirical generalizations must refer sooner or later to some aspects of concrete action or the situation of action."

Because of these differences in their purposes, their methodologies, and the "sights" they set to make their observations, the two disciplines interpreted the concept of "group dynamics" differently, or more accurately, concentrated on different aspects of it. By definition "dynamics" refers to "motivating forces." Group therapists interpreted it as the latent dynamic causes of interaction among individual members of the group which produce and shape the group behavior. Social scientists interpreted dynamics to refer to the overt behavioral phenomena of the group and their effect on the individuals in them. Thus one side deals with the dynamic causes of group behavior; the other, with their dynamic effect. It is no wonder, then, that in reporting on their findings they used two different vocabularies; that by and large they failed to grasp the essential significance of each other's findings; that confusion rather than integration characterized the literature. But surely no complete understanding of group dynamics can be achieved without including the causes and the effects of group interaction. The two approaches should be considered complementary, never antagonistic.

Scheidlinger (10), who has summarized the literature in his book *Psychoanalysis and Group Behavior,* made the significant comment that group therapists on the whole reported on the therapeutic process in the group while the social scientists reported on group process as such. This is understandable on the basis that the group therapists wield a powerful dynamic instrument of their own, the therapeutic technique, which cuts boldly across the very group processes which the social scientist is studying per se.

Several authors among the social scientists have attempted to summarize the voluminous experimental literature. Two outstanding books are *Group Dynamics*, edited by Cartwright and Zander (5), and *Small Groups* by Borgatta, Hare and Bales (4). Borgatta et al. bring about some unity by organizing the material into topics. Cartwright goes much further in this direction by presenting the chief theoretical orientations among the experimentalists and giving us their different methodological approaches and then giving experimental findings as examples from each group. In his introduction Cartwright (5) explains why there is so much confusion and differently oriented students have worked with many different kinds of groups with many different scientific methods, for many different reasons. He indicates that his attempt to organize the vast material is incomplete because the work is still in its early stages, but he succeeds in illuminating the main trends.

Among the individual authors who have published findings on group functioning, Redl (9) is an exception in that he combines the two points of view. He is a trained analyst who has done a good deal of group work (as distinguished from group therapy) as part of school and camp life in a therapeutically oriented setting. In writing on the group dimension which he calls "contagion," he gives evidence which points in the direction of the conclusion I have drawn above. However, he was concerned only with the single phenomenon of group contagion, and did not at all deal with the interrelationship between group therapy and group dynamics. He lists the causes of contagion under two headings: Under the heading of "the situation" he places factors which account for the how and when of contagion. This seems to me to be the chief concern of the social scientists. Under his heading of "personality factors" fall those which account for the "why" of contagion. According to my way of thinking, this is the chief concern of the group therapists. This seems to me to illustrate one reason why there is such a disparity among the findings of the two approaches.

Once one has understood the reasons for these differences one may raise the scientifically important question of the comparability of their findings. Is the dynamic basis of all groups the same? For only if this is true, is it feasible to compare them. Catell (5) warned that "experimental results are uninterpretable and noncomparable unless they are understood in reference to the taxonomic foundations." The taxonomic foundations in this field are as yet far from established. We must therefore find out whether the basic dynamics are the same in all groups; and if they are, we must examine the specific points of similarity and difference between their situations before we attempt to understand the nature of the therapeutic group in sociological terms and certainly before we apply that information clinically. Only then can different types of groups be compared or the findings based on one type be appropriately modified and applied to another. Unfortunately not all writers on the subject have emphasized or even recognized this basic principle with the result that many misapplications of findings have been made to non-comparable situations. It is imperative that we determine, with much greater exactitude than has heretofore been done, the extent and the limits of the common ground between any two types of groups, and in that way establish a truer measure of comparability.

It will be my contention that at root level the dynamic basis of all groups *is* the same. Although one of the most frequent and apparently obvious arguments offered against the comparability of therapy with ordinary groups is the fact that the former are composed of emotionally disturbed people, careful psychological scrutiny disproves its validity. Even superficially this difference in composition is not a valid argument because there will be a good sprinkling of neurotics among the so-called normal groups, and the normal members in them will certainly have a certain number of neurotic character traits. Therapy group members, on the other hand, are by no means entirely neurotic in their functioning. Simply functioning in an analytic group requires a certain amount of ego strength. (I am excepting for the present groups of schizophrenics.) There is, moreover, a more profound argument for psycho-logical comparability between therapy and ordinary groups. Analytic group therapists will agree that members of all types of groups must interact with one another out of the repertoire of their habitual modes and patterns of attitudes and behavior. Group interaction must proceed through that part of the members' ego development that we call character or personality. It is, if you will, ego interaction. Now psychoanalytic research has established the fact that character formation is the same, in principle, for normal and neurotic individuals. Beyond the normally developed ego functions, character structure is developed in an individual's early years as a compromise between the gratification of his inner needs and the demands of his social environment. It is the sum total of the individual's protective devices against too much pain and anxiety from within and without. The sum of such compromises forms his basic behavior patterns, his way of life, and is the basis of his interaction with other human beings. The patterns of neurotics, because of the greater anxiety under which the patterns were established, may produce poorer choices, may be more rigidly adhered to, be less adaptive, and give less gratification or cause more friction with the environment, but they will not be different in kind from those in normal people. Neurotics will, like normal people, interact through their ego defenses. They will, like normal people, often repeat, in present relationships, patterns which were more appropriate in past situations. These common ways of human interaction form the dynamic basis for all types of interaction and will be present in all types of groups. For this reason the composition of groups gives them a common ground. This reasoning will, I believe, serve until experimental proof is established or the hypothesis disproved.

On the basis of it we may amend Bales's appropriately cautious warning. He says in his paper on Phases of Problem Solving, "These results do not apply to groups where the major emphasis is on expressive personality interaction" and again, "They do not apply to groups of seriously disturbed persons" (5). This sound warning may be modified to read, "They do not necessarily apply" to such groups. According to my hypothesis, they *could* apply; but before such application is attempted, they must be evaluated in the light of the specific group situations. For instance, many compulsive neurotics might function just as well in a problem-solving group as normals, although groups consisting of members with neurotic reading problems could not be compared to normal problem-solving groups which require reading as a major function. My contention is that, broadly speaking, all kinds of groups are comparable on a characterological basis as to their composition, but the specific extent and limitations of their situations must be examined before absolute comparability is assumed.

The exceptions mentioned above lead us to the examination of those determinants which most vitally affect my contention's validity and supply us with a sound basis for deciding in how far findings made on one type of group may be safely applied to another. I submit that the purpose for which the group has come together is the most vital of such determinants. It is the group goal which determines the nature of its leadership, its particular composition, its internal structure, its methods of locomotion, and so on. If this is true, then the group goal is that element in the situation that must be most carefully analyzed when the question of comparability is being decided upon.

To sum up: comparability of different kinds of groups cannot be ruled out because the dynamic basis of all groups *may* be presumed to be the same, nor can it be taken for granted until the specific elements in the group situation are carefully analyzed. It is only when the degree of comparability is established that the findings on ordinary groups may be applied to therapeutic groups.

Now we are in a position to examine some of the major findings of the experimentalists in relation to therapeutic groups. We shall be asking two questions. To what extent can we apply to therapeutic groups findings derived from experimental or field study of other types of groups? And what part does the group-dynamic process play in the movement of the therapeutic group toward its goal? In other words, what is the relationship between group process and therapeutic process?

Since the nature of leadership occupies a rather prominent position in the studies of both therapists and experimentalists, it seems appropriate to begin with some detailed examination of this topic. One important conclusion of the experimentalists, with which the therapists will agree, is the emergence of a new definition of leadership. Leadership has come to be defined in dynamic rather than in static terms. No longer is it considered to be the function of the personality alone, nor of just the situation, but rather of the relationship between the personality and the situation. For instance, Bales (2) contends that leadership depends on an individual's access to the resources necessary to achieve the group goal, his identification with it, and his degree of influence on the other members. The very acceptance of this new definition ties in with our conclusion that when studying any group dimension in different kinds of groups, one must do so in terms of the specific situation of each group (particularly the goal).

Therefore, if we are to study leadership in normal and therapeutic groups we shall want to know in how far the effect of the goal on the specific conditions of leadership differs in the two situations. In ordinary problem-solving groups, for example, the goal is concrete and external, and the members have as much or nearly as much access to the resources for solving the problem as does the leader. For this reason the leader in such groups may be an *ad hoc* appointee or be elected. The goal for therapy groups is internal, emotional, and the resources for reaching it are so complex and technical that the members must choose a professional leader. In fact they choose the therapist, and it is he who decides whether or not they should join a group. Such a difference in the group situation cannot help but have an appreciable effect on the nature of its leadership, so that one cannot unquestioningly apply results from the one to the other. Furthermore, the goals of the therapeutic group are inextricably bound up with the most basic psychological needs of its members, whereas those of problem-solving groups—in fact, of most ordinary groups—are seldom of paramount importance to them. Field study groups are closer to therapy groups in this respect, but their goals pertain usually to only one important segment of the members' needs. Few other types of groups are so intimately, so vitally, and so completely involved with the members' total life situation as are therapeutic groups. These differences have a powerful effect on the responsibilities of the leaders and on the nature of their leadership. We must expect to allow for such differences when we consider applying results from other kinds of groups.

Let us test out some specific experimental findings gained from normal groups to see whether they confirm the principles we have been evolving. White and Lippitt (5), in their well-known study of group atmosphere as established by the leader in problem-solving groups, came to the conclusion that a democratic atmosphere has a better effect in production and interaction than a laissez-faire or an autocratic atmosphere. Preston and Heintz (8) came to a similar conclusion, also using problem-solving groups. They feel that the more distribution without leadership intervention, the better is the production and the interaction. Kahn and Katz (5) in a field study with industrial workers agree.

Can these results be applied to therapy groups? I believe that *they can,* but *not without modifications* based on the group goals. It is true that the contemporary literature on group therapy stresses the importance of the members as adjunct therapists. It is also true that there would be therapeutic effect (though not necessarily therapy) if the therapist simply allowed the normal group-dynamic processes to function without intervening. I do maintain, however, that analytic group therapy with its goal of solving pathogenic conflicts through analysis of transference and resistance would be seriously interfered with if White's and Lippitt's results were applied without modification.

We may leave aside Lippitt's point that production is increased because production in a therapeutic group is obviously of a different nature from that in a problem-solving group. But his finding that interaction is better in a democratic atmosphere, and Preston's and Heintz's finding that distribution of leadership without intervention of the leader makes for better interaction, must be examined most carefully. Interaction is indeed an important factor in goal locomotion in *both types* of groups. But in the light of the goals, one must define "good interaction" for each if one wishes to compare them. In problem-solving groups, "good interaction" is friendly interaction. Inimical feelings must be avoided if cooperation toward the external goal is to be paramount. In the therapeutic group "good" interaction is free interaction in which the whole range of underlying feelings comes into play. Often this means that the leader must work toward the expression of varying degrees of hostile feelings in order to facilitate self-understanding and the development of sounder relationships. Helping to set aside conscious antagonisms does not require the same degree of technical skill as removing defenses against unconscious hostile feelings. Any member can do it. Therefore the distribution of leadership must be more restricted in a therapy group. The leader must keep his finger on the pulse of every member and be ready to make the interpretations necessary to bring the hostile reactions to consciousness. The same comments might be made with regard to other unconscious feelings. For example, overprotectiveness of one member to another which might well be utilized in a problem-solving group would call for analytic intervention on the part of the group therapist. The leader must be free, therefore, to intervene and to exert his functional authority through his technical skill. The need to do so puts limits on the distribution of leadership in the therapeutic group.

Moreover, the members of the therapeutic group have chosen their leader with the idea of being able to rely on his personal maturity. Treatment principles may prescribe periods of accepting and then examining their dependency needs. They might rightfully be dependent on him for a relatively long period of treatment, even though his aim is to make them independent eventually. The leader cannot relinquish this function, nor other seemingly authoritative interventions, for the sake of group democracy. Leader distribution increases gradually as the members become free enough from their neurotic unconscious motivation to carry on themselves.

It may be worth while at this point to adduce an example from a group therapy session. In the mixed therapy group to which I refer, Jim was perhaps the chief "adjunct therapist." He had the insight and the courage to make many good interpretations. He was more willing than most patients to bring his impulses into the group for inspection, and often insisted that others do likewise. There was no question that he brought lifelikeness and vividness to the group proceedings which helped us "locomote" to our goal. For example, when Alice spoke rather vaguely about a new love relationship, he insisted that she give us the specific details. When she tried to answer she was forced to face squarely and to present to the rest of the group more meaningful material to which they could relate themselves. He also tended to keep the focus of the group talk related to the group experience itself. Once when Grace was telling us about the difficulties she was having with a romantic relationship, he said to her, "Why not you and me go out and fuck?" She had to examine her relationship with him.

In the first situation the leader could encourage Jim's leadership. The second comment, however, illustrates the point that the therapist–leader must put limits on a patient's leadership. If the therapist did not intervene and at least momentarily draw the leadership back to himself, Jim would have led the group away from its goal of understanding the meaning of their emotional relationships. He and Grace might have moved toward acting out instead. The therapist, however, drew upon his training and tried to make this experience an insightful one for all of them. He said, "Try to tell us, Jim, just what you think you might do in such a rendezvous?" With great effort, Jim who usually talked glibly tried to put impulses he usually acted out into words and feelings instead of plunging into action. This made him very anxious, but it helped him experience the difference between feeling and acting on impulse. It also helped Grace understand the true motivations of the men in whom she was so often disappointed. At one point in this case, a more democratic distribution of the leadership, and in another, reserving leadership for the therapist made for goal locomotion.

In order to clarify this problem of democracy in group leadership it will be necessary to take a small detour, for the problem has been inadvertently complicated by some confused thinking in both camps. Cartwright (5) has pointed out a fallacy of some of the group-dynamics researches which I believe also holds true of some enthusiastically democratic group therapists. He says that ideological considerations have somehow insinuated themselves into scientific matters, although ideology has no place in scientific experiment. It seems to me to have none in clinical matters either. Democracy is hardly the first duty of a doctor to his patient, even though we prefer him to administer treatment in a democratic manner. He has been selected and will be paid to apply his training and skill with due realistic authority. Here we come upon what I believe is a semantic confusion which adds to the misleading effect of the fallacy Cartwright mentions. To be realistically authoritative is not the equivalent of being authoritarian, which, in our culture at least, is rarely realistic. There need be no mutual exclusiveness between authority and democracy as there must be between authoritarianism and democracy.

The problem, although misnamed, does have some subtler implications for the leader of the therapeutic group. Every therapist in a democratic society has been taught a sound respect for the humanity of his partners in the therapeutic relationship. This respect must be evident in his attitude and will show up in the *way he makes his comments,* not in leaning over backward to be on a par with them in the very area in which he must offer superiority. It is just here that the intrusion of ideology plus semantic error has confused the clinical issues, for group therapists sometimes do reveal unconscious authoritarian motivations which stem from unresolved fantasies of omnipotence, or from remaining status conflicts. Such attitudes are undesirable because they are antitherapeutic, not because they are undemocratic. Every therapist is committed to analyze both his own omnipotent needs and the patient's needs to have him be omnipotent. Group therapists who are too aggressive and controlling and those who suffer from reaction formations to these tendencies fail to live up to their realistic functions. But this is a question of the leader's maturity and his techniques—not one of democracy.

To sum up: if we are to compare normal with therapeutic groups and to consider applying the experimental findings which have been made on the former to the management of the latter, then we must qualify those findings according to the specific requirements deriving from the differences between their separate goals. The present paper attempts to lay the theoretical groundwork for such modifications, but the final solution must come through further experiment with therapeutic groups.

A similar conclusion may be reached for the signally important group function of communication. Let us take Bavelas' findings (3) as an example around which to study the conditions differentiating the therapeutic from the problem-solving group. On the basis of experimental work with task-oriented groups he concluded that freedom of communication makes for better results than communication that is interfered with by leaders controlling the whole system of communication. When we examine the conditions carefully we find that in a problem-solving group verbal communication is largely in terms of ideas and is taken at its face value. There may be evidences of latent emotional meaning, but this remains rightfully incidental as far as locomotion toward the goal is concerned. The leaders and the members operate on the same overt ideational level.

In the therapeutic group the situation is very different. Locomotion toward the integral goal of characterological change requires that latent emotional communication play a central role. Feeling communication is focal; that of ideas, secondary. For a long period the members communicate in their usual way on an overt level, relatively unaware of latent emotional meanings. The leader whose training has taught him the language of the unconscious (and the preconscious) helps translate them. Through his personal analysis he is also cognizant of his own latent feelings and must handle them. Only gradually do the members learn this technique and as they do they can help to interpret their own and one another's communications. It is true that certain members, as for example, schizophrenic individuals, may be far keener than the therapist at catching unconscious elements in the members' participations, but they are seldom aware of more than a single segment of such productions, whereas the therapist must keep the total psychodynamic picture of each patient in mind.

Moreover, members are also unable, from lack of experience or because of the intrusion of their own unconscious needs, to time their interpretations correctly. The therapist has to be ready to intervene when a member makes an interpretation which, whether it be correct or not, also reflects an unconscious motive. In uncovering this unconscious motive (let us say, of hostility) the leader will help the interpreter understand himself, and may also help the recipient of the interpretation become willing to accept it instead of reacting to its unconscious hostile purposes. In order further to help the recipient assess for himself the core of truth in another member's interpretation the therapist may have to help the recipient eliminate further resistance stemming from inner sources. The leader–therapist, in other words, *must* guide the whole system of communication. One might even go so far as to define therapy as the process of changing the basic nature of communication among members. As everyone knows, this is a delicate and intricate task which requires long professional training. Of necessity it puts a greater distance between the leader and the members than exists in most nontherapeutic groups. This by no means contraindicates his leaving the communication to the members, but it does indicate the necessary limits to which the principle of "free" communication can be applied in the therapeutic group. Accordingly, the findings of Bavelas must be rather markedly modified if they are to be applied in therapeutic groups.

To put this another way: the resistance of human beings to understanding the unconscious emotional meaning of their communications creates a formidable difference in the situation of the two kinds of groups. It is a distinction which cannot be ignored by anyone who compares them. Therapists cannot ignore resistance without blocking the road to their goal. They must therefore be much more involved in the whole system of communications than the leaders of ordinary groups. Thus, our study of communication also demonstrates the validity of the principle that comparison between different kinds of groups is feasible only in terms of the specific situations, and that findings made on one type of group often require modification when they are applied to another.

The second question we asked referred to the relationship between the therapeutic process and the group-dynamic processes per se, as these function side by side in the therapeutic group.[3] Careful inspection reveals that on the whole the group processes tend to enhance the therapeutic process, but that in certain situations and at certain times they work against the therapeutic goal. They can never substitute for it.

The analytic therapist tends naturally to focus on the therapeutic process and until recently has often ignored the group-dynamic processes. This neglect has not seemed to interfere seriously with his therapeutic aim. Experience has shown that skilled use of the therapeutic process will achieve his aim. Since the group processes are natural ones, they will function regardless of whether or not the therapist is aware of them, and for the most part they will nevertheless help locomote the group to its goal. In those instances when they work in an opposite direction, the therapeutic process will effectively counteract them.

In one group for example, the therapist had enlisted the natural forces of the group to develop a climate and standards of its own and had guided them toward permissiveness and freedom of emotional expression. In this group there were a number of impulsive characters with a tendency toward acting out and one rigid compulsive character. It soon became the fashion to use four-letter words indiscriminately. This habit was interpreted by the majority to fit in with the free atmosphere. The compulsive became extremely anxious. The phenomenon of group pressure to accept group standards was about to put him in the dilemma of joining in or leaving the group. Either solution would have been antitherapeutic for all. The therapist had to relieve the pressure and change the standards. He had, on the one hand, to protect one patient from too much pressure until he was able to work through his defenses. On the other hand, he had to help the "freer" members to examine their own motivation in their consistent choice of flamboyant language. As therapy progressed, all members were able to see that neither had had as free a choice as they had thought. Flexibility and real choice could now become the new standards and the leader could leave these to the natural group processes with little further interference. In this typical case the leader had to wield the group forces in two directions. He had to help develop therapeutic group standards, but see to it that individual differences did not succumb to the natural force of group pressures.

Group-dynamics investigators have probably made more progress in measuring the dimensions of cohesiveness than in that of any other group force. The role of this phenomenon in therapy groups also illustrates the interrelationship of the therapeutic and the group processes. Experience with

[3] My conclusions are based on readings in both fields, my own experience since 1938, and the examination of protocols of other group therapists. They were: J. Hirsch, Brooklyn Child Guidance Center; H. T. Glatzer, Ph.D., New Rochelle Guidance Center; and at the Postgraduate Institute for Psychotherapy: H. Papanek, M.D., S. Gottlieb, A. Kadis.

therapeutic groups has shown that cohesiveness plays an important role in these too. It has, like many other group factors, a certain therapeutic value, but at some points it interferes with the progress of the group. The therapist who wishes to understand the full implication for his goal of this natural group force will discover that the sources of cohesiveness are different in the therapeutic from those in the ordinary group. In most ordinary groups cohesiveness increases rapidly with the mutual identification among members, growing out of their activity in carrying out the work necessary for reaching the goal. Cohesiveness is also increased by the satisfaction of the members' unconscious needs. Playing and winning games, building a clubhouse or campaigning for a cause quite obviously satisfy certain aggressive or libidinal needs. In problem-solving groups certain unconscious satisfactions may also work toward cohesiveness, but on the whole artificial stimulation toward that end becomes necessary.

In the therapy group the situation is quite different. The natural forces tend, during the early sessions, to hinder rather than facilitate cohesiveness. The members are not aware at first of what satisfactions will come to them. They are anxious, and in their anxiety often wish for an exclusive relationship with the leader. Some would have preferred to avoid the group. These are usually more anxious about belonging than hopeful of gaining satisfaction from the group because their neurotic problems have so often interfered with their ability to achieve it. It is the leader who must use his therapeutic skill to develop the particular kind of cohesiveness that will best serve his aim.

This difference in the nature of cohesiveness leads us to another distinction between ordinary and therapeutic groups. Ordinary groups strive for an overt cohesiveness based on friendliness, mutual interests, and cooperation, which can usually be achieved through the channeling or repression of negative feelings. The goal of therapy requires that such negative feelings be brought out into the open, their sources understood, and worked through. For example, it is up to the leader to help the patients recognize and express their jealous need for exclusive possession of the leader in order that they may be enabled to form deeper relationships with the members. This makes for cohesiveness indirectly. He will also have to help them examine their suspicions of one another. If there are many paranoid trends in the group this will take rather a long time. Meanwhile if the leader has used his dynamic techniques well, the members will begin to get satisfaction from mutual understanding. Due to these two therapeutic developments, a feeling of belonging begins to develop, leading to a very strong degree of cohesiveness. It will develop later than in natural groups but rest on a sounder substructure.

At a later stage when the forces making for cohesion in ordinary groups may well begin mounting an extraordinarily strong cohesiveness takes place in the therapeutic group, and the leader may make full use of it. The safe family-like atmosphere of the group which derives from the developing transferences is a tremendous force for cohesion. Even the hostilities engendered by them do not interfere with it because they are accepted and dealt with therapeutically.

At some point in this process, however, the therapeutic goal demands a loosening of the forces of cohesiveness, as Papanek (7) has pointed out. The therapist must work toward the resolution of the transferences, for they are distortions. Moreover, he is interested in helping his patients develop good relationships in their total life situations. He has used the group relationship as a means to this end. Now he must prevent the means from becoming an end in itself. It can become so comfortable and easy for the members that they cling to their "family" group rather than venture forth into outside relationships. The therapeutic technique can in itself achieve this end, but the therapist who understands and can deal with the dynamic group processes will have better control than those who ignore them. In some therapeutic groups where there is a tendency to overstress the familial nature of the group and to use the group to provide a new and better family instead of analyzing the transference distortions, the continued satisfactions can lead to stickiness and overcohesiveness.

Many other group dynamics cut across the dynamics of the therapeutic process. We need only think of the way in which the development of an individual member's role playing is utilized for goal locomotion in ordinary groups, while it is broken down by analysis in therapeutic groups. For example, the "perfect lady" becomes a leader in a social group. In a therapeutic group it is often discovered that her perfect behavior forms a compulsive facade which binds her anxiety but leaves her empty and frightened underneath. The intellectual is a leader in a problem-solving group, but his reliance on ideas to the exclusion of feelings is treated as a defense in the therapeutic group. (I do not imply, of course, that the positive values of such character traits are broken down. The effort is only to remove the rigidity of the structure.) However, space permits us to examine only these few at present.

In retrospect we may, I think, conclude that the clinician who is skilled in the use of his therapeutic tools will not be unable to achieve his goals, even though he may not be cognizant of the full range of group-dynamics findings. He is bound to become acquainted with them in his own fashion in meeting with his therapeutic groups. However, knowledge of their viewpoint will assuredly broaden his foundations and provide him a fuller understanding of the nature of groups and provoke his interest in the dynamic basis of all kinds of groups. It may also add to his skill in using the therapeutic potentialities of the group processes themselves. He will therefore enrich his conception of his work and probably develop greater precision in executing it. The sociologist, on the other hand, who does not know the relationship of the therapeutic process to the group processes, will not be crippled in his research on the nature of other types of groups, but he may be misled, if he develops clinical interests, into confusing the therapeutic effect of group work with therapy as such.

In summary, we may say that, although we had to limit our discussion to a very few of the group-dynamic elements, these will serve to illustrate the following hypotheses: (1) that all types of group are comparable because they have a common dynamic basis in the psychology of ego interaction; (2) that findings derived from studies of other types of groups may be applied to therapy groups *only* if due account is taken of the differences in their situations and appropriate modifications are made; and (3) that group and therapeutic processes are on the whole mutually reinforcing but at times tend to work in opposite directions.

While the present attempt to establish these working hypotheses is based on clinical experience, my hope is that it will serve to stimulate experimental validation of them. Such scientific validation should shed further light on the relationship between the group processes and the therapeutic process; minimize errors in the application of results from one type of group to another; and, most important, increase the mutual understanding and eventual integration of the knowledge produced by these two main approaches to the understanding of the nature of groups.

BIBLIOGRAPHY

1. Bach, G.: *Intensive Group Psychotherapy.* New York: Ronald Press, 1952.
2. Bales, R. F.: *Interaction Process Analysis—A Method of Study of Small Groups.* Boston, Mass.: Addison & Wesley Press, 1950.
3. Bavelas, A.: Communications Patterns in Task-Oriented Groups. *Acoustical Society of America, 22*:75, 1950.
4. Borgatta, E.; Bales, R.; Hare, P.: *Small Groups.* New York: A. Knopf, 1955.
5. Cartwright, C. and Zander, A., eds.: *Group Dynamics.* Evanston, Ill.: Row Peterson Co., 1953.
6. Freud, S. (1922): *Group Psychology and the Analysis of the Ego.* New York: Liveright, 1949.
7. Papanek, H.: Combined Group and Individual Therapy in Private Practice. *Am. J. Psychother., 8,* 1954.
8. Preston, M. and Heintz: Effects of Participatory and Supervisory Leadership. *J. Abn. & Soc. Psychol., 44*:345-355, 1949.
9. Redl, F.: The Phenomenon of Contagion and "Shock Effect" in Group Therapy, In: *Searchlights on Delinquency,* ed. K. R. Eissler. New York: International Universities Press, 1949.
10. Scheidlinger, S.: *Psychoanalysis and Group Behavior.* New York: Norton, 1952.
11. Wolf, A.: The Psychoanalysis of Groups. *Am. J. Psychother., 3, 4,* 1949-50.

3

Some Aspects
of Group Dynamics

Lewis H. Loeser, M.D.
Newark, N.J.

[The definition of a *group* and a number of broad issues of group dynamics and process are explored here. Loeser delineates five essential properties of groups, particularly focusing upon the core property of *relationship of size and function*. He very interestingly notes some of the dynamic factors underlying the very special significance and therapeutic usefulness of the four- to eight-member group. His paper would appear to deal with important issues falling within the complex interface between the spheres of group dynamics and group structure.]

Our interest in the subject of group dynamics derives primarily from intensive work with therapeutic groups and to a lesser degree from observational studies of educational and social groups. In the course of our clinical studies we have, over a period of years, introduced experimental variables into standardized group situations. We have utilized tape recordings and observers as a check on experimental results. While our interest has been primarily clinical,[1] we have found ourselves concerned with problems of group dynamics to an increasing degree.

It would seem advisable at the onset to point out the degree of confusion which exists on the definition of a group. What, precisely, is a group? In what way does it differ from an aggregate, a collection of people, a gang, or a troop?

From "Some Aspects of Group Dynamics" by L. H. Loeser, *International Journal of Group Psychotherapy*, 1957, 7, 5–19. Copyright 1957 by the International Journal of Group Psychotherapy. Reprinted by permission.

[1] Loeser, L. H.; Furst, W.; Ross, I. S.; Bry, T.: Group Therapy in Private Practice, a Preliminary Evaluation. *Am. J. Psychother.*, April, 1949.

To this observer it appears to be highly necessary that workers in the field of psychiatry and psychology agree on a uniform concept of the group, its properties and its functions, and be selective in the use of specific terms. The use of the word "group," for example, to denote any or all aggregates of people, regardless of form or function, should be avoided by the scientist. Six people sitting in the waiting room of a station are not a group. The same six people sitting on a committee and carrying out a specific function do constitute a group.

Let us study a highly efficient group, a true group, and compare it in function and properties, in behavior and reactions, to a low efficiency, or "poor" group. What functions, or to be more precise, what properties are present in a true group which are not present, or are quantitatively less present, in a "poor" group? What precisely permits us to say: "This is a true group, or an efficient group" and "This is a poor group," or "This aggregate of people is not at all a group"? What criteria do we use in making these judgments?

ESSENTIAL PROPERTIES OF A GROUP

The literature indicates a certain degree of agreement on this problem, though there is variation on emphasis and scope. Our study would suggest that there is inherent in all true groups, in varying degree, some five essential properties. The functioning of the group depends on the extent to which these five properties are quantitatively present. These are, possibly in the order of importance:

1. Dynamic interaction (among members)
2. A common goal
3. Relationship of size and function
4. Volition and consent
5. A capacity for self-direction

1. Dynamic Interaction among Members

There must be some type of relationship and subsequent interaction based on such relationship which may be either positive or negative: if deeply unconscious, we imply attitudes and reactions based on transference factors; if more conscious, we deal in terms involving rapport, empathy, love and hate. The dynamic interaction must, of necessity, be directed among group members and not toward a leader. To the extent that the interaction occurs between a leader and an aggregate of people, the group function diminishes. When all interaction is directed toward the leader, we may have a troop, classroom, or audience, but not a true group.

2. The Common Goal

A collection of people can function as a group only in the presence of a common goal. In the absence of some form of stated common goal,

goal-searching may in itself become the common goal for a limited period. The ultimate absence of a common goal is destructive to group functioning; a loosely defined goal is threatening; a clearly established goal is facilitating.

3. Size and Function

There is a direct relationship in all true groups between size and function. Groups of certain sizes are best equipped to carry out certain functions. Any disproportion of a serious degree reduces quantitatively the efficient functioning of the group. Recognition of this basic principle has been established by law and custom throughout the ages, although the basis of such action has, for the most part, been unconscious.

In our work we have come to think of the relationship between size and function in physiological terms. As the size of the group increases or decreases, certain fundamental changes in pattern of function take place of a predictable, observable nature. This subject will be enlarged upon later in this paper.

4. Volition and Consent

Except under most unusual conditions, an efficient group functions only in terms of volition and consent of its members. Groups composed predominantly of captive, involuntary members do not truly function as a group, except, possibly, in terms of rebellion. Numerous articles in the group therapy field derive from captive or involuntary groups, and the consequent preoccupation with problems of management and with the subject of hostility and aggression reflects the absence of volition and consent on the part of the group members.

5. A Capacity for Self-Direction

There is inherent in every true group, a capacity, a willingness, or an intent to govern, to control, or to direct the destiny of the group in terms of self-direction. In this sense there is an incorporation of democratic principles and attitudes implied in the function of any true group. A collection of people who have surrendered their prerogatives and privileges to a leader or to a rigid set of rules have diminished their group function in proportion to what they have given up. Our concept of the meaning of democracy borders closely to, and is likely related to, our basic definition of group functioning. In this sense all efficient small groups function on a democratic basis. As one swings in the scale from democratic principles toward authoritarianism or tyranny, we not only surrender democratic principles, but we no longer function as a group. We become followers or adherents, or subjects, but not group members.

Dreikurs, in a recent article, discusses this phenomenon at length and at one point states, "The therapeutic group cannot exist save in a democratic atmosphere and in turn it creates a democratic atmosphere."[2] In reality these words can be applied to all true groups, and to the extent that the democratic concept is missing, to that extent true group function is absent.

One cannot take liberties with this concept. As the true group is made smaller or larger, in terms of its functions, it becomes less true. As one introduces leadership or strict rules or diffuses the common goal, to that extent it functions less and less as an efficient group. It may serve some proper function just the same, but it no longer approaches perfection or high efficiency. In the same sense as a group in terms of function deviates increasingly from perfection, the application of the term "group" becomes, for the scientist, more and more strained. As psychic interaction ceases, as leadership increases in strength, as size changes or as goals disappear—we may then be dealing with a troop, or an audience, or a gang, or a collection; many terms are available. However, in terms of scientific accuracy, the use of the word group becomes less and less justified as we deviate from the concept of the true group.

SIZE AND FUNCTION

It would be profitable at this point to investigate the various types of groups (in terms of size) and to discuss certain properties which appear to bear a relationship to size. It is my thesis, and the evidence seems to be reasonably clear, that there exists a definite relationship between size, form and function. This relationship has been recognized from time immemorial but has seldom been expressed in explicit terms.

Numerous examples are available to us, all of which bear testimony to our conscious and unconscious recognition of the relationship between size, form and function. These include size of juries, lawmaking bodies, religious groups, committees, etc. As we examine the subject of the size of groups, it becomes apparent that certain natural subdivisions occur, each with their own individual properties and characteristics. A study of variously sized groups leads the observer to certain classifications based on size. These are as follows:

1. Dyad
2. Triad
3. 4 to 8 (the ideal therapeutic group)
4. 8 to 30 (the ideal educational group)
5. 30 to several thousands (the audience group)
6. Crowds, masses (unlimited numbers).

There exist in reality no sharp borderlines between these groups. Nevertheless there is a reasonable basis for delimiting the above classifications and a justification for examining them as separate entities.

² Dreikurs, R.: Group Psychotherapy and the Third Revolution in Psychiatry. *Int. J. Soc. Psychiat.*, *1*:(3), 1955.

The Dyad

Group function begins with the dyad. We are familiar with this in terms of marriage and in the therapeutic relationship of doctor to patient. In these examples we have the most intimate type of dyad relationship. The dyad has certain characteristics which are peculiar and exist in no other size group. It is, for example, capable of developing the highest degree of spiritual values, as in marriage and friendship. Individuals of mediocre talents and propensities are capable in a dyad relationship of building up group standards on a plane far higher than either would be capable of in individual activities. Conversely, hostile and aggressive reactions can develop in a dyad to a more intense degree than in any other group setting. This is partially accounted for by the fact that in a dyad, responsibility for actions and behavior is fixed and obvious. There can be no evasions or misconceptions and no great amount of defects can be covered up. This acts, of course, to reinforce positive values so that credit is placed where it belongs, but it likewise reinforces negative values in the destructive sense.

While the dyad can function on a nonauthoritarian mutual interaction basis it need not necessarily function on this level and numerous examples of dyad relationships in which dominance and submission, sadism and masochism, aggressive and passive individual behavior are known to all of us. Despite these distortions, the dyad is outstanding in that it is capable of producing the most intimate, the highest spiritual qualities and the closest relationships that can exist within any group form. This characterization is fully utilized in the therapeutic relationship of psychiatrist to patient. The dyad, however, is also the most fragile of the groups for it can be disrupted completely by the actions of any one member of it. The forces that hold the dyad together can shift readily into forces which tend to disrupt it, and it is incapable of reviving itself after the loss of one member. It is, then, both the strongest and the weakest type of group with which we have to work.

In the preceding paragraph we have implied the fact that in the dyad groups, libidinal drives are most likely to develop and influence behavior. This would seem to be an important aspect of group functioning which warrants further scrutiny. Our peculiar make-up (endocrine, psychological, or more likely combinations of both) is such that libidinal drives, either heterosexual or homosexual, are directed toward one other person. In the dyad relationship full opportunity exists for the fulfillment of such drives. The dynamic impetus given to relationships arising directly from such factors provides an intensity of feeling that reaches its height in the dyad group and which diminishes in intensity as the group enlarges. This is just as true for negative feelings arising out of libidinal drives. Hostility directed against a partner may reach a state of intensity far greater than can exist in a larger group relationship. Thus the dyad relationship can give rise to a lifetime of married bliss or of hostility and unhappiness.

As the group becomes larger, as we go from triad to quartet, to quintet, libidinal drives become diluted in intensity. In a true group where some degree of interaction and reciprocal relationship exists among all members, libidinal drives and relationships based on it are diluted to what might be called comfortable or workable or safe quantities.

One of the values inherent in group therapy derives from the above observation. In a therapeutic group of from five to eight members, the dilution in intensity permits reasonable amounts of such tension to reach the surface in a controllable and relatively safe manner. In actual practice this takes on more significance in terms of the negative sense rather than the positive. By far the greater amount of time in therapy is spent in the handling of negative feelings, such as hostility and aggression rather than positive, libidinal drives. The dilution of transference relationships in this sense makes possible the handling of the analysis and subsequent working through of many forces which in the dyad relationship of individual therapy would be extremely painful and at times disturbing.

The Triad

As we consider the basic properties and functions of a triad, certain concepts of considerable interest emerge. There is introduced into the group an added relationship which may actively strengthen or weaken the functioning of the group. The third person, actually any one of the three, takes on unusual powers which are inherent in no other member of any other size group. He may, for example, sit in judgment, act to reconcile or to arbitrate, evaluate or obstruct. He may easily reinforce the group by such action and make it strongly cohesive, or he may destroy or impair group functioning by negative action. He is free to choose either partner for concerted action should they disagree and thus wield a balance of power; or he may be excluded by the other two and be rendered impotent. The triad then represents for each member a potential source of strength but equally represents a source of potential danger. Role playing thus becomes precarious and unstable and, in general, humans reject whenever possible the triad grouping as a comfortable size for group function. The expression, "Three's a crowd," is a simple folk expression but represents reasonably well the attitude of ordinary mortals toward a triad group with its inherent implications.

Our experience with the triad group, on a therapeutic level, would bear out these general conclusions. We have, on an experimental level, operated with triad therapeutic groups from time to time. Our triad groups in general did not do well. Problems of rivalry and jealousy consumed a great deal of time and actively interfered with the therapeutic process. Problems of management intruded into the therapeutic process to a degree entirely different from those seen in the larger therapeutic group of six to eight members. Observers constantly felt that problems arising out of sibling rivalry, whether related to the therapeutic process or not, reduced cohesiveness and lowered efficiency of the group as a whole. Another surprising feature was the almost complete absence of reassurance and support that is found constantly in the larger therapeutic group.

Is there a legitimate function for a triad group? There are, but not many. In a setting in which the group is called upon to carry out a specific task of guarding a project or of supervising the work of others a triad group might, by its very nature, function quite efficiently. It is less open to outside influences, and the balance of power factor tends to maintain a high degree of integrity in its supervisory role. Aside from this type of function, essentially supervisory or investigative, the triad group has, in my opinion, very few other functions that cannot be carried out more successfully by groups of other sizes.

The Four-to-Eight Group

As we progress from the dyad and triad to the quartet and larger, the next natural subdividion is the four-to-eight grouping. It is unfortunate that the English language does not contain a specific word for this size group, for it probably has a wider range of usefulness than any other size group.

It is, first of all, the largest group that can function without a leader and without strong rules and regulations. As we enlarge beyond the eight members, all groups, social, musical, therapeutic or whatever their function, tend to do one of two things. They either openly or tacitly select (or evolve) a leader, or they set up rules and regulations to govern their conduct. A strong leader may obviate rules, or conversely, rigid and accepted rules may replace the leader.

If, by chance (and in particular where there is no common goal), groups larger than eight do not possess rules or a leader, they inevitably break up into subgroups and thus no longer function as a group. This phenomenon can be observed in its simple form in social groups.

We have given considerable thought to the phenomena described above. Why is it that six or seven people can function as an efficient cohesive group without rules or strong leadership but ten or twelve people cannot? Many theories have been advanced but none can be considered as entirely proven. We have much to learn on this point. It is certainly no accident that seven is the magic number for a therapeutic group. Observers over a wide area using diverse methods and approaching this subject from many points of view have reached common agreement on this point. For the properties of a four-to-eight group lend themselves peculiarly and accurately to the goal of psychotherapy. Let us list these properties:

1. It is large enough to dilute libidinal drives to safe and easily handled quanta.
2. It is large enough to provide a variety of intragroup transference potentialities to suit the needs of each patient at any given time.

3. It is large enough to avoid the strong positive and negative polarity of reaction of the dyad and triad and hence is more enduring. It cannot be destroyed by one or even two people.
4. It is large enough to permit heterogeneity and diversification of psychodynamic types and thus implement the group interaction process.
5. It is large enough to permit acting out in a diluted and workable manner.
6. On the other hand it is small enough to be handled by a therapist with a minimum of leadership and control. The therapist can maintain his uncritical, permissive and passive role, all of which are necessary for effective therapy.
7. It is small enough to operate without strong or numerous rules or regulations. Beyond a few simple rules such as hours, meeting places, etc., very few regulations need to be introduced.
8. It is small enough to permit each member a reasonable amount of attention and time, but large enough to remove the tensions of face-to-face talking. The passive individual can remain inconspicuous until his confidence is built up before he need take on an active role.

For precisely the above reasons, in areas other than group therapy, the four-to-eight group has ideal properties. It is, for example, the appropriate group for intimate social entertaining. It is likewise the largest group that can, in the field of music, function without a leader. Many other examples may be given to illustrate further the wide adaptability and variety of function inherent in the four-to-eight group.

The Eight-to-Thirty Group

While our focus is primarily the small group, the properties and functions of the larger groups are also of interest. The eight-to-thirty group is primarily of interest to us as the ideal group for educational purposes. As we progress in size from the eight group upward, the need for leadership increases proportionately, and the teacher can take over this role without sacrifice of other qualities. The eight-to-thirty group is large enough to permit active leadership but small enough to permit member participation. It is large enough to dilute interaction factors, which in the educational process would likely be deterring, but small enough to permit modest amounts of identifications. Acting out can be tolerated in reasonable amounts, though only if not excessive. It is thus ideally adapted to the educational process.

The Mass

This is the assembly that lends itself to audience type of participation. By its very size, it can exist only in the presence of fixed and rigid rules such as seating arrangement, time schedules, imposed silence, etc. It can be held together as a group only by someone acting in a performer or director role, taking the central spotlight position and completely dominating the action. It is relatively incapable of action, being slow to move in any direction or to change course. It is, however, responsive to emphatic influences, both negative and positive. Judgments of a group of this size are far more likely to be influenced by emphatic reactions than by considered intellectual processes of thought. It can thus be influenced and stirred emotionally by great performers and artists, but it can likewise be influenced to serious mistakes in judgment by demagogues and politicians. Unlike smaller groups, the larger group can be skillfully used by unscrupulous people to a degree unlikely in the small group. The small group can set us checks and balances, can inquire, doubt or ask for proof. The large group, forced to preserve order at the expense of free inquiry, must sacrifice the checks and balances at the expense, frequently, of truth.

As groups enlarge in size, an interesting phenomenon takes place in terms of transference factors and relationships. Small group relationships are predominantly in terms of transference factors, that is, strongly influenced by unconscious and, at times, illogical attitudes. The relationships are also more likely to spread laterally to other members of the group. Relationships based on sibling and parental identifications, unconscious but strong, are the rule.

As we go to the larger groups collateral transference relationships become weaker until, as in the audience group, we may have no relationship whatever to any other member of the group, but only to the leader or performer. The relationship which extends outward to the performer, the leader, or the speaker, consists predominantly of empathic forms of identification. We can then understand the great potential power wielded by the central figure in an audience size group, for virtually all relationships in the group relate to the one central figure. If the central figure is sufficiently endowed to generate positive empathic reactions, he is thus in a position of tremendous power to do good or evil, to entertain or to bore, to arouse emotion or to calm unrest.

Crowds, Masses, Mobs

Opportunity for direct observation on groups larger than the audience group has been limited. Since our primary interest is in dynamics of small groups we will leave this area to those better equipped to throw light on this subject.

SOME DYNAMICS OF GROUPS

Acting Out

My associate, Thea Bry, has, among others, given considerable thought to the subject of "acting out" and its significance in group dynamics.[3] It has

[3] Bry, T.: Acting Out in Group Psychotherapy. *Int. J. Group Psychother. 3*:42–48, 1953.

been our experience that acting out is best handled and most appropriately utilized by the four-to-eight group. Smaller groups do not tolerate acting out well for the threat to group solidarity is too immediate and resources for effective control are lacking. Groups larger than eight tend to submerge acting out by the introduction of strong leadership and rules. In this sense then, the very small group cannot tolerate acting out, the very large group will not.

The Group Reaction

For several decades observers have discussed, without arriving at specific conclusions, the existence of a group reaction which may be independent of, and superior to, or different from, the reactions of the individual members of the group. Can we postulate a "group mentality," which is more than, or different from the sums of the individuals?

A long and reasonably varied experience working with groups would permit this observer to answer the above question on both a "yes" and "no" basis. I am convinced that for the most part, under most circumstances, small groups do not have any appreciable degree of group reaction above and beyond that of the collective individuals. On the other hand, at certain times and under certain conditions, groups may take on properties and resort to actions such as to justify the concept of the group mentality.

What are these certain times referred to? They are always during periods of strong emotion, either pleasant or unpleasant. In this emotional atmosphere a form of feedback reaction is set up, leading to a secondary effect resembling the reverberating circuit. In many instances the chain of events and mechanisms involved can be traced back in detail. There results a building up of emotional tensions to a point where, in the end, individual reaction is submerged and group responses begin to take over. In this state, characterized physically by the reverberating circuit concept, groups may act, react, perform either positively or negatively in a way entirely foreign to, and unlike the normal mode of response of any individual of the group. A group mentality takes over, as it were.

I do not think that under normal circumstances this phenomenon is observed. In general our normal ego functions are directed at preserving the role we assume in any group, to permit us to function and to be relatively uninfluenced by external forces such as the group. Only under severe emotional stress, in the presence of a group setting in which the feedback mechanism and reverberating circuit are available, do we see a breaking down of our isolated roles and a taking over by the "group ego," as it were.

It is my distinct impression that there exists a dynamic balance between "role playing"[4] and group reaction representing a surrender to the influence

[4] By the term "role playing" I am referring to a predominantly unconscious process of acting out a role within the group. In this sense, role playing is defined as a neurotic defense mechanism with a specific function, in this case to maintain equilibrium against the threat of the group reaction.

of the group. It would appear as if one important function of role playing is to prevent, or perhaps hold to a minimum, any overt manifestation of group reaction and that there normally exists a state of equilibrium between role playing and the group reaction. We are, except in very predictable and safe circumstances reluctant to be carried away by any group reaction. When we do, we very clearly want to know where we are going and why. The preservation of our role in the group insures, or tends to insure, us against the impact of "group emotion."

As we observe manifestations of the group mentality, in particular as we see it in therapeutic and social groups, certain phenomena occur in sufficient frequency to be noted. In addition to the decrease of role playing referred to above, there is always an increase of tension. This increase may be either pleasant or unpleasant. Under all circumstances the amount is increased. In addition there is a distinct tendency toward uniformity of thinking. Differences disappear, leaving only one prevailing attitude; or under certain circumstances two such attitudes when intragroup splitting into two factions has precipitated the tension. Most pronounced is the lowering of critical faculties and suppression of sound judgment values. The latter is probably responsible (as well as other factors) for the potential excesses inherent in group behavior, as in lynching, but eqully responsible for high order of cooperation and inspirational guidance of successful group action.

What can be said about the nature of the phenomena referred to previously as the "feedback mechanism"? As observed in therapeutic and social groups it is usually generated by directing attention toward sensitive material, material relating to strong emotional ties and is most likely manifested after a period of tension has existed for an uncomfortable period. The subject involved may be unrelated to the previous material. Most important, it requires an early and definitive response, frequently a repeated response on the part of at least one other person. It is fed back, as it were, to the original source, generating a secondary response, is again fed back, and a tertiary response is noted. As a rule other group members become involved emotionally at this point, and what I have referred to as the "reverberating circuit" is now beginning.

The reverberative circuit represents a circular, around the group, reaction of high intensity. It may manifest itself in many ways, by collective anger, by laughter, by silence. The presence of a highly contagious form of emotion is then manifest. The group at this point has lost many of its former qualities. It is no longer a collection of individuals, each playing his own role. It is now a collective organism, reacting for the most part as a whole, relatively uncritical, capable of either a high or low order of behavior, more uniform throughout in make-up, with individual roles effectively suppressed. At this point a group mentality may be said to exist and group reaction is present.

In the analytic sense, the group reaction would seem to represent a surrender of both ego and superego to a new authority, the group. Only the id remains untouched, functioning under the protective authority of the newly formed "group ego," restrained only by the thinly organized "superego of the group." No wonder, then, that groups at this point are capable of excessive actions, for good or evil, far beyond the potentialities of any isolated member.

The phenomenon of group reaction is, as I have previously pointed out, opposed to and always subject to the role-playing needs of the individuals making up the group. As a result group reaction is always transient. In the end the individual ego reasserts itself, tensions drop, and each member in the end reverts back to his individual role. In this way homeostasis is implied, pathological behavior is avoided (usually) and the balance maintained. I see it as differing not at all from a body mechanism such as the function of respiration with its homeostatic system of checks and balances. The functioning group, the true group is no exception; there is a constant trend toward equilibrium.

An interesting property of the group reaction, discussed in detail by many early writers is the high degree of suggestibility present in individuals who are implicated by the total group reaction. In this reaction the individual having in effect surrendered his ego and superego to the group, loses his powers of critical judgment to a degree bordering on the hypnotic state.

THE LITERATURE

In the preparation of this paper I have not been unmindful of the mass of experimental and recorded data now available to the worker in this field. Strodtbeck, in a recent publication, estimates that over 1,400 articles dealing with small group studies have appeared in the last fifty years, the greater number in more recent years.[5] Many deal with minute fractions of the total problem and are difficult to orient into the larger picture. Others would appear to have direct bearing on the material with which we are dealing. I would like to call attention to a few relatively recent publications which will be of particular interest to the student of group dynamics. Those wishing to prusue this subject further are referred to the excellent bibliography of Strodtbeck and Hare of 1954.[6]

The problem of selection and synthesis of this published mass of material is one of enormous magnitude, perhaps well beyond the resources of the average worker in the field and certainly beyond the resources of the clinician. Partial attempts at synthesis have been made. A recent article by Roseborough has as its purpose "to review the present state of empirical knowledge in the field of small group study . . ."[7] Theoretical and interpretative work has not

[5] Strodtbeck, F. L.: The Case for the Study of Small Groups. *Am. Soc. Rev., 19,* December, 1954.

[6] Strodtbeck, F. L. and Hare, A. P.: Bibliography of Small Group Research (1906-1954). *Sociometry, 17*:107-178, 1954.

[7] Roseborough, M. E.: Experimental Studies of Small Groups. *Psychol. Bull., 50*:275-303, 1953.

been covered in this review, nor has systematic treatment of small group phenomena. The author deals predominantly with a series of papers in which independent variables are specified for investigation, variables such as group vs. individual comparisons, group functions and authority relationships, the effect of cultural variables on group relationships, size of groups in terms of function, the effect of personality variables on group function, etc. Many of the papers cited by Roseborough, confined as they are to small fragments of laboratory research, are difficult to fit into a unified pattern. Test results are frequently marginal, correlations are not always conclusive, and disagreement is occasionally seen in interpretations. Nevertheless this review is suggested as a profitable entry into the field of small group study by clinicians interested in exploring the area of group dynamics.

Cartwright's and Zander's recent volume entitled *Group Dynamics* is to be recommended.[8] It is a collection of studies of the small group drawn from a variety of research centers. The authors divide their material into six sections: theoretical, research, formation of groups and cohesiveness, group pressures and standards, the problem of goals, group structure, and problems of leadership. Each section is preceded by an introduction which tends to tie together the subsequent articles in an attempt at synthesis. The articles are, as one would expect, uneven. Some are direct and communicate readily on first reading; others give the impression of foundering in semantic confusion. This, I might add, is a fault too frequently observed in related literature. Too often do we find simple, direct concepts that could be expressed in terse and clear manner obscured by complicated and involved presentation. Cartwright and Zander have this in mind when they say "some of the obvious disparities of terminology when dealing with the same phenomena derived from the special languages that are brought to the study of groups. It may be expected that these purely semantic problems will be solved as research techniques become standardized and interdisciplinary work proceeds."

A partial and reasonably successful attempt at synthesis is demonstrated in a series of chapters in the recent volume of Gardner Lindzey. Chapters by Kelly and Thibout, Borgatta, Homans and Ricker, and others are certainly of value in orienting the reader in this difficult field.[9]

A recent issure of the *American Sociological Review* (December, 1954) is devoted exclusively to the subject of small group research. Edited by Strodtbeck, who contributes an excellent introduction, it contains a series of articles bearing directly and some less directly on the subject of group dynamics. Of particular interest is the paper of Harp and Bush on reactions to group pressures and the paper of Riley, Cohn and Riley on interpersonal orientations in small groups.

[8] Cartwright, D. and Zander, A. F. (eds.): *Group Dynamics: Search and Theory.* Evanston: Row, Peterson and Co., 1953.

[9] Lindzey, G. (ed.): *Handbook of Social Psychology.* Cambridge: Addison-Wesley Pub. Co., 1954.

Certain very broad references contain material of orientation value. The original articles by Simmel, dealing with the relationship between size and function, are classical and deserve careful study. Without experimental data and based almost entirely on observational and historical data, Simmel's perceptions and understandings are remarkable.[10]

Parsons, in his book dealing with *The Structure of Social Actions,* is worthy of careful study, some chapters bearing clearly on our subject.[11] MacDougal's famous volume on *The Group Mind* is perhaps outdated but contains many stimulating ideas to the present-day reader. The volume of G. C. Homans would be recommended, particularly the chapter by R. K. Merton.[12]

Invaluable contributions to the field of group dyanmics have resulted from the work of the Michigan group headed by Lippitt, the Harvard group including Homans, Borgatta, Bales,[13] and others.

There is, as one can readily see, no limit to the number of references one might cite in this complex field. The problem is not one of finding relevant material but rather a problem of interpretation and synthesis. In a sense we are predominantly dealing with minute aspects of knowledge. The problem of sorting, identifying and correlating these splinters into an integrated concept is one of great complexity. There is great need at this time for the working through of basic concepts. We have a plethora of fragmentary data but unified concepts of group function are sorely lacking. This article has been written in the hope that it may inspire further and more rewarding research into a unified concept of group dynamics.

[10] Simmel, G.: *Am. J. Sociol.,* *8*:158–196, 1902.
[11] New York: McGraw Hill, 1937.
[12] Homans, G. C.: *The Human Group.* New York: Harcourt, Brace and Co., 1950.
[13] Bales, R. F.: *Interaction Process Analysis.* Cambridge: Addison-Wesley Press, 1953.

II

NONTHERAPEUTIC T–GROUPS: AN IDEAL OBSERVATIONAL MEDIUM FOR THE STUDY OF GROUP DYNAMICS

4

Some Dynamic Processes Observed During an Unstructured Group Laboratory Experience

Morton Kissen
Institute of Advanced Psychological Studies
Adelphi University
Garden City, Long Island, New York

[A number of group dynamic tendencies observed during the course of an unstructured laboratory experience are outlined in this chapter. Essential processes such as the initial group anxiety, the focal conflict between individuation strivings and group "suction," the "fight-flight" stage, the narcissistic struggle for "pecking order" positions, the radical "polarization" impact of leader absence, and a number of typical group defense mechanisms against anxiety and feelings of depression are descriptively and analytically explored. The fact that these dynamic patterns can be seen to fall into a "developmental" sequence consisting of six relatively discrete phases is hypothesized as substantiating the need for an ego psychological conceptual model of group phenomena.]

This chapter summarizes the processes observed by the author during his involvement in the experiential laboratory portion of a group dynamics seminar held at the Menninger Foundation. The essential structural characteristics and theoretical rationale underlying the use of such groups for the training of psychiatric professionals have been described by Appelbaum (1963, 1966) and Horwitz (1967). Each group had approximately 15 members and met for 20 sessions of 1½ hours each. A recorder who was present during the entire sequence of meetings silently observed and recorded the interactions of group members and did not respond when alluded to or even when directly addressed by the group members.

The basic empirical recording process in many ways approximates that described by Whitaker and Lieberman (1964). In addition to the neutral recorder-observer, every member of the group was required to keep a running process recording of the events taking place in the group meetings. The diaries thus obtained were to be used as the empirical raw data for a subsequent more extensive analytic summary to be written by each member after the termination of the experiential portion of the seminar. Thus a number of empirical recording methods were used, which could potentially allow for an objective cross-check on the reliability of descriptive observations and inferences regarding group dynamic processes observed during the seminar.

In addition, the second half of the seminar consisted of a more didactic and conceptual discussion of the common experiences of the group members who were now clustered into larger classes of approximately 20 members each. The original four experiential groups were thus combined randomly into three theoretical discussion groups. During the course of the conceptual integration activities provided by these larger groups, it was possible via a sharing of experiences for the group members to compare notes and to elaborate on the common thematic preoccupations and dynamic processes that had almost universally occurred in all four experiential laboratory groups.

What follows is a descriptive review of the dynamic patterns observed during a typical laboratory group. Certain processes of group development, particularly as elaborated on in the theoretical writings of Bion (1959) and of Bennis and Shepard (1956), are reflected in the thematic content of this summary.

SUMMARY OF PROCESS RECORDINGS

The initial stage of any social encounter is usually an anxiety-laden experience for its participants. There is a rather pervasive feeling of strangeness which makes it difficult for a smooth interaction to occur. The natural reaction to such discomfort seems to be some attempt at familiarizing the various aspects of the experience. This could be clearly seen during the first few group sessions. Many unknown factors had to be clarified, and a flood of questions were posed by the seminar participants, questions about the purpose of the seminar as well as what was expected of its individual members.

Some thought this might be a seminar in which one discusses professional problems, much as one would at lunch with one's colleagues. Others felt this was to be a therapeutic group and related it to group therapy experiences they had previously undergone. A seminar atmosphere was initially set up in which psychological issues were discussed in a highly intellectualized and abstract fashion, much as they might have been discussed in any didactic classroom setting. Each member attempted to maintain a distance from the other individuals in the group. Although the participants made awkward attempts toward getting to one another, they experienced an overall hesitancy to speak and reveal themselves, especially since there seemed no way of predetermining how others would receive any statement one might make. The many instances of hostile banter between individual members made revealing oneself even more threatening.

The leader described the general atmosphere of suspiciousness that seemed to pervade the early sessions. However, he was also an unknown element and hence was reacted to cautiously. The group's preoccupation with deciphering the puzzle posed by the leader's presence was manifested in a concern about his aggressive powers. Pseudohostile feelers were directed at him with the express hope of clarifying the sort of person he was. Superficially, he gave the impression of being a rather mild-mannered person with a benign, albeit somewhat detached, attitude toward the group; participants wondered, however, whether he could tolerate spontaneous forms of self-expression. Since he had been designated as "leader," group members tended to view him as an authority figure, perhaps similar to the supervisors they were working with outside the group. His interpretations were seen as attempts to manipulate the group into moving toward some goal he desired. Some members spoke of "good supervisors," persons confident enough in their own capacities that they could tolerate criticism leveled at them, even from people having less training and experience than themselves.

The ambiguity surrounding the entire experience caused much of the initial discomfort. Each individual engaged in a struggle to find some role that would facilitate interaction with the others. Thus, each person tested out a series of interactional styles, seeking the most comfortable one. The seating pattern as well as the extent and qualitative aspects of the members' conversational styles became rough measures of their positions within the group on a dominance scale. One had to decide how much to give of oneself to the germinal process of group formation.

Obvious differences between members created jagged edges that had to be smoothed out during the early stage of the group's development. Thus, the group was primarily composed of first-year psychiatric residents from Topeka State Hospital. There was a small splinter group, however, consisting of a psychology trainee and two group work trainees from The Menninger Foundation. The residents usually initiated the early discussions, centering around experiences that were familiar to them during their professional training at Topeka State Hospital. Gradually, however, the boundaries separating them from the nonpsychiatric members were removed. This seemed to occur as the group became increasingly aware of the experience of anxiety they all were sharing. The movement toward unanimity and consensus was counterbalanced by an equally powerful striving toward individuation. Thus, although the group seemed to be moving toward an integration and a blurring of the differences between the members, many events occurred that hinted at desire by individual members to retain their identities.

A good example of the ambivalence surrounding the group integrative process was an assertion by one of the women that no effort had been made to incorporate the females into the group. While ostensibly crying out for a greater effort to integrate the women into the group, she in fact called attention to their femaleness as well. It was as if she said, "Look, we women are *different* from you men, and yet you make no effort to react to our difference from you."

This ambivalence could also be seen in the fear of many members that their uniqueness and individuality would have to be sacrificed during the process of group formation. Thus, some members emphasized that their previous group experiences made them a bit more comfortable in making an observation or suggesting a course of action. One member stated that he had undergone analysis and hinted thereby that he was more at ease than the others with the "dynamics" side of "Group Dynamics."

Still more subtle forms of individuation strivings could be seen in the various expressions of individual personality patterns. One member belabored an emphasis on his "maverick" tendencies, making frequent reference to what he saw as the oppressive and incorporative quality of The Menninger Foundation, and emphasizing its apparent discouragement of individualistic activities. Other members accomplished the same thing by monopolizing the conversation through glib banter, although this was more typically a defense against dealing with emotional issues. Taking a centrally located seat, coming late, and presenting a group-related dream also seemed to be partially related to individualistic strivings. Another quite subtle form of such strivings was probably present in the attempt to say something that might cue an intervention by the leader. The hostile scapegoating and jealousy that frequently followed the leader's commenting, "This person has just expressed something that the whole group is struggling with," was ample evidence that a narcissistic reward had been dished out, suggesting that a narcissistic striving had been present in the rewarded person as well as in his resentful colleagues.

Balanced against the narcissistic and individualistic strivings was an equally powerful pressure toward cementing a unified group out of its disparate elements. The need for a consensus was most clearly revealed whenever a decision, minor or major, was being discussed. This need also emerged when an attempt at clarification of some fuzzily perceived idea was being worked over by the group. Repression by the group of some salient fact, such as whether or not the leader had made a particular statement, or what the theme had been at a previous meeting, frequently outlined the consensual bent more clearly. The same force toward consolidation could be seen in the occasional spontaneous interruption of a discussion that appeared to be of a specialized nature. It is tempting to hypothesize that the almost habitual opening of the meeting with a discussion of the weekly lecture was some such effort toward unifying the group about a commonly shared experience, forgetting for the moment the useful defensive purposes that such an emotionally neutral topic can hold. A more basic consolidating mechanism, however, occurred through a constant tendency of the group to fall back on the experiences in its own history. For example, the earliest attack on the leader occurred via an outwardly humorous comment by one member with regard to certain characteristics of the leader that reminded him of a "Nincompoop." The group responded with almost boisterous laughter. Although subsequent recurring allusion to the "Nincompoop" comment may be viewed as a provocative attack on the leader, its solidifying nature should not be overlooked. Here was a humorous anecdote about an experience that all of the members had shared, and that would make no sense at all to a stranger. Thus, a commonly shared group experience was captured through a metaphor. Similarly, a particular joke or story told by one of the members frequently tended to become institutionalized and incorporated into the group storehouse of memories and experiences.

The potent nature of this integrative force was clearly revealed by the lack of absences, as well as by the group's reaction when an infrequent absence did occur. The absentee was typically greeted by a hostile silence or some other intensive confrontation with the fact that his actions have taken him along a separatist course. A similar reaction occurred whenever any individual narcissistic action was discerned by the group. It must be noted, however, that while individual pleasure seeking was forbidden during this gradual process of group solidification, a greater tolerance for spontaneity and self-expression "within the group context" seemed to be building up. This reached its climax during one session in which a sort of group "free association" occurred. Despite some tendency to inhibit the spontaneity of the group associative process, a general feeling of relaxation and pleasure seemed to have been shared by all. Thus, narcissistic pleasures could be experienced provided that they were channeled through the *group* medium.

The profound disintegrative effect of the leader's two-week absence was astonishing, as though all the props had been pulled out from under the group's integrative efforts. The group could no longer maintain a consensus and promptly splintered into two groups during a crucial decision-making session. A few members decided to show up for the next few meetings; the bulk of the group said that they would not attend. Having been reminded by the leader's absence of the transient nature of the group, everyone seemed to sense its ultimate demise. The members who did not show up for the subsequent sessions seemed to be making haste to prepare the funeral arrangements. This could be clearly seen in the pervasive denial that many of them manifested of having had any attachment to the group. One member, in particular, insisted that the group was far less involving than certain professional groups he attended where his ties seemed to be more permanent.

Other members manifested repressive defenses, frequently making statements such as, "I must be blind, I haven't the foggiest idea of what is going on." The members who did attend the meetings also seemed to have been using denial, but in a different manner. They refused to admit that the group was going to end and assumed that it would continue in some actual or spiritual sense.

It was fascinating to discover that despite the surface disintegration of group ties, a similar underlying experience was moving all the members. This became clear when the group reunited and began to look together at their common experience. Despite the outwardly different modes of handling the anxiety (attending vs. nonattending), the same anticipation of loss had been experienced by all members. The group now seemed capable of moving closer together. Despite a regressive preoccupation with food and eating and the pervasive work of mourning that had to be done, during the meeting after the leader's return the group was stronger than it had been. It seemed ready to reflect upon some of the memories and institutions that had been built up during its period of consolidation. I remember commenting during the first reunion meeting, after a period of much hostility and competition between the two camps, "I'm sorry that Dr. X isn't here; he probably could bring us together again." This particular member was the focus of the "Nincompoop" metaphor, a primary example of an institution created during the group's integrative stages. During later meetings other group members seemed more and more prone to look back on the proceedings that stood out as figure from ground in the group's common storehouse of memories.

Certain patterns of group interaction became more clear as a result of the seminar. Thus, certain defensive mechanisms familiar to me from a knowledge of individual psychotherapy came through on the group level. Repression was frequently manifested by the members' inability to recall what was going on in the group, or what theme the group had previously been discussing. Displacement of feelings onto a scapegoat who carried the burden for the whole group was very common. The group would frequently sit back and passively observe a few members acting out certain feelings that were present in everyone. Two members, in particular, tended to act out, through a sort of "Mutt and Jeff" routine, the sibling rivalry patterns that were salient at a particular moment. The same mechanism allowed for a general avoidance of participation in the feelings generated by the group. One could often observe the group subtly feeding fuel into a neutral ongoing discussion, attempting to keep it from dwindling, and thereby avoiding a confrontation with their feelings. Intellectualized discussions were maintained well beyond the period of their interest for a similar purpose. Humor was occasionally used as a defense against aggressive feelings, as well as in a counterdepressive fashion.

It was also possible to observe a great deal of hostility as well as heightened ties between particular members. One member expressed the desire to cement a closer friendship to me by describing a dream in which he took me fishing with him. I responded likewise by denoting that member as the person best able to bring the group closer together again. Some members, on the other hand, were highly antagonistic toward comembers. One member frequently called another the "assistant leader." After the leader stated that one particular member had made a crucial statement, I consistently reacted in a hostile fashion, saying, "I don't see what is so brilliant about his statement." A male member frequently reacted hostilely whenever one of the females in the group behaved in what he considered a "motherly" fashion.

DEVELOPMENTAL ANALYSIS

The experiential portion of the seminar thus offered an ample opportunity for observation of a number of group-as-a-whole dynamic patterns. There was clearly a sort of developmental progression that took place with subtly discernible shifts from one dynamic phase to another. Although these phases were complexly intertwined and often temporally overlapping, they were nevertheless discretely observable in the thematic content of the group discussion at various times. The phases can hence be thought of as points along a group developmental continuum. Figure 1 presents a schematic outline of the six discernible phases of the group's development.

Phase I: Anxiety-Dependency

In this earliest phase of the group's development the members find themselves threatened by the ambiguity and lack of structure implicit in the group situation. A rather pervasive feeling of anxiety is evident in the silences and hesitant verbal interactions that occur during this phase.

Most of the initial interactions between the members are directed at familiarizing themselves with each other and particularly with the leader who sits so silently and yet imposingly before them. Since there are no explicit structures and guidelines for behavior, a desperate attempt is made at imposing some form of structure upon the group interaction process. The leader and all the members are initially strangers, but this is clearly not an acceptable state of affairs for the group members. A certain quality of "fantasied familiarity" (Day, 1967) pervades the interaction between peer

FIGURE 1 Six phases of group development

I	II	III	IV	V	VI
Anxiety-dependency phase	Individuation versus group suction phase	Power phase	Group-system formation phase	Polarization phase	Reintegration and termination phase

group members. Thus, the group seems to split off into pairs and triplets, each containing members who have either had previous social contacts or who in some fantasied or empathic sense are able to identify with each other.

The anxiety underlying this early form of subgrouping and "cuddling" is clearly not dispelled by the makeshift familiarization interactions between the members. The leader's mysterious qualities seem to have somehow been overlooked in the anxious attempts at getting to know each other and the basic structural rules of the group situation in general. Hence, what next ensues is a preoccupation with the silent, verbally ungiving leader who shares with the members virtually nothing of either himself or his expectations of the group. The members busy themselves with attempts at engaging the leader in some form of dialogue. The magical wish that the leader will somehow relieve their anxiety by an active structuring intervention reflects the deeply regressive dependency needs that have been brought to the surface by the group situation. The craving is clearly for a strong authority figure—not unlike Freud's (1918/1946, 1922/1965) descriptions of the primal horde leader—who will somehow cut the group's anxiety via masterful clarificatory activity.

Unfortunately, the leader's sparse interpretive communications are clearly not the food being sought by the members. His interpretations are typically greeted by befuddlement and a sense of disappointment. The members begin to act more and more as helpless children unable to get sufficient gratification from a frustrating parent figure.

Phase II: Individuation versus Group Suction

A very basic conflict evident in the early thematic preoccupations of the group members is that between the need for belongingness and inclusion in the incipient group formation process and the fear that the group suction process will somehow lead to a loss of individuality and sense of identity.

From a dynamic standpoint, it can be argued that the group exerts a regressive pull on the members, which consequently stirs up a sense of anxiety and a strong need to erect defensive structures against these regressive feelings. Scheidlinger (1974) has recently argued that there is a sort of "mother-group" feeling occurring in therapeutic groups that somehow transferentially represents the powerful preoedipal mother figure who is both dreaded and idealized by the members. A similar process can be inferred to have occurred in the present group. Thus, the fact that some members reacted in a highly dependent manner and were quick to join in on the developing "groupiness" and others reacted in a more reserved and detached manner can, according to Scheidlinger, be derived from the nature of the early resolution of their particular ambivalent relationships with the preoedipal mother. The group itself thus symbolically represents a composite of the members' projected mother imagoes. Ambivalence toward being incorporated into the group represents a very basic conflict with regard to its desirable enveloping and protective attributes and at the same time its more noxious suction and identity-diffusion potential.

Comfortable and ego-syntonic characterological defenses such as intellectualization, rationalization, and displacement are often used by members to cope with the anxiety engendered by the group experience and to establish a firmer sense of their own individual identities. Narcissistic preoccupations and interpersonal competitiveness offer a similar opportunity for individualization and hence a protective buffer against the inherent danger of group incorporation.

Phase III: Power Relationships

The narcissistic orientation of the members, evident in their efforts to capture the attention of the leader and other members through extended monologues and other forms of idiosyncratic behavior, tends to play itself out in the form of a subtle jostling for position and a highly politicized mode of group interaction. The leader is clearly the most powerful member of the group, despite his general verbal recalcitrance and inactivity. A number of members, however, attempt either to usurp his power via their own seemingly powerful interactive activity and replace him or to mimic his interpretive efforts.

The process of scapegoating becomes visible during the power phase, with particular members being selected for brief or prolonged victimization. Although the group members hesitantly attack the leader (often through some form of humorous metaphor), their primary hostility is directed at their peers. It can be inferred that a kind of "identification with the aggressor" (Freud, 1937/1966) process is taking place in the group with the members tending to interact in both an identificatory and projective mode. Thus, members identify with the leader (who is viewed in a projectively distorted manner as a dangerously aggressive and powerful figure) and victimize other members in much the same manner that they imagine the leader would himself like to deal with the members.

The concept of the "fight–flight" stage (Bion, 1959; Rioch, 1970) of group development would appear applicable to this power phase. The latent anxiety and group tension is displaced and channeled into aggressive scapegoating and a politically combative stance. Depending on their particular characterological defensive structures, some members will attack others, and others will become the victims of the group attack. The group as a whole is most vulnerable to dissolution and failure during this phase. Much depends on the sensitivity and interpretive acumen of the leader, who must both illuminate what is going on in the group and protect the group's selected scapegoats by placing himself more directly in the line of fire. The group thus behaves as though it were a sort of "primal horde" (Freud, 1946) obsessively preoccupied with the fantastically distorted aggressive characteristics of its leader.

A successful resolution of this conflictual process often leads to an ultimately firmer sense of group cohesion and a rather clear-cut crystallization of the role functions of particular members and of the implicit power hierarchy within the peer group. The term *pecking order* would appear to aptly describe this hierarchical alignment of power relationships.

Phase IV: Group-System Formation

A number of authors (Durkin, 1974; Swogger, 1974) have attempted to conceptually articulate the complex and intricate fabric of a group's formative interactions by utilizing systems theory formulations and hypothetical constructs. The essential notion is that, at some point in the interactive history of the members of a group, it becomes a fluid and smoothly interconnected systemic structure rather than a mere aggregate of disparate individuals.

The process these theorists have labeled *summing*, which can be viewed as analogous to the erection of solid, impermeable boundaries between the members, thus ultimately shifts to a softening of these individuation and identity-maintaining barriers to communication and a relatively fluid and intimately connected mode of group communication, labeled *systemming* (Durkin, 1974).

In the present group, the key "system" moment appeared to occur during the phase previously described as a sort of group free-association period in which humor, commonly accepted group metaphors (which would have been incomprehensible to strangers who had not participated in the group experience), and a general reduction in the rigidity of individual defensive structures and resistance to primary process thought content all contributed to a sort of group "regression in service of the ego" (Hartmann, 1961) or "condenser phenomenon" (Foulkes & Anthony, 1965).

There can be no doubt that a solider, more cohesive group had formed with a general softening and increased permeability of the boundaries separating one member from another.

Phase V: Polarization and Division

The leader, of course, can seldom be fully integrated into the group-system formation and in many ways stands out as a specially articulated and unusually important element of the group. It is not surprising, therefore, that his absence can precipitate a major break in the smoothly efficient interpersonal relationships beginning to develop in the group.

His absence is both an unconscious reminder of the impending demise of the group and a structural impediment to group cohesion. As Freud

(1922/1965) noted, the members become a group by identifying with the leader who represents a composite of their projected ego ideals. Without the leader much of the group's cohesiveness, which has, at least in part, been derived by identificatory interactions with him, begins to dissolve. The group, subsequently tending to become fragmented and polarized, splits into two seemingly dissociated factions or subgroups. Since both subgroups are reacting to the dynamic impact of the leader's absence, an unconscious collusion between the split-off factions allows the group ultimately to remain intact and to perpetuate itself until its formally designated ending. The polarization essentially relates to the differential "defenses against depressive anxiety" utilized by the various group members. Thus, whereas some members deny such feelings by an intensification of their emotional involvement with the peer group, others deny these feelings by a temporary physical withdrawal from the group. Bennis (1961) deals more comprehensively with the issue of the depressive impact of leader absence on the group dynamic process and the defenses utilized by the members to ward off such feelings.

Phase VI: Reintegration and Termination

In the final phase, the group reunites and begins to work toward its formal termination. The psychological issue of separation is centermost in all the members' minds and hence becomes a latent thematic preoccupation of the group as a whole. A concern with death and endings in general is evident in the group discussion. A pervasive sense of unhappiness is implicit in the emotional fabric of the group interaction and is either directly reflected in the members' outward expressive demeanor or defended against via counter-depressive maneuvers. In the latter case, there is an air of forced gaiety in the group proceedings.

A need to summarize and reminisce over the various key events in the group's history can be discerned in the interaction during this phase. The individual who has been chosen to adopt the role of group historian comes to the fore and becomes a significant interactant. A review of the memorable events in the group's history seems to allow for a more thorough internalization and integration of the group experience, which ultimately facilitates the ongoing process of separation and mourning.

IDENTIFICATION, EGO AUTONOMY, AND THE "DEVELOPMENTAL" ASPECTS OF THE GROUP PROCESS

Any group experience that is truly "developmental" will lead to an increment in the individual group member's capacity for autonomous ego functioning. The concept of ego autonomy, extensively elaborated in the writings of Hartmann (1950, 1961) and Rappaport (1958), largely relates to a freedom of the ego from undue influence by either internal or external stimuli of a pressured and coercive nature.

Truly autonomous individuals must be prepared to give up a pleasurable dependency attachment to various significant objects in their external world. The members of an unstructured group are required more and more to perform such a task as their group experience approaches its termination date. Ideally, there has been an opportunity for a thorough internalization and integration of the group experience prior to its termination.

The leader's availability as an identification figure contributes to the consolidation and integration process, particularly during the later phase of the group experience. Each member is offered the more realistic attributes of the leader, who is now more verbally active and hence a more visible social modeling presence within the group. The members are encouraged to try in the future some of the stylistic techniques of group leadership they have observed during the course of the laboratory experience. Thus, the members have been offered an ego autonomy-enhancing identificatory role model, the internalization of which has enhanced the potential effectiveness of their own subsequent functioning as group therapists.

The concept of identification, although a highly complex one (Kissen, 1974), can be assumed to significantly relate to the interactive processes occurring in unstructured groups. Identificatory relationships can further be surmised to play an important but somewhat different role during the various phases of a group's development. Thus, the group process gradually shifts from a proneness to utilize more primitive forms of identification, consisting of a fairly large element of projective distortion, to a more veridical and realistic form of identification relationship. The earlier and more regressive form of identificatory relation can be labeled, after Klein (1946) and Kernberg (1975), *projective identification*. Such identifications tend to be highly distorted, at least in part, due to the excessive amount of libidinal and aggressive emotional energy invested in them. As the group develops, however, a greater and greater capacity exists in the members for autonomous ego functioning and hence for identificatory processes of a more objective and realistic nature. White, in a classic theoretical paper (1963), has described the relationship of the concept of identification to the development of a capacity for competence, mastery, and ego autonomy.

Recently there has been a greater conceptual interest in the "ego psychological" features of unstructured group process experiences (Saravay, 1975). A thorough exploration of the concept of identification and its relevance for the developmental aspects of group dynamics and group therapeutic experiences will most certainly help to elucidate some of the complex variables in this area of study.

CONCLUSION

The six phases of group development outlined in this chapter in some ways overlap and in some ways differ from previous group dynamics theories of development (Bennis & Shepard, 1956; Bion, 1959; Day, 1967; Martin & Hill, 1957). It is important, however, that the present analysis corroborates the existence of some form of empirically discernible developmental phasic sequence in the group-as-a-whole interactive processes of an unstructured laboratory group. There is thus also some reason to believe that a somewhat similar development sequence occurs in psychotherapy groups and perhaps even in more structured activity groups in which, to use Bion's terminology, the "work" group aspects camouflage the latent and more dynamic "assumptive" group tendencies.

Although experienced group therapists may find a different serial order to the idiosyncratic progression of thematic phases in particular groups than the one described in this chapter, they will nevertheless probably be able to corroborate both a number of the group dynamics processes given here and the fact that some form of group-as-a-whole developmental sequence occurs in each of their groups.

The timing, quantity, and dynamic content of interpretive interventions must hinge on the therapist's accurate awareness of the particular developmental phase and hence degree of ego autonomy that has been attained by a given group. What is thus being proposed here is an ego psychological model of group development not essentially different from the conceptual ideas of Zetzel (1970) which were elaborated within the framework of individual psychoanalysis. Although such a model has only recently begun to be articulated, the repetitive corroboration of the existence of empirically reliable and valid developmental sequences in a broad variety of group interactions makes such a conceptual approach both imminent and necessary.

REFERENCES

Appelbaum, S. A. The pleasure and reality principles in group process teaching. *British Journal of Medical Psychology*, 1963, *36*, 1–7. (This book, chap. 12)

Appelbaum, S. A. The Kennedy assassination. *Psychoanalytic Review*, 1966, *53*, 393–404. (This book, chap. 13)

Bennis, W. G. Defenses against depressive anxiety in groups: The case of the absent leader. *Merrill-Palmer Quarterly*, 1961, *7*, 3–30. (This book, chap. 7)

Bennis, W. G., & Shepard, H. A. A theory of group development. *Human Relations*, 1956, *9*, 415–437. (This book, chap. 10)

Bion, W. R. *Experiences in groups.* New York: Basic Books, 1959.

Day, M. The natural history of training groups. *International Journal of Group Psychotherapy*, 1967, *17*, 436–446. (This book, chap. 9)

Durkin, J. *Group systems therapy: The structure of thinking and feeling.* Unpublished manuscript, Lincoln University, 1974.

Foulkes, S. H., & Anthony, E. J. *Group psychotherapy: The psychoanalytic approach.* Baltimore, Md.: Penguin Books, 1965.

Freud, A. [*The ego and mechanisms of defense*] (C. Baines, trans.). New York: International Universities Press, 1966. (Originally published, 1937.)

Freud, S. [*Totem and taboo*] (A. A. Brill, Ed. and trans.). New York: Vintage Books, 1946. (Originally published, 1918.)

Freud, S. [*Group psychology and the analysis of the ego*] (J. Strachey, Ed. and trans.). New York: Bantam Books, 1965. (Originally published, 1922.)

Hartmann, H. Comments on the psychoanalytic theory of the ego. *Psychoanalytic study of the child* (Vol. 5). New York: International Universities Press, 1950.

Hartmann, H. *Ego psychology and the problem of adaptation.* New York: International Universities Press, 1961.

Horwitz, L. Training groups for psychiatric residents. *International Journal of Group Psychotherapy*, 1967, *17*, 421-435. (This book, chap. 5)

Kernberg, O. *Borderline states and pathological narcissism.* New York: Jason Aronson, 1975.

Kissen, M. The concept of identification: An evaluation of its current status and significance for group psychotherapy. *Group Process*, 1974, *6*, 83-97. (This book, chap. 16)

Klein, M. Notes on some schizoid mechanisms. *International Journal of Psychoanalysis*, 1946, *27*, 99-110.

Martin, E. A., Jr., & Hill, W. F. Toward a theory of group development: Six phases of therapy group development. *International Journal of Group Psychotherapy*, 1957, 7, 20-30. (This book, chap. 11)

Rappaport, D. The theory of ego autonomy: A generalization. *Bulletin of the Menninger Clinic*, 1958, *22*, 13-35.

Rioch, M. J. The work of Wilfred Bion on groups. *Psychiatry*, 1970, *33*, 56-66. (This book, chap. 8)

Saravay, S. M. Group psychology and the structural theory. A revised psychoanalytic model of group psychology. *Journal of the American Psychoanalytic Association*, 1975, *23*, 69-90.

Scheidlinger, S. On the concept of the "Mother Group." *International Journal of Group Psychotherapy*, 1974, *24*, 417-428. (This book, chap. 21)

Swogger, G. A. *Systems approach to small groups—the group as system.* Unpublished manuscript, Menninger Foundation, Topeka, Kan., 1974.

Whitaker, D. S., & Lieberman, M. A. *Psychotherapy through the group process.* New York: Atherton Press, 1964.

White, R. W. Ego and reality. A proposal regarding independent ego energies. *Psychological issues* (Vol. 3, No. 3), New York: International Universities Press, 1963.

Zetzel, E. R. A developmental model and the theory of therapy. In E. R. Zetzel (Ed.), *The capacity for emotional growth.* New York: International Universities Press, 1970.

5

Training Groups for Psychiatric Residents

Leonard Horwitz
The Menninger Foundation
Topeka, Kansas

[The essential format, structural characteristics, and typical thematic preoccupations of laboratory groups specially constructed as experiential learning opportunities for mental health professionals are described. The author emphasizes the basically didactic (as opposed to therapeutic) purposes of these groups and notes that they offer the members an opportunity to directly experience and integrate certain characteristic dynamic phenomena that almost universally occur in all groups, to internalize a model of group therapeutic technique (via identificatory interactions with the leader), and to gain some insight into their own personality dynamics and structure. A number of methods by which the leader can modulate the degree of regression that often occurs in such groups are presented.]

A seminar in group dynamics has been a part of the first-year curriculum of the Menninger School of Psychiatry for more than five years. Originally an elective, the value of the seminar to the residents has earned it a place as a required course. This training was first started with the idea of helping the resident improve his skills as a group leader in the various hospital groups he led, particularly the clinical-administrative meetings with other section personnel. As group psychotherapy programs began to grow in the training

From "Training Groups for Psychiatric Residents" by L. Horwitz, *International Journal of Group Psychotherapy*, 1967, *17*, 421–435. Copyright 1967 by the International Journal of Group Psychotherapy. Reprinted by permission.

Grateful acknowledgment for their critical reading of the manuscript and their helpful suggestions is extended to Drs. Otto Kernberg, Phyllis Kreinik, Bruno Magliocco, Herbert Modlin, Douglas Sheafor, and Saul Siegel.

institutions, the course came to be viewed more as an opportunity for the resident to be a participant in a time-limited, therapy-like group and thus to learn more about the feelings of patients in groups and about the major processes which occur in the functioning of therapy groups. Although the format of the course has undergone changes in certain details, the backbone of the training continues to be the unstructured group.

It has become clear during the past two decades that the unstructured group is a microcosm or laboratory of human behavior which may be studied from several points of view. Depending on the interests and objectives of the participants and the leader, the training group may be used to teach laymen about the dynamics of groups, or it may concentrate upon personal learning and insight, or it may, as in this instance, afford an opportunity to understand the processes involved in group psychotherapy. The course also exemplifies certain phenomena and techniques used in psychiatry generally. This paper describes some typical events in the life of such a training group, the rationale and technique of conducting it, and the probable coutcome of such a course.

EVENTS IN THE LIFE OF A GROUP DYNAMICS CLASS

Although group dynamics classes for psychiatrists may be conducted differently with regard to foci of interest and the kinds of interventions made by the leader, there is one uniform aspect of all these groups which produces certain predictable results. The common feature is the lack of any set structure, of clearly defined roles for participant or leader, and of an agenda behind which anxieties may be hidden.

One of the mysteries of the training group, and a major source of anxiety for the participants at the outset, is the question of what to talk about. A group of about ten members, largely psychiatric residents,[1] is assembled for the first time and is given a brief orientation and "contract" by the leader. They will meet once a week for twenty weeks. Sessions will last for ninety minutes. At the end of the session, each participant will record in his diary a summary of the session and some of his main impressions. The leader remarks: "Our aim is to learn about group psychotherapy by becoming a group. I will make comments about my observations of the group when I feel it will be helpful. Now I will turn it over to you to get started."

Most of the participants, having been together for a few months as first-year residents at the same hospital or neighboring hospitals, have already met. But there are usually brief introductions around the table, more notable for what is withheld than for what is told. Then what?

---

[1] Although the course is given mainly for psychiatrists in their first year of training, a number of other trainees in the various training programs of the Menninger School of Psychiatry also may participate: Students in pastoral counseling, psychosomatic medicine, clinical psychology, and social work.

The major initial preoccupation is with the leader and the fact that he has already indicated that his main role will be that of observer. They speculate whether he is really serious about this or is just playing a waiting game. If we are patient enough, they think, perhaps he will stop being coy and start being the real teacher that he should be. They turn to each other for help in their common misery. But their queries are almost invariably addressed to those who have some obvious differences from themselves, perhaps to find common ground, hopefully to find an ally, often to assimilate and neutralize the threatening stranger. A woman in the group, or a native of a foreign land, or perhaps a trainee in another discipline usually becomes the object of their interest. Typically, they ask, "What is the state of psychiatry in Argentina and did you have any experience with groups?" A pastoral counselling trainee is asked about the role of prayer in counselling with his parishioners. When the leader suggests that their questions directed at experts in these unusual fields could also be an expression of their wish to get the leader to answer questions, he is hardly heard. These interpretations are not the kind of "food" they came to get.

Resentment about being observed is another underlying theme at the outset. In one group it was expressed via the issue of whether participants should be allowed to take notes during the session. The reality objection was the reduced spontaneity of the note-takers and their unwillingness to carry their load of active participation. A less direct discussion of the problem appeared in the context of irritation with television camera crews who happened to be visiting the school at the time; the school authorities, the students complained, were placing public relations ahead of the main goal of teaching. Another vehicle of the same theme has been a preoccupation with school examinations. The group argued that examinations were demeaning to postgraduate students, fostered unhealthy competition with peers, and created needless anxiety. When the comment was offered by the leader that they were uneasy about the kind of "rating" they might get from him, even though ratings would not be made, the group shifted to another topic.

After the initial fear and suspicion have subsided, the group has the task of getting itself out of the hole into which it has dug itself, i.e., of overcoming its regressively dependent and hostile attitudes associated with having a leader who refuses to lead, a teacher who will not teach, an expert who keeps his own counsel. The leader's interpretations, largely focused upon feelings being expressed toward him or defenses against such feelings, both tend to promote the regression yet at the same time to encourage a movement toward resolution. The leader listens carefully for expressions of hostility toward him, usually spoken metaphorically, and consistently interprets their presence as well as the frustrations and fears which give rise to them. He is alert to the scapegoating of other members, both to protect individuals from being unduly victimized and to uncover anger toward himself.

As the leader encourages the verbalization of such thoughts, he is implicitly communicating an accepting attitude toward such feelings. They are at first proffered tentatively and then with greater confidence. Each experience of ventilating anger, dissatisfaction, and criticism of the leader provides the members with the conviction that retribution is not in the offing and tends to promote a more realistic perception of the leader.

Anger and dissatisfaction with the leader is invariabley manifested by fantasies or behaviors which express rebellion against the structure or contract set by the leader, minimal though it may be. Supposedly legitimate latenesses, which members may initially excuse quite readily, on closer examination often express resentment about the waste of time involved in coming to the group, the seeming fact that the leader is not teaching anything about group dynamics, or perhaps dissatisfaction with the leader's interference in the last meeting. One member absented himself from a meeting to attend a musical comedy which had come to town and blandly explained his behavior to the group on the basis of the pleasure principle: the liveliness of the entertainment was more appealing to him than the dullness of a group meeting. The group effectively pointed out the many facets of this behavior: the patent hostility which he tended to deny, his need to avoid submitting to an inferior, "patient" role, his wish to find himself in the center of controversy in order to avoid being overlooked. The group's shock and dismay were partly a reaction against their own repressed wishes to behave in the same way. Other vehicles for the expression of anger are proposals that the time of the meeting be changed, failure to record post-meeting impressions in one's diary, and challenging the wisdom of not being given reading assignments. (The members know that the unstructured group experience is followed by a series of didactic sessions based on selections from the group psychotherapy literature.) More direct expressions of resentment against the leader consist of complaints that he says too little or, sometimes, too much; frequently his interpretations are attacked as invalid or, at best, unprovable.

The middle phase and major work of the group consists of reaching some resolution of the authority problem. The polarities of dependency and counterdependency are represented by subgroupings and most often find expression in terms of factional disputes over the problem of structure. The dependent bloc wants more direction, perhaps an agenda, and searches desperately for someone in the group with expertise. Whoever has read a book on group behavior is elevated to the position of wise man. The dependents will find much comfort in any of the leader's contributions, even if his remarks are only prods or requests for more elaboration. The counter-dependents on the other hand resent the leader's participation and oppose the effort by anyone to impose structure. They stand for free, uninhibited, and spontaneous expression of feeling. If a more timorous soul should suggest that each member give a thumbnail sketch of his background and interests, these avant-garde "abstractionists" raise their voices in protest. If there is a suggestion that the group be polled on whether or not to change the meeting time, they oppose the sterile mechanics of voting.

Movement toward resolving the group's underlying dependent wishes occurs when the members begin to find agreement about their common, shared striving for nurturance accompanied by recognition of their real capacity to utilize their own resources. To some extent they are able to give up their perception of the leader as an authoritarian person who is trying to rub their noses in the dirt. They do not have to be so sullen nor so passively angry. The leader is now seen less as a manipulator, and they feel less like puppets of his will. Concomitantly, they become more accepting of their own responsibility to use the group for learning purposes and are less prone to discount observations made by others or themselves. One group worked on the problem of why they were so upset over a particular member's absence. They wondered whether they were like a "poker" group which can function despite absences provided there is a minimum attendance, or like a "bridge" group in which a missing member precludes the game. They came to the pithy and accurate observation that they were "a poker group with bridge group feelings." The group begins to rely upon its expertise, not born of desperation but based upon a more realistic appraisal and better utilization of their capacities.

Group dynamics classes typically deal briefly with the problem of intimacy, closeness, and distance from peers. How free can we get in sharing our feelings toward each other, both positive and negative? One group found much comfort and pleasure in healing the dissensions that had been present both among themselves and with the leader. They enjoyed the camaraderie and new-found warmth, but a subsequent meeting found them discussing the problem of handling the homosexual patient who makes sexual advances to his doctor. The consensus was to "tell him to cut it out" firmly and decisively, an expression of their own struggle to take distance from threatening positive feelings toward the leader and each other.

As termination approaches, there are inevitable feelings of reluctance to disband and anger about not having learned enough. Accusations are directed toward the leader for not having directed the group more skillfully, against themselves for having been maladroit or resistant students, and against their colleagues for failing to contribute more. The question of ratings once again arises, and the fear that this group did not measure up to previous ones becomes a concern. Usually such criticisms and self-criticisms are replaced by a more realistic appraisal of the benefit derived from the group.

THE LEADER'S ORIENTATION AND TECHNIQUE

The leader's technique in any unstructured group is largely conditioned by his teaching objectives as well as by the goals, both latent and manifest, of the group members. The primary objective of the leader is to teach the method of group psychotherapy. But it may be questioned how one can attempt to illustrate a treatment approach when treatment is not actually being offered. The course is described in the school's bulletin as a seminar in group dynamics in which the members learn about group processes by being participant-observers in their own group. The course is not advertised as treatment, nor is it intended to be such. However, it is clear that many of the residents, particularly since the course is given in the first half of their first year when anxieties about new professional experiences are at their height, regard the sessions as an opportunity to find some relief for their anxieties. They appreciate the opportunity to ventilate and to share their common concerns, and they hope to enhance their acquisition of that valuable commodity in psychiatry, personal insight.

The issues which arise in an unstructured group are substantially the same as those which appear in any therapeutic group. The feelings about authority figures—the wish to be dependent in conflict with the fear of submission, the wish to be directed as against the fear of exploitation, the wish to be the leader's favorite as against the fear of antagonizing one's peers—occur in all these goups and constitute the major dimensions of work. Insofar as therapy and training groups both explore the feelings generated in the individual by finding himself in an unstructured group, there are basic similarities between them.

The distinguishing feature of the two types of groups lies in the relative emphasis upon personal insight. If a patient group avoids personal insight, it is a manifestation of resistance. But this kind of training group is free to take it or leave it, without destroying or perverting its goals. The members are free to explore only the group phenomena: group themes, group conflicts, group resistances, etc. In so doing, they may perceive, or the group may point out, individual modes of handling various kinds of affects; but this aspect is optional and the group must determine how far it wishes to go in this area. For example, when the group is attempting to move in the direction of greater intimacy, they may encourage the members of minority groups to discuss the customs of their particular religious sects or nationalities or racial groups in the hope of dissolving boundaries and finding common bonds. But despite the seeming unanimity of such a theme at the moment, there are inevitable counterforces and individuals will range variously around the dimension of intimacy. Some will insist vehemently that the group should go further, perhaps wishing to go too far too fast and thus alienating members who are interested; some insist upon their right to privacy and wish to remain aloof; some may seek out and exaggerate dissension and hostility as a defense against further movement toward intimacy. The leader need only interpret the conflicting wishes within the group as a whole regarding their desires to move closer to each other. How much he, or any member, should go beyond this to interpret or clarify individual modes of reacting is a matter of choice for the group.

In general, little attention is devoted to individual or intrapersonal dynamics in these groups. Partly this is a function of the relatively brief number of sessions. Partly it is due to the inhibition which one would expect among members who are classmates and hence tend to have extragroup contacts, both professional and social. But mainly, despite the common wish for a therapeutic experience, there is a natural enough reluctance to look inward, particularly when the group provides the freedom not to do so. The leader, of course, encourages the expression of feelings about various events in the group's life, but he uses such behavior to illustrate a variety of group phenomena without necessarily attending to the individual dynamics which are also being evidenced.

What are the group processes to which the leader attends? Foremost is the common group tension or group focal conflict described by Sutherland (1952), Whitman and Stock (1958), and Whitaker and Lieberman (1964). It is assumed that every group session touches on one or more themes which express a common conflict, a wish countered by a fear. Ideally the group theme is developed by the verbalizations of the majority of members. But often it finds expression through one or two *spokesmen* who are either passively permitted or actively encouraged by the group to verbalize their feelings. A rebellious member may be subtly prodded to criticize the leader, to suggest revisions in the contract, or to absent himself from the group for invalid reasons. One of the more difficult concepts for the novice to grasp is the phenomenon of the group acting as a whole when it seems on the surface to be operating as an aggregate of separate individuals. The emergence of a particular individual as the leader of the group at any one time must always be understood as a confluence of his personal needs and the needs of the group. Too often it tends to be understood by the group in terms of the idiosyncrasies of the individual alone. Redl (1963) has described this phenomenon as *role-suction* and has given several apt illustrations.

Other group phenomena include scapegoating, which inevitably develops, usually as a displacement from the leader onto one or more of the members, and polarization, which consists of a split within the group over an important issue, such as the extent to which the group should be structured. The proponents of each point of view tend to see such a conflict solely as an external affair with each individual unambivalently striving for his special values. But the division of the group into polarized factions or subgroups usually expresses two arms of a conflict *within each individual.* Other, more specific group phenomena consist of attending to the meanings of seating arrangements, body postures, and similar nonverbal expressions of feeling and conflict.

A central problem in all groups, training or therapeutic, concerns the degree of regression to be encouraged by the leader. As in individual treatment, the leader may regulate the regressive pull by the role he takes: the more silent and frustrating he is, the greater the regression. The more like an analyst he behaves in confining his comments to interpretations, the more frustrated the group will feel and the more preoccupied they will become with fantasies about the leader: what is he thinking? does he approve of them? does he prefer one to the others? Frequently their fantasies will take a projective turn and they will suspect, for example,.that the leader's statement that he plans to miss the next meeting is some kind of trick to elicit their reactions. Conversely, if the leader's interventions are more than just interpretive, if he gratifies to some degree the members' wishes for guidance and support, if he answers some of their questions when the anxiety level is rising, the regressive reactions tend to subside. A leader may typically be asked by the group, when they introduce themselves around the table in the initial meeting, to say a few words about himself, which he may or may not choose to do. Or when the leader announces that he plans to be absent next time, he may or may not explain the reason for his absence. The choice made in such instances will either enhance or minimize regression.

A second determinant of the regressive pull is the degree to which the leader interprets leader-transference as opposed to peer-transference. The two transferences are usually similar and often run parallel to each other, differing largely in intensity. A member is not only concerned about what the leader's impression of him is but about the opinions of his fellow members as well. He is not only resentful of the leader's position as an authority figure but he opposes those in the group who take on leadership positions. He is not only fearful of the leader's potential for hostile attacks but sees others in the group as similarly threatening. It is not just the leader who has obligated him to a contract; the group gradually places demands upon him, too.

The more the focus upon feelings toward the leader, the more regressive the transference is likely to become in the sense of uncovering progressively deeper layers of attitudes and conflicts toward authority figures. Some workers believe that group classes for psychiatrists should deal largely with the transference to the leader. Appelbaum (1963), in fact, has conceptualized the entire process in terms of the gradual emergence of the reality principle, i.e., learning to accept one's own capacities for problem-solving rather than remaining in a hostile dependent stance toward the leader who is expected to feed answers to the group. When the group has learned to accept this responsibility, according to Applebaum, it is ready to terminate.

In contrast, writers like Bennis and Shepard (1956) view the dependency problem as only the first of two major phases of the unstructured training group. (They do not confine their work to the training of psychiatrists, but this aspect is probably not crucial.) They contend that when the group is able to assimilate the "trainer" as a member with special resources, but someone who is incapable of doing their work for them, the group moves into dealing with the problem of greater closeness to peers. They begin to have the task of sharing their observations about each other in a constructive and helpful way based upon their experiences together in the preceding sessions. This is the "feedback" phase which occupies a large share of some human relations training groups.

Whether the group remains leader-centered or becomes more peer-centered depends largely upon the leader's orientation. After some reduction has occurred in both the exaggerated view of the leader's potency and in the hostile dependency toward him, the leader is generally faced with two alternative routes. He usually is able to interpret the events in the group with primary emphasis upon feelings toward himself, as he did earlier, or he may begin to emphasize concerns about interrelationships among members. Thus, for example, in a meeting occurring at about the midpoint of a particular group's life, the discussion first centered around the feelings of comfort the members experienced in being with their confreres in the group as opposed to members of other groups. Then, in a somewhat labored way, they began to express their feelings about an absent member whose absence had been planned and seemed legitimate to them. They emphasized his positive contributions to the group, his ability to make penetrating and helpful observations about what was going on, while meeting their criticisms of his role as leader's assistant. It was obvious that their reluctance to speak freely in this session had two main determinants. Insofar as the absent member was a displacement figure from the leader, they avoided negative comments which would too easily be interpreted as criticism of the leader. But insofar as he was just another member, they were leery about focusing their attention upon him, particularly their criticisms, because it would be moving the group into a phase of greater intimacy and closeness, something which they both wanted and feared. The leader could have emphasized the fear of expressing anger toward himself or he could have focused on their reluctance to express negative (or positive) feelings about each other. The latter course, provided he was correct in assessing that the feelings about the leader were not the paramount issue, would contribute to some reduction in transference feelings to the leader and encourage increased interaction among members. Focusing upon the leader, on the other hand, would lead to the further uncovering of unconscious fantasies about authority figures.

The problem in conducting such groups, as in doing psychotherapy, is that of encouraging enough regression to induce tension and work while avoiding excessive frustration and anger. But an additional factor, the time limitation of twenty sessions, makes it necessary to help the group avoid a greater regression toward the leader than can be reasonably resolved by the end of the course. Both factors previously mentioned, verbal participation by the leader and focus upon peer transference, should be used to regulate the degree of regression.

Since this group is primarily didactic in its ultimate purpose, the leader must be especially conscious of the technical devices he uses. His interventions must not only help the group deal with its conflicts and resistances but also give his students a model to emulate. A frequent resistance in the early stages is the group's reluctance to deal with significant events which they initially perceive as minor occurrences: lateness, absences, etc. The leader has the obligation in the early stages to be unconventional enough to raise these issues. It is usually possible to illustrate that the "unavoidable" lateness resulted from a reluctance to attend in the first place. Soon the group will take over this function as part of a growing identification with the leader. By encouraging discussion about such matters as seating arrangements, the group becomes attuned to some of the nonverbal aspects of their functioning. For example, at the height of one group's wish to be given more direction from the leader, the group seated itself in a cluster at some distance from the leader; inquiry into the meaning of the choice of seats revealed a fairly unanimous wish for more activity by the leader. Hopefully, such interventions will serve as examples for the student therapist.

OUTCOMES OF THE TRAINING GROUP

Group phenomena are experienced by the members and are learned *in vivo* and not simply as abstract concepts. An important adjunct to the course is the reading group of ten sessions which follows the unstructured group experience. The reading assignments are discussed whenever possible in terms of the recently completed group experience. Concepts like dispersion, cohesion, rule-suction, focal group conflicts, etc., are examined in the light of the real-life situations which they all have shared.

A training course illustrates general clinical phenomena and general therapeutic techniques as well as those relevant to groups. First, with regard to clinical modes of thinking, a lesson of paramount importance is that there are multiple levels of communication, that one should not be content with simply attending to manifest content. The question the clinician should always be asking is: why is the patient raising this point in this way at this time? What is occurring in the here and now which is being expressed indirectly or obliquely and is perhaps just outside the ken of consciousness? The central concept in dynamic psychiatry of transference and its communication via the metaphor is an essential lesson to be learned in a training group. In one of its early sessions, one group became interested in the problem of whether a physician should perform a complete physical on a patient simply because the patient expects him to do so despite his own conviction that the procedure is unnecessary for proper diagnosis and treatment. The minister in the group was asked if he used prayer when he counselled with a parishioner simply because the latter expected it. These preoccupations were not too far from their concern about their own wish for the leader to take over more active control of the group while at the same time fearing that he might accede to these wishes to the detriment of their learning experience. The group's reaction to the leader's translation of these metaphors is often one of great surprise. Gradually, however, they begin to acquire the attitude that all is not what it seems, and this lesson is one of the most valuable dividends of the course. Ganzarain (1958) reached a similar conclusion in his controlled experiment in teaching psychiatry to medical students. One group received ordinary didactic instruction while the other group had a course of group psychotherapy. The latter students not only profited from the therapeutic aspects of the course but seemed to have a better, more vivid grasp of certain clinical concepts, particularly transference.

Another psychodynamic principle, more easily learned in the abstract than understood in a life situation, is that of the multiple and shifting meanings of a given piece of behavior. One group had an opportunity to explore the many different facets of their silences. They were able to see that silence not only represented an angry reaction to oral frustration but also that it was a protest against the perceived necessity to submit to a passive, compliant role, that it signaled a wish on their part to be "fed" by the leader, and that it was a defense against their own hostile impulses as well as their fear of possible counterattack. This kind of complexity is easily demonstrated in a group situation because the differing character structures of the members tend to elucidate the spectrum of motives applying to a single piece of behavior: several genotypes underlying one phenotype.

In terms of clinical techniques, the participant has an opportunity to observe an experienced clinician dealing with a group of "patients." Basic to any educational and growth process is an identification with one's mentors, and the model the students perceive unquestionably helps many of them in their search for a proper professional approach in dealing with their patients. When the students in one training group were asked which of the leader's techniques they found themselves using with their own patients, each member, as might be expected, stressed a particular facet of the leader's technique with which he identified himself. Frequent reference was made to the prodding intervention which the leader used to encourage further elaboration: "Would you care to say more about that?" This remark embodies the attitude mentioned above that behaviors are complexly motivated and that one should seek to explore beyond the face-value of a comment.

Each student mentioned particular techniques designed to encourage freedom of expression, particularly of negative feelings toward the leader or toward each other. They spoke of learning to tolerate better the hostility of their patients, to refrain from retaliation, and to view the attacks usually as something to be understood rather than as personal criticism. They saw the importance of using nonverbal expressions of interest, curiosity, and the effort to understand as a means of eliciting material from their patient.

Some stressed the leader's neutrality in the face of conflicts of opinion by dissident factions and the importance of trying to elucidate feelings rather than expressing one's own biases or values. On this latter point, they were able to learn that neutrality is not synonymous with complete inhibition of one's feelings. A common misconception of the novice in psychiatry is that the doctor should maintain an attitude of cool and detached interest, a caricature of the psychoanalyst who suppresses *all* of his affective responses. One member stated: "The group leader participated more than I thought he would. This was particularly true of his nonverbal behavior. In clinical situations I have identified particularly with the leader's openness. On the ward and in group discussions on the ward, I have participated more freely and made less attempt to blunt my affect in response to patients' statements."

While the acquisition of insight into one's personality is not an objective of the course, it often turns out to be a by-product. Beginners in psychiatry are beset by many anxieties concerning the new field they are entering and the new professional identity they must begin to acquire. They are often eager for a therapeutic experience and are particularly intent on learning more about themselves. To the extent that the group consciously attempts to give "feedback" to each other, to share impressions and observations about their behavior in the group, there develops some degree of increased self-understanding. For the most part, the learning consists of an underlining of, or new emphasis on, facets of functioning of which they already were aware. Many are surprised to observe the extent of their own hostility. Some report that what they formerly regarded as a penchant for humor turned out to be vitriolic sarcasm, particularly in the way others responded to it. Some were surprised to learn that their passive compliance was a thin defense against strong competitive and aggressive wishes. More often than not, such things are self-observations. Occasionally, certain maladaptive character traits are pointed out which the person has not been aware of before. By some students, these observations are dismissed lightly or ignored or repressed, while others may take these observations seriously and attempt to understand them more fully.

SUMMARY

Classes in group dynamics consisting primarily of an unstructured group experience are an important part of the curriculum in the Menninger School of Psychiatry. Offered in the first year, the course is viewed partly as an introduction to group psychotherapy but partly also as a general introduction to clinical concepts and clinical techniques, taught and learned in a real-life situation as a supplement to the more abstract, didactic courses. Although the course is not offered as psychotherapy and is not intended as such, many of the issues which arise resemble those occurring in a therapeutic group. The emphasis, however, is upon understanding group issues, and the leader confines himself largely to group-relevant interventions. The extent to which the group delves into self-understanding is a matter of choice for the members. Two major dimensions govern the extent of the regressive pre-occupation which develops around the leader: the degree of frustration which he induces by limiting his participation and the extent to which his interpretations focus upon leader–member as opposed to member–member transference. Because of the relatively limited amount of time available to resolve regressive transference reactions, the leader strives for a more diluted and less intense relationship with himself than he would encourage in a therapeutic group.

REFERENCES

Appelbaum, S. A. (1963), The Pleasure and Reality Principles in Group Process Teaching. *Brit. J. Med. Psychol.*, 36:1-7.

Bennis, W. G., and Shepard, H. H. (1956), A Theory of Group Development. *Human Relations*, 9:415–437.

Ganzarain, R. (1958), Group Psychotherapy in the Psychiatric Training of Medical Students. *Internaltional Journal of Group Psychotherapy*, 8:137:153.

Redl, F. (1963), Psychoanalysis and Group Therapy: A Developmental Point of View. *Amer. J. Orthopsychiat.*, 35:135-147.

Sutherland, J. D. (1952), Notes on Psychoanalytic Group Therapy. I. Therapy and Training. *Psychiatry*, 15:111-117.

Whitaker, D. S., and Lieberman, M. A. (1964), *Psychotherapy through the Group Process.* New York: Atherton.

Whitman, R., and Stock, D. (1958), The Group Focal Conflict. *Psychiatry*, 21:269-276.

6

Transference in Training Groups and Therapy Groups

Leonard Horwitz
The Menninger Foundation
Topeka, Kansas

[In this chapter, Horwitz makes an important but rather difficult distinction between the transferential processes in t-groups and those occurring in therapeutic groups. A key difference is that the leader transference, by necessity, is far more diluted in t-groups. Rather than a mysterious "blank screen" analyst who elicits projective fantasies and interprets group themes, a more realistic and peer-related leadership figure is needed. Horwitz hypothesizes that the more realistic and tangible nature of the leader's presence in t-groups will allow for a minimization of unresolvable transferential reactions and regressive fixations in such time-limited groups whose primary focus needs to be of an educational rather than a therapeutic nature.]

Human relations training groups, or sensitivity groups, have attained increasing popularity during the past fifteen years in America and abroad. Under the sponsorship of the Laboratory for Group Development in Bethel, Maine,[1] the technique of using the small unstructured group to study group processes and for acquiring personal insights has gained wide acceptance in a variety of settings. Frank (1964), in the only focused attempt to describe and conceptualize the similarities and differences between training groups and therapy groups, noted certain clearcut differences in goals and processes

Grateful acknowledgment is made to Drs. Warren Bennis, Dorothy Stock, Otto Kernberg, Howard Baumgartel, Jerome Frank, and Stephen Appelbaum for their careful reading of the manuscript and for the many helpful suggestions they made.

[1] The major summer laboratory conducted by National Training Laboratories, National Education Association, Washington, D.C.

between them. He based his observations on an experience at Bethel as a member of a training group (t-group) in the mid-1950s.

Frank emphasizes the major difference in objectives: Training groups attempt to help members become more sensitive to their own functioning and to the important events occurring within the group so that they may become more effective as members and as leaders of their groups back home. Therapy groups aim to help their members attain insight into their functioning in interpersonal situations of *all* kinds and thus help to relieve neurotically determined distress. As Frank (1964) describes it, there was a de-emphasis in the training group on learning about oneself.

> Training groups are composed of individuals trying to learn new skills from the trainer. Therapy groups attempt to modify more pervasive and more central attitudes than training groups, so they put relatively more emphasis on unlearning old modes of behavior as compared to learning new ones, and take longer to achieve their aims. (p. 18)

A second distinction Frank makes is that teaching membership skills in the training group focuses on interpretations about the group as a whole, rather than about individual motivations. Feelings of members are elucidated only insofar as they shed light on and illustrate group process. Therapy groups, of course, focus primarily on individuals and their underlying motives and conflicts. A third important difference lies in the role of the central figure. In therapy groups, the initial dependence on the therapist is greater and is never completely resolved. "The therapist can never become fully a member of the group, though he may approximate this, whereas trainer and member of a training group can become genuinely indistinguishable" (p. 18).

There has been a steady trend toward de-emphasizing the study of group process in t-groups in favor of enhanced personal insight. Some writers have referred to sensitivity training as "psychotherapy for normals" (Weschler, Massarik, & Tannenbaum, 1962) although many decry this therapeutic trend in t-groups. Shepard (1964) described the shift as follows:

> Implicit recognition that individual development was the lasting consequence of training led to increased focus on individual dynamics. Group level interventions were replaced by more personally oriented interventions . . . NTL [National Training Laboratories] began to focus on the problem of "giving and receiving feedback" and in recent years, personal feedback has seemed to be the most important feature of the T-group. (p. 16)

Although there has been a shift towards personal insight, Bethel groups do *not* typically aim at uncovering and resolving unconscious conflict. Rather, they attempt to help the individual perceive more clearly his or her own mode of interaction which may impair effectiveness. Perhaps one could say that t-groups aim to impart insights concerning the more conscious or preconscious levels of personality functioning.

With this shift in emphasis toward more insight giving in training groups, a natural question is whether training techniques have begun to shift in the direction of those used in a therapeutic group. More specifically, has the trainer begun to use transference reaction to him- or herself as a vehicle for uncovering personal dynamics as is done in therapy groups? On the basis of the training group literature, as well as my own experience in a few Bethel t-groups, it appears that such a shift in trainer role has not occurred. My purpose is to examine the differences in leader roles in the two groups, particularly in the use of transference, and to explore the consequences of the difference in method.

Before delineating these differences, I wish to emphasize that neither group psychotherapy nor human relations training may be adequately represented by a single point of view. Practitioners in each field span a wide range of methods, techniques, and theories. Most therapists operate within a psychoanalytic frame of reference and hence emphasize transference, although there are distinct variations in their use of leader versus peer transference and the strictness with which they attempt to maintain their role of a projection screen. Similarly, trainers differ widely in their "visibility" (Whitman, 1964) within their groups. The modal points to be used in our comparison will be the training group described by Bradford (1964) and the therapy group formulated by Sutherland (1952) and Ezriel (1952).

First, how is transference, particularly with regard to the leader, conceptualized in the therapy group? Therapists clearly and explicitly view their role as a transference figure—a screen upon which wishes and fears are projected, brought into awareness by interpretation, with the object of resolving them. They encourage transference reactions (1) by confining their participation as much as possible to creating a permissive atmosphere in which free expression of feelings and fantasies are received uncritically, (2) by promoting an attitude of reflection about the meaning of individual and group behaviors, and (3) by restricting their remarks to interpretations of group themes and individual variations around them. The role approaches that of the psychoanalyst whose thoughts and feelings remain relatively unknown to the patient and whose silence tends to induce considerable frustration with a resulting emergence of regressive tendencies which then become the subject of analysis and interpretation. This model of the therapist who limits therapist-group interaction and who is often seen as quite depriving is, of course, varied according to the capacity of the group to tolerate the anxiety induced by such a procedure.

ROLES OF TRAINER IN A T-GROUP

The central figure in the human relations training group, on the other hand, plays multiple roles (Bradford, 1964). The group may be permitted to struggle with its transference reactions toward the trainer, but transference is not consciously and explicitly promoted. Little, if any, explicit reference to this cornerstone conception of psychotherapy appears in the literature. Certain generic issues, like members' reactions to the trainer, the prototypes of dependency and counterdependency, the distorted attitudes toward authority figures, are observed by all writers of the Bethel school, though there is an assiduous avoidance of the term.[2] Benne (1964) recommends, for example, that the trainer sometimes should remain impassive and enigmatic to encourage the expression of fantasies about the trainer, which can then be corrected. But the consensus is that the trainer should serve other functions than simply one of observer and interpreter. First, the usual laboratory setting generally reduces transference reactions. All participants, including the trainer, are addressed by their first names. Since they usually spend two weeks together on a "cultural island," trainer and participants see each other during coffee breaks, evening social hours, and other real-life situations where the trainer emerges as a real person. Second, a trainer role that tends to attenuate transference reactions is that of the person who "models" the ideal of openness in expressing one's feelings. Thus she or he may at times share personal feelings of perplexity, anxiety, or confusion about what is transpiring in the group partly to encourage others to express their reactions freely and partly to help the group resolve unrealistic fantasies of the omniscient leader. Finally, the trainer sometimes is "teacher," who may deliver a "lecturette" or summarize some shared event that has special value as a generalization about group behavior.

While training groups attend to problems regarding group process, therapy groups have little, if any, interest in the dynamics of groups per se. Learning group dynamics in a therapy group is incidental to its major purpose of enhanced personal insight. Thus, while both groups seek personal insight for their members, the training group in addition attempts to teach important dimensions of group functioning. Problems of membership requirements and their changes during the life of the group, the dynamics of decision making, and the growth of group norms are studied in the training group as they are experienced. Such problems may also be part of the data generated in a therapy group, but they are not a focus of learning for the patients. Both trainer and therapist, for example, must always be alert to restrictions in group norms, particularly as they tend to interfere with free communication of feelings. The woman, for example, who emphasizes the "intellectual

---

[2] In a personal communication, Bennis correctly points out that such terms as *parataxic distortion* or *valid communication,* which are common in training literature, denote the same process as tranference reactions. He also notes that tranference occurs *despite* the trainer's attitude. The trainer's method may enhance or discourage its development, but it will appear in some form and to some extent. Dorothy Stock, also in a personal communication, made a similar point regarding the use of nonanalytic terminology in training literature since the laboratory method had its origins in the fields of social psychology and education.

brilliance" of the male members tend to freeze the men into highly restraining roles. Their attempts to fulfill her expectations result in intellectual muscle flexing. Both therapist and trainer are likely to call attention to the inhibiting effect of such a statement, but the trainer will also attempt to show that rigidifying norms in a group may easily be established, particularly early in a group's life, and such events must be carefully scrutinized.

Members of one t-group were asked several days after the group had started about whether they would be willing to accept a new member. They sensed that the trainer's preference was to accept the new person, and though disposed favorably to the idea, they were not enthusiastic about it. One member, who vehemently opposed the proposal, finally enlisted many others on his side. In an instance of this kind, both training and therapy groups have the opportunity to explore feelings about newcomers, the leader's power, and submission to a powerful peer. For the training group, it was an excellent illustration of an important facet of group dynamics: The numerical majority is often secondary to the "emotional" majority in the decision-making process. Such lessons are not relevant to the objectives of a therapeutic group because patients do not attempt to understand the dynamics of groups, but such a situation provides the trainer with an opportunity to clarify and point up a principle of group dynamics. Such teaching makes for some attenuation of transference to the trainer. These interventions, insofar as they reveal trainers as real people with particular styles of teaching, tend to make them less of a projection screen than are more silent therapists. Furthermore, this kind of spoon feeding also reduces the oral frustration within the group and contributes to reduction of the more regressive fantasies of the members.

THE TRAINER AS A MODEL

In addition to the role of teacher, the trainer often moves gradually in the direction of a membership role so that toward the end of the life of the group the contributions and status of the trainer approach those of a peer. This develops largely through "modeling" behavior, by which the trainer exemplifies the ideals of openness and a willingness to face uncomfortable, conflictful situations without smoothing them over. Of course, the group therapist also confronts uncomfortable issues in the group but does it without blurring his or her identity as the central figure in contrast with the trainer who moves into a membership role.

How trainers move from the position of central figure toward that of member may be illustrated by several examples of trainer behavior. Not infrequently during the inevitable rituals of self-introductions around the table in the first session, trainers will be asked to introduce themselves and describe their background as the other members do. More often than not, they comply perhaps responding more briefly than the others, to avoid frustrating the group. In so doing they contribute to the reduction, at least in part, of the members' preoccupation with the mysterious leader who has let the group know that she or he does not intend to lead. A therapist would probably interpret the meaning of the request for self-introduction, rather than meet the request.

One kind of recommended trainer behavior is a willingness to express "his own situationally induced feelings of discomfort, anger, uncertainty, and helplessness with the group" (Benne, 1964, p. 19). Such expressions serve two major purposes: One, they presumably help members to express more easily their own feelings, which may be too threatening to reveal. They also help limit the regressive fantasies that inevitably develop in the unstructured group in which the central figure is seen as magically endowed with unusual powers for both good and evil and against which various defenses must be erected. The group therapist, on the other hand, would attempt to interpret the group's regressive and dependent wishes toward himself or herself without abdicating the special role as the central figure. Thus, as a trainer, one presents oneself as a real person, with the same kind of weakness and fallibility common to the other members; as a therapist, one does not reveal these inner thoughts and feelings, but rather helps the patients to modify their dependency position by making them more aware of it.

The following example of a membership-modeling intervention used by the trainer is offered by Bradford (1964). A t-group came into one of its early sessions to find that the nameplates on the table had been shuffled around in a way to suggest that somebody was attempting to manipulate the seating arrangement. Resentment simmered, but the group was fearful of dealing with the issue. The trainer forthrightly said that he felt "pushed around," and his frankness permitted the group to uncork its anger. In a similar situation, the therapist would undoubtedly try to encourage and elicit feelings about such an event and try to uncover the meanings of behavior without imparting her or his own feelings to the group. A byproduct of the trainer's intervention would be to enhance his image as a member and further help to strip him of his "projection screen" qualities.

Trainers also participate in giving personal feedback to members. It has already been pointed out that Bethel groups are increasingly moving away from a concern with group issues and are focusing on personal learning via the feedback process. Personal feedback by trainers to members undoubtedly contributes to their membership status but can be made "safely" only insofar as the omniscience attributed to the trainers has been resolved, or at least reduced.

EFFECTS OF TRAINER'S MEMBERSHIP STATUS

The trainer never fully achieves the ideal of becoming a coequal or peer with the others. The powerful dependency strivings are not that easily neutralized, and hence the members will not permit the trainer to become just another member. Thus, feedback from the trainer must be carefully attuned to the trainer's perceived position in the group. The therapist, on the other hand, operates in a more protected position, usually giving interpretations within the safety of a group theme; that is, the therapist shows each individual his or her particular reaction to the common group tension (Ezriel, 1952).

This movement toward increasing membership status of, with consequent attenuation of transference reactions toward, the trainer raises the question of the effects of such an approach in contrast to what develops in the usual therapy group. In my experience with both kinds of groups, the outstanding difference between the training group and the therapy group is the reduced preoccupation of members with the trainer as compared with that of patients with the therapist. While both groups develop magical expectations of the central figure, their intensity—as well as the elaborate fantasies concerning what the central figure is thinking or planning and why this person is behaving as he or she does—tends to be substantially reduced in the training group. The therapy group encourages the development of regressive transference reactions toward the leader; in contrast, the t-group attempts to keep them in check by having the trainer play a memberlike role and focus comments on peer relations rather than trainer–member relations. In this way, members of the t-group go through a relatively abbreviated period of dealing with their dependency problems toward the trainer and begin to focus on their relationship to each other and the problems of intimacy and closeness; they learn from this emphasis on peer relationships about their characteristic modes of interaction.

Another development in the therapeutic group largely absent in the t-group is an explicit termination process. Regressive developments as termination approaches in a therapeutic process are well known. Dependency feelings characteristic of the beginning reappear, anger at not having been magically cured surges up, and depression over having to give up a valued relationship occurs. But the training group, not having developed an intense transference relationship with the trainer, reveals little of these phenomena.[3] The t-group literature concerning characteristic problems of bringing a training group to a close is relatively sparse.

The method that attenuates transference reactions to the leader and

---

[3] Dorothy Stock in a personal communication states:

I think there is a termination process in t-groups, but it is not focussed around the leader. Two things I have noted: first, a mourning over the impending separation from one's peers; and second, disappointment at not having achieved all one's individual goals and for not having dealt as hoped with all the issues which came up during the course of the group. I have seen groups which dealt with both these issues admirably and realistically, making the last few sessions very productive and satisfying. Groups which don't [deal with both issues realistically] seem prone to reunions.

abbreviates the period of concern about them in the group seems to me consistent with the aim of giving personal feedback to members during a relatively brief series of sessions in t-groups as compared with therapy groups. The definite time limit and predetermined number of sessions in a t-group (usually about 20 sessions) will in iteslf set limits upon the degree of dependence on the central figure that is likely to develop. Several writers have noted the kind of self-regulation that tends to develop in time-limited groups (Berman, 1953). The leader's "membership" role seems to reinforce this decreased dependency on the leader and consequent increased reliance on peers for personal learning primarily by means of feedback.

FEEDBACK IN A TRAINING GROUP VERSUS INSIGHT IN A THERAPY GROUP

The feedback process is designed chiefly to enable participants to become more aware of some of their characteristic modes of interacting which become apparent to others in a close relationship but are hidden from the participants themselves. It is a process of communicating one's perceptions of others in a setting where members are ideally attempting to help each other and where the observations are gauged approximately to the level at which the member is ready to accept them.[4] Usually, the feedback received by a member in a t-group has a special impact on her or him because it generally is derived from a consensus of observations and because the sheer weight of numbers, combined with an effort to give responsible help, usually produces a significant effect on the member. The extent to which these insights produce significant behavioral change is a question still to be answered.

A dramatic instance of feedback occurred in one t-group in connection with a member's efforts to dominate and control the group. The initial comments to him concerned his drive for power and his lack of any genuine interest in others, despite his superficial solicitousness. Finally one member said he thought Jim was contemptuous of the others in the group, of their opinions, abilities, and what they had to offer him. Jim opened his notebook, which contained a voluntarily kept personal diary, and read a paragraph describing his impressions after the initial meeting. He had written that not a single person in the group showed any leadership ability and none could hold a responsible position in industry as he did. He then acknowledged to the group that he had heard similar criticisms from others and he even admitted

---

[4] A common myth that has grown up about t-groups is that feedback is nothing more than a "no-holds-barred" attack upon a fellow member. While angry outbursts may occur, the trainer takes pains to point up the difference between such retaliations and the more deliberate and constructive efforts involved in the feedback process. It is not a means of "tearing down defenses," as some have described it, but rather a genuine effort to encourage growth and change by enhancing self-understanding.

some explosive and sadistic behavior toward his wife. His subsequent behavior in the group became considerably less "phony" and pseudosympathetic, and there was little doubt that the group's feedback had produced, or at least reinforced, an important personal insight.

How does the feedback process in a Bethel group compare with the insights that develop in a therapeutic group? In the kind of group psychotherapy described by Sutherland (1952) and Ezriel (1952), the therapist attempts to uncover a common group tension or an underlying conflict shared by the entire group although expressed in an idiosyncratic manner by each member as a function of his or her own character structure. It is similar to the orientation described by Whitman and Stock (1958) in their discussion of the group focal conflict. Thus, in the group dealing with dependency conflict in its initial phases and looking toward the leader for omnipotent and magical solutions, some will ask the therapist what to discuss, some will ask for instruction about the theory of group psychotherapy, while others may silently and expectantly await the therapist's magical words to rid them of their anxiety. The therapist must interpret this group theme while at the same time pointing out to individual members their own characteristic mode of expressing their wishes and fears. Although various kinds of distortions, projections, and manipulations occur in the behavior of members toward each other, therapists use these behavioral data in relation to the common tension toward themselves.

For example, in one therapeutic group I conducted, much of one meeting consisted of a heated argument over the obscene language of one member, a young man. During the argument, it became increasingly clear that the "offender" (who was also his most vocal proponent) perceived the therapist as a bourgeois and repressive individual who kept him from talking as freely as he wished. This perception he displaced onto persons in the group who most closely approximated his image of the therapist. One of his antagonists, a young woman who argued for more gentlemanly language, was struggling against her own introject of the evil, seductive father who has little control over sexual and aggressive impulses. (This patient had suffered a brief psychotic episode during which she had the delusion that her father was going to rape her.) The common tension that involved the group in this instance was the fear lest their sexual impulses get out of hand. The young man defended himself against these impulses by projecting a severely repressive superego onto the group, only to struggle vigorously against it. The prudish woman, on the other hand, unable to tolerate her own sexual wishes, was doing battle with the projected licentiousness which she saw ready to run rampant in the group. The therapist attempted to show that despite their polarized positions, they were struggling with transference distortions based on the same fear of sexuality—one by projecting id wishes and the other by projecting superego injunctions. When they became aware of these distortions, they were able to begin dealing with these internal, repressed conflicts. The level of insight into unconscious motives that the therapist aims for is considerably deeper than the insight that occurs in a training group.

Therapeutic and training groups emphasize two different methods of insight giving. The training group depends more on personal feedback from one's peers, while the therapy group depends largely on the therapist's interpretation of transference to him- or herself. It is interesting to speculate whether or not it would be profitable to use the transference approach with a brief, time-limited group, such as a t-group, to enhance the objective of personal insights. If the trainer were to confine that role to observer and interpreter and thereby encourage the development of transference reactions, the group would undoubtedly become more preoccupied with and develop more intense feelings toward the central figure. Then the group might spend a considerable portion of the twenty-odd sessions expressing and coming to terms with their frustrated dependency needs and their wishes to be given a few omniscient observations about themselves from the trainer. Efforts to learn about themselves from the group's observations would certainly decrease inasmuch as the expert leader would understand more about their behavior, motives, and latent preoccupations than anyone else present. To the extent that the group did acquire insights from the central figure, it would be within the context of the common problem within the group.

The feedback method, on the other hand, encourages peer observation in the form of mutual evaluations in which members have the opportunity of hearing a consensus opinion about their roles in the group. It appears to have some special advantages over the transference method for a brief time-limited group. First, feedback is in no way restricted to a group theme, and therefore is likely to encompass a wide range of behaviors and observations. Rather than emphasizing individual modes of relating oneself to the authority figure in the group, the t-group permits a wider range of observations: a person's overreadiness to rush to the defense of those who are attacked, another's habit of quickly acceding to pressure from others, or another's tendency to stir up hostile interactions by subtly getting others to do battle. Second, the feedback method exploits the power of peer pressure. A common occurrence in a t-group is the report by a member who has just been evaluated by the group that he or she has heard these observations many times before, by spouse, colleague, supervisor, or friend. But the previous comments were rarely as telling in their impact as the group consensus. The power of group opinion, especially in an atmosphere of mutual care and trust, carries with it considerable persuasive force.

A final, and perhaps crucial, advantage of transference attenuation in the t-group is the trainer's wish to avoid the depth of regression the therapist seeks to elicit. The therapist aims to promote regressive responses from the patient in order to bring into awareness the unconscious conflicts that impair personal functioning. The therapist is best able to do this by refraining from excessive participation, by taking the role of a projection screen, and by frustrating to some degree the patient's conscious and unconscious wishes. The trainer, on the other hand, would see such behavior as creating an "artificial" authority problem and seek to resolve the authority transference as quickly as possible by interpretation and also by playing roles that tend to remove the aura of mystery surrounding the more neutral andless "visible" therapist. The trainer is content to work with more superficial and more conscious layers of the personality than is the therapist.

My conclusion is that the use of transference is appropriate for the intensive, uncovering approach of a therapeutic group, but is best attenuated and minimized in a training group. Where the objective is restricted to helping one gain insight about one's major blind spots in relating to others in groups, and where a time limitation exists with regard to the life of the group, the feedback technique seems to be the method of choice.

SUMMARY

Human relations training groups have increasingly focused over the past few years on personal insights into individual members' characteristic modes of behavior. While such groups also deal with group issues, these have become of secondary interest in the usual Bethel t-group. Since the t-group is coming to be used to acquire enhanced understanding about oneself, although at a more superficial level than in a therapy group, the problem is posed as to why the central vehicle of psychotherapy, transference, is not emphasized as the major tool of the typical training group. The group therapist encourages the development of transference, particularly to herself or himself, by acting primarily as observer and interpreter of group and individual conflicts and resistances. This behavior facilitates regressive reactions toward oneself, which are fundamental in uncovering unconscious conflict. The trainer, on the other hand, not only interprets but often moves in the direction of a "member" role, by modeling behavior and contributing personal reactions to group events as a way of helping the group to understand and learn about itself. These memberlike behaviors contribute to attenuated transference reactions and diminished preoccupation with the central figure, to a decrease in regressive reactions, and to increased interaction and interdependence among the members. To achieve the goal of maximum learning about blind spots and distortions in one's personal interactions in a brief time-limited group, the "memberlike" role of the trainer seems preferable to the transference role of the therapist.

REFERENCES

Benne, K. D. Comments on training groups. In L. P. Bradford, J. R. Gibb, & K. D. Benne (Eds.), *T-Group Theory and Laboratory Method*. New York: John Wiley & Sons, 1964.

Bennis, W. G., & Shepard, H. A. Theory of group development. *Human Relations,* 1956, *9,* 415–437.

Berman, L. Group Group psychotherapeutic technique for training in clinical psychology. *American Journal of Orthopsychiatry,* 1953, *23,* 322–327.

Bradford, L. P. Experiences in a t-group. In L. P. Bradford, J. R. Gibbs, & K. D. Benne (Eds.). *T-Group Theory and Laboratory Method.* New York: John Wiley & Sons, 1964.

Ezriel, H. Notes on psychoanalytic group therapy: II. Interpretation and research. *Psychiatry,* 1952, *15,* 119–126.

Frank, J. D. Human relations training groups and therapy groups. In L. P. Bradford, J. R. Gibb, & K. D. Benne (Eds.), *T-Group Theory and Laboratory Method.* New York: John Wiley & Sons, 1964.

Shepard, H. A. Explorations in observant participation. In L. P. Bradford, J. R. Gibb, & K. D. Benne (Eds.), *T-Group Theory and Laboratory Method.* New York: John Wiley & Sons, 1964.

Sutherland, J. D. Notes on psychoanalytic group therapy: I. Therapy and training. *Psychiatry,* 1952, *15,* 111–117.

Weschler, I. R., Massarik, F., & Tannenbaum, R. The self in process: A sensitivity training emphasis. In I. R. Weschler & E. H. Schein (Eds.), *Issues in Training.* Washington, D.C.: National Training Laboratories, 1962.

Whitman, R. M. The t-group in terms of group focal conflict. In L. P. Bradford, J. R. Gibb, & K. D. Benne (Eds.), *T-Group Theory and Laboratory Method.* New York: John Wiley & Sons, 1964.

Whitman, R. M., & Stock, D. The group focal conflict. *Psychiatry,* 1958, *21,* 269–276.

7

Defenses against "Depressive Anxiety" in Groups: The Case of the Absent Leader

Warren G. Bennis
Massachusetts Institute of Technology, Cambridge

[In this fascinating and extremely important paper, Bennis highlights four characteristic defense mechanisms utilized by the members of an unstructured laboratory group to cope with depressive feelings associated with the absence of the leader. The use of mechanisms such as fantasy projection, manic denial and idealization, scapegoating, and restitution of the lost object (all complexly related to the more general defense mechanism of *projective identification*) allows for a dilution, masking, and distortion of the basic feelings of unhappiness experienced by the members in response to the leader's absence. A comparative analysis of the thematic content evident in process recordings obtained from both leader-absent and leader-present meetings is offered by the author as an empirical substantiation of his group dynamic hypotheses.

It has often been noted that groups—particularly those which have as their major purpose therapy or self-study[1] —utilize a variety of mechanisms for

From "Defenses against 'Depressive Anxiety' in Groups: The Case of the Absent Leader" by W. G. Bennis, *Merrill-Palmer Quarterly of Behavior and Development*, 1961, 7, 3-30. Copyright 1961 by the Merrill Palmer Institute. Reprinted by permission of the author and the Merrill-Palmer Quarterly of Behavior and Development.

This is part of a larger study sponsored by the National Institute of Mental Health. Senior investigators of this project are Elvin Semrad, M.D., and Eugene Cogan, Ph.D. Acknowledgments are due to the aforementioned for some of the formulations, and particularly to Eugene Cogan, Ted M. Mills, Philip Slater, Herbert Shepard, Edith Varon, and Howard Perlmutter for critical readings and suggestions.

[1] Jaques points out that this phenomenon exists in more formally structured groups as well (12).

warding off anxieties. To the group observer or leader these defensive maneuvers the group constructs appear as a set of fictions and myths, collectively shared, which tend to deflect the group members from experiencing threatening anxieties (22). I intend in this paper to explore the mechanisms of secondary identification—chiefly "projective identification" (12, 15)—as they serve defensive—anxiety-reducing—needs, and to propose tentatively some hypotheses relating generally to defense mechanisms in groups.

Under consideration here will be a group, meeting together for a period of fifty weeks with the avowed purpose of learning "group dynamics" by using their own group as the focus of study. Due to a variety of circumstances, the group leader had to be absent for four of the first eleven meetings and on two other occasions later in the group experience. I will attempt to illustrate how the group coped with this loss in terms of specific defenses employed.[2]

THE GROUP SETTING

Nineteen psychiatrists, all first- or second-year residents from two hospitals, participated in the group experience for an hour and a half each week for fifty weeks. The major goal for the group, made explicit by the leader, was to arrive at an understanding of group dynamics through participation in a group which would attempt to understand its own processes. The group leader was a psychoanalyst, clinical director of a well-known psychiatric hospital and well acknowledged for his experience and success in conducting groups of this sort (21). His orientation (the observations and interpretations he made) was guided by psychoanalytic theory although primarily based on the "here and now" interaction rather than genetic factors. The group leader's particular style lent itself very neatly to formulations concerning depressive anxiety since one of his major roles was that of a leader, who, in his words, "deprives and refuses." The behavioral consequences of his formulations took the following forms: (a) he spoke only infrequently during the group meetings—typically under five interventions per meeting, and those only a sentence or two; (b) he provided minimum and ambiguous structure; (c) he did not reward and occasionally punished by reminding the group of their responsibilities (summaries and papers were assigned); (d) his remarks were geared to the shared and unconscious fantasies of group members and were

[2] Implied in this approach and throughout the paper is the contention that the group provides a useful crucible and analogue for understanding intrapsychic processes and that concepts applicable to the person unit may equally apply to the group unit (16, 19, 23). Kelley and Thibaut point out: "Thus, whereas some authors (e.g. Dashiell) suggest using individual problem solving as a model for analyzing group process, Bales suggests the opposite—that group process be used as a model for individual thought process. Undoubtedly both views have merit" (13, p. 738).

thereby frequently ambiguous and readily misunderstood. In addition to the anxiety which the leader evoked, the fact that the residents were relative strangers to each other and were just beginning their responsible positions with the concomitant threat of impressing their peers, all fed into heightening their anxieties. Finally, the group leader himslef was viewed by some as a "realistic authority figure" since it was felt that his judgment might ultimately influence their professional careers.

The group meetings took place at a hospital in a comfortable room where the residents could be seated around a table with the leader at the head. Seated around the periphery of the room and behind the table each week were a number of observers (three or four psychologists who made up the research group) and a female secretary who took complete notes, noted arrival and departure times, seating arrangements, and all material which the tape recorder could not accurately pick up. All the meetings were electronically recorded, typed onto hectograph sheets, and then duplicated. The protocols and tape recordings, which were discussed each week by the leader and the research group, provide the data for this paper.

In this group, a fortuitous factor occurred during the early part of the group life, creating antecedent conditions where the study of depressive anxiety could be undertaken.[3] The leader was absent for four of the first eleven meetings. The protocols reflected the potent effects of his absence: the pervasive themes were absence or silence (of group members or leader), loss and responsibility to the group. A content analysis of the first twelve meetings reveals that between 60 and 70 per cent of the material centered around these issues. From data collected in another part of the study, we know that the group leader, over time, was idealized by the group members, that he was seen as omnipotent, that he represented the group's ego ideal.[4] How could this leader who, when present, refused and deprived, who structured a situation which inevitably led to anxiety, who was absent for so many of the early meetings, emerge so idealized, so well respected and loved? In an attempt to obtain more understanding of this question, we turned to defenses against depressive anxiety.

In order to dramatize the potent effects of the leader's absence and to provide the reader with some inkling of the major preoccupation of the group during this bereavement period, I will summarize and quote briefly from one meeting. (Further elaboration follows; what is of moment here is an example which distills the group's dominant tone.)

During the tenth meeting when the group leader was present (he had been previously absent three times), the group began with a discussion of Yom Kippur, the Day of Atonement. One of the group members had read

---

[3] Other students of group behavior have examined similar phenomena using different theoretical constructions (5, 10, 17).

[4] "Inspecting the data shows a systematic increase over time in the tendency for group members to select the Leader as ego-ideal" (4, p. 3).

Abraham's article on "Kol Nidre" and opened the meeting with his own puzzlement over the meaning of the prayer:

X: [Abraham] spent a great deal of time trying to interpret "Kol Nidre" with reference to the Oedipal situation and with reference to the rejection of the father figure by the brothers. Have any of you who are Jewish here heard any discussion of the "Kol Nidre?" (Pause) It's quite a paradoxical prayer.

Y: It's very interesting that you should mention the rejection of a father by the brothers; that's pretty much the theme that I made out of last week's meeting.

Later on in this meeting there was a lengthy discussion about whether the leader was a member of the group or not. One member of the group visualized the group as an "organism, an individual and a rather immature individual because it's less than three months old." He also visualized the leader as "something outside the group." This fantasy accurately reflects the helpless condition of the group in the face of the leader's impending absence and past absences. The leader's interpretations, which follow below, provide the most graphic illustration of the group's problem: the loss of the leader. (These comments were spaced over the entire length of the meeting.)

Are you saying that every part of our body has a job to do?
Are you implying that when a member isn't here somebody else has to do his work?
You mean on a gun team, if the ammunition bearer is not there, it continues to function?
I was going to ask the neurologists if a man can function without one prefrontal gyrus.
Is it true that phantom limb cases don't actually believe they've lost the part?
Perhaps you can title this meeting "The Whole Clamors for Its Parts."

The above remarks were made by the leader at meeting 10 to prepare the group for his impending absence the following week as well as to direct the members to work on their feelings of loss already experienced.[5] How the group handled this loss, the vicissitudes of emotions and defenses employed in response to depressive anxiety, will be considered after a closer look at the background of the absences and the group's reaction to them.

[5] Edith Varon has raised the question of whether in fact the leader's interpretations (a particularly high number for him) did not evoke the depressive anxiety, a kind of "self-fulfilling prophecy." As will later become clearer, the leader was interpreting the latent meaning of the phenotypic behavior; he was not inducing anxiety, simply interpreting it. Subsequent material from the protocols, which will be presented, argues plausibly for this reasoning.

THE ABSENCES

The leader announced at the first meeting that he would have to be away during certain weeks. (The group began the middle of July and the leader's absence was due to the customary August vacation.) He mentioned four dates when he would be away and it was up to the group to decide whether they wanted to meet or not. Table 1 shows leader absence (LA) during the first sixteen meetings. Over the span of fifty meetings there were six LA meetings. Of these six LA meetings, one—meeting 7—was unanticipated by the entire group due to a misunderstanding; another—meeting 15—was anticipated by the residents of one hospital, but due to faulty communications, residents of the other were not notified. After the fifteenth meeting there were no other LA meetings until meeting 34. Member absences averaged about 6 per meeting, with a range from 2-8 after the sixteenth meeting. Major attention in this paper will be focused on the first twelve meetings as it was during this period that the leader's absence had its most severe effects due to the embryonic state of the group. (Later on I will discuss briefly meeting 34 [LA], but only as a device for comparison with the earlier LA sessions.)

TABLE 1 Leader and Member Absences

Meeting	Members absent	Leader absent	
1	0	P	
2	1	P	
3	6	P	
4	9		A
5	6	P	
6	13		A
7	3		A
8	5	P	
9	2	P	
10	8	P	
11	10		A
12	1	P	
13	5	P	
14	6	P	
15	11		A
16	6	P	

Note.—The group did not meet for 2 weeks between the 6th and 7th meetings. On the 7th meeting the group expected—through a misunderstanding—an LP meeting, but the leader was absent. Three of the 9 members who were present at meeting 4 were not present at meeting 3 and expected an LP meeting. At meeting 11 only 2 members who were present knew that it was an LA meeting; the others expected an LP meeting.

DIFFERENCES BETWEEN LA AND LP MEETINGS

If we examine an LA session and the LP session immediately following it, we discover some interesting patterns. (Thus, for present purposes, meetings 4 and 5, meetings 6 and 8, and meetings 11 and 12. Meeting 7 was excluded from this analysis because, while the leader was absent, he was, in fact, expected to be present.)

First of all, at the three LA meetings under consideration, there was a consistently higher rate of absenteeism: only 5 out of 18 members were present during meeting 6; 8 were present at meeting 11. (One member later joined the group, giving it 19 members at full component.)

Another factor which seems to discriminate between these LA and LP meetings was that the former in all cases lasted longer, and with greater activity and interaction. The average number of typed pages per LA meeting was 43; per LP meeting, 23. This may have been due to the fact that the leader's absence created uncertainty as to when the meeting precisely began and when it ended. Usually the members would start only after ten or fifteen minutes of kidding, joking, informal side-chatter, etc., and would stop when the tape recorder had used all its tape. (The observers and tape recorder were present at all meetings.)

Group affectivity, also, showed remarkable contrasts between these LA and LP meetings. There was a greater release of positive feelings toward group members during the LA sessions. One of the group members said during meeting 12:

... but it seems to me that, that last meeting was the first time anyone had said anything nice about anyone else, and I just wondered whether we shy away from that sort of thing more intently than we do against expressing negative feelings.

The post-meeting responses collected during the course of the study reflected the positive affect manifested during the LA meetings in comparison to the LP meetings (3).[6] A good part of the LP meetings was spent in discussing how meaningful, important, pleasant, cohesive, and friendly the LA meetings had been. When the members were asked by those who had been absent during the LA meeting what accounted for this climate, they attributed it to the smaller size of the group or to the illuminating topics under discussion.

---

[6] Post-meeting responses were factor analyzed into two pure factors: identification with the leader and member cathexis. This last factor consists of variable descriptions: (a) Satisfaction with the meeting, .65 factor loading; (b) Relaxation, .58; (c) Lack of anger, .43; and (d) Warm and friendly feelings, .83. Group cathexis scores for meetings 4 and 11 (LA meetings) were higher—in the positive affect direction—than any other meetings up through meeting 12. (The group cathexis score for meeting 11 was 50; for meeting 12 (LP), 37; almost 1.5 standard deviation difference.)

Little mention was made of the leader's absence except for its intellectual connections. (Two members claimed they might try LA sessions with the groups they were leading.)

Another difference between these LA and LP meetings, perhaps the most important, concerns the introduction of unconscious material in the form of dreams. Only two times during the first twelve meetings was dream material brought into the group; in both cases, during LA meetings. This will be discussed in detail below.

One final contrast between these LA and LP meetings will be mentioned although this does not exhaust the differences observed. It was found that there existed in all cases a more pervasive element of depression in the LP meetings. This was manifested in the longer periods of silence and statements expressing the depression. Let us now turn directly to the specific defenses.

DEFENSES AGAINST DEPRESSIVE ANXIETY

In *Group Psychology and the Analysis of the Ego* (7), Freud took as his starting point the relationship between the group and its leader. The essence of this relationship was described in terms of mechanisms of identification: between group members and leader and among group members. Freud did not explicitly develop the concept of identification beyond that of identification through introjection, although it is clear that where he differentiated between the Army and the Church, his discussion foreshadowed the mechanism of projective identification. In the first case, the soldier replaces his ego ideal by the leader who becomes his ideal; in the second case, the Christian takes Christ into himself as his ideal and identifies himself with Him. The recent movie, "Bridge on the River Kwai," offers an excellent example of the former mechanism: the troops replace their ego ideals with the brave Colonel Nickerson, thus gaining a binding cohesion. The communion ceremony represents the latter case, identification through introjection. Melanie Klein (15) and her associates have called the former process identification through projection.

In short, projective identification is a secondary or defensive mechanism which utilizes some external object in order to relieve certain internal anxieties—in this specific instance, anxiety over a lost object. Identification by projection implies both splitting off parts of the self and projecting them into another person or object. Klein goes on to elaborate the mechanism of projective identification into defenses against paranoid anxiety, which put bad objects and impulses into particular members, and defenses against depressive anxiety, which tend simultaneously to split off the good from the bad objects and to heap resentment on the bad and idealize the good. According to Klein: "When the depressive position arises, the ego is forced (in addition to earlier defences) to develop methods of defence which are essentially directed against the 'pining' for the loved object. These are fundamental to the whole ego-organization" (14, p. 316).

Let us now turn directly to the assortment of defenses utilized by the group under study, attempting to apply Klein's formulations for the individual to the group process whenever appropriate. Four mechanisms will be presented: (a) *fantasy projection*, where masked symbols are utilized to dissipate energy away from the actual source of anxiety; (b) *manic denial and idealization*, where the source of anxiety is denied and good impulses are projected into other objects; (c) *scapegoating*, where the bad impulses are absorbed by other objects; and (d) *restitution of the lost object: peer group replacement*, where impulses concerning the absent leader are projected onto an appropriate group member. These four defenses are not empirically independent from one another or mutually exclusive; however, for analytic purposes, they will be discussed separately. After a brief illustration of these four defenses against depressive anxiety as they occurred in the group, meeting 34 will be discussed in order to illustrate a nondefensive form of identification with the leader.

Defense through Fantasy

Perhaps the most economical device to relieve depressive anxiety is dream material. We know that dreams provide the instrument whereby primitive elements may be analyzed. This group took no chances that painstaking dream-work could be done: dreams were brought into the group meeting on two occasions and only when the leader was absent; both dreams, as we shall see, were centrally involved with feelings toward the leader. The importance of the dreams could be gauged by the amount of time spent discussing them. In both cases, the narrative of the dream and the subsequent associations dominated the bulk of the meeting, taking well over half of the time.

In meeting 6, the group discussion was auspiciously started by an individual who said that he awoke that morning with a heavy depression and almost did not come to the group meeting. This same individual, the week before, had been attacked when he said that he did not particularly want to come to the LA meeting the following week because his assumption was that if the leader was going to be absent, the meeting would not be held. In meeting 6, he related his depression to the leader's absence:

So there I was feeling tired, sort of a depressive thing . . . and the two thoughts that came after that were: first, depression means object loss usually, on an intellectual level; and the next thought was "Dr._____ isn't here this week," so I kind of assumed that what I felt was a depression because of a transference phenomenon—that this was a sort of an object loss, in a sense.

We will return to this statement later in the discussion of *manic denial* but for the moment we can say that this remark was deflected by the four other members of the group. (Only five members were present at this meeting.) It did, however, precede and to some extent precipitate the introduction of a dream by a member who had been completely quiet the week before—a dream which was clearly related to the absent and deserting leader.

At the beginning of the meeting, in fact before the group formally opened, there was a brief discussion about vacations. The resident who eventually introduced the dream material was bemoaning the fact that he had only two or three days of vacation time available to him. He then mentioned laughingly "going to Miami Beach for the winter." Another resident responded, "What a dreamer," to which the resident who produced the dream responded, "Well, you can dream." (The group leader was on vacation during this period of protracted absences.)

After about a third of the meeting had elapsed, the same resident turned to the resident who earlier had discussed his depressed feelings over the leader's absence and said:

You know when you were talking before, something came to my mind and I just couldn't help smiling. It's, ah, I don't know why a dream that I had last night came to my mind, it was about groups. I don't know why. I'll just throw it out here, but no, ah, there was this one patient and, ah, I may be letting myself wide open I don't know.

This patient was doing poorly; in other words, his defenses sort of crumbling, you know. We felt that we were treating him, not as a group, but a few people and we felt that he shouldn't be pressed, because we might really produce a complete break so we decided that maybe the thing to do was to give him a little inspirational group therapy and then somebody brought a record and in this record was Billy Graham recording one of his meetings. Then there was the patient and two other men and one girl and they all held hands and started playing the Billy Graham record. When the record started there was a background of rock and roll music and then this group of the patient and then the other two men and the girl, they got up and started doing a rock and roll—that was the inspirational group.

That this dream appears to be related to the group's problem of dealing with a deserting leader is highly plausible both in terms of the dream content as well as the group's ultimate associations to the dream. The "patient doing poorly" seems to represent the "sick group" with only five members present. The "rock and roll" music was associated to by several members when they claimed that rock and roll had been mentioned by some group members the week before. They tried to remember the context and could not, but did remember who had introduced the phrase.

(Upon reading over the previous week's protocol it became apparent that rock and roll had some relationship to the group, most probably its leader. During a skittish part of that meeting the group talked about "a sort of spontaneous fountain that will bring forth and all we have to do is sit and drink."

I think you are referring to the rock pile.
I think the "rock pile" is interesting since rocks were the original god figures
    when people used to worship gods all the time.
This is too deep.
Rock of Ages, Rock of my Fathers.
Rock and roll.

These statements were made by different group members. Thus, it would appear that rocks [fathers] may very well be connected with the leader.)

Following the narration of the dream, there was a temporary struggle about how to deal with the dream. One group member felt that it was not "appropriate" for the group, but if it were, it should be related to the hospital where they were experimenting with "administration through team relationships." The other group member, who felt it was not appropriate, tried to suppress the analysis of the dream in terms of its relationship to the group by a number of means:

1. *Claimed it was not appropriate*: (To the producer of the dream) "Why did you bring this up? It seems to me maybe it's not appropriate for us to talk about the content of the dream."
2. *Prematurely and hurriedly analyzed the dream*: "Unless you're different from other residents, I might speculate that maybe we're all sort of having a problem with closeness and relations with groups and relations with patients and that certainly we all, I'm sure, feel this way, and it seems to me that's what the dream's about."
3. *Displaced dream from group to outside, safer symbol*: "I think your dream may well have been related to this approach [team administration] rather than to this group here or groups."

This last statement launched a long discussion on teamwork in hospitals with particular reference to supervision. I have remarked elsewhere that "when the content of a discussion deals with organizational relationships of a hierarchical nature, it typically relates to the leader problem in the group" (1). In this case the residents spent the rest of the group meeting discussing their supervisors, generally in negative terms. Their supervisors were authoritarian, "have an unlimited number of votes" (said with a sad laugh); or "he interjects his personality, and then he pulls it out, puts it in, and then he pulls it out, and sometimes when you think that you're running the thing, he'll step in and take over, and then again, when you're looking for him, he's not there, he'll sit back. . . ." This last statement is a perfect description of the group leader as the members see him: he's in and out, when you want his help he's not there, he's ultimately powerful, etc.

Later on in the meeting the same supervisor was referred to as "writing orders on my patients and changing them" and "not only is he on vacation, but he isn't coming back." (This was met with great laughter.) Later it was stated that this supervisor "was inaccessible today as he was in Rome."

Now it is fairly clear that this dream, a direct derivative of the group situation, was transformed into an object external to the group (team relationships and the supervisor) and this transformation tended to alleviate the depressive feelings aroused by the loss of the leader. In fact, we can see that every attempt to relate material from the meeting to the group leader was quickly sabotaged. Note how this happened when the person who initiated the meeting on the theme of the loss of the leader was quickly squelched; also, how the dream was at first avoided and later projected onto a safer object.

Dreams, which were brought in during two LA meetings (and only then), we propose, were used to externalize grief and suffering in two ways: by dissipating energy tied up with the displaced object and by exploiting, at a remote level, dream symbols which are masked derivatives and reminders of the more primitive elements of the group processes.

Manic Denial and Idealization[7]

Among the most common defenses against anxiety is denial. When we observe a denial pattern which is shared by the group and perpetuated to a degree that is unrealistic, we have some reason to wonder about the source of anxiety. For an example of manic denial, as it occurred in this particular group, let us look back at the same meeting referred to above (meeting 6). Recall the opening of the meeting when one group member related his depression to the leader's absence. What followed his opening remarks could be seen as a pattern of attempts to ignore the content, even though it is reasonable to assume that it would be natural for the members to have some negative feelings toward a leader who was absent. Some of the following remarks are examples of manic denial:

It seems to me that we don't know Dr. _____ well enough, we haven't had enough—at least from my hospital, we haven't had enough—in connection with him to feel any loss.

As for him leaving, I had no conscious anger or anything, whatsoever; as a matter of fact, I said, "The guy's going on vacation probably." I don't know, I assumed he was.

After this followed a discussion on vacations which seemed to serve the group's need to escape from the topic of the leader's absence as well as

[7] "Another way in which depressive anxiety may be alleviated by social mechanisms is through manic denial of destructive impulses, and destroyed good objects, and the reinforcement of good impulses and good objects, by participation in group idealization. These social mechanisms are the reflection in the group of denial and idealization shown by Melanie Klein to be important mechanisms of defense against depressive anxiety" (12, p. 486; 14).

validate the possibility that the leader himself was really on vacation. However, the depressed individual again related his "tiredness" to the absent leader. This was met by a statement which argued—on intellectual grounds— for the legitimacy of denial.

Well, I've had fellows say to me, "Well, you've done this because you've had some sort of relationship with your father." I don't think that we really can deduce anything like that here, nor is that even a valid thing to try to get to here, but we can, I personally feel that we can, arrive at a more clear picture perhaps of why we, as individuals, act as we do. Or *how* we act, rather; how we, as individuals, act, not why, but how we act.

Not being deterred by this remark, the depressed individual perseverated on his "lost" feeling and then related how his own father died when he was an infant. That this statement corresponds so closely to the group's own problem—the group leader "dies" during the infancy of the group life—may explain why it was immediately brushed aside by other group members:

I wonder if you really can work that sort of thing out here.

You don't seem that depressed to me, actually.

Following this discussion, the group wandered off into a discussion of group goals: what was expected of them, what they expected. Shortly after this, the group dealt with the dream discussed above and proceeded to have an enjoyable, active meeting on psychiatric administration and the foibles of authority figures.

The following week (meeting 7) the leader was expected back (due to faulty communication) but did not appear. At this time, the five members who had been present at the previous LA meeting proceeded to celebrate it with long testimonials about how rewarding and stimulating it had been. Not only was the meeting considered gratifying, but some felt it was improved because the leader was absent:

A: The impression I have is that the leader was a necessary, is a necessary, was necessary to the group interaction in the early stages, to promote the kind of thing we were here for. Now I may be wrong, that would be the impression I have from what you said, and yet, on the basis of our meeting here, I don't think we would have done as well with the leader present.

B (who had not been present at the previous meeting and had been for the most part silent): But he is present.

A: I was just, that was my impression.

C: He wasn't present.

B: He is now.

B, who was apparently attempting to get the group to examine the impact of the leader's absence-presence (10), was ignored with silence. Someone then asked A if he thought the group did in fact require a leader. A did not answer directly.

Later in the group meeting, a fairly silent member who up to that time had not spoken intervened with a good deal of emotion in his voice and told the group:

I don't know, but my own feeling is that there is only one person here who is expressing real feelings. That's you [referring to the depressed individual]; I don't believe anybody else aside from him expresses feelings sincerely. He is the only one who is crying.

This was followed by laughter and then an attempt to smother this threatening material by indicating to the speaker that one can express feeling without crying. Immediately following this, the speaker who had attacked the group for not crying said that he did not think it was possible for him to attend the group meetings because he had no car, and that he was not sure, if he had a car, that he wanted to attend. The group then responded to him by attempts to arrange transportation for him. Then he said, "I will come if they come [referred to a ride]. Or if you plan, as Sam said, for Dr. _____ [the leader] to send his car." This was received by spontaneous laughter from the group. The humor here contains a hollow gallows quality, in effect saying: "We cannot even get our leader here. Can you imagine his sending his car to pick *us* up?"

Meeting 8, which followed an unexpected LA meeting, stayed mainly on the topic of "how wonderful" meeting 6 had been, with an acceleration of testimonials.

I think we can see from these few examples that manic denial is always accompanied by idealization of some other object. Early in the group life—and particularly in this group where the leader was so frequently absent—idealization would probably focus on objects apart from the leader. This suspension of object choice would lead to the hypothesis that the initial forms of projective identification (manic denial) would use a variety of other objects until the group members became ready to substitute the leader's ego ideal for their own. Examination of the group protocols up through meeting 12 indicates that one of the chief interpersonal tensions existing in the early life of the group was the imbalance and asymmetry of members' willingness to share in the same object. It's as if the group members were saying to one another: "Let us advance to this object equitably and simultaneously. Anyone who seriously seems to be setting up his own private identification with the leader will be hurt."[8]

[8] Those members of the group who were initially attacked consisted of two members who had been in the leader's previous group for the last half of the meetings and who

We can observe the mechanism of manic denial and idealization during the fourth meeting, the first time the leader was absent. The members were expressing some concern about the apparent goallessness of the group when one member said:

Well, perhaps it's like neuroanatomy, I was confused up until the final, and then all the tracks and sections appear at different levels, and sort of fit into a whole, just for the period of examination—and then it fell apart. . . . Well, perhaps at the end, the last session, we'll sort of look upon this as sort of a contiguous whole, as we walk out.

Following this comment, the group members enshrined a number of people, "all greats in psychiatry," as a source for structuring the rest of the group meetings. There was frequent allusion to individuals they had worked for and lecturers in psychiatry and past supervisors, all of whom had been excellent and instructive.

It appears then that one mechanism for dealing with depressive anxiety is a parallel device: manic denial of the loss accompanied by idealization of other objects. These objects may be the group itself, "greats in psychiatry," other members of the group, and ultimately, the group leader. (It should be mentioned that the idealization may have occurred in this group despite the leader's absences and the production of depressive anxiety. The causal connection cannot be clearly documented here for, in fact, as was mentioned earlier, the leader can, indeed, be considered a "great" in psychiatry—certainly in the Boston area where his reputation as a very prestigeful figure is taken for granted.)

Hostility, Scapegoating, and Paranoia

One of the more common phenomena observed in group and organizational life is scapegoating, usually thought to be misdirected or inappropriate hostility. Scapegoating can be thought of as a special case of defense against depressive anxiety. As Jaques points out, "The primary defense mechanism against the onset of depressive anxiety was that of retreat to the paranoid position" (12, p. 492).

The interesting aspect of scapegoating and hostile behavior is that it exists concurrently with the idealization phenomenon. In fact, we can say that idealization and scapegoating proceed *pari passu*: that as the need to project good impulses increases, an equal and opposite need exists to project into external objects bad impulses and wishes. What is more interesting perhaps

---

had had some previous identification with the leader and his group, and who indicated their positive feelings to the leader. The other scapegoated member was very vocal in announcing his strong allegiance to the leader. (He announced, for example, that he did not think the group should or would meet without the leader present.)

than the acknowledged fact of scapegoating is the question of the particular objects selected as targets for attack. These objects, I propose, are not random. What appears to be the case, instead, is a quiet collusion between the attacked and attacker; a shared unconscious phantasy which permits the attacked to drain off the guilt associated with loss (in the particular instance of depressive anxiety) and which provides the attacker with a "legitimate" channel for expressing his anger at the lost object. We see at the unconscious level, then, a group cooperating in setting up the guilty party (who in some magical way created the loss) and the plaintiff who feels wronged (deserted in this case).

A striking example of this can be seen in meeting 11 (LA) when a group member attacked the group recorder (who was reporting a five-minute summary of the previous meeting) for allegedly attacking another member of the group who was not present. Actually, the recorder's remarks indicated precisely the opposite: that the group member in question was an important and "good" group member. Then the group attacked the protector of the alleged attacked one for a long period. It appeared that the "protector" attacked (quite unrealistically) the observer for criticizing an innocent victim, thus, in turn, reaping the group's hostility.

The incidence of scapegoating and paranoiac behaviors was so ubiquitous in the group that a number of hypotheses about object choice of the scapegoat can be made concerning depressive anxiety.

1. Those individuals who will be selected as scapegoats will tend to be individuals who attempt to set up an identification with the leader *before* the main portion of the group is ready. This will occur during the early stage of group life.
2. Those individuals who will be selected as scapegoats will be those individuals who resist an identification with the leader *after* the main body of the group has replaced him for their own ego ideal. This will occur late in the group life.[9]
3. Those individuals who will be selected as scapegoats will tend to be individuals who have had in their own development some guilt associated with a lost significant figure. They will evoke hostility as a way of draining off guilt associated with an earlier loss; a loss for which they feel in some degree responsible. (In this group, the two members who were attacked regularly reminded the group of the fact that the group leader was absent and/or they were angry or depressed by his absence. In both cases, the fathers of these two men died during childhood.[10]

[9] Further research is being conducted on this problem: W. G. Bennis and R. Burke, Leadership and Identification in Small Groups—in preparation.

[10] "In other words, a central problem involves the way in which the presence of children influences adult functioning, especially in relation to the adult's own unresolved problems from childhood" (11, p. 113). In this paper the authors establish a connection

Restitution of the Lost Object:
Peer Group Replacement

Two theoretical considerations will provide the necessary structure for the analysis of this defense—perhaps the most complicated, from a dynamic point of view.

First, Rochlin has proposed that in most cases, following an emotional trauma due to an important lost object, the individual creates some sort of unique restitution of the lost object (18); the derivative transformations of the original lost object vary considerably from other persons to inanimate objects which symbolically represent the lost object.

Secondly, let us consider Freud's discussion of the myth of the primal horde: "These many individuals eventually banded themselves together, killed [the father], and cut him in pieces.... They then formed the totemistic community of brothers all with equal rights and united by the totem prohibitions which were to preserve and to expiate the memory of the murder" (7, p. 112). The horde's act, according to Freud, was soon distorted into a heroic myth: instead of murder by the group, the myth held that the father had been overthrown singlehandedly by one person. In this attribution of the group act to one individual (the hero) Freud saw the "emergence of the individual from group psychology." His definition of the hero is ". . . a man who stands up manfully against his father and in the end victoriously overthrows him" (8, p. 9).

The unique restitution of the lost object coupled with the unconscious wish to overthrow the (father) leader and displace him with one of the (brothers) group members can now be put in terms of our conceptual framework. One way of handling anxiety concerning loss of significant group members—in this case, the leader—is to elevate a group member, as a replacement, into this position. In other words, *group members projectively identify with another group member by projecting onto him their own rebellious impulses as well as utilizing the replacement to mask the loss of the absent leader.*

How this replacement emerges and on what grounds a particular group member is selected as the replacement (Freud attributed this to the youngest son) can only be partly illustrated by the data presented below. Much more research remains to be done before any definitive statements can be made. However, our tentative speculation is that an unconscious collusion between the replacement leader and other group members eventuates in which characteristics of the replacement resemble those characteristics of the lost leader

---

between the onset of mental illness and certain anniversary (death) dates. In this connection, the loss of the leader in the group under study represented the trigger, it appears, for early traumatic events to reassert their way to consciousness; a type of anniversary event without reference to specific times.

about which group members feel most ambivalent. We will turn to the protocols presently in order to illustrate this defense, but for the moment, let us examine some of the conditions under which this defense may or may not be manifested.

In the group under discussion, a number of conditions mitigated against a total replacement of the leader and a strong identification with a peer replacement. In the first place, the group had not met a sufficient period of time for the "heir apparents" or "contenders" to emerge (20). Moreover, with the unstable and inchoate nature of the group in its early stage, it is doubtful whether group members would invest one of their peers with differential power. This is particularly true in light of the suggestions made above concerning the equilibration of distance toward the leader. And, most important, no matter what the fantasies of the group members, the leader was not permanently lost; he would return.

Despite these forces, other forces were also operating in the group to create a *pro tem.* leader. Examples which will be presented below show that the group tried valiantly to replace the lost leader. And this occurred most openly during LA meetings and always collapsed at the following LP meeting. The elevation of the surrogate leader was always accompanied by a manic cohesiveness which was short-lived (2),[11] most probably due to apprehension about the returning leader as well as jealousy stirred up by the bestowal of power on a peer. As suggested above, characteristics of the replacement in this case resembled, or were perceived as resembling, characteristics of the absent leader: i.e., the replacement was quiet, thoughtful, controlled, psycho-analytically oriented, and neutral. As we shall see, this defensive reaction was only partially successful.

A few excerpts from LA meeting 11 followed by LP meeting 12 will illustrate the role of the replacement leader and group members' attitudes towards him.

LA Meeting 11

A (replacement leader): You, you, you're always coming back to the leader again, the importance of the leader; now I grant that this is very important and, ah, I miss his presence, I think, not as much as anybody else but I miss it. But I think there's also an interaction among members which is, is just as important, ah, and, ah, B said that he had come in today to be the center of the stage, more or less, to be the Romeo [allusion to a reported dream].

A (later on): To some extent to bring the feelings which you brought in, ah, which arise in connection with, ah, feelings toward other members and toward the leader as well, which, ah, I would think that the leader's absence, as you say, promotes, ah (pause). But I, I don't think it's as bad

---

[11] Supporting evidence may also be found in Philip Slater's "Totemic Process in Groups" (unpublished manuscript, 1960).

as you think it is. It seems that we can see two camps: one, the type, ah, whose interests are identified mainly with the activities of the leader and centered about the leader, how the leader affects the group, and how the group as a whole responds to the leader—which you represent, C. B and D represent the opposite extreme that they're individuals and they're going to fight for their rights and they're going to express what they feel, and they're not going to lose their identification in any way. I think, I myself tend to fall in that category, but I know, I know better, ah (laughs), ah, that I haven't gone to the opposite extreme yet.

C: You know, A, as far as I'm concerned, your comment, there's more to it than that because at the earliest meetings, I recall that I came to the group with all sorts of emotional feelings and, ah, and, ah, expressed them; and then I've, ah, noticed that you, you, you've, ah, tended to be very controlled in the meeting and I've told you this, ah, a couple of times, and it's, ah, an admirable thing, I think.

C (to A, later on): No, the point is that I'm identifying with you.

B: Because you think his control is admirable, you mean?

C: Yeah, because I have the feeling that, ah, A usually understands what's going on at the meeting.

(Pause)

B: And he only speaks at appropriate times, and says worthwhile things.

E: In other words, ah, ah, A is a better father figure for you.

B: A better psychiatrist.

(Pause)

E: Well, that's a father figure.

B: It's also ego ideal in this group.

E: Yeah, that's what I mean, I mean, his [C's] ego ideal is more incorporated in A than it is in any of the other members in the group.

B: Well, A probably comes the closest to doing that, of anybody.

E: So that is the way he allays his anxiety when, in the leader's absence, he uses A for his ego ideal. This is the way he controls his anxiety. Maybe that's why he said what he said.

D: Ah, ah, you know, I, I, I missed this point, I think, completely. What, what is it again? B, what's the point here? C, C sees in A his ego ideal as a psychiatrist? Therefore, in the absence of the leader . . . .

B: That was E.

E: I say, ah, *perhaps,* I didn't say this is a way of . . . .

D: Yeah, you always say "perhaps," so what difference does it make?

E: I think it makes a lot of difference.

F: Anger, anger.

E: Yeah, I'm really angry.

When we pierce through the above intellectualizations, anger, and confusion, we see the group struggling to create a replacement out of the available peer group resources to dampen their loss reactions. That this was a tenuous and unstable resolution can be detected from the above excerpts wherein the ambivalence of both the group and the heir apparent is manifest. The uneasiness of the head that wears the crown becomes so exacerbated that it topples completely the following week when the group leader returns.

LP Meeting 12 There was at first some reminiscence about the warmth and tenderness of the preceding meeting. That there was some confusion about the affective memory can be observed by C's remark very early in the meeting:

C: I was particularly interested in this, ah, business of the, ah, positive feelings, since I was right in the middle of it and took rather a beating.

E: Well, C, I, I was wondering about that myself, ah (pause). I think it was brought up in the last meeting that, ah, I don't know who said it or use the exact word, but, ah, it was implied that, ah, it seemed that group members were able to express themselves better with Dr. _____ being absent, I guess; the reasons, I don't know.

B: The meeting before, before the last one, we had a very angry meeting when Dr. _____ was here; and we had a very contrite meeting when he wasn't here. Last meeting we had a more of a sort of, well, at first it was angry and then we were talking intimately, that's when he wasn't here. Now this meeting, we've talked about mostly being intimate with ourselves, and nobody has anything to say.

D: It's like having a new doctor, changing doctors. I was thinking that before. I thought to myself that it's, ah, it's like visiting with a new, it's like being interviewed by another doctor today, and, ah, going through that more than one patient says, said to me, who had been in and out of mental hospitals so many times: "I've been through this since—over and over again." We're always, it seems, faced with the problem of bringing last week's absent members up to date for integrating them. I don't think we'll ever, ever get to that point until we, we do something about our attendance; until we are a warmer group.

(Long Pause)

B: You sounded very gloomy just reading your report this morning.

D: Well, I won't blame it on my car or on the weather.

(Pause)

B: You feel gloomy?

D: Yes, I do, B, and, and I'm not going to tell this new doctor why.

Recall that D, the previous week, was cited by the replacement leader as one who shared generally his own feelings about the group's independence from the leader; D also was a main supporting member of A during the previous meeting and his "gloominess" in this meeting probably stemmed from "changing doctors"; i.e., objects of identification. In a capsule we see the pain of reshifting energy from one to another object, the energy transformation accompanied by mourning.

Shortly after this exchange the group members begin to chisel away at the temporary scaffolding of the replacement they had constructed the week before.

B (one of A's main supporters of the preceding meeting): I was thinking about your statement [to C] of identifying with A and this sort of made me mad because to me A is the antithesis of what I would like to see in this group. A, A, ah, is very controlled and he does, you, you know very little about A. [Read B's statement of the previous week.] Actually what he feels is unknown; over and over again it comes out that he felt this way during the meeting and he felt this way last meeting, but he wouldn't say it, which all means to say that when you look at A during the meeting, he may be seething or he may not be, but he doesn't tell you, ah, whereas at the beginning [to C] you told some rather personal things, ah, but then later on, you decided A was the best way to be, and this seemed to me just, just a retreat rather than an advance. I'd rather have A do what you're doing than you do what A does; so we all become A's and we're all doing nothing except sit around and impress each other with our, with our competence and our knowledge, and ability to control ourselves.

(Long Pause)

C: Well, the thing I said last week, ah, the thing I admired about A's behavior is that, ah, he seems to be quite well adjusted to the group and at the same time he seems to understand a lot of what's going on.

B: Yeah, I agree, he does seem to be, I'll agree that he is. Maybe I mean what's "well-adjusted to the group" mean? That means that everything in the group does, doesn't bother you one way or another?

C: Well, I feel that he doesn't go to extremes one way or another.

B: Doesn't express extremes, or he doesn't go to the extremes, really? (Mumbling) I'm not sure how you can tell with somebody who doesn't tell (laughs) how it affects him.

This exchange was followed by long gloomy periods, marked by lengthier pauses than usual, finally interrupted by a group member who asked the leader why the group was so gloomy this session.

The striking aspect of the exchange above is, of course, the mercurial disenchantment of B, just the week before A's most admired devotee ("And he only speaks at appropriate times and says worthwhile things. . . . A better psychiatrist.") And B's sentiments were shared to a greater or lesser degree by other group members. Just those traits which seemed to endear A to the group the previous week, by some curious alchemy, now appeared to alienate him.

Some speculations which emerge from our theoretical framework may provide a partial explanation for this phenomenon. The first obvious point is that the replacement can only function and succeed under conditions where the real leader is *permanently* absent. What is identified with during the leader's absence—as unresolved vestiges of the lost leader—is eclipsed considerably by the real leader's return. Feeding into this are two correlative notions. First, that those members who presumably deserted the leader for the replacement leader feel "taken in" by the replacement. It's as if they were saying: "We've been conned. He isn't the real leader at all; just an imposter." The wish to overthrow the leader, shared by all group members, is a fraud in reality. The forbidden act—seen now as perpetuated solely by the "fallen" hero—forces group members to project their bad impulses on the unsuccessful replacement. This would partly account for their repulsion toward the replacement. Second, the guilt associated with their abortive desertion of the leader and promotion of a peer "behind his back" may account for the gloominess which prevailed from the very beginning of the meeting, as well as account for the reparations paid to the leader subsequent to the attack on A. (B, for example, shortly after his disaffection from A goes on to reveal "deeprooted feelings and fears" concerning the leader.)

We can now summarize the complicated vicissitudes of this defense somewhat more concisely. As a way of alleviating the depressive anxiety over the lost leader, the group searches for a unique restitution of the lost object by selecting one of their own peers as a replacement. Selection of the peer replacement, I propose, is not accidental but is a strategic and complicated decision among members to select a replacement who is perceived as representing those traits of the lost leader about which the group members feel most ambivalent. This unique restitution through "succession" by a peer group replacement serves a number of needs through projective identification: (a) anxiety over loss is warded off by a replacement; (b) revenge toward the lost leader is projected onto the replacement; (c) the wish to overthrow the real leader is projected onto the replacement.

In conclusion, some material from this defensive behavior has led to a provocative and tentative speculation which has some general implications for the study of loss and identification in groups. Recall that A was attacked for precisely those characteristics which were attributed to the leader, but which could not be directly criticized due to inhibitions against aggression toward the leader. Thus, we see the projection of bad impulses onto the failing replacement and the concomitant idealization of the leader. An excerpt of B tends to corroborate this notion.

B: Our feelings toward the leader are so deep-rooted. I'm always thinking about that. I very seldom say anything to D₁. _____ ; I can't bring myself to. I, as I was thinking about it, I am pretty sure I know why. The leader represents a person to me so much that gives approval that I can hardly bear to say anything to somebody like that—especially in this kind of group where he does not give a reply. And I find it very difficult to be, ah, to feel I will be rejected by the leader, ah, that, that, that is as I thought about it. Then I thought to myself, "Well, I probably can talk to the leader and if I make an effort I could." But I'd have to make that effort sort of consciously over time. It strikes me that everybody's relation to the leader's going to be that type of a thing. Not necessarily anywhere near the same dynamics, but you ask, why don't we accept the leader as a group. And I'll say because if you, you could find out why every member had the feelings toward it, then you could find out.

(Pause)

C: Somehow or other, we don't accept him, more or less; that's I think pretty much, ah, actual observation.

B: Well, I'd love to do something about it.

In this case, the unique restitution, a peer group replacement, while not wholly a successful venture, was probably a stronger adaptation to the loss than the three aforementioned defenses.[12]

Freud has pointed to a defensive identification wherein a substitute for "a libidinal tie is made by means of the introjection of the object into the ego" (7, p. 65). Now we can speculate that A, who had succeeded in this introjection (an identification with the aggressor), or is perceived by group members to be "like the leader," can be utilized by group members both as a savior while the leader is absent and the culprit during the leader's presence.

Let us strengthen the case for this speculation by quoting from Freud's *Group Psychology and the Analysis of the Ego* at some length:

Another such instance of introjection of the object has been provided by the analysis of melancholia, an affliction which counts among the most remarkable of its existing causes the real or emotional loss of a loved object. A leading characteristic of these cases is a cruel self-depreciation of the ego combined with relentless self-criticism and bitter self-reproaches. Analyses have shown that this disparagement and these reproaches apply at bottom to the object and represent the ego's revenge upon it. The shadow of the object has fallen upon the ego, as I have said elsewhere. The introjection of the object is here un-mistakably clear (7, p. 68).

Now, if we use the individual as a model for the group, we have Resident A, whose characteristics were introjected as a unique restitution to ward off

---

[12] The primal horde hypothesis cannot, of course, be accepted at face value. And yet the fact that large formal organizations provide automatic rules for succession indicates that certain restrictions have to be made against revolt. "It may be that the revolt represents a realization of important fantasies individuals hold in all organizations, that the emotions involved are undercurrents whenever rebellious and submissive tendencies toward existing authorities must be controlled. These are the themes of some of our great dramas—*Antigone, Billy Budd, Hamlet,* and our most recent folk tale, *The Caine Mutiny"* (2, p. 425).

anxieties about the loss of the real leader. Upon the return of the leader, the reproaches which apply to the absent leader fall upon the introjected replacement leader. Freud goes on:

> But these melancholias also show us something else.... They show us the ego divided, fallen into two pieces, one of which has been altered by introjection and which contains the lost object. But the piece which behaves so cruelly is not unknown to us either. It comprises the conscience, a critical faculty within the ego, which even in normal times takes up a critical attitude towards the ego.... We have called it the "ego ideal" (7, p. 68).

The transformation to the group now becomes clearer. The introjected object pales in the eyes of group members before the competing ego ideal, the leader, and critical rage vents itself against the introjected for two reasons: (a) because it does not measure up to the standards of the ego ideal ("A isn't my idea of a good psychiatrist."); and (b) because the revenge which cannot openly be expressed toward the deserting leader can be projected onto it.[13]

These aforementioned mechanisms represent the most pervasive elements in group life for dealing with depressive anxiety. There are others, of course, which cannot at this time be analyzed. And other mechanisms of projective identification are concerned with different sources of anxiety. For example, Anna Freud's discussion of "identification with the aggressor" and "altruistic surrender" are probably related to "paranoid–schizoid" anxiety. What ultimately is needed is a typology of anxieties and characteristic mechanisms (in terms of projective identification) associated with the anxieties. Other forms of projective identification noticed but not discussed in detail here are "identification with work"—a form of an identification with the aggressor—and homosexual tendencies which were only touched upon in the discussion of idealization.[14]

COMPARISON WITH LATER LA MEETING

I mentioned earlier that it might be instructive to discuss an LA meeting which occurred much later in the group's experience, meeting 34. The

---

[13] It should be made clear here that this introjection of the characteristics of the replacement is a *super-ego* incorporation. "An ego which with the aid of the defense-mechanism of projection develops along this particular line introjects the authorities to whose criticism it is expressed and incorporates them in the super-ego. It is then able to project its prohibited impulses outwards" (6, p. 138).

[14] The dream which was reported in meeting 11 (LA) was clearly homosexual in nature with group members singing in a chorus and appearing as young girl dancers. Save for one group member, all faces were more or less bland and identity-less; the leader was seen as at least three characters in the play: Romeo, the dreamer's mother, and the dreamer's wife. This meeting gave rise to very positive feelings among members which

following excerpts best illustrate the emotional climate of the group during this meeting.

M: Then that raises the question, what, what, what is it we want and we expect and can't have?

N: Being taken care of. I think that, ah, ah, you see it much more strikingly in patients, ah, but it seems to me that, ah, we haven't, ah, maybe never will completely give up the idea of being taken care of. I sat here and thought of that and tried to connect it with the going back—in psychoanalytic theory I guess that it would be made more possible to get, give up this idea by understanding what had happened in the beginning. [He is referring to the beginning of the group meetings.]

(Later On)

O: So that even when the leader isn't here, he's still here just as much really.

Q: Yeah.

O: And we use what he said before rather than needing him sitting here and making comments now. He's still here, and every one of our relationships is that.

Q: Because he's a hub?

O: Yeah.

Q: It's taking a big piece of cheese.

N: You mean you don't believe in the old saying, "Out of sight, out of mind"?

(Laugh)

R (later on): I'll tell you of a chance observation I had to make for what it's worth. Z was a resident here last year, left in June and came back, ah, some time the middle of last week, on a visit, he'd gone into the service, he asked me how things were going here, and I told him, well, it seemed to me, now with three months left, that I had to go through some process of assimilation of all that had gone on. He said, well, his experience that hadn't occurred in the last three months, when he had gotten into the service, he found himself with groups, talking like the leader with individual patients, talking like, I don't know all the figures he mentioned, but Dr. _____ stood out in my mind because he found himself making comments like, like Dr. _____ had been making, and operating much like him.

S: Which is trying, which is solving the problem of loss by identification.

---

embarrassed some by its closeness. And during the meeting, one of the group members was thought to be taking over the leader's role; and in fact, one member did, with some finality, sit in the leader's chair when the meeting was under way, expressing the members' cohesiveness against the leader.

(Very Lengthy Pause—Restless Coughing and Noise)

M: Perhaps, ah, it's almost as though, ah, we kind of learned the psycho-analytic approach, and what it means here, in a way, when we first began talking about what's going on here, and then we got to talking about, ah, why is it going on. Ah, we're sort of thinking now in terms of going back to earlier relationships, and wondering what happened to us that, ah, that makes this happen, you know (pause), we sort of learned an approach.

(Pause)

O: I wonder, is there any difference in, ah, the way people feel now, versus the way they felt before when the leader wasn't here, and this, I don't know.

N: You, you're, you're having a different feeling, aren't you?

O: Yeah, yeah.

N: I think I am, too.

Q: One thing I think, ah, we can, we can, ah, accept the loss a little more realistically than we could, before we acted out, ah, we did all sorts of things, immature things.

N: You mean we admit the loss now instead of just trying to deny it?

(Chatter)

N: Now we can tolerate it.

S: Instead of just chatting on, you feel unhappy in a sense.

N: Yeah, I feel a loss.

S: That's what I was thinking about these, ah, what does it mean to work through losses and things, essentially what it probably means is that you face up to the fact essentially of feeling loss and then, ah, you, you somehow accept it but you, that doesn't mean the feeling goes away.

N: No, that's what X keeps harping about all the time.

Q: I was talking to Y about, I mean, doesn't necessarily mean you didn't need him, ah, we'd miss him probably, but that we still operate and function without him, it doesn't mean that we could collapse, without him.

N: The psychotic person becomes crazy at this point, when, ah, they suffer loss.

S: It's not because the person is gone, but because they're let down, or they can't go on, and that sort of stuff.

N: The sick patients.

T: But these fantasies still go through our minds too, ah, at some time or another.

S: What is what the working through the loss is.

These excerpts require very little comment; the group members have done that for us. The desperate need for constructing defenses, directed against pining for the loved object, seems to have diminished. The group seems to have acquired what for Freud was the essential aspect of a primary group: "a number of individuals who have substituted one and the same object for their ego ideal and have consequently identified themselves with one another in their ego" (7, p. 80).

The work of mourning continued as an obligato throughout the life of the group; decathexis proceeded, memory by memory. Note in this meeting there was some reference to the "beginning" and the members' initial attitudes toward the leader. Also of interest is their "operating" like him, taking on his characteristics. The comment on "out of sight, out of mind" is a classic imitation of the folk aphorism customarily employed by the leader. They "learned an approach." Concomitant to, and a part of, the mourning, was a development of giving and taking among group members, a communal brotherly milieu. (A good deal of discussion, not reported here for space reasons, dwelt on "kibbutzim" and communal living.) Finally, there was the direct recognition of the leader's significance and their learning from him. In meeting 35 when the leader returned, one of the members said:

T: Has anybody told Dr. _____ how much we missed him last week?

U: We sure have.

(*Laugh*)

S: And I was wondering if we weren't talking about this all the time.

M: We really talked a lot about that last week, about the ending of the group and what would be beyond there, beyond the pleasure principle.

S: Yeah, we seem to feel a little bit depressed, mourning, ah, has a different tone for meetings. Long ago when Dr. _____ was absent, there seemed to be more hostility and outward expression of anger, and, ah, now it seems to be a little more tender.

T: Well, you know.

"Reality," as Freud said, "passes its verdict—that the object no longer exists—upon each single one of the memories and hopes through which the libido was attached to the lost object, and the ego, confronted as it were with the decision whether it will share this fate, is persuaded by the sum of its narcissistic satisfactions in being alive to sever its attachment to the non-existent object" (9, p. 166).

SUMMARY

Briefly stated, the central idea of this paper was an attempt to ex-trapolate the Freudian formulations of identification in order to account for defensive (projective) identification behaviors. The particular type of projective identifications treated here related specifically to depressive anxiety, anxiety over the lost object. The group under study provided an interesting crucible for this analysis because the group leader was absent for a substantial number of early meetings.

Simply stated, projective identification is a process of splitting off good and bad impulses and dynamically projecting them onto and into social objects. The interplay among these projections determines a good share of group life. Four mechanisms of projective identification were delineated in this paper: (a) *Fantasy projection,* where dream symbols dissipated energy away from the source of anxiety into disguised, external, and hence, safe objects; (b) *Manic denial and idealization,* where the source of anxiety was denied, and, aided by good impulses, projected onto figures who could, in this case, take the place of the protective leader; (c) *Scapegoating,* where the bad impulses related to the absent leader were absorbed and deflected by "innocent" group members; (d) *Restitution of the lost object: peer group replacement,* where a replacement ego is introjected in the service of dampening anxiety concerning the loss of the real leader.

These mechanisms, in more muted and indirect ways, are probably present in all social organizations where loss of significant objects is encountered.[15] Indeed, it would seem that problems of "loss" and "succession" in formal organizations might be more fully understood if they could be analyzed in terms of how the membership managed anxiety attendant on loss.

[15] Howard Perlmutter raises the question: "What is the difference between losing a member of the group and losing a leader? I do not think they really are quantitative differences but important qualitative ones. My main impression is that there are more *persecutory* feelings in the loss of the leader than there are in the loss of a member" (personal communication). This is a fair question and can be put to empirical test. Plans are being made for experimental investigation of this question. Equally fascinating questions arise in terms of loss: temporary–permanent, excusable–inexcusable, imposed–elected, accidental–intentional, abdication–overthrow. These all may have different effects. The effects of group composition must also be taken into account. The group under consideration here is, after all, a highly sophisticated one; one in which the value-orientation prescribes a verbal, intellectual effort to understand the dynamics of the unconscious. I would guess that specific defenses might well be related to the particular composition of the group, that a less well-educated membership would tend to use less intellectual defenses, e.g., more scapegoating. This is a question well worth exploring and about which I can now only be tentative and circumspect.

REFERENCES

1. Bennis, W. G. Decision-making in groups. *Group Psychother.,* 1957, **10,** 287–298.
2. Bennis, W. G. and Shepard, H. A. A theory of group development. *Human Relat.,* 1956, 9, 415–437.
3. Cogan, E. The course of group development: group reaction to the leader and to fellow members. In *The use of group process in teaching group dynamics.* Boston, Mass.: Group Psychology Project, Harvard Medical School, 1958. (Hectographed).

4. Cogan, E. and Shapiro, D. Object choice and group development. Paper read at Amer. Psychol. Ass., Washington, D.C., Sept., 1958.

5. Foulkes, S. H. and Anthony, E. J. *Group psychotherapy.* Penguin Books, 1957.

6. Freud, A. *The ego and mechanisms of defense.* New York: International Universities Press, 1946.

7. Freud, S. *Group psychology and the analysis of the ego.* (Trans. J. Strachey.) New York: Liverwright, 1949.

8. Freud, S. *Moses and monotheism.* New York: Vintage Books, 1955.

9. Freud, S. *Collected papers.* Vol. 4. London: Hogarth Press, 1956.

10. Herbert, E. L. and Trist, E. L. The institution of an absent leader by a students' discussion group. *Human Relat.,* 1953, **6**, 215–248.

11. Hilgard, J. R. and Newman, M. F. Anniversaries in mental illness. *Psychiatry,* 1959, **22**, 113–121.

12. Jaques, E. Social systems as a defense against persecutory and depressive anxiety. In M. Klein *et al.* (Eds.), *New directions in psychoanalysis.* New York: Basic Books, 1956. Chap. 20.

13. Kelley, H. and Thibaut, J. Experimental studies of group problem solving and process. In G. Lindzey (Ed.), *Handbook of social psychology.* Vol. 2. Cambridge, Mass.: Addison-Wesley, 1954. Pp. 735–785.

14. Klein, M. *Contributions to psychoanalysis, 1921–1945.* London: Hogarth Press, 1950.

15. Klein, M. On identification. In M. Klein, *et al.* (Eds.), *New directions in psychoanalysis.* New York: Basic Books, 1956. Chap. 13.

16. Newcomb, T. N. Sociology and psychology. In J. Gillan (Ed.), *For a science of social man.* New York: Macmillan, 1954. Pp. 227–256.

17. Powdermaker, F. B. and Frank, J. D. *Group psychotherapy.* Cambridge, Mass.: Harvard University Press, 1953.

18. Rochlin, G. Loss and restitution. In *The psychoanalytic study of the child.* Vol. 8. New York: International Universities Press, 1953. Pp. 288–309.

19. Schutz, W. C. The group mind revisited. Paper read at Eastern Psychol. Ass., Philadelphia, April, 1958

20. Semrad, E. V. and Arsenian, J. On the concept of billets–the functioning of small groups. Paper presented to Group Psychology Project, Harvard Medical School, 1958.

21. Semrad, E. V., Arsenian, J., and Standish, C. T. Experiences with small groups in teaching group psychology. *Group Psychother.,* 1957, **10**, 191–197.

22. Shepard, H. and Bennis, W. G. A theory of training through the use of group methods. *Human Relat.,* 1956, **9**, 403–414.

23. Warriner, C. K. Groups are real: a reaffirmation. *Amer. sociol. Rev.,* 1956, **21**, 549–554.

III

PHASES OF GROUP DEVELOPMENT

8

The Work of
Wilfred Bion
on Groups

Margaret J. Rioch
Group Relations Conference Committee
Washington School of Psychiatry

[This chapter offers perhaps the best available summary of Bion's very important and influential theory of group development. In a clear and concise fashion, Rioch describes Bion's key conceptions of the *basic assumption* (dependency, fight–flight, and pairing) and *work* groups. Emphasis is given to the complex and simultaneous inter-twinings of these two forms of group process within the fabric of any given segment of group interaction. The concept of *valency*, as it relates to the quality and degree of vulnerability of particular individual members and leaders to specific basic assumptions, is also explicated.]

The shift in perspective from the individual to the group is difficult to make in actual practice although it is often given lip service. It is like a shift to a higher order of magnitude, which is not easy when the lower order is in itself very complex and by no means thoroughly understood. But the shift is necessary in order to grasp social phenomena. From this perspective it is often possible to see the problems of the individual or the pair in a new light. This is well known to family therapists, who find an individual child or a marital

From "The Work of Wilfred Bion on Groups" by M. J. Rioch, *Psychiatry*, 1970, *33*, 56–66. Copyright 1970 by The William Alanson White Psychiatric Foundation. Reprinted by special permission of the William Alanson White Psychiatric Foundation, Inc.

relationship more comprehensible when seen in the framework of the entire family.

The Washington School of Psychiatry-Tavistock Conferences provide opportunities for members to study behavior in large groups of 50-60, in small groups of 10-12, and in intergroup situations. No particular theoretical framework is prescribed, and staff members come with various theoretical points of view and from various professional orientations, including sociology, psychology, psychoanalysis, and business administration. But Bion's concepts have been especially useful to the staff since they formulate group psychological processes in integrative terms. A. K. Rice, who has directed most of the British and American conferences since 1962, was strongly influenced by his membership in a training group conducted by Bion in 1947-48, as well as by Bion's theories.[1]

Much of the material on which Bion based his theories and many of the examples which he gives come from the small groups which he conducted at the Tavistock Clinic. He does not deal exclusively with these, however, but also discusses large social institutions such as the army and the church. His interest in group processes was stimulated when, as an officer in the British Army during World War II, he was engaged in the selection of men for leadership roles and in charge of a rehabilitation unit of psychiatric patients. He began at that time to think of treatment of the whole society of the hospital not as a makeshift to save psychiatric manpower, but as the best way to get at the malady as he perceived it, namely the inability on the part of the patients to function adequately as members of society or, in other words, as group members. He saw this inability with reference both to the hospital community and to society at large.

Because Bion's name is so much associated with groups and because he emphasized the phenomena of total fields rather than of individuals he is sometimes thought of as having reified the idea of the group or as having talked about the group as a mythical entity instead of talking about human behavior. This is not the case. He defines a group as a function or set of functions or an aggregate of individuals. It is not a function of any one part separately, nor is it an aggregate without a function.

For example, if a dozen strangers are lying by chance in the sun on the same beach they do not constitute a group according to this definition. But if someone in the water cries for help and the twelve individuals respond by trying to save the swimmer from drowning in some kind of concerted action, however rudimentary the concertedness may be, they have become a group in that they now have a function. This may last for only a few minutes or it may turn into an organization of life savers which goes on for years.

Although Bion thinks and speaks of instincts, he does not postulate a

---

[1] The work summarized [in this chapter] is found chiefly in W. R. Bion, *Experiences in Groups.*

herd instinct or a group mind. He thinks that ideas of this kind are often developed by people in groups, but that when they occur they are symptomatic of regression. In his opinion groups bring into prominence phenomena which can best be understood if one has some experience of psychotic phenomena as well as of normal and neurotic behavior. The belief that a group or group mind exists, as something other than a function of a number of individuals, appears to Bion to be a distorted figment of the imagination which emerges when people are threatened with a loss of their individual distinctiveness.

He emphasizes that people do not have to come together in the same room to form a group. In his view a hermit in a desert is inevitably a member of a group and cannot be understood unless one knows what the group is from which he has separated himself geographically. People have to come together in a room in order that group phenomena may be demonstrated and elucidated but not in order that they should exist. This is similar to the situation in psychoanalysis in which the patient has to enter into a therapeutic relationship with the analyst in order that the analyst may demonstrate and analyze the transference, but not in order that transference phenomena should exist.

Bion's central thought is that in every group two groups are present: the "work group" and the "basic assumption group." This may all sound less mysterious if one says that in every group there are two aspects, or that there are two different ways of behaving. Bion's terminology is a short cut which may lead to the belief that he thinks of each group of ten people as consisting of twenty invisible people sitting in two separate circles and talking, now in normal rational voices and now in another voice as in O'Neill's *Strange Interlude*. And in fact he does think in this kind of metaphor. At the same time he is quite clearly aware that it is a metaphor, which some of his less poetic readers tend to forget. He does not mean that there are two groups of people in the room, but that the group behaves as if that were the case, and he considers that this is the unconscious fantasy of the people in the group.

His concept of the work group will be described first and then that of the basic assumption group. The work group is that aspect of group functioning which has to do with the real task of the group. This exists in a committee which has come together to plan a program, or a staff of an organization which proposes to review the activities of the past year, or a small group met to study its own behavior. The work group takes cognizance of its purpose and can define its task. The structure of the group is there to further the attainment of the task. For example, if a group needed to collect dues it would appoint a treasurer. But it would not appoint a finance committee unless there were real matters of policy to be taken care of by such a committee. The number of vice presidents would be limited by the functions which vice presidents had to perform. The number of meetings would be dictated by the amount of business which had to be conducted. The leader of the work group is not the only one who has skills, and he leads only so long as his leadership serves the task of the group. The members of the work group cooperate as separate and discrete individuals. Each member of the group belongs to it because it is his will and his choice to see that the purpose of the group is fulfilled. He is therefore at one with the task of the group and his own interest is identified with its interest. The work group constantly tests its conclusions in a scientific spirit. It seeks for knowledge, learns from experience, and constantly questions how it may best achieve its goal. It is clearly conscious of the passage of time and of the processes of learning and development. It has a parallel in the individual with the ego, in Freud's sense, in the rational and mature person.

Groups which act consistently like the one just described are very rare and perhaps even non-existent in pure culture. A large part of Bion's theory has to do with why groups do not behave in the sensible way just described as characteristic of the work group. Man seems to be a herd animal who is often in trouble with his herd. Ineffective and self-contradictory behavior seems at times to be very common in groups—even though highly effective functioning is common at other times. The work group is only one aspect of the functioning of the group. The other aspect is the one which Bion calls the basic assumption group.

Bion is probably best known popularly for the names which he coined for the three kinds of basic assumption groups—namely, the dependency, the fight-flight, and the pairing groups. It should be emphasized that he himself used the word "adumbrated"—that is, vaguely outlined—to characterize his classification of these groups, and it may well be that the classification should be made differently or that other categories should be added. This is not the main point.

It is important to understand what the term *basic assumption* means, for otherwise one may get lost in the description of the three kinds which Bion adumbrated and forget the more important point, which is the commonality of all three. Basic assumption means exactly what it says—namely, the assumption which is basic to the behavior. It is an "as if" term. One behaves as if such and such were the case. In pre-Columbian days seafaring men operated on the basic assumption that the world was flat and that they might fall off its edge. Therefore they did not venture very far from the coast. So on many different levels, by observing the behavior of individuals and of groups, one can tease out the basic assumptions on which they operate. Bion uses the term to refer to the *tacit* assumptions that are prevalent in groups, not to those which are overtly expressed. The basic assumptions of the basic assumption groups are usually outside of awareness. Nevertheless, they are the basis for behavior. They are deducible from the emotional state of the group. The statement of the basic assumption gives meaning to and elucidates the behavior of the group to the extent that it is not operating as a work group.

According to Bion there are three distinct emotional states of groups from which one can deduce three basic assumptions. The first of these is the dependency basic assumption.

The essential aim of the basic assumption dependency group is to attain security through and have its members protected by one individual. It assumes that this is why the group has met. The members act as if they know nothing, as if they are inadequate and immature creatures. Their behavior implies that the leader, by contrast, is omnipotent and omniscient. A group of sick, miserable psychiatric patients, for example, and a powerful, wise, loving, giving therapist easily fit this picture. The power, wisdom, and lovingness of the therapist are, of course, not tested. The patients are often united in the belief that if they sit long enough, the wise leader will come forth with the magic cure. They do not even need to give him adequate information about their difficulties for he knows everything and plans everything for the good of the members. In this emotional state the group insists that all explanations be extremely simple; no one can understand any complexity; no one can do anything that is difficult; but the leader can solve all difficulties, if he only will. He is idealized and made into a kind of god who will take care of his children. The leader is often tempted to fall into this role and to go along with the basic assumption of the group.

But since no one really can fill this role and since anyone who is doing his job will refuse to fill it, he can never succeed in meeting the group's expectations. In failing to be the omniscient and omnipotent leader of these people who are presenting themselves as inadequate weaklings, he inevitably arouses their disappointment and hostility. The members will try for a long time to blind themselves to this and will try not to hear what he says in interpreting their dependency to them. They often try quite desperate maneuvers to wring his heart and to force him to take proper care of them. One of the most frequent maneuvers is to put forth one member as especially sick and requiring the special care of the leader. Such a member may actually be pushed by the others into a degree of distress which he had not really felt at all, but the group needs someone who will wring the leader's heart or else show him up to be an unfeeling demon. The interesting thing is that whereas the group seems to be concerned about this poor person and his trouble, it is actually more concerned about the group aim to get the leader to take care of it and to relieve its feelings of inadequacy and insecurity. A person who falls into this role can very easily be carried away by it until he oversteps the bounds, and then he may find himself abandoned by the group.

When the leader of such a group fails to meet expectations, as he is bound to do, the group searches for alternative leaders. These are often eager to accept the role, and to prove that they can do what the original leader could not do. This is a temptation which the group offers to its more ambitious members. When they fall for it, they are usually in for the same fate as the original leader.

One of the frequent concerns in the dependency group has to do with greed. This is understandable enough since in manifesting the kind of childlike dependency characteristic of this basic assumption, the group members are perpetuating a state appropriate to an earlier stage of development and each one is demanding more than his share of parental care. There is often conflict in this group between the dependent tendencies and the needs of the individuals as adults. Resentment at being in a dependent state is present as well as a desire to persist in it. Although anger and jealousy are expressed, they do not usually arouse a tremendous amount of fear because of the basic assumption that a super-being exists in the form of the leader, who will see to it that the irresponsibilities of the members will not go too far and will not have dire consequences. There is often conflict between the desire to express feelings irresponsibly and the desire to be mature and consider consequences. The basic assumption dependency group in pure culture does not exist any more than the work group in pure culture. But the more it tends to be dominant over the work group, the more the relationship of the members to the leader takes on the characteristics of a religious cult. The work function will often then be felt as a challenge to a religion. Some of the same phenomena will occur which have occurred in the world in the conflict between science and religion, as if the claims of science were challenging the claims of religion. The words or writings of the leader become a kind of Bible and the group engages in exegesis of his works. This tends to happen particularly if the leader has already demonstrated his human inability to satisfy the demands of the group for a deity. His written words or remembered words may then be taken in place of his person.

The outside world often looks cold and unfriendly to the basic assumption dependency group. Sometimes when the members feel deserted by their leader, they forget their internal squabbles, close ranks, and snuggle up to each other like little birds in a nest. A warm groupiness develops which gives a temporary sense of comfort and security. To challenge this is heresy and is persecuted as such.

The second basic assumption group is that of fight–flight. Bion joins these together as two sides of the same coin. The assumption is that the group has met to preserve itself and that this can be done only by fighting someone or something or by running away from someone or something. Action is essential whether for fight or for flight. The individual is of secondary importance to the preservation of the group. Both in battle and in flight the individual may be abandoned for the sake of the survival of the group. Whereas in the basic assumption dependency group the sick person may be valued for his ability to engage the leader as a person who will take care of others, in the fight-flight group there is no tolerance for sickness. Casualties are to be expected.

A leader is even more important than in other basic assumption groups because the call for action requires a leader. The leader who is felt to be appropriate to this kind of group is one who can mobilize the group for attack or lead it in flight. He is expected to recognize danger and enemies. He should represent and spur on to courage and self-sacrifice. He should have a bit of a paranoid element in his makeup if he wishes to be successful, for this will ensure that if no enemy is obvious, the leader will surely find one. He is expected to feel hate toward the enemy and to be concerned not for the individual in the group but for the preservation of the group itself. An accepted leader of a fight–flight group who goes along with the basic assumption is one who affords opportunity in the group for flight or aggression. If he does not do this, he is ignored.

This basic assumption group is anti-intellectual and inimical to the idea of self-study; self-knowledge may be called introspective nonsense. In a group whose avowed purpose or work task is self-study, the leader will find when the group is operating in basic assumption fight–flight that his attempts will be obstructed either by expressions of hatred against all things psychological and introspective, or by various other methods of avoidance. The group may chitchat, tell stories, come late, be absent, or engage in innumerable activities to circumvent the task.

In groups engaged in more overt action, it is possible to observe the close connection of panic and the flight–flight group. Bion contends that panic, flight, and uncontrolled attack are really all the same. He says that panic does not arise in any situation unless it is one that might as easily have given rise to rage. When the rage or fear are offered no readily available outlet, frustration arises which in a basic assumption group cannot be tolerated. Flight offers an immediately available opportunity for expression of the emotion in the fight–flight group and meets the demands that all basic assumption groups have for instantaneous satisfaction. Attack offers a similarly immediate outlet. Bion thinks that if the leader of such a group conforms to the requirements of the fight–flight leader he will have no difficulty in turning a group from headlong flight to attack or from headlong attack to panic.

The third basic assumption group is that of pairing. Here the assumption is that the group has met for purposes of reproduction, to bring forth the Messiah, the Savior. Two people get together on behalf of the group to carry out the task of pairing and creation. The sex of the two people is immaterial. They are by no means necessarily a man and a woman. But whoever they are, the basic assumption is that when two people get together it is for sexual purposes. When this basic assumption is operative, the other group members are not bored. They listen eagerly and attentively to what is being said. An atmosphere of hopefulness pervades the group. No actual leader is or needs to be present, but the group, through the pair, is living in the hope of the creation of a new leader, or a new thought, or something which will bring about a new life, will solve the old problems and bring Utopia or heaven, or something of the sort. As in the history of the world if a new leader or Messiah is actually produced, he will of course shortly be rejected. In order to maintain hope, he must be unborn. Bion emphasizes the air of hopeful expectation which pervades the group. He says it is often expressed in clichés—such as, "Things will be better when spring comes"—or in simple-minded statements that some cure-all like marriage or group therapy would solve all neurotic problems. Although the group thus focuses on the future, Bion calls attention to the present, namely the feeling of hope itself, which he thinks is evidence that the pairing group is in existence even when other evidence is not clear. The group enjoys its optimism, justifying it by an appeal to an outcome which is morally unexceptionable. The feelings associated with this group are soft and agreeable. The unborn leader of this group, according to the basic assumption, will save it from feelings of hatred, destructiveness, and despair—both its own feelings and those of others. If a person or an idea should be produced by such a group hope will again be weakened, for there will be nothing to hope for. The destructiveness and hatred have not really been reduced and will again be felt.

These then are the three basic assumption groups which Bion describes. It is clear enough how different they all are from the work group. Although each one has its own characteristics, the basic assumption groups also have some characteristics in common. Basic assumption life is not oriented outward toward reality, but inward toward fantasy, which is then impulsively and uncritically acted out. There is little pausing to consider or to test consequences, little patience with an inquiring attitude, and great insistence upon feeling. Basic assumption members often are confused, have poor memories, are disoriented about time. They do not really learn and adapt through experience but actually resist change, although they may shift very readily from one basic assumption to another. Often there are reminiscences about the good old days. The language of such groups is full of clichés, or repetitive phrases, and of vague and loose generalizations. Another important aspect of the basic assumptions is that they are anonymous. They are not formulated by any one member in the group and cannot be attributed to any one member. No one wants to own them. There is a kind of conspiracy of anonymity, which is facilitated by the fact that identities and names get mixed up; statements are attributed falsely or vaguely. The basic assumptions seem to be the disowned part of the individuals, and individuals seem to fear the basic assumptions as if they might take over and leave nothing of the mature, rational persons in the group. Since the basic assumptions are anonymous, they can function quite ruthlessly, which is another reason why they are feared. There is much vicarious living in a basic assumption group, particularly through roles, so that often a person becomes fixed in a role which the group needs for its own purposes and then cannot get out of it. Basic assumption groups also constantly attempt to seduce their leaders away from their work function.

Neither the work group nor the basic assumption group exists in pure culture for very long. What one sees in reality is a work group which is suffused by, intruded into, and supported by the basic assumption groups.

One can make an analogy to the functions of the conscious ego, which are suffused by, invaded by, and supported by the irrational and unconscious aspects of the personality. So it seems that the basic assumptions represent an interference with the work task, just as naughty, primitive impulses may interfere with the sensible work of a mature person. And this is one important side of the picture. There is another, more positive side to the basic assumptions, however, which Bion emphasizes just as much as the negative aspects, and that is the sophisticated use of the proper basic assumption by the work group. For example, a work group such as a hospital can and should mobilize the basic assumption dependency in the service of its task of taking care of sick patients. Bion identifies the church as that major institution in society which mobilizes and uses in a sophisticated way the basic assumption dependency; the army as that one which mobilizes basic assumption fight–flight; and the aristocracy as that one which is most interested in breeding and therefore mobilizes pairing. Whether or not the aristocracy can still be considered to exist, even in England, as an important institution is an open question, along with what takes its place if it does not. Bion himself does not think that the aristocracy can be considered to be a real work group which uses its basic assumption in a sophisticated way, for if the work group characteristics were dominant in the aristocracy then the interest in breeding would be manifest in some such way as a subsidy of scientific genetics research. But this is obviously not the case. If we consider the army, for example, it is clear that the relevant basic assumptions badly interfere with its function if they get out of hand. Fight–flight when engaged in simply as irrational basic assumptions leads to panic or ill-conceived attack. However, when mobilized in a sophisticated way, fight–flight represents the motive force for battle and for organized withdrawal. As indicated earlier, both the work group and the basic assumption group are abstractions; they are concepts which are useful in thinking about ways of functioning which occur in groups. Bion's idea is that both are occurring simultaneously, but to varying degrees, in all groups.

It is necessary now to introduce another one of Bion's concepts, namely that of valency. This is a term which is used to refer to the individual's readiness to enter into combination with the group in making and acting on the basic assumptions. A person may have a high or low valency depending on his capacity for this kind of combination, but in Bion's view it is impossible to be a human being without having some degree of valency. The thing that Bion is trying to do with all his concepts and constructions is to produce useful ways of thinking about man in his function as a social animal. In his concept of valency he is saying that everyone has the tendency to enter into group life, in particular into the irrational and unconscious aspects of group life, and that people vary in the amount of tendency they have in this direction. Bion thinks of this tendency as something which is manifested on a psychological plane to be sure, but which is so basic to the human organism that it should not be thought of as purely psychological. He thinks of it as biological and speaks of it as analogous to tropism in plants rather than as analogous to more purposive behavior. By borrowing a word from physics rather than from psychology or sociology he emphasizes the instantaneous and involuntary aspects of the kind of behavior he is talking about, which he calls instinctive. Valency in the basic assumption group corresponds to cooperation in the work group. But whereas cooperation requires thought, training, maturity, and some degree of organization in a group, valency requires none of these. It simply occurs spontaneously as a function of the gregarious quality in man.

Individuals vary not only in the degree of valency which they manifest but in the kind to which they have the strongest tendency. With some it is toward basic assumption dependency; some toward fight-flight; some toward pairing. Every human being has the capacity for all three, but usually one or another valency predominates. This has nothing to do with whether a person has been psychoanalyzed or not. It is not possible to analyze valency out of a human being as one is supposed to be able to analyze neurosis. For effective functioning in groups, however, and especially for leadership functioning, it is desirable to know oneself well enough to know to which valency one tends. An effective society uses the valencies of its members to serve its various purposes. For example, the educator can find a good outlet for his valency toward basic assumption dependency. The combat commander can use appropriately his valency toward basic assumption fight-flight. The valency toward basic assumption pairing finds a useful expression in individual interviewing and, of course, in family life. There are various types of chairmen and directors of organizations. One type will be solicitous for the welfare of his members and will take a special interest in the weaker ones or in anyone who is sick or disabled. Another will see his main function as fighting for the interests of his organization against any outside or inside attack. Another will find that he does his job best by going around after hours to each one of his members separately, convincing each one of what he wants done. When the meeting takes place everyone is already in agreement and the decisions have all been made. Any and all of these ways can be effective, though each one may be more appropriate at one time than at another.

In the naive or unconscious fantasy, the leader of the dependency group has to be omnipotent; the fight leader has to be unbeatable and the flight leader uncatchable; the leader of the pairing group must be marvelous but still unborn. But in the mature work group, which is making a sophisticated use of the appropriate basic assumptions, the leader of the dependency group is dependable; the leader of the fight-flight group is courageous; and the leader of the pairing group is creative.[2]

---

[2] For these formulations the author is indebted to a personal communication from A. K. Rice, who wrote approximately these words in *Learning for Leadership*, p. 72.

For effective functioning the basic assumptions must be subservient to and used in the service of the work task. They make good servants and poor masters. The various tales about fantastic machines, demons, genii, and so forth, who perform miraculous tasks for their masters until one fine day they take over and go on a binge of destruction, are mythical representations of the capacity of human beings for harnessing tremendous energy effectively and at the same time of the danger of such energy when it is not harnessed. *The Lord of the Flies* provides another illustration of what happens when the work group is weak and the irresponsible basic assumption group takes over.

The work task is like a serious parent who has his eye on intelligent planning. The basic assumptions are like the fun-loving or frightened children who want immediate satisfaction of their desires. What Bion emphasizes is that both exist and that both are necessary. The basic assumption group, however, exists without effort. The work group requires all the concentration, skill, and organization of creative forces that can be mustered to bring it into full flower. The writers who derogate groups as tending to reduce the intellectual abilities of the individuals in the group are, according to Bion, talking about the basic assumption functions, not work group functions. Bion holds to a very consistent middle way between the glorification and the derogation of the group. The latter is to be found in Jung's statement, "When a hundred clever heads join in a group, one big nincompoop is the result, because every individual is trammelled by the otherness of the others"[3] Bion holds that a group, like an individual, may be stupid and cruel or intelligent and concerned. He does not hold that great achievements are always those of the individual working in solitude. He says that in the study groups he has been in he has made interpretations of behavior just because he believes that the group can hear them and use them, and experience has borne him out. In his own words, he attributes "great force and influence to the work group, which through its concern with reality is compelled to employ the methods of science in no matter how rudimentary a form" (p. 135).

Individuals seem to fear being overwhelmed by their valency for group life; or one might put it that they fear being overwhelmed by the basic assumptions. It is not uncommon in self-study or therapy groups to hear phrases like "the fear of being sucked in by quicksands," or "the fear of being homogenized," which express the fear of being immersed in the group and thus losing one's individuality. Bion thinks that there is not actually so much danger as people think there is of being overwhelmed by the basic assumptions. He has a healthy respect for people's capacities to function on a work level. He thinks that in groups met to study their own behavior, consistent interpretation of the basic assumption tendencies will gradually bring them into consciousness and cause them to lose their threatening quality. The parallel here to the psychoanalysis of unconscious impulses is

[3] Quoted from a letter from C. G. Jung (Illing, p. 80).

clear. Presumably, the more the basic assumption life of the group becomes conscious, the more the work task can emerge into effective functioning.

But the individual in a group is not always convinced of this. Bion thinks that the task of the adult in establishing adequate contact with the life of the group or groups in which he lives is truly a formidable one. His first, second, and often third attempts are likely to be failures and to result in regression. When individuals in a group feel that they have lost or are about to lose their individual distinctiveness, they are threatened by panic. This does not mean at all that the group disintegrates, for it may continue as a fight–flight group; but it does mean that the individual feels threatened and very likely has regressed.

Bion says clearly that he thinks of the value of a group experience as the conscious experiencing of the possibilities of the work group. This must be differentiated from the coziness and so-called closeness of feeling in the basic assumption group. The work group which Bion is talking about does not depend upon great amounts of love or warm feelings or an oceanic oneness of the group members. It does depend upon the increasing and developing ability of each individual to use his skills responsibly in the service of the common task. It is not anything like the "togetherness" which is a function of the fear of being alone or on one's own. In the work group, each individual is very much on his own and may have to accomplish his own part of the task in a very lonely way, as for example someone who is sent upon a secret mission or someone who has to make the ultimate policy decision where the buck stops. The reluctance to take the final responsibility for decisions and actions can be seen as a basic assumption dependency phenomenon and is not a characteristic of the work group member, especially not of the work group leader.

The anxiety which one tends to feel in groups and the difficulties with which group membership faces one stem from the double danger of either being isolated like a sore thumb of the total body which may be amputated, or being swallowed up by the total body and losing oneself. When the basic assumption group is strong, the individual tends to feel either in danger of being victimized and extruded, or swallowed up in the anonymous unanimity of group feeling. The usual case, even when work elements are present, is that the individual is wavering somewhere in between the two dangers, with an uneasy sense that he is in a dilemma out of which no right way can be found.

When anxiety becomes severe the group may, as Bion says, resemble the mysterious, frightening, and destructive Sphinx. The Sphinx was made up of disparate members. She had the seductive face of a woman and a body composed of parts of powerful and dangerous animals—the lion, the eagle, and the serpent. To those who wished to pass by her she posed the riddle: "What walks on four legs in the morning, two at noon, and three in the evening?" Those who could not answer she flung to their deaths over the cliff, and that included everyone until Oedipus came by and told her that it was man..

Oedipus had been to Delphi to try to find out who really were his parents; and later too, to his sorrow, he searched for the murderer of the king. He sought after knowledge even when it meant his own undoing. Not by chance was it this man who, as the legend has it, grasped immediately the concepts of time, change, and development implicit in the riddle of the Sphinx. So long as we think in static terms that there *is* an entity which walks on four legs or which *is* the personality or which *is* the group, we can never grasp the complex and apparently disparate phenomena of the world, in time, in which we live. When Oedipus grasped the complexity in an intuitive vision of the whole, the fearful Sphinx threw herself off the rock. But unfortunately she constantly climbs back up again and waits with a new riddle for a new Oedipus to come by.

When the Sphinx lies in wait with her dreadful question, representing the frightening complexity and uncertain behavior of the world, especially the world of groups, one feels terrified at what John Fowles calls "the eternal source of all fear, all horror, all real evil, man himself" (p. 448).

But the same man or the same group which has filled the world with horror at its capacity for evil can also amaze by its capacity for good. If the Sphinx were to ask, "What is it that on Monday is wrangling, cruel, and greedy; on Tuesday is indifferent and lazy; on Wednesday is effectively and intelligently collaborative?," one could easily answer, "That is man and it is also ten men in a group." If she asked, "What made the difference?," a few partial answers could be given. One of them is that on Wednesday the group had a clear goal to which all of its members wanted to devote themselves. Another is that the roles of the members were clearly defined and accepted. Still another has to do with the boundaries between this and other groups. But if the Sphinx were to go on and press about what to do in order that the Wednesday behavior should become more constant and the Monday and Tuesday behavior less frequent, we *might* find ourselves with no satisfactory answer hurtling over the cliff.

REFERENCES

Bion, W. R. *Experiences in Groups;* Basic Books, 1959.
Fowles, John. *The Magus;* Dell, 1967.
Illing, Hans A. "C. G. Jung on the Present Trends in Group Psychotherapy," *Human Relations* (1957) 10:77–83.
Rice, A. K. *Learning for Leadership;* London, Tavistock Publications, 1965.

9

The Natural History of Training Groups

Max Day
Harvard Medical School Department of Psychiatry
Massachusetts Mental Hospital Center, Boston

[Day presents an interesting conceptualization of certain characteristic phases in the life history of an unstructured laboratory group. The typical group is seen as moving through states of fantasied familiarity, transient victimization, more focused victimization, exaggerated perfect unity, and, ultimately, individualization. Day stresses the significance of "scapegoating" as an essential group dynamic process which can both facilitate and disrupt the overall group unity and ultimate capacity for more therapeutic levels of activity. The latter portion of a laboratory group is viewed as being pervaded by considerable evidence of both transferential activity and the therapeutic alliance to leaders and peers. Such "readiness" for therapeutic work—although not usually taken advantage of in such groups—reflects their very great efficiency and potency.]

The progress of the formation of the therapeutic envelope (Day, 1963)—that mesh of interpersonal relationships, inner conflicts, and outer contexts within which group therapy can take place—appears to follow a recurrent series of steps. These steps represent changing maneuvers for dealing with the basic issues of helplessness and the need to feel effective, both of which must be accepted and satisfactorily worked out for a goup of people to be able to engage in therapy or other ventures which require similar closeness.

The literature is pretty well agreed that groups have a beginning, middle, and end phase. The dynamics that mold the beginnings interest us here.

From "The Natural History of Training Groups" by M. Day, *International Journal of Group Psychotherapy*, 1967, *17*, 436–446. Copyright 1967 by the International Journal of Group Psychotherapy. Reprinted by permission.

Foulkes and Anthony (1957) find that the patients flounder in their self-consciousness, "confess" symptoms, feel cut off, magically expect the conductor to be the "expert," reluctantly turn to their peers for help and make apologetic revelations of symptoms with some relief. George Bach (1954) finds a beginning phase of testing out to make oneself familiar with the possibilities and limitations of the group situation. Alexander Wolf (1949, 1950) pays recognition to phases by setting his groups tasks titrated to fit their needs at each stage. In the opening phase, he deals with the resistances to group therapy by analyzing them either in the group or individual situation and by offering explanations of the group approach. Christopher Standish and Elvin Semrad (1951), in writing of groups of psychotics, describe the testing out phase as being loaded with hostility, often displaced to the environment of the hospital. Agreement in this phase fosters a good deal of group unity which permits the advent of the second stage: the expression of anxiety-laden psychotic material.

Training groups offer the most commonly repeated experiments in the opening phase carried out by different leaders with diverse memberships. The general patterns of development observed in these can help us understand the underlying dynamics of how groups coalesce, how the therapeutic envelope forms. Training groups which run for an academic year begin with fantasied relationships, flower into testing out, congeal into exaggerated togetherness, and then move on to individualization. This paper will focus on the techniques used by people in a group to get close to one another.

FANTASIED FAMILIARITY

In the beginning, people busy themselves with who they are, how the leader works, and how the group will function. Almost at once they turn to the leader for guidance. His attitude implies he will not necessarily give immediate satisfaction. He observes without interfering except to protect the safety and integrity of the group or to identify and clarify matters which the group cannot yet penetrate. He provides the general guidelines for spontaneous but appropriate interaction. This sets in motion the striving of old yearnings to come to the surface and also the need to be reasonable about everyone's needs and comforts. It implies the members have the potential to satisfy themselves and others. In response to this attitude, the members turn to the group with a vengeance and begin to express many feelings and attitudes about the group which originally and in the unconscious were intended for the leader.

Great anxiety about the intense yearnings to get close and merge becomes apparent, as well as all sorts of defenses against these wishes. The group will apparently flounder about. This is not to be credited to the analytic attitude, since such flounderings may be observed in formally run groups as well. In their helplessness and loneliness, the members show a mixture of three kinds of reactions: tentative feeling out reactions, correct intuitions, and fantasied relationships.

The feeling out reactions may be prudent or they may appear flamboyant and exhibitionistic in character. Each individual's style becomes clear and meaningful as it is later seen to stem from solutions to conflicts in his own development.

The correct intuitions motivate closeness and distance—the counterdance of the porcupines, to paraphrase Freud—which each one seeks in the group. The intuitions often cannot be proved until much later. Presumably, intuition is inborn, although molded by experience.

Fantasied recognitions of familiarity represent a universal technique seen in every family when a child is born. Every family plays the game of seeing whom the child resembles at a time when anger toward the intruder must be kept in abeyance. Biological resemblance is often fleeting, changing from day to day, but it is used as a rationalization for recognitions of closeness. Even when a child is adopted, the parents may praise the agency's cleverness in choosing a child who resembles the family stock. This game often appears again when a son marries and the family begins to see the new daughter-in-law as resembling the man's mother. This is a useful form of extending credit to the newcomer until the relationship has developed.

Fantasied recognition happens quickly, is often not recognized for what it is, and may be quickly submerged. It is seen frequently in the leader's countertransference to the group, since he is helpless in the group and, unlike the other members, may not react openly, except as it is appropriate. He may scan the faces for one which reminds him of someone pleasant or unpleasant from his own past. He may focus his confidence or concerns on that one or use such a fantasy to deny concerns about a given individual.

Group members may not verbalize the recognition fantasy, though relying on it, until much later. They may say with certainty, "We Harvard men are all closer and the rest of you are out in the cold"; or confess later, "I saw you at once as mean but it isn't so." Members are preoccupied with finding a familiar face, attitude, station in life, work, past history, faith, or common misfortune, and when these are not readily available, they are manufactured. The source of the fantasy is in the depths of the personality, and the fantasy itself can teach much about the meaning of the current danger to the person as well as about his past solutions under such circumstances. Eventually, when mutual interactions have led to genuine bonds following upon work together, these fantasies of familiarity or prejudices are dropped.

TRANSIENT VICTIMIZATION

The members' fantasy is that the leader's intention is to frustrate them. This view is intensified by his analytic attitude. They identify with this view of him and get even for their old hurts as well as for their current frustration by looking for a victim. This may be the leader himself, another member, or an outsider. Members identify with the position of aggressor and of scapegoat at different times.

Prospects for the role of scapegoat are the ones who dare take a stand against the leader or the group. They try to be different by insisting on their individuality, by refusing to do the required work, or by open expressions of antagonism to the leader and his views. They want to be accepted despite their extreme attitude and because of their stand. These two phenomena merge, the vengeance and individuality stand, much as the appearance of an optical illusion, where foreground and background change places continually the longer one watches.

The challengers are bound to fail. Each one has to retire in apparent defeat to lick his wounds, since the group is living out its victimization fantasy. The attacker is relieved that his anger can be tolerated and that he cannot now win out. The group may be frightened of having hurt someone and by the possibility of being hurt in return. For a while, freedom of interaction may be stifled as people try to be more tactful. Secretly, all are comforted by the stability of the victim who remains intact, by the permission given to show such feelings, and by having been allowed to live out this fantasy.

If the member shows that he cannot take the attack, attacks on him may increase and the leader may have to intervene or the member will be forced to leave the group. Whether a member is overprotected by the leader or leaves the group, either outcome has serious consequences for the group's being able to deal with its aggression and creativity. Ideally, such a situation can be used as a fruitful approach in opening up a group.

The group may choose the leader as a scapegoat. He then has to bear the punishment for a variable time without retaliation if the group is to remain together and coalesce. This can be as painful for the members as for the leader. If he retaliates, he may succeed in breaking up the group.

The members want a leader so that they can shift onto him their burden of values and demands of conscience. Such shifts make it possible for the members to lighten their inner burden of superego demands and at the same time have an opportunity to see the other sources of demands or conflicts that are within the personality. With the lifting of the individual superego lids in the group, there has to be an outpouring of pent-up anger. The leader's permissive analytic attitude encourages this process and permits the projection of unacceptable parts of the self, whether forbidden sexual or aggressive wishes or oppressive values, onto other members. Small wonder, then, that there is such an intensity of feeling, such anger and acting out and victimization, in group life.

This process of bringing the fantasies forth resembles the play of a child in which variants of a trauma are acted out again and again in different versions until the trauma has been mastered. The trauma in the group seems to be the weakness and helplessness that each member feels in the setting. Not all the members have to try out the weak and helpless roles overtly. This depends upon the pressure of the anxiety within each member, on the member's flexibility in participating, on his ability to identify with others, on his rigid need for a certain posture, and on the activity and passivity of each member in relation to the others. In smaller groups, there is more rigidity in choice of role. In larger groups, there is more fluidity, so that several people may occupy a specific function.

There may be a return to this way of relating later on in the group at moments of loss or relative loss, especially of the leader but also of other members. When the leader is absent, whether he announces it in advance or has to be absent with little notice, the group may feel that he is testing them, albeit for their own good, to give them a different kind of experience, that he is checking up to see who is most anxious, who has changed, and so on. Similarly, when a new member is introduced, feelings are entertained by the group that the leader no longer cares for them else he would not introduce new members. The introduction of a new member is experienced as a victimization by the leader. In retaliation, the new member is initiated, is given a trial by torture. If he is helped to accept this, and if the older members are helped to see what they are doing, he can become a member. If he is too frightened, he may be forced to leave the group. It is as if the torture fantasy is the oldest mode of joining oneself to another human being and must be lived through emotionally on the occasion of union or loss.

MORE FOCUSED VICTIMIZATION

As a climax to the transient victimization of the testing out period, there is often an excessive concern about some unusual member, who may in fact be very sick emotionally, may be very uncomfortable about being in the group, or may merely be very quiet. As his unusual characteristics come to the attention of the group, they first express concern and then attack him. If he is very sick or uncomfortable in the group, he may withdraw. If he is merely subbornly quiet, he can usually demonstrate his mettle by withstanding the attacks of the members. In either case the membership must be helped to face their concern about their individual helplessness. When they can accept this, they can usually help the member feel at home so that the group may proceed with its work. If the extreme member leaves, he needs to be helped to return and work out these issues of closeness; his extreme behavior is usually a defense against having to come close to the others. If he will not return, the group must be helped to give him up. In this process, they are aided to face their own fears of helplessness, ineffectiveness, and closeness.

EXAGGERATED PERFECT UNITY

As the members realize that they cannot only keep attacking one another, and also that members can take it and survive, they are more ready to put themselves in the position of victims of the leader in his therapeutic work. As they move from the conscious wish to be helped to its unconscious determinants, they progressively move from the idea of being analyzed to the wish to be exposed, to be hurt, and to be victimized. The earliest unconscious fantasy shared by the members is that to become a group is to become victims of the leader. Training groups pass on this myth to subsequent groups. When asked what the group was like, they smile knowingly, almost gloatingly, and say, "You'll find out." Preconscious versions of this fantasy are that the leader will spitefully interfere with their professional futures if they are bad or that he will exploit them and make himself famous by publishing books and articles based upon them. Gradually, step by step, the members pin on the leader his role of torturer.

Then the members huddle closer together. Consciously, they may feel they have successfully mastered certain travails in common and can feel closer on the basis of experience. And in a sense this is so. They now have to live through another version of negotiation at getting closer. The positive side of dependency needs begins to come out, needs for one another and for the leader. Different members can tolerate expressions of different versions of these needs, depending on their own family background and personal history. Some members can express these needs more in relation to the leader, some more in relation to other members. As the members see that these issues can be tolerated and faced in the group, they can begin to reveal some of their hidden alliances, not so much to discard them as to make them manifest. Revelation alone weakens their strength in interfering with the work of a group to a certain extent. They are usually in abeyance until a later date when they can be studied in greater detail for their more infantile determinants.

As a step in the direction of concentrating energy in the group, some members will defensively spill material pertaining to the group outside of it and hurt one another in some fashion. This raises the issue of confidentiality. As it is investigated, the membership defines what belongs inside the group and what belongs outside of it. Gradually, rules are laid down to deal with this issue, rules which tend to grow in intensity and become exaggerated. People begin to see changes and progress in others which they ascribe to the group. Actually, some of these changes may merely be due to greater comfort and relaxation within the group. Absentees are missed more. People may refuse to begin a meeting until every member is present. There is sadness when the people are away, even if only for vacation. There is relief when the whole membership is present. This leads to a compulsive, stifling kind of closeness, of fusion, and also a picture of helplessness: "We cannot function unless everybody is here." Gradually, people begin to rebel against this group-imposed conformity. The notion grows that there is a greater need for individuality, yet members are reluctant to give up this fantasy of closeness. For some members, its existence stretches on for a greater period of time than for the rest of the group. If the leader shares in the belief that this exaggerated closeness is indeed a reality, he may incur the wrath of those members who begin to chafe at its existence, and their justified anger at this imposition of infantile bonds will be a detriment to the work of the group. In any case, both kinds of people—those who want closeness and those who rebel against it—do not value their own ability; both hold their own talents and their ability to produce in low esteem, and all show very little leadership, since their individuality is submerged in conformity or rebellion. Toward the end of this period, there is encouragement of and pressure on silent members to reveal themselves and to participate along with everyone else, which is useful therapeutically. However, some of the encouragement is given grudgingly, and at the least withdrawal, the group angrily complains, "You haven't changed," or "We haven't cured you after all," with absolute seriousness. One can see glimmerings behind this larger group fantasy of the more individual version—the transference bond—that supplies the energy for this fantasy of unique closeness to the therapist or to other members who are significant to a given member. The forms of the fantasy are personal, such as playing chess with the leader and trading queens with him, writing a paper with him, or being supervised by him. Gradually, there has been a shift, consciously, from unity for a few members to unity for the whole group including the leader. Unconsciously, there has been a shift from an intesne dyadic or triadic relationship with the leader to include other members of the group. Finally, there is the comfort that the leader does not fall in with this fantasy and allows members an opportunity to grow.

INDIVIDUALIZATION

Each person with his own special qualities begins to become apparent to the other members in the group as an individual. People begin to realize that they have been unaware of the impact which they have had on other people. They also see that the other individuals are different from how they have seen them. For example, the group realizes with anxiety that their pet scapegoat who used to save them much effort by revealing himself endlessly to their attacks now stimulates them beyond belief with revelation of his own painful feelings, so that they feel impelled to do the same, to reveal themselves. The member who was seen to have leadership qualities and was apparently able to challenge the leader now shows himself to have problems in certain areas. The pet silent member is no longer so silent and can take care of himself when under attack. People begin to see that it is hard to have total group involvement for any given issue or any one member. They are more willing to settle for respectful interest in all members, with special interest in some, without feeling that they are betraying the whole group. Most members have thus developed transference objects within the group at a preconscious level. At the end of the thirty-week or forty-week experience, they are able to pick out certain members who have special significance for them in a special way that is reminiscent of their own past. Because it is a training rather than a therapy group, however, and must terminate, all the manifestations of transference are usually not verbalized. On the other hand, it is interesting that individualization is often pushed further than one would expect in that length of time, as if hastened on by the imminent termination.

DISCUSSION

Repeatedly, one sees in training groups an opening phase of fantasied closeness which rapidly disappears, followed by transient victimization climaxing in focused victimization, followed by intense, exaggerated unity, which then is followed by a more realistic appraisal of the self and others. By the time this last-mentioned phase has been reached, the membership has been through a welter of emotional storms and feels many bonds of unity, particularly with the leader and certain members but, in a more general way, with most of the rest of the membership, which cannot be accounted for in terms of what has been learned or won by each member. As a matter of fact, what has developed, on the one hand, is a series of transferences in various directions and, on the other hand, a working relationship which one can correctly call a therapeutic alliance. The transference states and therapeutic alliance together make up the individualization which one eventually sees.

This sequence is seen regularly in individual therapy. The fantasied closeness is briefer and perhaps unnoticed, since contact with the therapist is more intense and it is needed less. With many patients, we see a period of testing out, and then a period of exaggerated expectations of the therapist. Sometimes, in very dependent or trusting patients, the first period is passed so quickly that it is not noticed, and the patients immerse themselves at once in the exaggerated, dependent acceptance of everything that the therapist might say. With others, the period of testing out goes on for ever so long and frequently recurs. The group process seems to magnify this kind of individual reaction so that it can be seen in bold relief. The overlapping of similar primitive feelings highlights the dramatic, even bizarre, intensity of the reactions. It is similar to Japanese block-printing, which is done in stages. As each color is applied independently, one can make out only in part, or not at all, what the final picture will be, but, in the end, one can almost see what each layer of color contributed. Similarly, group phenomena may illuminate the process of getting closer emotionally in a way not visible in individual therapy.

A comparable sequence occurs during the process of falling in love. In love at first sight, the two individuals leap into exaggerated unity at once, foregoing the need for testing out. Later on these same people may get reverberations from having missed the chance to test the partner out. For most other people, the steady work of forming a relationship overcomes doubts and hesitations but never leads to an intensity which approaches the delirium of love at first sight. Neither sequence is a true adult relationship. That occurs only when there is further individualization within the marriage. One can also see a similar sequence of developments in the aim-inhibited relationship of friendship.

One wonders how a group can possibly form after such periods of fantasy, victimization, and fusion. Yet it does. It does so repeatedly, and seems to do so because of the successful passage through these treacherous maneuvers. They appear to be necessary steps in the process of binding oneself to the leader and reviving old personal transferences which fit into a particular group. By the time the members have individualized in the group, they are attached by transferences directly to varous individuals and directly or indirectly to the leader. In this way, individual needs can be used for the purpose of the group even though the individual is seeking for satisfaction in the working out of his own dilemmas.

Traditionally, we have looked on the development of the group as following Freud's model (1921) of the group of brothers who want to be cared for by father and yet want to overwhelm and replace him. But these same phenomena can be viewed in another and more primitive way. The attempt at leadership, which the group opposes and them victimizes, and the intense fusion bear witness to earlier determinants for these phenomena, having to do with the earliest relationship to the mother. Characteristically, these qualities are exaggerated to what looks to the beginner like pathological levels in the group.

SUMMARY

Systematic progression through the phases of fantasied familiarity, transient and focused victimization, and exaggerated unity leading to individualization are seen repeatedly during the period of group coalescence. Various phases or maneuvers may be exaggerated in a given group, depending upon its composition. These are attempts to deal in safety with the problem of getting close. Early closeness fantasies are revived and lived out but not worked through as necessary prelude to the mobilization of transferences, the development of a therapeutic alliance, and individualization in a group. The sources of these developments in the individual and their vicissitudes in the group are examined.

REFERENCES

Bach, G. R. (1954), *Intensive Group Psychotherapy*. New York: Ronald Press.
Day, M. (1963), The Therapeutic Envelope. Paper presented at meeting of American Group Psychotherapy Association, January 1963.

Foulkes, S. H., and Anthony, E. J. (1957), *Group Psychotherapy*. Baltimore: Penguin.

Freud, S. (1921), Group Psychology and the Analysis of the Ego. *Standard Edition*, 18:69–143. London: Hogarth Press, 1955.

Standish, C. T., and Semrad, E. V. (1951). Group Psychotherapy with Psychotics. *J. Psychiat. Soc. Work*, 20:143–150.

Wolf, A. (1949), The Psychoanalysis of Groups. *Amer. J. Psychother.*, 3:16–50; 4: 523–558.

10

A Theory of
Group Development

Warren G. Bennis
and
Herbert A. Shepard
Massachusetts Institute of Technology, Cambridge

[The phases of group development are comprehensively outlined in this influential and quite important contribution. Sullivanian and Freudian theoretical concepts are skillfully utilized by the authors in their account of the developmental stages empirically observable in the typical unstructured laboratory group. Such groups are seen as shifting from an initial preoccupation with power relationships and the issue of response to leader authority (in which the dependent members are in conflict with the counterdependent members) to a concern with the more peer-related issue of intimacy (in which the overpersonal members are in conflict with the counterpersonal members). Conflict resolution and positive group developmental shifts are seen to occur as a fortunate result of interactive behavior by key unconflicted members as well as of the occurrence of significant "barometric" events, such as the group revolt against the leader and the need to perform an interpersonal evaluation task just prior to the ending of the group.[1]]

If attention is focused on the organic properties of groups, criteria can be established by which phenomena of development, learning, or movement

From "A Theory of Group Development" by W. G. Bennis and H. A. Shepard, *Human Relations*, 1956, 9, 415–437. Copyright 1956 by Plenum Publishing Corporation. Reprinted by permission.
[1] This theory is based for the most part on observations made over a 5-year period of teaching graduate students "group dynamics". The main function of the seminar as it was set forth by the instructors was to improve the internal communication system of the group, hence, a self-study group. See (18).

toward maturity can be identified. From this point of view, maturity for the group means something analogous to maturity for the person: a mature group knows very well what it is doing. The group can resolve its internal conflicts, mobilize its resources, and take intelligent action only if it has means for consensually validating its experience. The person can resolve his internal conflicts, mobilize his resources, and take intelligent action only if anxiety does not interfere with his ability to profit from his experience, to analyse, discriminate, and foresee. Anxiety prevents the person's internal communication system from functioning appropriately, and improvements in his ability to profit from experience hinge upon overcoming anxiety as a source of distortion. Similarly, group development involves the overcoming of obstacles to valid communication among the members, or the development of methods for achieving and testing consensus. Extrapolating from Sullivan's definition of personal maturity we can say a group has reached a state of valid communication when its members are armed with

"... referential tools for analyzing interpersonal experience, so that its significant differences from, as well as its resemblances to, past experience, are discriminable, and the forsight of relatively near future events will be adequate and appropriate to maintaining one's security and securing one's satisfactions without useless or ultimately troublesome disturbance of self-esteem" (19, p. 111).

Relatively few investigations of the phenomena of group development have been undertaken.[2] This paper outlines a theory of development in groups that have as their explicit goal improvement of their internal communication systems.

A group of strangers, meeting for the first time, has within it many obstacles to valid communication. The more heterogeneous the membership, the more accurately does the group become, for each member, a microcosm of the rest of his interpersonal experience. The problems of understanding, the relationships, that develop in any given group are from one aspect a unique product of the particular constellation of personalities assembled. But to construct a broadly useful theory of group development, it is necessary to identify major areas of internal uncertainty, or obstacles to valid communication, which are common to and important in all groups meeting under a given set of environmental conditions. These areas must be strategic in the sense that until the group has developed methods for reducing uncertainty in them, it cannot reduce uncertainty in other areas, and in its external relations.

[2] "Unfortunately, relatively little research has yet been devoted to analyzing the relationships between group goals and the associated group functions." D. Cartwright and A. Zander (3, p. 313). The best attempt to date, and one we have relied on a good deal is by H. Thelen and W. Dickerman (21). The Thelen and Dickerman paper was based on training groups at the National Training Laboratory for Group Development at Bethel, Maine. These groups were similar in function and goals to the seminar groups at M.I.T.

I. THE TWO MAJOR AREAS OF INTERNAL UNCERTAINTY: DEPENDENCE (AUTHORITY RELATIONS) AND INTERDEPENDENCE (PERSONAL RELATIONS)

Two major areas of uncertainty can be identified by induction from common experience, at least within our own culture. The first of these is the area of group members' orientations toward authority, or more generally toward the handling and distribution of power in the group. The second is the area of members' orientations toward one another. These areas are not independent of each other: a particular set of inter-member orientations will be associated with a particular authority structure. But the two sets of orientations are as distinct from each other as are the concepts of power and love. A number of authorities have used them as a starting-point for the analysis of group behavior.

In his *Group Psychology and the Analysis of the Ego,* Freud noted that "each member is bound by libidinal ties on the one hand to the leader . . . and on the other hand to the other members of the group" (6, p. 45). Although he described both ties as libidinal, he was uncertain "how these two ties are related to each other, whether they are of the same kind and the same value, and how they are to be described psychologically." Without resolving this question, he noted that (for the Church and the Army) "one of these, the tie with the leader, seems . . . to be more of a ruling factor than the other, which holds between members of the group" (6, p. 52).

More recently, Schutz (17) has made these two dimensions central to his theory of group compatibility. For him, the strategic determinant of compatibility is the particular blend of orientations toward authority and orientations toward personal intimacy. Bion (1, 2) conceptualizes the major dimensions of the group somewhat differently. His "dependency" and "pairing" modalities correspond to our "dependence" and "interdependence" areas; to them he adds a "fight–flight" modality. For him these modalities are simply alternative modes of behavior; for us, the fight–flight categorization has been useful for characterizing the means used by the group for maintaining a stereotyped orientation during a given subphase.

The core of the theory of group development is that the principal obstacles to the development of valid communication are to be found in the orientations toward authority and intimacy that members bring to the group. Rebelliousness, submissiveness, or withdrawal as the characteristic response to authority figures; destructive competitiveness, emotional exploitiveness, or withdrawal as the characteristic response to peers prevent consensual validation of experience. The behaviors determined by these orientations are directed toward enslavement of the other in the service of the self, enslavement of the self in the service of the other, or disintegration of the situation. Hence, they prevent the setting, clarification of, and movment toward group-shared goals.

In accord with Freud's observation, the orientations toward authority are regarded as being prior to, or partially determining of, orientations toward other members. In its development, the group moves from preoccupation with authority relations to preoccupation with personal relations. This movement defines the two major phases of group development. Within each phase are three subphases, determined by the ambivalence of orientations in each area. That is, during the authority ("dependence") phase, the group moves from preoccupation with submission to preoccupation with rebellion, to resolution of the dependence problem. Within the personal (or "interdependence") phase the group moves from a preoccupation with intermember identification to a preoccupation with individual identity to a resolution of the interdependence problem.

II. THE RELEVANT ASPECTS OF PERSONALITY IN GROUP DEVELOPMENT

The aspects of member personality most heavily involved in group development are called, following Schutz, the dependence and personal aspects.

The dependence aspect is comprised by the member's characteristic patterns related to a leader or to a structure of rules. Members who find comfort in rules of procedure, an agenda, an expert, etc. are called "dependent." Members who are discomfited by authoritative structures are called "counterdependent."

The personal aspect is comprised by the member's characteristic patterns with respect to interpersonal intimacy. Members who cannot rest until they have stabilized a relatively high degree of intimacy with all the others are called "overpersonal." Members who tend to avoid intimacy with any of the others are called "counterpersonal."

Psychodynamically, members who evidence some compulsiveness in the adoption of highly dependent, highly counterdependent, highly personal, or highly counterpersonal roles are regarded as "conflicted." Thus, the person who persists in being dependent upon any and all authorities thereby provides himself with ample evidence that authorities should not be so trustingly relied upon; yet he cannot profit from this experience in governing his future action. Hence, a deep, but unrecognized, distrust is likely to accompany the manifestly submissive behavior, and the highly dependent or highly counter-dependent person is thus a person in conflict. The existence of the conflict accounts for the sometimes dramatic movement from extreme dependence to extreme rebelliousness. In this way, counterdependence and dependence, while logically the extremes of a scale, are psychologically very close together.

The "unconflicted" person or "independent," who is better able to profit from his experience and assess the present situation more adequately, may of course act at times in rebellious or submissive ways. Psychodynamically, the difference between him and the conflicted is easy to understand. In terms of observable behavior, he lacks the compulsiveness and significantly, does not create the communicative confusion so characteristic of, say, the conflicted dependent, who manifests submission in that part of his communication of which he is aware, and distrust or rebellion in that part of his communication of which he is unaware.[3]

Persons who are unconflicted with respect to the dependence or personal aspect are considered to be responsible for the major movements of the group toward valid communication. That is, the actions of members unconflicted with respect to the problems of a given phase of group development move the group to the next phase. Such actions are called barometric events, and the initiators are called catalysts. This part of the theory of group development is based on Redl's thesis concerning the "infectiousness of the unconflicted on the conflicted personality constellation."[4] The catalysts (Redl calls them "central persons") are the persons capable of reducing the uncertainty characterizing a given phase. "Leadership" from the standpoint of group development can be defined in terms of catalysts responsible for group movement from one phase to the next. This consideration provides a basis for determining what membership roles are needed for group development. For example, it is expected that a group will have great difficulty in resolving problems of power and authority if it lacks members who are unconflicted with respect to dependence.

III. PHASE MOVEMENTS

The foregoing summary has introduced the major propositions in the theory of group development. While it is not possible to reproduce the

[3] Schutz has developed a test, Fundamental Interpersonal Relations Orientations (FIRO), which is capable of measuring "conflictedness" and "independence" with respect to each of the dimensions, dependency and intimacy, as well as a third, "assertiveness" or the degree to which an individual will make his views felt in expressing himself in a group. See (16).

[4] For a brilliant discussion see F. Redl (15). Redl, following Freud's formulation, illustrated that it is possible for group action to come about as a result of the exculpation of guilt, as the unconflicted frees the conflicted personality individual by the magic of the initiatory act. It is also probably true that individuals may also "like" and feel more compatible with those individuals who do not stir up defended areas. For example, the highly ambivalent person who polarizes his conduct along unswerving submissive lines may react negatively to an individual who represents the opposite pole of the ambivalence, the highly rebellious individual. No doubt this is oversimplified and schematic, for evidence is obtainable that shows the opposite to be true; i.e., where individuals seek in others those aspects of their personality which are less accessible to consciousness. Read H. Lasswell's article (11), written in 1932 but very modern in its conception. He shows here how the id, ego, and super-ego were delineated in an executive's staff. The evidence, then, seems to indicate that we can be made both anxious and comfortable with individuals who embody our unconscious forces probably depending upon the threat to self-esteem.

concrete group experience from which the theory is drawn, we can take a step in this direction by discussing in more detail what seem to us to be the dominant features of each phase. The description given below is highly interpretive, and we emphasize what seem to us to be the major themes of each phase, even though many minor themes are present. In the process of abstracting, stereotyping, and interpreting, certain obvious facts about group process are lost. For example, each group meeting is to some extent a recapitulation of its past and a forecast of its future. This means that behavior that is "regressive" or "advanced" often appears.[5]

A. Phase I: Dependence

(i) Subphase 1: Dependence-flight The first days of group life are filled with behavior whose remote, as well as immediate, aim is to ward off anxiety. Much of the discussion content consists of fruitless searching for a common goal. Some of the security-seeking behavior is group-shared—for example, members may reassure one another by providing interesting and harmless facts about themselves. Some is idiosyncratic—for example, doodling, yawning, intellectualizing.

The search for a common goal is aimed at reducing the case of anxiety, thus going beyond the satisfaction of immediate security needs. But just as evidencing boredom in this situation is a method of warding off anxiety by denying its proximity, so group goal-seeking is not quite what it is claimed to be. It can best be understood as a dependence plea. The trainer, not the lack of a goal, is the cause of insecurity. This interpretation is likely to be vigorously contested by the group, but it is probably valid. The characteristic expectations of group members are that the trainer will establish rules of the game and distribute rewards. He is presumed to know what the goals are or ought to be. Hence his behavior is regarded as a "technique"; he is merely playing hard to get. The pretense of a fruitless search for goals is a plea for him to tell the group what to do, by simultaneously demonstrating its helplessness without him, and its willingness to work under his direction for his approval and protection.

We are talking about the dominant theme in group life. Many minor themes are present, and even in connection with the major theme there are differences among members. For some, testing the power of the trainer to affect their futures is the major concern. In others, anxiety may be aroused through a sense of helplessness in a situation made threatening by the protector's desertion. These alternatives can be seen as the beginnings of the

---

[5]It should be understood that the trainer's behavior and certain ground rules under which the group operates are important forces in the group's development. A rationale for and description of these aspects are presented in another paper. See H. A. Shepard and W. G. Bennis (18).

counterdependent and dependent adaptations. Those with a dependent orientation look vainly for cues from the trainer for procedure and direction, sometimes paradoxically they infer that the leader must want it that way. Those with a counterdependent orientation strive to detect in the trainer's action elements that would offer ground for rebellion, and may even paradoxically demand rules and leadership from him because he is failing to provide them.

The ambiguity of the situation at this stage quickly becomes intolerable for some, and a variety of ultimately unserviceable resolutions may be invented, many of them idiosyncratic. Alarm at the prospect of future meetings is likely to be group-shared, and at least a gesture that may be made in the direction of formulating an agenda for subsequent meetings.

This phase is characterized by behavior that has gained approval from authorities in the past. Since the meetings are to be concerned with groups or with human relations, members offer information on these topics, to satisfy the presumed expectations of the trainer and to indicate expertise, interest, or achievement in these topics (ex-officers from the armed services, from fraternities, etc. have the floor). Topics such as business or political leadership, discrimination and desegregation, are likely to be discussed. During this phase the contributions made by members are designed to gain approval from the trainer, whose reaction to each comment is surreptitiously watched. If the trainer comments that this seems to be the case, or if he notes that the subject under discussion (say, discrimination) may be related to some concerns about membership in this group, he fails again to satisfy the needs of members. Not that the validity of this interpretation is held in much doubt. No one is misled by the "flight" behavior involved in discussing problems external to the group, least of all the group members. Discussion of these matters is filled with perilous uncertainties, however, and so the trainer's observation is politely ignored, as one would ignore a *faux-pas* at a tea-party. The attempts to gain approval based on implicit hypotheses about the potential power of the trainer for good and evil are continued until the active members have run through the repertoire of behaviors that have gained them favor in the past.

(ii) Subphase 2: Counterdependence-flight As the trainer continues to fail miserably in satisfying the needs of the group, discussion takes on a different tone, and counterdependent expressions begin to replace overt dependency phase. In many ways this subphase is the most stressful and unpleasant in the life of the group. It is marked by a paradoxical development of the trainer's role into one of omnipotence and powerlessness, and by division of the group into two warring subgroups. In subphase 1, feelings of hostility were strongly defended; if a slip were made that suggested hostility, particularly toward the trainer, the group members were embarrassed. Now expressions of hostility are more frequent, and are more likely to be supported by other members, or to be met with equally hostile responses.

Power is much more overtly the concern of group members in this subphase. A topic such as leadership may again be discussed, but the undertones of the discussion are no longer dependence pleas. Discussion of leadership in subphase 2 is in part a vehicle for making explicit the trainer's failure as a leader. In part it is perceived by other members as a bid for leadership on the part of any member who participates in it.

The major themes of this subphase are as follows:

1. Two opposed subgroups emerge, together incorporating most of the group members. Characteristically, the subgroups are in disagreement about the group's need for leadership or "structure." One subgroup attempts to elect a chairman, nominate working committees, establish agenda, or otherwise "structure" the meetings; the other subgroup opposes all such efforts. At first this appears to be merely an intellectual disagreement concerning the future organization of group activity. But soon it becomes the basis for destroying any semblance of group unity. Fragmentation is expressed and brought about in many ways: voting is a favorite way of dramatizing the schism; suggestions that the group is too large and should be divided into subgroups for the meetings are frequent; a chairman may be elected and then ignored as a demonstration of the group's ineffectualness. Although control mechanisms are sorely needed and desired, no one is willing to relinquish the rights of leadership and control to anyone else. The trainer's abdication has created a power gap, but no one is allowed to fill it.

2. Disenthrallment with the trainer proceeds rapidly. Group members see him as at best ineffectual, at worst damaging, to group progress. He is ignored and bullied almost simultaneously. His interventions are perceived by the counterdependents as an attempt to interrupt group progress; by the dependents, as weak and incorrect statements. His silences are regarded by the dependents as desertion; by the counterdependents as manipulation. Much of the group activity is to be understood as punishment of the trainer, for his failure to meet needs and expectations, for getting the group into an unpleasant situation, for being the worst kind of authority figure—a weak and incompetent one, or a manipulative, insincere one. Misunderstanding or ignoring his comments, implying that his observations are paranoid fantasies, demonstrations that the group is cracking up, references to him in the past tense as though he were no longer present—these are the punishments for his failure.

As, in the first subphase, the trainer's wisdom, power, and competence were overtly unquestioned, but secretly suspected; so, in the second subphase, the conviction that he is incompetent and helpless is clearly dramatized, but secretly doubted. Out of this secret doubt arises the belief in the trainer's omnipotence. None of the punishments meted out to the trainer are recognized as such by the group members; in fact, if the trainer suggests that the members feel a need to punish him, they are most likely to respond in injured tones or in tones of contempt that what is going on has nothing to do with him and that he had best stay out of it. The trainer is still too imposing and threatening to challenge directly. There is a secret hope that the chaos in the group is in fact part of the master plan, that he is really leading them in the direction they should be going. That he may really be helpless as they imply, or that the failure may be theirs rather than his, are frightening possibilities. For this reason subphase 2 differs very little in its fundamental dynamics from subphase 1. There is still the secret wish that the trainer will stop all the bedlam which has replaced polite uncertainty, by taking his proper role (so that dependent members can cooperate with him and counterdependent can rebel in the usual ways).

Subphase 2 thus brings the group to the brink of catastrophe. The trainer has consistently failed to meet the group's needs. Not daring to turn directly on him, the group members engage in mutually destructive behavior: in fact, the group threatens suicide as the most extreme expression of dependence.[6] The need to punish the trainer is so strong, however, that his act of salvation would have to be magical indeed.

(iii) Subphase 3: Resolution-catharsis No such magic is available to the trainer. Resolution of the group's difficulties at this point depends upon the presence in the group of other forces, which have until this time been inoperative, or ineffective. Only the degenerative aspects of the chain of events in subphases 1 and 2 have been presented up to this point and they are in fact the salient ones. But there has been a simultaneous, though less obvious, mobilization of constructive forces. First, within each of the warring subgroups bonds of mutual support have grown. The group member no longer feels helpless and isolated. Second, the trainer's role, seen as weak or manipulative in the dependence orientation, can also be perceived as permissive. Third, his interpretations, though openly ignored, have been secretly attended to. And, as the second and third points imply, some members of the group are less the prisoners of the dependence–counterdependence dilemma than others. These members, called the independents, have been relatively ineffective in the group for two reasons. First, they have not developed firm bonds with other members in either of the warring subgroups, because they have not identified with either cause. Typically, they have devoted their energies to an unsuccessful search for a compromise settlement of the disagreements in the group. Since their attitudes toward authority are less ambivalent than those of other members, they have accepted the alleged

---

[6] Frequently groups select issues capable of fragmenting the group; e.g., desegregation in a group of northern liberals and conventional southerners. Thus we see evidence of what is so typical during this subphase, the "self-fulfilling prophecy." That is to say, certain strategic topics are predestined to splinter the group, which only serves to confirm its uselessness and disparateness.

reason for disagreement in the group—for example, whether a chairman should be elected—at face value, and tried to mediate. Similarly, they have tended to accept the trainer's role and interpretations more nearly at face value. However, his interpretations have seemed inaccurate to them, since in fact the interpretations have applied much less to them than to the rest of the group.[7]

Subphase 3 is the most crucial and fragile in group life up to this point. What occurs is a sudden shift in the whole basis of group action. It is truly a bridging phase; if it occurs at all, it is so rapid and mercurial that the end of subphase 2 appears to give way directly to the first subphase of Phase II. If it does not occur thus rapidly and dramatically, a halting and arduous process of vacillation between Phases I and II is likely to persist for a long period, the total group movement being very gradual.

To summarize the state of affairs at the beginning of subphase 3: 1. The group is polarized into two competing groups, each unable to gain or relinquish power. 2. Those group members who are uncommitted to either subgroup are ineffective in their attempts to resolve the conflict. 3. The trainer's contributions only serve to deepen the cleavage in the group.

As the group enters subphase 3, it is moving rapidly toward extinction: that is, splintering into two or three subgroups. The independents, who have until now been passive or ineffectual, become the only hope for survival, since they have thus far avoided polarization and stereotypic behavior.[8] The imminence of dissolution forces them to recognize the fruitlessness of their attempts at mediation. For this reason, the trainer's hypothesis that fighting one another is off-target behavior is likely to be acted upon at this point. A group member may openly express the opinion that the trainer's presence and comments are holding the group back, suggest that "as an experiment" the trainer leaves the group "to see how things go without him." When the trainer is thus directly challenged, the whole atmosphere of the meeting changes. There is a sudden increase in alertness and tension. Previously, there had been much acting out of the wish that the trainer were absent, but at the same time a conviction that he was the *raison d'être* of the group's existence—that it would fall apart without him. Previously, absence of the trainer would have constituted desertion, or defeat, fulfilment of the members' worst fears as to their own inadequacy for the trainer's. But now leaving the group can have a

---

[7] The ambiguity of the situation, particularly the vague and uncertain role of the trainer, tends to induce black–white reaction patterns on the part of the highly ambivalent group members. What results, as Frenkel-Brunswik has stated, is the "neglect of reality and seeking for unqualified and unambiguous over-all acceptance and rejection of other people. The maintenance of such solutions requires the shutting out of aspects of reality which represent a possible threat to these solutions" (5). Another highly interesting approach is J. C. Flugel's *The Psycho-Analytic Study of the Family* (4).

[8] Putting this in Newcomb's A–B–X system we see that the less attraction between A and B, the more strain toward symmetry "is limited to those X's [our independents] co-orientation toward which is required by the conditions of the association" (13).

different meaning. General agreement that the trainer should leave is rarely achieved. However, after a little further discussion it becomes clear that he is at liberty to leave, with the understanding that he wishes to be a member of the group, and will return if and when the group is willing to accept him.

The principle function of the symbolic removal of the trainer is in its effect of freeing the group to bring into awareness the hitherto carefully ignored feelings toward him as an authority figure, and toward the group activity as an off-target dramatization of the ambivalence toward authority. The leadership provided by the independents (whom the group sees as having no vested interest in power) leads to a new orientation toward membership in the group. In the discussion that follows the exit of the trainer, the dependents' assertion that the trainer deserted and the counterdependents' assertion that he was kicked out are soon replaced by consideration of whether his behavior was "responsible" or "irresponsible." The power problem is resolved by being defined in terms of member responsibilities, and the terms of the trainer's return to the group are settled by the requirement that he behave as "just another member of the group." This phrase is then explained as meaning that he should take neither more or less responsibility for what happens in the group than any other member.

The above description of the process does not do justice to the excitement and involvement characteristic of this period. How much transferable insight ambivalent members require from it is difficult to assess. At least within the life of the group, later activity is rarely perceived in terms of submission and rebellion.

An interesting parallel, which throws light on the order of events in group development, is given in Freud's discussion of the myth of the primal horde. In his version:

> "These many individuals eventually banded themselves together, killed [the father], and cut him in pieces. . . . They then formed the totemistic community of brothers all with equal rights and united by the totem prohibitions which were to preserve and to expiate the memory of the murder" (6, p. 112).

The horde's act, according to Freud, was soon distorted into an heroic myth: instead of murder by the group, the myth held that the father had been overthrown single-handed by one person, usually the youngest son. In this attribution of the group act to one individual (the hero) Freud saw the "emergence of the individual from group psychology." His definition of a hero is ". . . a man who stands up manfully against his father and in the end victoriously overthrows him" (8, p. 9). (The heroic myth of Freud thus shares much in common with Sullivan's "delusion of unique individuality.")

In the training group, the member who initiates the events leading to the trainer's exit is sometimes referred to as a "hero" by the other members.

Responsibility for the act is felt to be shared by the group, however, and out of their experience comes the first strong sense of group solidarity and involvement—a reversal of the original version, where the individual emerges from the group. This turn of events clarifies Freud's remark concerning the libidinal ties to the leader and to the other group members. Libidinal ties toward the other group members cannot be adequately developed until there is a resolution of the ties with the leader. In our terms, those components of group life having to do with intimacy and interdependence cannot be dealt with until those components having to do with authority and dependence have been resolved.

Other aspects of subphase 3 may be understood by investigating the dramatic significance of the revolt. The event is always marked in group history as "a turning-point," "the time we became a group," "when I first got involved," etc. The mounting tension, followed by sometimes uproarious euphoria, cannot be entirely explained by the surface events. It may be that the revolt represents a realization of important fantasies individuals hold in all organizations, that the emotions involved are undercurrents wherever rebellious and submissive tendencies toward existing authorities must be controlled. These are the themes of some of our great dramas—*Antigone, Billy Budd, Hamlet,* and our most recent folk-tale, *The Caine Mutiny.* But the event is more than the presentation of a drama, or an acting-out of frantasies. For it can be argued that the moments of stress and catharsis, when emotions are labile and intense, are the times in the group life when there is readiness for change. Leighton's analysis of a minor revolution at a Japanese relocation camp is worth quoting in full on this point:

> "While this [cathartic] situation is fraught with danger because of trends which may make the stress become worse before it gets better, there is also an opportunity for administrative action that is not likely to be found in more secure times. It is fairly well recognized in psychology that at periods of great emotional stir the individual human being can undergo far-reaching and permanent changes in his personality. It is as if the bone structure of his systems of belief and of his habitual patterns of behavior becomes soft, is fused into new shapes and hardens there when the period of tension is over. . . . Possibly the same can be true of whole groups of people, and there are historical examples of social changes and movements occurring when there was widespread emotional tension, usually some form of anxiety. The Crusades, parts of the Reformation, the French Revolution, the change in Zulu life in the reign of Chaca, the Meiji Restoration, the Mormom movement, the Russian Revolution, the rise of Fascism, and alterations in the social sentiments of the United States going on at present are all to some extent examples" (12, p. 360).

Observers of industrial relations have made similar observations. When strikes result from hostile labor–management relations (as contrasted to straight wage demands), there is fluidity of relationships and a wide repertoire of structural changes during this period not available before the strike act.[9]

So it is, we believe, with the training group. But what are the new values and behavior patterns that emerge out of the emotional experience of Phase 1? Principally, they are acceptance by each member of his full share of responsibility for what happens in the group. The outcome is autonomy for the group. After the events of subphase 3, there is no more attribution of magical powers to the trainer—either the dependent fantasy that he sees farther, knows better, is mysteriously guiding the group and protecting it from evil, or the very similar counterdependent fantasy that he is manipulating the group, exploiting it in his own interests, that the experience is one of "brain-washing." The criterion for evaluating a contribution is no longer who said it, but what is said. Thereafter, such power fantasies as the trainer himself may have present no different problem from the power fantasies of any other group member. At the same time, the illusion that there is a struggle for power in the group is suddenly dissipated, and the contributions of other members are evaluated in terms of their relevance to shared group goals.

Summary of Phase I

The very word development implies not only movement through time, but also a definite order of progression. The group must traverse subphase 1 to reach subphase 2, and subphase 3 before it can move into Phase II. At the same time, lower levels of development coexist with more advanced levels. Blocking and regression occur frequently, and the group may be "stuck" at a certain phase of development. It would, of course, be difficult to imagine a group remaining long in subphase 3—the situation is too tense to be permanent. But the group may founder for some time in subphase 2 with little movement. In short, groups do not inevitably develop through the resolution of the dependence phase to Phase II. This movement may be retarded indefinitely. Obviously much depends upon the trainer's role. In fact, the whole dependence modality may be submerged by certain styles of trainer behavior. The trainer has a certain range of choice as to whether dependency as a source of communication distortion is to be highlighted and made the subject of special experiential and conceptual consideration. The personality and training philosophy of the trainer determine his interest in introducing or avoiding explicit consideration of dependency.[10]

There are other important forces in the group besides the trainer, and

---

[9] See A. Gouldner (10), W. F. Whyte, Jr. (22). Robert E. Park, writing in 1928, had considerable insight on some functions of revolution and change. See (14).

[10] This is elaborated further in the accompanying paper, "A Theory of Training by Group Methods," by H. A. Shepard and W. G. Bennis.

these may serve to facilitate or block the development that has been described as typical of Phase I. Occasionally there may be no strong independents capable of bringing about the barometric events that precipitate movement. Or the leaders of opposing subgroups may be the most assertive members of the group. In such cases the group may founder permanently in subphase 2. If a group has the misfortune to experience a "traumatic" event early in its existence—exceedingly schizoid behavior by some member during the first few meetings, for example—anxieties of other members may be aroused to such an extent that all culturally suspect behavior, particularly open expression of feelings, is strongly inhibited in subsequent meetings.

Table 1 summarizes the major events of Phase I, as it typically proceeds. This phase has dealt primarily with the resolution of dependence needs. It ends with acceptance of mutual responsibility for the fate of the group and a sense of solidarity, but the implications of shared responsibility have yet to be explored. This exploration is reserved for Phase II, which we have chosen to call the Interdependence phase.

B. Phase II: Interdependence

The resolution of dependence problems marks the transfer of group attention (and inattention) to the problems of shared responsibility.

Sullivan's description of the change from childhood to the juvenile era seems pertinent here:

> "The juvenile era is marked off from childhood by the appearance of an urgent need for compeers with whom to have one's existence. By "compeers' I mean people who are on our level, and have generically similar attitudes toward authoritative figures, activities and the like. This marks the beginning of the juvenile era, the great developments in which are the talents for cooperation, competition and compromise" (20, pp. 17-18. Emphasis ours).

The remaining barriers to valid communication are those associated with orientations toward interdependence: i.e., intimacy, friendship, identification. While the distribution of power was the cardinal issue during Phase I, the distribution of affection occupies the group during Phase II.

(iv) Subphase 4: Enchantment-flight At the outset of subphase 4, the group is happy, cohesive, relaxed. The atmosphere is one of "sweetness and light." Any slight increase in tension is instantly dissipated by joking and laughter. The fighting of Phase I is still fresh in the memory of the group, and the group's efforts are devoted to patching up differences, healing wounds, and maintaining a harmonious atmosphere. Typically, this is a time of merrymaking and group minstrelsy. Coffee and cake may be served at the meetings. Hours may be passed in organizing a group party. Poetry or songs commemorating the important events and persons in the group's history may

TABLE 1 Phase I. Dependence–power relations*

	Subphase 1 Dependence-submission	Subphase 2 Counterdependence	Subphase 3 Resolution
1. Emotional modality	Dependence–Flight	Counterdependence–Fight. Off-target fighting among members. Distrust of staff member. Ambivalence.	Pairing. Intense involvement in group task.
2. Content themes	Discussion of interpersonal problems external to training groups.	Discussion of group organization, i.e., what degree of structuring devices is needed for "effective" group behavior?	Discussion and definition of trainer role.
3. Dominant roles (central persons)	Assertive, aggressive members with rich previous organizational or social science experience.	Most assertive counterdependent and dependent members. Withdrawal of less assertive independents and dependents.	Assertive independents.
4. Group structure	Organized mainly into multi-subgroups based on members' past experiences.	Two tight subcliques consisting of leaders and members, of counterdependents and dependents.	Group unifies in pursuit of goal and develops internal authority system.
5. Group activity	Self-oriented behavior reminiscent of most new social gatherings.	Search for consensus mechanism: Voting, setting up chairman, search for "valid" content subjects.	Group members take over leadership roles formerly perceived as held by trainer.
6. Group movement facilitated by:	Staff member abnegation of traditional role of structuring situation, setting up rules of fair play, regulation of participation.	Disenthrallment with staff member coupled with absorption of un-certainty by most assertive counter-dependent and dependent individuals. Subgroups form to ward off anxiety.	Revolt by assertive independents (catalysts) who fuse subgroups into unity by initiating and engineering trainer exit (barometric event).
7. Main defenses	Projection Denigration of authority		Group moves into Phase II

*Course terminates at the end of 17 weeks. It is not uncommon for groups to remain throughout the course in this phase.

be composed by individuals, or, more commonly, as a group project. All decisions must be unanimous during this period, since everyone must be happy, but the issues on which decisions are made are mostly ones about which group members have no strong feelings. At first the cathartic, healing function of these activities is clear; there is much spontaneity, playfulness, and pleasure. Soon the pleasures begin to wear thin.

The myth of mutual acceptance and universal harmony must eventually be recognized for what it is. From the beginning of this phase there are frequent evidences of underlying hostilities, unresolved issues in the group. But they are quickly, nervously smoothed over by laughter or mis-interpretation. Subphase 4 begins with catharsis, but that is followed by the development of a rigid norm to which all members are forced to conform: "Nothing must be allowed to disturb our harmony in the future; we must avoid the mistakes of the painful past." Not that members have forgotten that the painful past was a necessary preliminary to the autonomous and (it is said) delightful present, though that fact is carefully overlooked. Rather, there is a dim realization that all members must have an experience somewhat analogous to the trainer's in subphase 3, before a mutually understood, accepted, and realistic definition of their own roles in the group can be arrived at.

Resistance of members to the requirement that harmony be maintained at all costs appears in subtle ways. In open group discussion the requirement is imperative: either the member does not dare to endanger harmony with the group or to disturb the *status quo* by denying that all problems have been solved. Much as members may dislike the tedious work of maintaining the appearance of harmony, the alternative is worse. The house of cards would come tumbling down, and the painful and exacting work of building something more substantial would have to begin. The flight from these problems takes a number of forms. Group members may say, "We've had our fighting and are now a group. Thus, further self-study is unnecessary." Very commonly, the possibility of any change may be prevented by not coming together as a total group at all. Thus the members may subgroup through an entire meeting. Those who would disturb the friendly subgroups are accused of "rocking the boat."

The solidarity and harmony become more and more illusory, but the group still clings to the illusion. This perseveration is in a way a consequence of the deprivation that members have experienced in maintaining the at-mosphere of harmony. Maintaining it forces members to behave in ways alien to their own feelings; to go still further in group involvement would mean a complete loss of self. The group is therefore torn by a new ambivalence, which might be verbalized as follows: 1. "We all love one another and therefore we must maintain the solidarity of the group and give up whatever is necessary of our selfish desires." 2. "The group demands that I sacrifice my identity as a person; but the group is an evil mechanism which satisfies no dominant needs." As this subphase comes to a close, the happiness that marked its beginning is maintained only as a mask. The "innocent" splitting of the group into subgroups has gone so far that members will even walk around the meeting table to join in the conversation of a subgroup rather than speak across the table at the risk of bringing the whole group together. There is a certain uneasiness about the group; there is a feeling that "we should work together but cannot." There may be a tendency to regress to the orientation of subphase 1: group members would like the trainer to take over.

To recapitulate: subphase 4 begins with a happy sense of group belongingness. Individual identity is eclipsed by a "the group is bigger than all of us" sentiment. But this integration is short lived: it soon becomes perceived as a fake attempt to resolve interpersonal problems by denying their reality. In the later stages of this subphase, enchantment with the total group is replaced by enchantment with one's subgroup, and out of this breakdown of the group emerges a new organization based on the anxieties aroused out of this first, suffocating, involvement.

(v) Subphase 5: Disenchantment-fight This subphase is marked by a division into two subgroups—paralleling the experience of subphase 2—but this time based upon orientations toward the degree of intimacy required by group membership. Membership in the two subgroups is not necessarily the same as in subphase 2: for now the fragmentation occurs as a result of opposite and extreme attitudes toward the degree of intimacy desired in interpersonal relations. The counterpersonal members band together to resist further involvement. The overpersonal members band together in a demand for unconditional love. While these subgroups appear as divergent as possible, a common theme underlies them. For the one group, the only means seen for maintaining self-esteem is to avoid any real commitment to others; for the other group, the only way to maintain self-esteem is to obtain a commitment from others to forgive everything. The subgroups share in common the fear that intimacy breeds contempt.

This anxiety is reflected in many ways during subphase 6. For the first time openly disparaging remarks are made about the group. Invidious comparisons are made between it and other groups. Similarly, psychology and social science may be attacked.[11] The inadequacy of the group as a basis for self-esteem is dramatized in many ways—from stating "I don't care what you think," to boredom, to absenteeism. The overpersonals insist that they are happy and comfortable, while the counterpersonals complain about the lack of group morale. Intellectualization by the overpersonals frequently takes on

---

[11] This frequently comes about as a result of the intellectualization process that accompanies this subphase. Members raise the question, "Are we a group?" Any answer offered is distorted and tranformed into an attack on the inadequacies of social science research. The guise of intellectual concern only serves as a foil to indicate the failure and impotence of the group, another example of the "self-fulfilling prophecy."

religious overtones concerning Christian love, consideration for others, etc. In explanations of member behavior, the counterpersonal members account for all in terms of motives having nothing to do with the present group; the overpersonals explain all in terms of acceptance and rejection in the present group.

Subphase 5 belongs to the counterpersonals as subphase 4 belonged to the overpersonals. Subphase 4 might be caricatured as hiding in the womb of the group; subphase 5 as hiding out of sight of the group. It seems probable that both of these modalities serve to ward off anxieties associated with intimate interpersonal relations. A theme that links them together can be verbalized as follows: "If others really knew me, they would reject me." The overpersonal's formula for avoiding this rejection seems to be accepting all others so as to be protected by the others' guilt; the counterpersonal's way is by rejecting all others before they have a chance to reject him. Another way of characterizing the counterpersonal orientation is in the phrase, "I would lose my identity as a member of the group." The corresponding overpersonal orientation reads, "I have nothing to lose by identifying with the group." We can now look back on the past two subphases as countermeasures against loss of self-esteem; what Sullivan once referred to as the greatest inhibition to the understanding of what is distinctly human, "the overwhelming conviction of self-hood—this amounts to a delusion of unique individuality." The sharp swings and fluctuations that occurred between the enchantment and euphoria of subphase 4 and the disenchantment of subphase 5 can be seen as a struggle between the "institutionalization of complacency" on the one hand and anxiety associated with fantasy speculations about intimacy and involvement on the other. This dissociative behavior serves a purpose of its own: a generalized denial of the group and its meaning for individuals. For if the group is important and valid then it has to be taken seriously. If it can wallow in the enchantment of subphase 4, it is safe; if it can continually vilify the goals and objectives of the group, it is also safe. The disenchantment theme in subphase 5 is perhaps a less skilful and more desperate security provision with its elaborate wall of defenses than the "group mind" theme of subphase 4. What should be stressed is that both subphase defenses were created almost entirely on fantastic expectations about the consequences of group involvement. These defenses are homologous to anxiety as it is experienced by the individual; i.e., the state of "anxiety arises as a response to a situation of danger and which will be reproduced thenceforward whenever such a situation recurs" (7, p. 72). In sum, the past two subphases were marked by a conviction that further group involvement would be injurious to members' self-esteem.

(vi) Subphase 6: Consensual validation In the groups of which we write, two forces combine to press the group toward a resolution of the interdependency problem. These are approaching end of the training course, and the need to establish a method of evaluation (including course grades).

There are, of course, ways of denying or avoiding these realities. The group can agree to continue to meet after the course ends. It can extricate itself from evaluation activities by asking the trainer to perform the task, or by awarding a blanket grade. But turning this job over to the trainer is a regression to dependence; and refusal to discriminate and reward is a failure to resolve the problems of interdependence. If the group has developed in general as we have described, the reality of termination and evaluation cannot be denied, and these regressive modes of adaptation cannot be tolerated.

The characteristic defenses of the two subgroups at first fuse to prevent any movement toward the accomplishment of the evaluation and grading task. The counterpersonals resist evaluation as an invasion of privacy: they foresee catastrophe if members begin to say what they think of one another. The overpersonals resist grading since it involves discriminating among the group members. At the same time, all members have a stake in the outcome of evaluation and grading. In avoiding the task, members of each subgroup are perceived by members of the other as "rationalizing," and the group becomes involved in a vicious circle of mutual disparagement. In this process, the fear of loss of self-esteem through group involvement is near to being realized. As in subphase 3, it is the independents—in this case those whose self-esteem is not threatened by the prospect of intimacy—who restore members' confidence in the group. Sometimes all that is required to reverse the vicious circle quite dramatically is a request by an independent for assessment of his own role. Or it may be an expression of confidence in the group's ability to accomplish the task.

The activity that follows group commitment to the evaluation task does not conform to the expectations of the overpersonal or counterpersonal members. Its chief characteristic is the willingness and ability of group members to validate their self-concepts with other members. The fear of rejection fades when tested against reality. The tensions that developed as a result of these fears diminish in the light of actual discussion of member roles. At the same time, there is revulsion against "capsule evaluations" and "curbstone psychoanalysis." Instead, what ensues is a serious attempt by each group member to verbalize his private conceptual scheme for understanding human behavior—his own and that of others. Bring these assumptions into explicit communication is the main work of subphase 6. This activity demands a high level of work and of communicative skill. Some of the values that appear to underlie the group's work during this subphase are the follows: 1. Members can accept one another's differences without associating "good" and "bad" with the differences. 2. Conflict exists but is over substantive issues rather than emotional issues. 3. Consensus is reached as a result of rational discussion rather than through a compulsive attempt at unanimity. 4. Members are aware of their own involvement, and of other aspects of group process, without being overwhelmed or alarmed. 5. Through the evaluation process, members take on greater personal meaning to each other. This facilitates communication and creates a deeper understanding of how the other person thinks, feels, behaves; it creates a series of personal expectations, as distinguished from the previous, more stereotyped, role expectations.

The above values, and some concomitant values, are of course very close to the authors' conception of a "good group." In actuality they are not always achieved by the end of the group life. The prospect of the death of the group after much procrastination in the secret hope that it will be over before anything can be done, is likely to force the group into strenuous last-minute efforts to overcome the obstacles that have blocked its progress.[12] As a result, the sixth subphase is too often hurried and incomplete. If the hurdles are not overcome in time, grading is likely to be an exercise that confirms members' worst suspicions about the group. And if role evaluation is attempted, either the initial evaluations contain so much hostile material as to block further efforts, or evaluations are so flowery and vacuous that no one, least of all the recipient, believes them.

In the resolution of interdependence problems, member-personalities count for even more than they do in the resolution of dependence problems. The trainer's behavior is crucial in determining the group's ability to resolve the dependence issue, but in the interdependence issue the group is, so to speak, only as strong as its weakest link. The exceedingly dependent group member can ride through Phase I with a fixed belief in the existence of a private relationship between himself and the trainer; but the person whose anxieties are intense under the threats associated with intimacy can immobilize the group. (*Table II* summarizes the major events of Phase II.)

CONCLUSIONS

Dependence and interdependence—power and love, authority and intimacy—are regarded as the central problems of group life. In most organizations and societies, the rules governing the distribution of authority and the degree of intimacy among members are prescribed. In the human relations training group, they are major areas of uncertainty. While the choice of these matters as the focus of group attention and experience rests to some extent with the trainer, his choice is predicated on the belief that they are the core of interpersonal experience. As such, the principal obstacles to valid interpersonal communication lie in rigidities of interpretation and response carried over from the anxious experiences with particular love or power figures into new situations in which they are inappropriate. The existence of such autisms complicates all discussion unduly and in some instances makes an exchange of meanings impossible.

---

[12]Cf. S. Freud (9, pp. 316–57). The meaning of termination of treatment and of its consequences for the patient is discussed here.

TABLE 2 Phase II. Interdependence–personal relations

	Subphase 4–Enchantment	Subphase 5 Disenchantment	Subphase 6–Consensual validation
Emotional modality	Pairing–flight. Group becomes a respected icon beyond further analysis.	Fight–flight. Anxiety reactions. Distrust and suspicion of various group members.	Pairing, understanding, acceptance.
Content themes	Discussion of "group history", and generally salutary aspects of course, group, and membership.	Revival of content themes used in Subphase 1: What is a group? What are we doing here? What are the goals of the group? What do I have to give up—personally—to belong to this group? (How much intimacy and affection is required?) Invasion of privacy vs. "group giving". Setting up proper codes of social behavior.	Course grading system. Discussion and assessment of member roles.
Dominant roles (central persons)	General distribution of participation for first time. Overpersonals have salience.	Most assertive counterpersonal and overpersonal individuals, with counterpersonals especially salient.	Assertive independents.
Group structure	Solidarity, fusion. High degree of camaraderie and suggestibility. Le Bon's description of "group mind" would apply here.	Restructuring of membership into two competing predominant subgroups made up of individuals who share similar attitudes concerning degree of intimacy required in social interaction, i.e. the counterpersonal and overpersonal groups.	Diminishing of ties based on personal orientation. Group structure now presumably appropriate to needs of situation based on predominantly substantive rather than emotional orientations. Consensus significantly easier on important issues.

TABLE 2 (*continued*) Phase II. Interdependence—personal relations

	Subphase 4—Enchantment	Subphase 5 Disenchantment	Subphase 6—Consensual validation
		The personal individuals remain uncommitted but act according to needs of situation.	Communication to others of self-esteem of interpersonal relations; i.e. making conscious to self, and others aware of, conceptual system one uses to predict consequences of personal behavior. Acceptance of group on reality terms.
Group activity	Laughter, joking, humor. Planning out-of-class activities such as parties. The institutionalization of happiness to be accomplished by "fun" activities. High rate of interaction and participation.	Disparagement of group in a variety of ways: high rate of absenteeism, tardiness, balkiness in initiating total group interaction, frequent statements concerning worthlessness of group, denial of importance of group. Occasional member asking for individual help finally rejected by the group.	
Group movement facilitated by:	Independence and achievement attained by trainer-rejection and its concomitant, deriving consensually some effective means for authority and control. (Subphase 3 rebellion bridges gap between Subphases 2 and 4.)	Disenchantment of group as a result of *fantasied expectations of group life.* The perceived threat to self-esteem that further group involvement signifies creates schism of group according to amount of affection and intimacy desired. The counterpersonal and overpersonnel assertive individuals alleviate source of anxiety by disparaging or abnegating further group involvement. Subgroups form to ward off anxiety.	The external realities, group termination and the prescribed need for a course grading system, comprise the barometric event. Led by the personal individuals, the group tests reality and reduces autistic convictions concerning group involvement.
Main defenses	Denial, isolation, intellectualization, and alienation.		

Stating the training goal as the establishment of valid communication means that the relevance of the autistic response to authority and intimacy on the part of any member can be explicitly examined, and at least a provisional alternative formulated by him. Whether this makes a lasting change in the member's flexibility, or whether he will return to his more restricted formula when confronted with a new situation, we do not know, but we expect that it varies with the success of his group experience—particularly his success in understanding it.

We have attempted to portray what we believe to be the typical pattern of group development, and to show the relationship of member orientations and changes in member orientations to the major movements of the group. In this connection, we have emphasized the catalytic role of persons unconflicted with respect to one or the other of the dependence and interdependence areas. This power to move the group lies mainly in his freedom from anxiety-based reactions to problems of authority (or intimacy): he has the freedom to be creative in searching for a way to reduce tension.

We have also emphasized the "barometric event" or event capable of moving the group from one phase to the next. The major events of this kind are the removal of the trainer as part of the resolution of the dependence problem; and the evaluation-grading requirements at the termination of the course. Both these barometric events require a catalytic agent in the group to bring them about. That is to say, the trainer-exit can take place only at the moment when it is capable of symbolizing the attainment of group autonomy, and it requires a catalytic agent in the group to give it this meaning. And the grading assignment can move the group forward only if the catalytic agent can reverse the vicious circle of disparagement that precedes it.

Whether the incorporation of these barometric events into the training design merely makes our picture of group development a self-fulfilling prophecy, or whether, as we wish to believe, these elements make dramatically clear the major forward movements of the group, and open the gate for a flood of new understanding and communication, can only be decided on the basis of more, and more varied, experience.

The evolution from Phase I to Phase II represents not only a change in emphasis from power to affection, but also from role to personality. Phase I activity generally centers on broad role distinctions such as class, ethnic background, professional interests, etc.; Phase II activity involves a deeper concern with personality modalities, such as reaction to failure, warmth, retaliation, anxiety, etc. This development presents an interesting paradox. For the group in Phase I emerged out of a heterogeneous collectivity of individuals; the individual in Phase II emerged out of the group. This suggests that group therapy, where attention is focused on individual movement, begins at the least enabling time. It is possible that, before group members are able to help each other, the barriers to communication must be partially understood.

REFERENCES

1. Bion, W. R. "Experiences in Groups: I." *Hum. Relat.*, Vol. I, No. 3, pp. 314–20, 1948.
2. Bion, W. R. "Experiences in Groups: II." *Hum. Relat.*, Vol. I, No. 4, pp. 487–96, 1948.
3. Cartwright, D., and Zander, A. *Group Dynamics.* Evanston, Ill.: Row Peterson, 1953; London: Tavistock Publications, 1954.
4. Flugel, J. C. *The Psycho-Analytic Study of the Family.* London: Hogarth Press, 1931, 1938.
5. Frenkel-Brunswik, E. "Intolerance of Ambiguity as an Emotional and Perceptual Personality Variable." In Bruner, J. S., and Krech, D. (Eds.), *Perception and Personality.* Durham, N.C.: Duke Univ. Press, 1949 and 1950, p. 115.
6. Freud, Sigmund. *Group Psychology and the Analysis of the Ego.* Translated by J. Strachey. London: International Psycho-Analytical Press, 1922; New York: Liveright, 1949.
7. Freud, Sigmund. *The Problem of Anxiety.* Translated by H. A. Bunker. New York: Psychoanalytic Quarterly Press and W. W. Norton, 1936.
8. Freud, Sigmund. *Moses and Monotheism.* London: Hogarth Press, 1939; New York: Vintage Books, 1955.
9. Freud, Sigmund. "Analysis Terminable and Interminable." *Collected Papers,* Vol. V. Edited by J. Strachey. London: Hogarth Press, 1953.
10. Gouldner, Alvin. *Wildcat Strike.* Yellow Springs, Ohio: Antioch Press, 1954; London: Routledge and Kegan Paul, 1955.
11. Lasswell, H. "The Triple-Appeal Principle." *Amer. J. Sociol.,* Jan. 1932, pp. 523–38.
12. Leighton, A. H. *The Governing of Men.* Princeton: Princeton Univ. Press, 1946.
13. Newcomb, T. M. "An Approach to the Study of Communicative Acts." *Psychol. Rev.,* Vol. 60, pp. 393–404, 1953.
14. Park, Robert E. "The Strike." *Society.* Glencoe, Ill.: The Free Press, 1955.
15. Redl, F. "Group Emotion and Leadership." *Psychiatry,* Vol. V, pp. 573–96, 1942.
16. Schutz, W. C. "Group Behavior Studies, I–III." Harvard Univ., 1954 (mimeo).
17. Schutz, W. C. "What Makes Groups Productive?" *Hum. Relat.,* Vol. VIII, No. 4, p. 429, 1955.
18. Shepard, H. A., and Bennis, W. G. "A Theory of Training by Group Methods." M.I.T. mimeo, 1956; *Hum. Relat.,* Vol. IX, No. 4, pp. 403–14, 1956.
19. Sullivan, H. S. "Tensions, Interpersonal and International." In Cantril, Hadley (Ed.), *Tensions that Cause Wars.* Univ. of Illinois Press, 1950.
20. Sullivan, H. S. *Conceptions of Modern Psychiatry.* Washington, D.C.: William Alanson White Psychiatric Foundation, 1940, 1945; London: Tavistock Publications, 1955.
21. Thelen, H., and Dickerman, W. "Stereotypes and the Growth of Groups." *Educational Leadership,* February 1949, pp. 309–16.
22. Whyte, W. F., Jr. *Patterns for Industrial Peace.* New York: Harper, 1951.

11

Toward a Theory of Group Development: Six Phases of Therapy Group Development

Elmore A. Martin, Jr.
South Carolina State Hospital
University of South Carolina, Columbia
and
William Fawcett Hill
Utah State Hospital, Provo

[The theory of group development, previously largely elaborated upon within the framework of unstructured laboratory groups for normals, in this chapter is applied to psychotherapy groups for disturbed individuals. Such groups are seen as gradually evolving from an initial largely *autistic* (the authors, by such a term, would appear to mean *projective-transferential*) phase to a more mature phase of interpersonal relatedness and individualization. Psychotherapy groups are depicted as generally falling short of the most creative and integrative forms of group inquiry and relatedness typically seen in highly sophisticated t-groups.]

In this paper an attempt is made to encapsulate a dynamic, complex, and fluctuating phenomenon—the development of a psychotherapy group. This

From "Toward a Theory of Group Development: Six Phases of Therapy Group Development" by E. A. Martin, Jr., and W. F. Hill, *International Journal of Group Psychotherapy*, 1957, 7, 20–30. Copyright 1957 by the International Journal of Group Psychotherapy. Reprinted by permission.

Research projects supported by NIMH are acknowledged as having provided the possibility for collaboration on this article.

developmental process is divided into six discrete phases. Each phase is described in terms of the major therapeutic problem confronting the group and characteristic behaviors to be found at each phase level. In addition, the transitional stages between these developmental plateaus are also described in a manner which is meant to indicate the potentials within the group interaction for movement from one phase to another.

Involved in the theory and in the derived scale of group development is the assumption that therapy groups have distinct and common growth patterns which are describable, observable, and predictable. This untested assumption rests on empirical observations and theoretical conjectures. The proposed developmental continuum involves six phases through which any group would pass if it were to start at a condition of minimal groupness and continue until it has reached its optimum function. Groups would be different in the length of time spent in any one phase and in the specifics of the problems (and themes) they would face in any phase. Most groups would disband, and even have achieved their purpose, before reaching the ultimate level of development.

This theory of group development is offered as a tentative ordering of the complexities of group therapy phenomena because we believed that some systematic conceptualization of group development is essential and that to date the literature in this area is meager. It is our belief that any generalization about a therapy group can be meaningfully stated only in the context of some level of group development for that group. Similarly, research designs which ignore levels of group development are in jeopardy. A final observation concerns the therapist himself. Some theory of group development is necessary for a therapist to know where his group is now and in what direction it might move and what within the group are the potentials to which he might attend to maximize development.

The phases and their transitional periods can be thought of as points along a continuum and thus this developmental theory can be turned into a developmental scale. Figure 1 presents an eleven-point scale of group development.

PHASE I—INDIVIDUAL UNSHARED
BEHAVIOR IS AN
UNSHARED STRUCTURE

In this phase groupness is minimal. There is no identification with the group as such, although there may be some private and egocentric conceptions about the group being a source for personal advantage. *Esprit de corps* and cooperative ventures are latent. The characteristic most evident to an observer is the social isolation of the members. In groups of psychotic patients the behavior is primarily autistic or at best highly private and of preconceived orientations. In groups of neurotics or less regressed patients there are

PHASES	SCALE POINTS		TITLE OF PHASE
Phase I		1	Individual unshared behavior in an imposed structure
Transition from I to II		2	
Phase II		3	Reactivation of fixated interpersonal attitudes
Transition from II to III		4	
Phase III		5	Exploration of interpersonal potential within the group
Transition from III to IV		6	
Phase IV		7	Awareness of interrelationships, sub-grouping and power structures
Transition from IV to V		8	
Phase V		9	Consciousness of group dynamics and group process problems
Transition from V to VI		10	
Phase VI		11	The group as an effective integrative-creative social instrument

FIGURE 1 Scale of group development.

mutually compatible productions but as yet they are individualistic and egocentric and clearly not group relevant. In either case a group at Phase I is stimulated by past experiences or from endogenous, intraphysic material of its members.

The justification for calling this a group rests upon the presence of a therapist who must be perceived, however dimly, by members as someone different and special. Regularity of meeting time and place also are factors tending to produce groupness, even though it be minimal. Another factor is the consistency in membership and the seating arrangement where group members are physically confronted one with another. However, from the observer's point of view, the only functional evidence of groupness is the centrality of the leader who provides a focal point around which the members tend to revolve in their private orbits. This is not akin to a "dependency phase" such as is described by Dickerman and Thelen.[1] There is little cathexis on the therapist, although there is a tacit acceptance of him as the leader, and he is a centripetal agent in an otherwise centrifugal situation.

Thus in Phase I there is no interpersonal, group-relevant structure, and the group is essentially a congerie of social isolates held in loose association by a vague awareness of the therapist and his role. With regressed patients the reaction may be slight and with neurotics and "normals" the concern over the

---

[1] Thelen, H. A. and Dickerman, W.: Stereotypes and the Growth of Groups. *Educational Leadership,* 6:309–316, 1949.

therapist may take on obsessive qualities. Nonetheless, these are private idiosyncratic concerns over the leader and are not in terms of his behavior in this group.

TRANSITION FROM PHASE I TO PHASE II

At this stage there is an emergence of the therapist as leader of the group and his group role is publicly acknowledged. Also at this stage there is a diminution of autistic behavior[2] which is replaced by an asyndetic mode. By asyndetic we mean that some element in the statements of one member serve as a cue or trigger for statements made by the next speaker. The next speaker in turn is cued off by some element in the verbalizations of the preceding speaker and so on. This produces what might be called a verbal chain reaction and in this process a group can wander all over the place. The asyndetic process has both group-relevant and autistic aspects. The material that is cued off is highly personal and is not in the context of the previous speaker who provided the stimulus. Nonetheless, these productions do indicate that members have paid some attention to each other's verbalizations. Also these tangential productions do produce a sense of continuity which suggests some groupness.

The cathartic and pure id gratification of autistic productions eventually seem to lose some of their charm and the reality of the presence of others in the group must obtrude. The asyndetic process thus establishes some oblique social contacts although retaining highly egocentric gratification. The member's attempts to break down the autistic barriers in the transitional period abort and there is frequent regression to pure Phase I behavior. To break through to Phase II the therapist must capitalize on his centrality and provide patterns of behavior which are not asyndetic but give more recognition of the members as social beings.

PHASE II—REACTIVATION OF FIXATED INTERPERSONAL STEREOTYPES

In this phase no member is reacted to as an individual in his own right. Instead, members react to one another in terms of previously learned personality stereotypes. In Freudian terms the interactions would be seen as manifestations of transference phenomena. These fixated interpersonal perceptions are part of the mental impedimenta which the members brought with them to the group, and therefore do not represent learning that has occurred in the group. As contrasted with Phase I, we now have a publicly acknowledged awareness of the

[2] Autistic behavior does not completely disappear regardless of the phase level. In principle any of the higher phase level operations will have behavioral elements of lower phase operations. This is readily accounted for by a concept of regression brought about by the inevitable frustrations to be found in the group process.

existence of each other by the members of the group, but this is in terms of "ghosts" of earlier interpersonal experiences and lacks recognition of the complexities and individuality of the personalities present. From the observer's point of view the flavor of the interaction will be that of disregard for the needs and the individuality of the members, and of attributing to each other projected attitudes for which there is no consensual validation. The leader will also be "type cast" and because of family and cultural conditioning will be cast in some omniscient role, although there will, of course, be some ambivalence and negative transference. On the group level there will be manifest principally positive transference material. Therefore, it is at this point that the dependency modality becomes operant. The leader and members will thus be type cast and statements will be made about the leader describing him as "brainy" or "Mr. God" and members might be called "bigot" or "sweet" or whatever, without much relevance to reality. Much "normal" social exchange is maintained on this level, and therefore this should not be considered as necessarily pathological. In fact, before a reasonable amount of social and interpersonal data has been exchanged between persons, there is no other way of relating except on the basis of matching a new individual to preconceived stereotypes. Thus, the positive or therapeutic value of this phase lies in the socialization aspects.

TRANSITION FROM PHASE II TO PHASE III

As in all transitional periods, there is dissatisfaction with the current group operation and frustration with the inability of the group to develop new patterns. Operating on social stereotypes is inevitably going to break down because of the reality that members differ from their type casting. There will even be open resentment on the part of some members as to the way they are invariably reacted to by certain other members. Thus, insistence on their own rights and views would tend to move the group toward more realistic appraisals of each other. The leader remains in his strong transference position, but the *idiosyncratic perceptions* that members have of the leader begin to yield to a *group consensus*. The leader can aid and abet in this period by making the members more aware of discrepancies in this stereotyping of the leader. Secure and flexible leaders might even go further and present to the group through their behavior some of the incongruities in their own personalities. Certainly leaders who tend to role-play the group leader prevent the group in relating to the leader as a human being and thus maintain the "type-casting phenomena."

PHASE III—EXPLORATION OF INTERPERSONAL POTENTIAL WITHIN THE GROUP

While there are still many asyndetic processes and transference-dominated perceptions and even occasional autisms at this phase, the group can now, for the first time, deal with the "here and now" of group life, and the perceptions of each other's personalities and behavior. The group now adopts the spirit of active emotional exchange. From the point of view of the observer there is much time spent in the exploration of individual personalities, and a group value emerges which places much importance on the individual. In this rise of individualism two group styles of interaction have been discerned. One is a relatively calm approach by the group to the problems and personality of an individual member. The group may devote the whole session or more to a consideration of one member and then move on to consider another. The other style is more "give and take" wherein the focus is rapidly shifting, and there is a lot of interaction and trading back and forth of interpersonal perceptions. The former style seems to be more problem-oriented, whereas the latter is more affect-laden. In both cases the group task is to differentiate group members and give them recognition as individuals. The therapist's sophistication in the psychology of the individual members assures him of supremacy at this phase. He can aid them in articulating unconscious motivations and fantasies and can provide terminology and frames of reference for classifying individual behavior. While the therapist is still regarded more or less as omniscient, nevertheless, due to the nature of his function he is, if effective, less active in this phase. As the therapist exhibits skills which are obvious to the members, the high regard for the therapist shifts onto more realistic ground.

It is at this point that membership is valued and absences and tardiness are topics of considerable concern. Where the dropping out of one or two members is imminent, a hypochrondriacal concern for the health of the group becomes manifest.

Most therapists would not consider that the group task was therapeutic, or to state it slightly different, that therapy was taking place. In so far as a definition of therapy implies change and learning, then the abreaction of Phase I and the socializing of Phase II might be discounted as therapy and viewed more in the light of necessary steps in group development preparatory to therapy. Some therapists may tend to see the interactions at this stage as the essence and the goal of group therapy. Most therapy groups never progress beyond this, as the therapist is satisfied when the patients give emotional feedback to one another and show increasing awareness of their effect on each other. Undoubtedly therapy is taking place at this stage in that insights into the self are thrust upon the members by each other. Also some ego strengthening should take place where feelings of belongingness provide an antidote for anomie, and feelings of self-worth are engendered through the groups' concern for the individual. The sharing of fallibilities and ego-alien fantasies also convince the member that he is not so bad (or different) after all. The leader might at this stage confess to or act out some of his own personality flaws, but he should guard against insisting he is one of the gang and is almost as sick as the members. If he is to be effective, he must represent reality and mental health.

TRANSITION FROM PHASE III TO PHASE IV

While it is true that the complexity of individual personality is infinite, gratification in the exploration of individuality is probably governed by a law of diminishing returns. Thus, what was earlier exciting and novel tends to become less intriguing and rather repetitive. Some feeling develops that the members are confronted with the same old faces and the same old problems. At the same time, some awareness develops that there is a patterning of relationships in the group. The group, at this stage, suffers from ennui with rummaging through each other's psyche and tends to turn to considerations of the relationships that have developed among the group members out of this interpersonal inquiry. It is difficult, however, to shift from the purely unilateral to an interrelationship orientation. The therapist, at this time, can make the group aware of their boredom with the pursuit of the interpersonal and can point up this new area—relationship—which they might explore.

PHASE IV—AWARENESS OF INTERRELATIONSHIPS, SUBGROUPING AND POWER STRUCTURES

In the history of the group there is now available a great deal of data on each of the members, some of it stemming from fixated perceptions of Phase II and much from Phase III. At this point there is a growing understanding that more has taken place than exploration of individual personalities and that in the give and take of group interaction certain relationships have developed between members. For example, some members may have a "pairing relationship" (in Bion's terms), some relationships may be symbiotic, others hierarchial, others sadomasochistic complementarities, and so forth. The leader, because of his sophistication and powers of trained observation, can see the obvious and point out these relationships to the group. Thus the leader frees the members to articulate as well as become increasingly aware of these relationships. When members become skilled in identifying relationship dynamics they may even develop insight into their attempts to structure specific relationships with the therapist. Thus, certain members will be spotted as "teacher's pet" or "leader's assistant," and so forth.

What is happening here is a synthesizing process where the seemingly random interactions of interpersonal exchange are made more dynamic, orderly and lawful, because they are now seen as symptomatic of underlying relationships in the group. This matrix of interrelationships is the warp and woof of the group, and concern with this almost approaches a concern with the group itself; nonetheless, it does not quite meet the *group qua group* level of abstraction.

The relationships in the group during this stage become less unilateral and develop into subgroup alignments. Rationale for this phenomenon is set forth by Redl, Bion, and Hill.[3] To state briefly the rationale: members are concerned with obtaining emotional gratification and these needs tend to be dissimilar and sometimes antithetical. Certain members emerge who seem to be freer in their attempts to obtain emotional gratification and others with similar needs tend to sustain and support these spokesmen. Thus, subgroups tend to develop around the nuclei of these opinion and emotional attitude leaders. Obviously leadership is beginning to emerge. Also at this stage, the group is becoming polarized and rivalries develop. The group does not disintegrate, partly because of the overlapping membership within the subgroups and partly because the members realize that the group must be maintained if it is to provide for their emotional gratification.

From the point of view of an observer, the group seems to shift periodically from one emotional climate to another and certain members seem to be influential in these shifts. It is usually difficult for an observer to detect accurately which members are consistently aligned with which leaders. Nonetheless, an observer is aware of shifting centers of power and the operation of power structures.

The leader is, in a sense, external to the power struggle but is possibly part of a subgroup which is characterized by task orientations and acceptance of diversity. As has been stated above, leadership has now shifted largely into the hands of certain members. The therapist's task now is to identify for the group these attitude and opinion instigators and also, if possible, their supporters and to make the group aware of the vicissitudes and outcomes of the subgroup power struggle.

The therapeutic value of this phase lies in the ability of the members to perceive the effects that their emotional need-meeting have on their behavior. A new type of learning also may take place at this point which has direct implications for operating in the larger society. If we accept the concept of a group being a microcosm of society, then the subgroup phenomena and the shifting power structures parallel the social reality of the larger community, and the ability of a patient to see himself in relation to these power structures, and to see their impingement on him, is presumed to be therapeutic.

Most therapy groups, before their ultimate dissolution, probably do not get to the fifth phase. The reasons for this may lie in the fact that operation in the third and fourth phase is presumed to be the goal of therapy. It may

[3] Redl, F.: Group Emotion and Leadership. *Psychiatry*, 5:573–596, 1942; Bion W. R.: Experiences in Groups. *Human Relations*, 3:3–14, 1950; Hill, W. F.: Subgroup Dynamics Within Total Group Process. In: *Methods for Studying Work and Emotionality in Group Operation, Monograph—Human Dynamics Labs*, ed. H. Thelen et al. University of Chicago, 1954, pp. 149–168.

also be that many therapists do not have the skills to aid the group to go beyond this.

TRANSITION FROM PHASE IV TO V

The conflicting needs in the group, each need with its champion and supporters, inevitably leads to a high tension state in the group. In time the tolerance on the part of the members for this tension state decreases and dissatisfaction with this factional mode of operation increases. The solution to this problem lies in a total group orientation in place of the polarized and individual subgroup operation. Thus, attempts are made by group members to reach this group level, but due, in part, to the considerable conceptual difficulties this is not successful. Attempts to reach this group orientation are characterized by remarks like the following: "Why can't we get along together?" or "Do we have to struggle with that again?" or, more insightfully, "If all of us would try to understand the problem rather than choosing up sides we might get somewhere."

The therapist's task at this point is to make the group aware of its dissatisfaction with factionalism and to provide the group with some models and concepts for getting at group level abstractions. The therapist might introduce, at this time, techniques for getting at total group data such as role playing, use of an observer, and so forth, but the group will not be able to assimilate or use effectively such data at this time.

PHASE V—RESPONSIVENESS TO GROUP DYNAMIC AND GROUP PROCESS PROBLEMS

At this phase there is an awareness by the members of the group that the group is, in a sense, an organism. That one meeting of eight persons can be called a group and another meeting of eight different persons might be called a gathering, congerie or some "un-group" phenomenon indicates that "group" rests on some theoretical grounds which makes "group" a theory or theoretical construct. It is, incidentally, just as respectable a theory or construct as, for example, ego or social class. The important thing at this phase is that there is a sharing of this theory—group. Usually only the therapist has the skills and concepts necessary to investigate and understand the implications that a group has for its members. Thus the therapist's most appropriate behavior at this time is to provide concepts and frames of reference that aid in describing and comprehending group dynamics and group process. At first the group is dependent on the therapist for models and concepts but will eventually develop some skill in thinking in these terms. Again the dependency on the leader is more realistic although his skill and knowledge may tend to mobilize or maintain feelings of personal inadequacy and feelings of omniscience toward the therapist.

For the observer the group seems to be concerned with learning and applying concepts about how this group functions and in what ways other groups seem to be like this one. Individual problems become reinterpreted as group problems. Thus the dependency on the leader is not seen entirely as stemming from his greater knowledge or lesser pathology but as part of the process problem of the group. Similarly, a domineering person is not seen only as a person who has a personality problem which the members might try to alleviate, but also that his problem is simultaneously cause and effect of one of the group problems. It is, no doubt, difficult for a group to remain at this level of operation, and regression is common. A special condition obtains at this level also: after a while a group exhausts process and dynamics and must revert to lower level operations in order to generate or make manifest further process and dynamics. Thus, we may say that a group is at this phase when it demonstrates from time to time, and not infrequently, awareness of its silences, difficulties with the therapist, tabooed topics, difficulty in getting started, and similar group phenomena.

TRANSITION FROM PHASE V TO PHASE VI

Once the group has developed the ability to describe its own process and has found this desirable, there will naturally follow attempts to diagnose and remedy undesirable features that have been uncovered. Again the group does not have the skills for this which reside or should reside in the therapist, and thus these attempts will be met with frustration. Observations of process problems will carry with them implied requests for solutions. Thus remarks like the following may be heard, "Why does it take us so long to get started?" or "Why don't some of the people in the group participate more?" and so on. It is important at this point that the therapist make aware the fact that the members entertain the wish and the belief that group problem-solving can take place. The leader may suggest techniques such as having an observer, play back recordings, role playing, and so forth. When any of these are adopted the group will still have difficulty in utilizing the data in any diagnostic or problem-solving manner.

PHASE VI—THE GROUP AS AN INTEGRATIVE-CREATIVE SOCIAL INSTRUMENT

This is an ideal phase and one which a group would not be expected to operate in for a sustained period. Human relations training groups, which are run on quasi-therapy lines, have been observed to operate on this level for periods up to half an hour.[4] To operate at this level with any degree of consistency probably carries with it the assumption that the members are

[4] Thelen, H., et al., op. cit.

more effective and mentally healthy than the national average. Thus, therapy groups are most likely to disband before this level is reached, irrespective of whether the leader is able to aid a group in reaching it.

At this stage, the group has a pattern of distributive leadership and realistic individuation of role has taken place. Thus roles are assigned on the basis of competence; and degrees of incompetence are accepted and dealt with accordingly. Similarly, the group can proceed and make decisions acceptable to the group without compulsive consensus. The group can now regulate its process to a certain extent and the members feel that they are, to a similar extent, masters of their fate. Thus the group can select their goals and pace themselves in the achievement of them. Also the group can do cooperative problem solving, diagnose its own process problems, and develop techniques to handle them. The main concern is to have data on the social realities in its field of operation; this means data which are intrapsychic, intragroup and relating to the larger society in which the group is imbedded. The therapist becomes more like any other member, but this is because the members tend to become as capable as the therapist. The therapist still may be differentiated due to his experience and training, but not so much in the role of providing leadership, but as a resource person. His position might be best termed as *primus inter pares.*

Thus, while we still may have from time to time autisms and asyndetic processes, neurotic dependency, stereotypy in interpersonal perception and hypochondriacal concern over the health of the group, nonetheless, there is a dynamic state of tension which motivates the group to tackle its own problems in a cooperative, experimental, and creative fashion, thereby functioning as an integrative organism. When members can operate in this fashion they then, and probably only then, can leave the shelter of the therapy group and become really effective people, rather than merely adjusted people, in their own communities. Thus they can deal with the environmental stresses in a positive rather than passive manner and perhaps aid in the growth of their associates. Following the dictum of Kurt Lewin, that to have a healthy society we need healthy groups, implies that members of our society, be they in therapy or not, need some experience with primary groups which reach this level of operation.

IV

FREUDIAN CONCEPTS RELATED TO GROUP DYNAMICS

12

The Pleasure and Reality Principles in Group Process Teaching

Stephen A. Appelbaum
The Menninger Foundation
Topeka, Kansas

[Appelbaum presents anecdotal material, derived from a number of unstructured group experiences, that seems to suggest the usefulness of Freud's notions of the pleasure and reality principles as important group psychological explanatory concepts. Most unstructured groups, according to Appelbaum, initially regress to a primitive position in which pleasure strivings and the need for instant gratification are the order of the day. It is only with much reluctance that they learn to shift to a more realistic attitude in which there is greater capacity to delay gratification. A useful group experience will facilitate such a developmental and essentially ego psychological shift.]

The distinctions often drawn between education and psychotherapy, group and individual psychotherapy, and group psychotherapy and group dynamics are superficially plausible, and have been made to look even more so through institutionalization of them by disparate professions. Yet in important respects they are similar. All of them come about through learning and change in an interpersonal context. They have in common motivation, reward, and practice. They can all be measured, from moment to moment, as to how much attention is given to the process, how much to the content. Looked at

Reprinted from "The Pleasure and Reality Principles in Group Process Teaching" by Stephen A. Appelbaum, *British Journal of Medical Psychology*, 1963, *36*, pp. 1-7, by permission of Cambridge University Press.

in this way many of the differences seem to reside more in the goals of the teacher–leader–therapist (and his consequent techniques) and in the putative purposes prescribed by social and technical conventions than in intrinsic means by which the individual learns–changes–gets better.

As Freud put it, 'The contrast between individual psychology and social or group psychology, which at first glance may seem to be full of significance, loses a great deal of its sharpness when it is examined more closely. . . . In the individual's mental life someone else is invariably involved . . . and so from the very first individual psychology . . . is at the same time social psychology as well' (1921). In describing the teaching of psychotherapy Ekstein and Wallerstein write, '. . . both supervision and psychotherapy are interpersonal helping processes working with the same affective components, with the essential difference between them created by the difference in purpose' (1958). In comparing group psychotherapy and group dynamics 'training groups' Jerome Frank writes, '[they are] better viewed as points on a continuum than as differing in essence. Both are learning situations which have the aim of bringing about changes in their members' (1963).

Classes in group process, organized and taught as described below, provide a terrain in which education, group dynamics, and group and individual psychotherapy meet, without fixed borders. Such classes convene for the purpose of observing group phenomena as these are encouraged to develop in the class itself. It is assumed that some such phenomena are at least latent in all groups. But in groups constituted similarly to these classes, these phenomena become readily apparent. This is so because the absence of work (other than to observe the emergence and development of group process) makes conspicuous many aspects of small group dynamics which are usually masked behind rules of order, schedules of production, and highly directive leadership. As with projective tests and the encouragement of transference through limiting information about the therapist, the minimization of structure enables ordinarily latent behaviour to become manifest. Through attuning himself to the behaviour patterns and forces which he observes and experiences, the student develops a repertoire of phenomenological and inductive information with which to understand better his own and others' behaviour in a group, as well as the group's corporate behaviour.

Psychiatry has become interested in these classes for at least two major reasons: (1) Attempts to understand psychopathology have led to ideas not only about the interpersonal origin of symptoms and behaviour difficulties, but to the notion that inadequate interpersonal functioning, or styles of negotiating, are in themselves conditions to be treated. Logically, a small group which is organized so as to present a continuous challenge to social adaptation is a medium well suited for psychotherapy. Group psychotherapists can use the insights learned in training classes to make interpretative comments about group process, in addition to comments they may choose solely on the basis of knowledge of the individual. (2) Some psychiatrists, such as

Berman, look upon group process classes as similar to psychological treatment, in that both provide opportunities to appreciate experientially data which would otherwise be known only in the abstract (1953). In Bertrand Russell's terms, as applied by Richfield to the problem of the nature of insight, the student gains knowledge by *acquaintance* in addition to knowledge by *description* (1954).

To the extent that the educational–dynamic–therapeutic processes are similar, and apply both to individuals and groups, it would seem profitable to examine these processes, as they ensue in training classes, with reference to a concept prominent in the psychoanalytic understanding of individual personality development. The concept chosen is Freud's pleasure and reality principles (1911).*

Under sway of the pleasure principle the individual is dominated by a striving for pleasure and withdrawal from pain. It should be added that the English rendering of *lustprinzip* as 'pleasure principle' erroneously implies that the object of the fundamental rule of mental functioning is simply 'pleasure.' Rather, what is meant here, in keeping with what I believe is Freud's original meaning, is the infantile striving for direct and immediate tension release, for taking the shortest distance between two points regardless of the consequences, for behaving under the premise that gratification should be immediate, exactly what is craved, and should involve work only to the extent of fantasying what is wanted. As the result of interpersonal and physical frustration of this tendency, the reality principle develops: the individual learns to attend, remember, judge, delay, and think, and in other ways adapt himself to approximate as best he can under present circumstances the dictates of the pleasure principle.

This broad concept has, of course, many implications. But for heuristic purposes it is here applied narrowly to the life of a hypothetical group of people according to the following paradigm: wishes derived primarily from the pleasure principle—those saturated heavily with orality, passivity, and unreality—meet with frustration. Recognition of the reality of the group's situation follows upon the frustration and leads to the development of new means of satisfaction. A similar march of events may be observed in all treatment processes, often conceptualized as the repetition–compulsion, as the patient runs through a gamut of earlier modes of adaptation which are usually more infantile, passive, and inefficient for purposes of learning and change.

The group process classes as described in this chapter are organized as follows:† Prospective members enroll themselves by agreeing to a verbal contract which specifies time and place of around twenty hour-and-one-half

---

*R. L. Sutherland describes a parallel between infantile psychosexual development and the learning process in a school of psychiatry. He adds, 'But the same *motif* can be seen in any classroom or in the teaching of any new skill' (1951).

†For another explication of this method see Semrad & Arsenian (1951).

meetings, attendance requirements, the taking of minutes, possible work assignments, and the goal of studying the psychology of groups. They meet with a leader whose sole 'teaching' consists of helping them observe what happens under these conditions.*

Surround any group of people by walls, face them with each other and themselves without a clear purpose or task on which to focus, and they become uncomfortable. They turn to the leader for help with their discomfort. He suggests that their first problem is to decide who the recorder of minutes is going to be. Sometimes they perform this task with dispatch by some system such as going in alphabetical order. This done, an uncomfortable silence again falls. Sometimes, with a glance over their shoulder waiting for the leader to step in with a solution, they make work for themselves by flailing away at what seems at times to be an insurmountable problem of deciding how recorders are to be designated. Or, sophisticated and controlled, they solve this and other problems and then join together in a show of camaraderie and unity to take issue with the contract; then the leader asks if they know each other's first names. The banding together is revealed as premature and artificial, and they look to the leader again to lessen the discomfort.

In other educational experiences—early years of life, school, learning special skills—a prominent attitude of the student, often promoted through lectures and rote-memory examinations, is to receive instruction, doing only what work is necessary to digest what is fed. Group members seek to re-instate these familiar and congenial attitudes. They wait expectantly, no matter how busy they may appear. Where are the answers they not only crave but deserve, for they are here, signed up, with tuition paid? Instead of answers they get a contract which makes demands upon them. Or so the contract seems to them, for no matter how non-demanding, how sensible, how like their own desires it is, they attack it. If it specifies punctuality, their wish is to be late; if it requires attendance, they wish to be absent; if it sets forth a particular distribution of minutes, other ways become attractive; if it includes projects or papers for them to do, they are rebellious. The wrong solid food of the contract and its demands is spit out. 'Sooner or later', as one member put it, 'you must give us milk.'

Another theme is sounded: 'If you won't teach us, at least you can help us with our problems.' A meeting falls on a holiday or a member is going to be out of town. Should we meet anyway? Maybe we can meet another day, in

---

*In what follows license has been taken, for purposes of exposition, to present schematically and impressionistically material condensed from a number of groups in the author's experience with psychotherapy groups and teaching groups, in the Menninger School of Psychiatry, Brockton and Boston V. A. Hospitals, Division of Legal Medicine of the Commonwealth of Massachusetts, and Boston University. This illustrative exercise hardly exhausts the many issues and events which occur or the meanings which can be attached to them.

the morning, evening, dawn? Will the leader be there? Or, a persistently silent or truculent or disorganized or helpless member derails their discussion, or provides a screen for projections which make members uncomfortable. Somebody wants to bring a friend to a meeting, or a dog, to shut the blinds or refuse to take minutes. Though these are their problems, they turn to the leader for solutions, blandly disregarding the reality of their own capabilities in favour of hopes for an easy, pleasurable, being-taken-care-of solution.

They revert to another familiar attitude from earlier learning situations—currying favour with the leader. One member thinks: Surely the leader will like me best as I am the brightest one. Other members think: The others are so assertive, surely I'll be the favourite because I am the most tractable. They are treacherous, I am loyal; they are rebellious, I am easy to get along with; they misunderstand the leader, I am his interpreter. Each member wants to be the chosen one. Apparently talking to each other, they are using one another as vehicles to establish themselves with the leader. Notice how they look surreptitiously at the leader while they are ostensibly talking to other members. Under the sway of these wishes, communication at times become chaotic. They misunderstand each other, interrupt each other, forget what each one says. But wanting to be the favoured one with the leader is only half of the story; the other half is anger over persistent frustration by him, so the communication with him, verbally and through the minutes, is also marked by forgetfulness and misunderstanding. People are talking to and for themselves; their efforts, under a pall of disappointment and anxiety, are dispirited and confused.

If the leader will not relieve discomfort, teach them, solve problems for them, or love each one better than the other, then they will love each other. So pairs develop, mother-son, father-daughter, mother-daughter, father-son, brother-brother, brother-sister, each one a reversion to a past unity which now gives in fantasy promise of bringing about matters as they want them. Only the coin of these mergers fits with the present—sharing of smoking equipment, passing of notes, offering intellectual agreement and support. The leader systematically calls attention to these pairings with remarks that invite the members to bring the private exchanges into the common currency of the group. Members react, however, by feeling guilty at having cut off their fellows, and ashamed at the revelations of their liaisons. Though sometimes they hear the leader's remark as a welcome back to the larger group, more often it seems a rap on the knuckles.

This leader is really impossible. We are having a tough time, and it is his fault, so the least he can do is to relax the rules. With disappointment and rebellion they ask for license to enjoy the forbidden.

But what is forbidden? The one set of rules, the contract, has been breached, but all the leader did was point that out; it was some fellow members who expressed outrage and became the enforcers. One action, however, seems increasingly forbidden in the minds of the members. This is independent decision or initiative. The leader says he must leave the next meeting early. Though they are angry at this 'rejection', and mounful at this loss, no one asks where he is going, nor does anyone bring up the possibility of meeting earlier or at another time. When their attention is called to this, they are amazed at the idea of acting with such temerity. 'You didn't say we could', they complain, 'how were we to know'? In the next breath, however, they talk boldly of plans for a variety of independent actions, countermanding in advance the leaders fancied objections. Yet amidst their protestations they hint, then ask for the leader's permission. They seem to have yielded their own capabilities for deciding on right and wrong in favour of a new repository of ethics, the leader; who, to still their guilt, must give some signal that they can be irresponsible as they once were.

The leader, as an agent of a reality which members know but find difficult to acknowledge, becomes in members' eyes an inciter and a spoil-sport. He helps them to observe their patterns of injured social sensibilities, overpoliteness, scholarliness, feigned indifference, and bluster; and he encourages them to see wishes associated with the pleasure principle embedded within these attitudes. At the same time he systematically disappoints these wishes. If he were to ease their discomfort, there would be no need for them to learn how to do so themselves. If he were to solve their problems, their latent skills would fail to emerge. If he were to distribute his affection unequally, all those less favoured would be weighted with an increased burden of resentment and disappointment toward the leader and other members. And the most favoured member would lock himself in place, learning nothing new, as he exploited only those assets which got him to his enviable position. Instead, the leader treats them all with scrupulous equality, encouraging the idea that he is a person who loves them all, equally well. '[Education] makes use of an offer of love as a reward from the educators; and it therefore fails if a spoilt child thinks it possesses that love in any case and cannot lose it whatever happens' (Freud, 1911).

Skins gleam with perspiration, faces redden, lips curl, bodies fidget or slouch. Then physiological discharge becomes channelled into organized patterns. A female, refusing to talk for hours, sits with her legs steadfastly apart, coolly draining off her discomfort through symbolic bodily behaviour. Male and female begin sitting together, or studiously avoiding each other. Seating arrangements are changed, food is brought, members come late or leave early as a rash of 'unavoidable' events develop, and news filters back of paper work undone and sudden flareups with supervisors. But acting-out and acting-up meet with confrontation which aims to bring all events back into the arena of scrutiny, thus reminding them of the group's avowed purpose.

As this egocentric absorption continues to pay such small dividends, members more and more look for what can be done with the social reality around them. They are in a group of people, and carry within them a repertoire of emotionally charged experiences with groups. These begin with the family, extend through childhood gangs and adult professional organizations, achieve ethical stature in the ideal of the brotherhood of man, and often culminate in the fantasy of the children of God reunited in the Heavenly Hosts. So new in-groups hold promise of the satisfactions of the primary group. But an obstacle to the formation of new groups is that everyone continues to feel that others, not oneself, ought to yield. A compromise solution presents itself: If each can find something of himself in the other, they can make common cause without changing anything internally; in fact, each one's opinion of his 'rightness' is more confidently held as it is supported by others; each can go on pleased with himself as always, yet feel that he has achieved tolerant accord with his fellow men. So the group dissolves into boys versus girls, psychologists versus psychiatrists, those loyal to the group and those who question what all this 'groupiness' is about. Unlike the earlier pairing, the new units are larger, more complexly organized within themselves, and united by the common cause which is often buttressed by an intellectualized rationale. At war with non-selves, the several groups mill about, having made a step toward the reality principle of approximately the same magnitude as has been made between nations of the world.

The leader asks, 'How many groups are there now?' which serves to disrupt the new equilibrium. But then he goes on to help the group see that a similar process can be used to form one single, and more powerful, group. All that is necessary is one common cause, and that they all have, the problem of the leader, from whom nobody, and no groups or anybodys, can wring the satisfactions he wants. Individual attacks on him have occurred previously but have been dissipated through the fears of the attacker, or fended off by loyal lieutenants, or inveterate peacemakers. But now the group seems ready to push toward unification around their common problem. Like a clarion call a seemingly innocent quotation finds its way into the discussion: 'The bad that men do lives after them, the good is oft interred with their bones.' The leader asks the source of the quotation. The implications of a funeral oration over the body of the great leader, Caesar, brings anxious titters, but, in this together, they determinedly move ahead.

By turns the leader is criticized as cold, anxious, incompetent; too young or too old, too well-dressed or too informally dressed. When the leader picks up his contractual option of assigning work, there is a climactic and unified outpouring of anger at this unfair and demanding taskmaster. But a curious theme runs through these crashing chords. Notice how the subject of the leader's not appearing for a meeting comes into the discussion, and brings, not joy, but a sudden chill. Furtive eyes search elsewhere for the culprit, each one acting as if he is the one who has driven the leader away. A room full of Hamlets, they vacillate, the hollowness left by attempts at humour being filled with waspish snapping as the entente sags, becomes firm, then buckles again. It seems they want only to fight, but not to win. An *esprit de corpse,* as one recorder's slip of the pen illustrates it, seems not worth the price of guilt over the leader's symbolic murder. Not only is the band of parricidal brothers and sisters ashamed and guilty, but it seems they are looking past the leader's demise to what may lie in store for them. They have noticed how the strong, quick-witted 'assistant' leader fares. As his reward for interpreting the leader's remarks, helping weaker members, cutting down the bully, the obstreperous, the fool, he is driven outside, an alterantive for attacks on the leader, the next candidate for witch hunt and guillotine.

With disdain for consistency the group ceases in its disavowal of the leader's ability to give even bread, to discover they are getting cake. He may not be a teacher, but surely he is a psychotherapist. The goal of learning group dynamics seems far removed as a member blurts out his recognition that he acts towards the leader as he acts toward his father. In a rush of corroborative remarks about this 'gem', magic fills the air, and a surge of gratitude bubbles into locker room camaraderie. Rather than contend with the repercussions of ridding themselves of the leader, they install him as a wise, bountiful saviour. When he asks whether they think 'gems are a group's best friend', they are hurt and bewildered. But, though sullen and reluctant, they start again to flex their growing psychic muscles.

A piece of reality, hitherto overlooked, is discovered. They are able not only to make changes in defiance but with zest and exploration. Undeviating seating arrangements change, fluctuating ones become fixed, the colour of the paper on which minutes are typed becomes shocking orange, there is talk of altering the format of the minutes, and the traditionally silent recorder speaks. Members report they feel different toward the leader; he is less 'blanked out', more of a person. These strengthening exercises prepare them for the moment of truth when they are faced with making a major decision independent of the leader; let's say, to change a meeting time. To the extent that this decision is either a blustering rebellion or a sour alternative to the hope that the leader will step in and make it for them, they work fitfully, openly or covertly turning to the leader for acquiescence. To the extent that the decision is a response to the pull of present problems which requires present adaptive solutions, they make it independent of the leader. To the latter extent they achieve an emotional climax of satisfaction with a job well-done, of newness, and discovery. It is an achievement that stands them in good stead as yet a new piece of reality intrudes—they are approaching the end of the allotted life of the group.

Someone mentions the imminence of the group's ending. A heavy moment of silence ensues. A member adds he is going away and must miss the last meeting of the group. This time there is not talk of contract, injured feelings, or attack. Instead, long silences alternate with busy checking of dates and schedules. In trying to remember the originally stipulated number of meetings they accidentally add one more meeting to the total. And they recall the date of the last meeting as a week later than the one which appears on the calendar. They talk of extending the life of the group; if not with the leader then by themselves. As they leave the meeting they are bunched in solemn procession. The next meeting opens in a careening series of dialogues, witticisms bright and sharp which click through the air, hurried along by crackles of laughter. But as the tempo slows, then lurches, the leader asks what their feelings are, and the jerry-built denial collapses.

'Who needs him anyway?' is the theme as the leader is steadfastly ignored. Members move their chairs so that their back is turned toward him. He tries to speak, but someone always launches a comment before the leader can get under way. He asks, 'Does anyone besides me feel I am being left out?' Members turn back sheepishly, and in the ensuing discussion recognize they have tried to leave the leader rather than suffer the blow of his leaving them.

Sour grapes yields to a request for heartier fare. Discussion is organized around requests that, with the end in sight, the leader give up his accustomed role as a teacher of group process and give them something real such as a lecture on group process. Though earlier in the group's life they have systematically 'forgotten' the contract, the one piece of information directly given them, and though they ignore the possibilities for learning in the work assignment of writing their own view of topics related to the group, they insist it is learning that they want.

Is it still the small child talking, asking for implicit approval through a reward, or for a magic word that will ease the tension and erase the problems in a twinkling? Is this request only another means of denying the ending? There may be some of all these possibilities in it, for the reality principle does not dethrone the pleasure principle but rather safeguards it. And what reality is not determined in part by unceasing influence from the past? But perhaps they want something of the leader to take away with them, less as a talisman of faith that they will be kept secure than as an investment in themselves. This is what they say. They want a lecture and discussion in order to become better group therapists. They want to learn the meanings of material over which they have puzzled. They want to check their own impressions against those of the leader. They want to take his bag of tricks as their own. And they must somehow be right in this because their fellows feel the same way. They know this because they have learned to listen and hear each other, and, give or take some differences, they really are not bad fellows after all, and often have useful ideas. Further, they have a right to this information: for the leader is one of them, and they feel a claim on one another.

But if they want mastery over the present, using the tools available from the present, and want to avoid the loss of the leader by being like him, the leader's work is already mostly done. By taking him away as part of themselves, they have become stronger antagonists to loss and frustration. They have taken the best there was to be had, and, in the process, have learned much of what there was to learn.

Is this education or is it therapy? As an educational device, the group was encouraged to develop its adaptive functions in order to gain mastery (shift reliance from the pleasure principle to the reality principle) and to observe how, under these conditions, this happens. 'Education can be described without more ado as an incitement to the conquest of the pleasure principle. . .' (Freud, 1911). This, too, is a means by which therapy proceeds. The distinctions are more meaningful, it seems to me, in regard to goals, techniques, and the relative amount of emphasis paid to content and process. The principles are the same.

SUMMARY

Group process training classes have become of interest to psychiatry for the insights they offer to group psychotherapists, and for the opportunity they provide for all clinicians to learn experientially data otherwise available only in the abstract. These classes provide a terrain in which group and individual psychotherapy, group dynamics, and education meet without fixed borders. Despite manifest differences, institutionalized by disparate professions, a developmental process is assumed to be intrinsic to all of these disciplines, a process which can profitably be understood by the same means one understands individual psychological development. An attempt is made to view a series of trial adaptations of students in a course in group process training from the standpoint of Freud's pleasure and reality principles.

ACKNOWLEDGEMENTS

For critical reading of the manuscript and helpful suggestions I am grateful to Drs Ann Appelbaum, Riley W. Gardner, and Martin Mayman of The Menninger Foundation, and John Arsenian of Boston State Hospital.

REFERENCES

Berman, L. (1953). A group psychotherapeutic technique for training in clinical psychology. *Amer. J. Orthopsychiat.* **22**, 322.

Ekstein, R. & Wallerstein, R. S. (1958). *The Teaching and Learning of Psychotherapy.* New York: Basic Books, Inc.

Frank, J. D. (1963). *Theories of T-Group Training, National Training Laboratories.* (In the Press.)

Freud, S. (1911). Formulations on the two principles of mental functioning. In *Standard Edition,* Vol. 12 (1958). London: Hogarth.

Freud, S. (1921) Group psychology and the analysis of the ego. In *Standard Edition,* Vol. 8 (1955). London: Hogarth.

Richfield, J. (1954). An analysis of the concept of insight. *Psychoanal. Quart.* **23**, 390.

Semrad, E. & Arsenian, J. (1951). The use of group process in teaching group dynamics. *Amer. J. Psychiat.* **108**, 358.

Sutherland, R. L. (1951). An application of the theory of psychosexual development to the learning process. *Bull. Menninger Clin.* **15**, 91.

13

The Kennedy Assassination and the Oedipal Struggles of a Training Group

Stephen A. Appelbaum
The Menninger Foundation
Topeka, Kansas

[The intensely guilty emotional reactions of the members of a t-group during a meeting following the assassination of President Kennedy suggest to Appelbaum a phylogenetic hypothesis very much in line with Freud's original primal horde conception. He thus proposes that unstructured laboratory groups—and perhaps other forms of groups as well—relive in their own contemporary interactive behavior a primitive historical experience (the violent revolt of the brothers against the tyrannical primal father). Ontogenetic factors, too, such as the phallic–oedipal dynamics valent at the time are seen as influencing the group's movement toward an active revolt against the leader.]

A group dynamics class, convened for twenty meetings to study the psychology of groups through the method of observing itself, met for the ninth time two weeks after the death of President Kennedy. That meeting was spent in mourning, but with the leader of the group rather than the President the object of the members' feelings of loss, guilt, anger and fear. Even

Reprinted from *The Psychoanalytic Review*, Vol. 53, No. 3, 1966, through the courtesy of the Editors and the Publisher, National Psychological Association for Psychoanalysis, New York, N.Y., under the title "The Kennedy Assissination."

I am grateful to Dr. Martin Mayman of the Menninger Foundation for his helpful comments, and to the participants in the events described, especially to Dr. Lawrence Sack, who wrote the notes from which quotations are taken.

between patient and individual psychotherapist, such an early intense emotional involvement would not be expected. Its seemingly premature occurrence between student-psychiatrists and their teacher–group leader requires an explanation and offers an opportunity for increased understanding of group process and its relationship to psychoanalysis.

In *Group Psychology and the Analysis of the Ego,*[8] Freud suggests that a group comes about through identification of the members with one another, based upon an emotional tie with the leader. In *Totem and Taboo*[5] he suggests that the emotional tie is a legacy from the prehistoric killing of the leader–father by the band of brothers in order to break the father's sexual monopoly, and that this fateful act, followed by remorse and penitential renunciation of parricide and incest, supplies a basis for the group living which we call the family.

Along with Freud's other ideas concerned with applied psychoanalysis, the *Totem and Taboo hypothesis* is a source of lively disagreement. It professes to explain events otherwise unaccounted for by more parsimonious and more easily verifiable constructs. As an alleged historical occurrence which bears a possibly significant relation to the present, it carries a social and historical obligation.

Eissler writes, "As long as there is a shred of possible truth in the belief that the psychoanalysis of a people, by unearthing the unconscious factors at work in their history, may bring mastery to them, and lead to the sort of action that guarantees preservation, that possible truth ought to be pursued by means of intensive research."[3] How can such an investigation be pursued? Archaeological and anthropological studies provide one approach to the necessarily indirect test of the primal horde hypothesis. Observation of the behavior of animals, the psychoanalysis of individuals, as well as the behavior of groups may be other, quasi-independent sources of confirmation.

Group dynamics classes, or training groups, are designed explicitly to facilitate observing patterns and forces implicit in group formation and group behavior. This is done primarily by minimizing the structure ordinarily created by active leadership, schedules of production, and rules of procedure which ordinarily tend to obscure the dynamics of the group. These classes are structured for the most part to the limited extent of specifying the goal of studying the psychology of groups, agreements regarding time and attendance, and sometimes the taking of minutes or other work assignments. Rather than teaching didactically, the leader tries to dispel resistance to group formation and development and to promote understanding through introspection.

The eighth meeting of one of these training groups took place on Thursday, November 21, 1964, the day before the assassination of the President. Most of this meeting was devoted to the question of whether the group should meet the following Thursday, which was Thanksgiving. All other professional activities for that day had been cancelled except those necessary duties associated with day-to-day patient care, so some readers may find it strange that the group could have seriously considered meeting on a legal holiday. It is a testimonial to the quick and intense regressive pull in unstructured groups that logic and convention are so easily put aside under the pressure of transference thoughts and feelings. In this instance the members seemed to feel that the leader would look with favor on their meeting despite the holiday, and with disfavor on their not meeting. Members were torn between wishes to have a holiday and the discomfort of the leader's fantasied disapproval. The "danger" to any one of them of earning the leader's enmity could be minimized by his having allies; the safest solution of all would be to have unanimous agreement that there should not be a meeting. As noted in *Totem and Taboo,* "acts which are illegal to an individual . . . can only be justified when the whole clan shares the responsibility of the deed."[5] So the members of the group moved from the initial scrupulous interpretations of "the rules," and jockeying for favor with the leader, to a new intensity of friendliness and warmth in their feelings for each other. The group's recorder noted in his minutes, "More laughter and less hostility . . . more even participation of all members than previously . . . greater meaning in intragroup relationships . . ." Only thus united, it seemed, could they overcome their fear and decide that despite what I thought, it was all right to miss a week's meeting. This mundane decision, presented to me in seemingly innocent harmony, masked an underlying defiance and rebellion. The purpose which they held in common, and around which they had implicitly organized, was the wish to depose the leader entirely. In the language of the *Totem and Taboo* hypothesis, they had banded together for parricide. The next day the President was assassinated.

In describing the following meetings, two weeks later, I shall excerpt (in italics) from notes taken by the group's member–recorder, expanding on them from memory and from notes which I customarily jot down after each meeting.

The thoughtful and moderately lengthy report was read and received without the usual concern, and comments were confined to a few detached words on whether the laughter of the previous meeting was "nervous" or "real." They were unusually quiet. The first explanation which they offered for this quietness was the difficulty in getting started again after a long break. Then a member mentioned it was the end of the term in the School of Psychiatry, and this meant termination notes on patients and evaluative notes on themselves. "Ending is in the air," said one. This led to the memory that at the last meeting, during the discussion of whether to meet on Thanksgiving, sad reference had been made to the ending of the group. (It was, as you remember, only the eighth of twenty meetings.) At this point one of the female members disclosed that her father had recently died.

I remember noting all these references to separation and loss, and considering the possible relationship to the President's death, but remained unconvinced until the assassination was brought up explicitly, the comment

introducing it being, "a lot of history has gone on since we last met." During
the discussion which followed, they mentioned the similarity between leaders
of any kind and fathers, "if you believe in psychoanalytic theory." One
member made the slip of calling President Kennedy, *Doctor* Kennedy." They
seemed to recognize the metaphorical implications in regard to myself, and I
wondered whether this transference discovery would block or encourage the
development of the theme. It proved to be a precursor of much work to be
done.

   *The initial polite and slightly anxious climate gave way to a mood of
depression and apathy. The introduction of the subject of the assassination of
the President deepened the gloom . . . a mournful succession of comments . . . the group's mournful attitude.* Several members wore black or
nearly black ties. A young woman member failed to wear lipstick. The
conversation was halting. Attempts at levity fell flat. It was a heavy, labored
atmosphere, thick with gloom.

   *. . . Collective expression of guilt . . . in which individual expressions of
hostility toward others, particularly authority figures, was taboo. . . . Many
members were struggling with Doctor Appelbaum as an object of their
aggression . . . Expression and even acknowledgement of these feelings* [was]
much less acceptable than before.

   Much attention was paid to the assertion that everyone was to blame for
the President's death because of their participation in a society which indulged
naked aggression. As one member put it, "It was the fault of our social
structure." At this point there were downcast eyes and sideways looks. These
suggested to me that this member's assertion was less an indictment of the
nation than an implicit recognition of something about the social context of
group and leader which had brought them to this sorry moment.

   They reported worrying that the assassin could just as easily have been
one of their own patients to whom they had given a weekend pass. Often,
they said, they had misgivings about giving freedom to patients who had poor
control over their impulses. To me, it seemed that "the patients" stood for
their own impulses which they were sorry they had allowed some freedom.
They corroborated this impression by saying expressly, "It doesn't pay for us
to express anger."

   *The group became concerned with Doctor Appelbaum's health and noisily
laughed at assurances that he wasn't in danger.* One member revealed that he
had been driving behind me and that I seemed to have been in danger by the
way I had made a turn in the path of oncoming traffic. This observation was
not easily laid to rest, several times being referred to and embroidered. "Please
drive more carefully," someone said.

   The guilt implicit in this concern for my wellbeing was traced to their
previous anger with me. They at first debated briefly whether any of them
had ever really been angry with me, though in previous meetings they had
acknowledged unmistakable evidences of such anger. Denial of anger shifted to

an acknowledgement of how put out they were with me because of a questionnaire I had asked them to fill out at the first meeting (for research purposes). It seemed easier for them to admit being angry in response to something unpleasant which I had, in fact, inflicted upon them, than to acknowledge that the aggression stemmed in the first place from within themselves. Eventually, however, they achieved a consensus that at the last meeting they had indeed been defiantly united against me without my having done anything to deserve it.

The mourning process seemed partially successful, and toward the end of the meeting group members showed an increased ability to express hostile feelings to one another.

I remember thinking at several points that the group's mourning work was proceeding sufficiently well so that they might be able to go on to other matters. Such was not the case. It seemed that beyond the expression and working through of loss, worry, and guilt, there was a need to remain penitentially uncomfortable for the rest of the session. I finally suggested, when someone mentioned how unrelentingly sad the mood was, that they seemed to think that a great crime required a great penance. Toward the end of the meeting, when they briefly attacked fellow members, I attempted to redirect the anger toward myself by asking whether these digs at one another were diversions of their feeling that it was I who was to blame for the continued discomfort of this meeting (as mourners are angry at the deceased for "causing" so much pain.) They denied this. Possibly the denial was a continuation of their fear of acknowledging anger toward me. My impression, however, was that the denial, in an important respect, was accurate. They were constrained to carp at each other in order to advertise that the unity which had produced a disaster was no more. At the same time they could punish one another. In a way it seemed they appreciated the opportunity to "pay up" their conscience so as to be freed for further assertiveness. As the recorder put it, *The group members thanked the leader for indulging their masochistic needs...*

The two members who persisted in denying any morbid preoccupations were withdrawn and appeared uncomfortable.

Ordinarily groups proceed as in a dialectic, each thesis evoking an antithesis, before it can successfully discharge its tension. Two members, who had kept aloof throughout, and who tended to view the group's behavior in hyper-realistic terms so as to avoid emotional participation, had "expressed" their disagreement through silence. Finally, one of them ridiculed the group's immersion in sadness, worry, and taking me so seriously as an object of their feelings. I wondered to myself whether the group might be embarrassed by this hyper-masculine "tough-minded" attack by their colleague. They responded, however, with reiterations of their belief in what they had been experiencing. That this attack on the group was only another mode of defense against the feelings and reactions dealt with more openly by the others, was suggested by two remarks addressed to me by one of the dissenters before the official beginning of this meeting. He called attention to my arrival with, "You just made it on time." (Was he worried I might not be there? Was this attack on me designed to cover his fear?) He added, "We one-upped you this morning–we had a lecture [on group dynamics and group psychotherapy*] and now we know what's going on." (Was he telling me, in addition, that they needn't worry about my demise because I had outlived my usefulness?)

The impact of this meeting was, perhaps, best summed up by the recorder's comment that my interjected remarks *served as the army drum in the President's funeral procession to punctuate the mournful succession of comments signifying guilt and fear of aggression.*

DISCUSSION

The question posed by these events was: how can one understand such an intense mourning reaction directed at the teacher–leader in a classroom–group, especially when one would not ordinarily expect such a reaction as early as the ninth hour even in the potentially more personal one-to-one relationship of individual psychotherapy?

To those workers who allow and observe its emergence, the potential for quick, intense emotional arousal in groups, despite the seeming handicaps that members may be strangers to each other or enrolled as students, is well-known. To say that this is the nature of groups is merely to describe. The "nature," according to Freud[5,8,9] is the group's emotional, if not phylogenetic, duplication of the Oedipal situation. That is, the Oedipus complex arises in a family group situation which in some respects resembles the primal group. In the absence of structure which might maintain repression, or might obscure preconscious trends, people in a group always tend to feel themselves subordinates to somebody or something as an authority, and to play out in this situation aspects of the emotional patterns of the Oedipal configuration, along with many of its pre-Oedipal antecedents.

In previous papers this writer[1,2] offered an analysis of group development as a progression through infantile psycho-sexual stages, conceptualized as the shift from the pleasure to reality principles. Ordinarily, these developments show a back-and-forth, though steadily more mature, progression. The meeting before the assassination was an early, relatively timid experimentation with rebellion and deposition of the leader, probably influenced by oral-aggressive and anal aggressive issues prominent at the time. Full-blown phallic–Oedipal modes of attack usually occur only near the end of the series of meetings, and can be recognized by vivid imagery and themes (e.g., attacking bulls, references to my wife, quotation from the funeral oration over Caesar), and

---

*Seminars on group process are scheduled to follow the group dynamics experience. This lecture was independent of that teaching series.

spirited attack (e.g., "Why should we take notes anyway?" "He's wearing a clashing tie and shirt," "Where does that arrogant psychologist get off thinking he can teach psychiatrists?"). The present paper offers an instance of overwhelmingly stimulating external events bringing about the hurried cathexis of a phallic–Oedipal organization. The result was a confluence of experiences thrust on them by the present, aroused from their past, and expressed in the transference.

The role of women in such groups offers a further delineation of the Oedipal theme.* My tentative impression is that women tend to seek a protective haven of favoritism with the leader. Their anger with him seems more likely to come from what they feel is a "rejection" when evidence of favoritism or love is not forthcoming. The more psychologically feminine a woman the more easily she slips into this role; the more masculine her identification the more she tends to resist this role or even side openly with the rebellious "brothers." (This crude generalization, of course, fails to describe many styles of behavior; for example, an inhibited woman resists these and other roles without its implying much about her sexual identity.) At those moments when the group has achieved sufficient coherence and strength to mount a vigorous phallic attack on the leader, women in the group seem to become more seductively sexual; they wear more make-up and dress better. At such times seemingly extraneous references to sex find their way into the discussion. Before one meeting whose major theme was getting along without me and my "gimmicks," a member brought a magazine to the group and displayed suggestive pictures of women. During that meeting the group referred for the first time to the fact that it had only one woman member; it discussed sex instruction, made biblical allusions to death and reincarnation, and in reference to the attacks on me, one member asked, "Does there have to be a murder before there can be a birth?" For what this observation may be worth for comparative purposes, I have at such times noticed in myself an openness toward appreciation of the female students as sexual women.

One can say that all these data are accounted for by the familiar ontogenetic-transference understanding of the workings of the Oedipus complex, that what are replayed in unstructured groups are erotic and aggressive experiences originally occurring in the matrix of the family group. Reference to phylogenetic constructs, as in the *Totem and Taboo* hypothesis, would therefore be unnecessary. Hartmann[10] writes that though phylogenetic constructs may be valuable as a source of clues, they are of doubtful value in leading to a system of hypotheses resting on empirical verification.

Freud too, was cognizant of the need for such verification: ". . . I regard it as a methodological error to seize on a phylogenetic explanation before the

---

*All of the groups of this kind that I have observed have had a minority of women members; other workers might report different observations in groups dominated by women.

ontogenetic possibilities have been exhausted." Nonetheless, he forthrightly declared, in the same passage, "I fully agree with Jung in recognizing the existence of this phylogenetic heritage . . ."[7]

Though this assertion has been repudiated by many analysts since Freud, it is not easily laid to rest. One reason is the observation of those dream symbols whose universal meaning is regularly corroborated in psychoanalysis but which yield few personal associations, e.g., hat = phallus. It is as if these symbols stem from a memory system independent of life experience. Relevant to this point are the various philological and psycholinguistic studies demonstrating that words are carriers of universal meanings, transcending present-day cultures and languages.[12] And having once traced behavior to the Oedipus complex, are we not obliged to consider what the pre-history of the Oedipus complex itself may be? Why should there be a family organization as we know it? Why the prohibition against incest? Is the model of instincts played out upon the environment in itself sufficient to explain the intensity of Oedipal fantasies, even in families where, as far as one can tell, threats and seductions are minimal?

Freud faced these issues in his discussion of primal fantasies; "the individual," he said, "reaches beyond his own experience into primeval experience at points where his own experience has been too rudimentary. It seems to me quite possible that all the things that are told to us today in analysis as fantasy—the seduction of children, the inflaming of sexual excitement by observing parental intercourse, the threat of castration (or rather castration itself)—were once real occurrences in the primeval times of the human family, and that children in their fantasies are simply filling in the gaps in individual truth with prehistoric truth."[6]

This issue comes forth in regard to unstructured groups as one attempts to account for the quickness and intensity of emergence of the gamut of Oedipal behaviors regularly observed. Ordinarily, similar issues arise so flagrantly in individual psychotherapy only after time-consuming lifting of repressions.

Further, the dramatic coalescing of members when the phallic struggle is at its height, with its requirement of unanimity if the attack is to be strong and concerted, seems to have little in common with the infantile experiences of most people. The individual, caught up in his ambivalence toward the father over love for the mother (or vice versa in its inverted form), rather than seeking unity and comradeship, feels himself locked into a lonely struggle for separate relationships. As Freud pointed out in *Group Psychology and the Analysis of the Ego*,[8] it is only the inhibition of such one-to-one sexual aims which makes group formation possible. One may claim that the experience of aim-inhibited group formation is learned from latency onward as part of the solution of the Oedipal conflicts, and that this development forms the basis for Oedipal resurgence in the training groups. But, in the early period of group development noted here, it is ordinarily the infantile, pregenital experience which is duplicated. If there is insufficient basis in past environmental experience to explain these events, it would seem justified to consider the hypothesis of the band of brothers, with its supporting evidence from anthropology and sociology.[5] As Freud[6,7] points out, it need not be an "either-or" problem. The emotional configurations may be activated not only because they are spurred by a person's early experience but also as if they were a tropism from antiquity.

If one were to embrace the *Totem and Taboo* hypothesis as a theoretical construct, one would be likely to embrace, also, a series of anthropological, genetic, historical, as well as psychological postulates. One would probably want to subscribe to such statements as that of Pirenne: "History is in its essential aspect continuity ... that proceeds from generation to generation without man's being capable of escaping therefrom and which therefore connects our times with the most distant epochs,"[11] and with that of Freud's in *The Interpretation of Dreams*: "Behind this childhood of the individual we are promised a picture of phylogenetic childhood—a picture of the development of the human race, of which the individual's development is in fact an abbreviated recapitulation influenced by the chance circumstances of life ... Dreams and neuroses [neuroses in this passage refers not to a clinical entity, but to unconscious motivation] seem to have preserved more mental antiquities than we could have imagined possible; so that psychoanalysis may claim a high place among the sciences which are concerned with the reconstruction of the earliest and most obscure periods of the beginnings of the human race."[4] One might subscribe also to the "assumption of a collective mind, which makes it possible to neglect the interruptions of mental acts caused by the extinction of the individual ..."[5] and entertain the notion that a part of the problem of the transmission of psychological disposition ... "seems to be met by the inheritance of psychical disposition ..."[5] or through subliminal learning: "... no generation is able to conceal any of its more important mental processes from its successor. For psychoanalysis has shown us that everyone possesses in his unconscious mental activity an apparatus which enables him to interpret other people's reaction, that is, to undo the distortions which other people have imposed on the expression of their feelings. An unconscious understanding such as this of all the customs, ceremonies and dogmas left behind by the original relation to the father may have made it possible for later generations to take over their heritage of emotion."[5]

I anticipate the objection that either phylogenetic, ontogenetic, or transference explanations are a less parsimonious approach to explain the data described here than the simple explanation that most people, meeting as individuals or groups for the first time after such an event, would feel a need to share reactions. To my mind, it is just this universality and depth of feeling, so apparent on that fateful weekend, that requires a psychological explanation. Shorn of his fantasy implications, John Kennedy the man was, after all, personally unknown to the population at large, doing a job that affected people socially, politically, and economically and not always to the mourner's satisfaction. Specifically, in regard to this group's reaction, by the time of the described meeting two weeks after the fact, each of the members had been through a number of such discussions and mournings. One might have expected them again to touch on the subject, but I thought they felt constrained—far more than one would expect in the ordinary run of events—to "work through" what was initially an unconscious representation of those events.

REFERENCES

1. Appelbaum, S. A. The Pleasure and Reality Principles in Group Process Teaching. *British Journal of Medical Psychology*, Vol. 36, 1963. pp. 49–56.
2. _____. An Application of Group Psychology to International Relations. *In Press*.
3. Eissler, K. Freud and the Psychoanalysis of History. *Journal of the American Psychoanalytic Association*, Vol. 11, 1963. pp. 675–703.
4. Freud, S. The Interpretation of Dreams (1900). *Standard Edition of the Complete Psychological Works of Sigmund Freud*, Vols. 4 and 5, London: Hogarth Press, 1953.
5. _____. *Totem and Taboo* (1913). *Ibid.*, Vol. 13, 1955.
6. _____. *Introductory Lectures on Psychoanalysis* (1916). *Ibid.*, Vol. 16, 1963.
7. _____. *From the History of an Infantile Neurosis* (1918). *Ibid.*, Vol. 17, 1955.
8. _____. *Group Psychology and the Analysis of the Ego* (1922). *Ibid.*, Vol. 18, 1955.
9. _____. *Civilization and its Discontents* (1930). *Ibid.*, Vol. 21, 1961.
10. Hartmann, H. Some Comments on the Formation of Psychic Structure. *Psychoanalytic Study of the Child*, Vol. 2, New York: International Universities Press, 1946.
11. Pirenne, J. Des origines a' l'Islam. *Les grands Courants de l'Histoire Universelle*, Vol. 1, 3rd ed. Neuchatel, Editions de la Baconniere. Paris: Albin Michel, 1945.
12. Thass-Thienemann, T. Psychotherapy and Psycholinguistics. *Topic. Probl. Psychother.*, Vol. 4, 1963. pp. 37–54.

14

Notes on Freud's "Primal Horde" Concept and its Relevance for Contemporary Group Psychoanalysis

Morton Kissen
Institute of Advanced Psychological Studies
Adelphi University
Garden City, Long Island, New York

[An updating of Freud's classical group psychological conception of the primal horde is offered via an integration of that concept with contemporary ego psychology and an ontogenetic, rather than phylogenetic, theoretical structure. Examples of the occurence of primal-horde-like rebellions in a variety of unstructured and structured groups are presented. The primal horde phenomenon is seen as an essential process facilitating both necessary group developmental shifts and therapeutic gains. A number of empirically testable hypotheses are suggested for future group dynamic and group psychoanalytic research.]

Many of Freud's group psychological conceptions have been integrated into modern group psychotherapy theory and practice. Thus, a number of authors (Kissen, 1974; Scheidlinger, 1968) have updated and extensively studied concepts such as identification and regression. Their relationship to contemporary group psychology is assumed to be one of great significance and is seldom questioned.

However, the primal horde hypothesis developed in Freud's classical group psychological writings (1918/1946, 1922/1965) has not had a similarly respectable history. Despite its relevance to group psychotherapy and psycho-analysis, it has seldom been seriously treated either clinically or theoretically in the recent group psychotherapy literature. The writings of Appelbaum (1963, 1966, 1967), who has clearly taken Freud's primal horde hypothesis quite seriously as an explanatory principle capable of illuminating certain dynamic trends observed in unstructured laboratory groups, are a noteworthy exception.

In this chapter an attempt will be made both to explore conceptually the original primal horde notion and to describe a number of group process phenomena that seem to logically require such a hypothetical construction. In contrast to Freud's emphasis on phylogenetic conjecture and mythologizing, an ego psychological conceptual model will be utilized to explain the primal-horde-like phenomenon that is repeatedly observed in a variety of unstructured and structured laboratory group situations. The relevance of such a phenomenon for a modern group psychoanalytic treatment approach will be touched upon, and hypotheses for future group dynamic research will be mentioned.

FREUD'S ORIGINAL PRIMAL
HORDE CONCEPTION

Freud (1918/1946) hypothesizes that at one time in history there existed a social grouping in which a horde of brothers were governed in a highly authoritarian fashion by a father who totally controlled and overpowered them and restricted their sexual pleasures. In elaborating upon this hypothesis, he states,

> The Darwinian conception of the primal horde does not, of course, allow for the beginning of totemism. There is only a violent, jealous father who keeps all the females for himself and drives away the growing sons. . . . One day the expelled brothers joined forces, slew and ate the father, and thus put an end to the father horde. Together they dared and accomplished what would have remained impossible for them singly. Perhaps some advance in culture, like the use of a new weapon, had given them the feeling of superiority. Of course, these cannibalistic savages ate their victim. This violent primal father had surely been the envied and feared model for each of the brothers. Now they ac-complished their identification with him by devouring him and each acquired a part of his strength. (pp. 182–183)

Freud had a way of presenting provocative and controversial hypotheses in such a pictorially vivid and graphic fashion that they take hold upon the mind of the reader, often with greater clarity and definiteness than Freud meant to convey. There is no doubt that his conceptualization of the dynamics underlying the oedipal conflict was in many ways interwoven within the fabric of this early account of a possible historical event that has left its imprint upon subsequent group psychology. Concepts such as castration anxiety, repressed sexualized oedipal longings, and displacement—helpful in explicating the dynamics of phobic and hysterical neuroses—are clearly related to this historical account of the origins of totemism and incest taboos.

In Freud's later writing on this subject (1922/1965), he is more circumspect and careful to emphasize the fact that he is merely elaborating on a suggestive hypothesis and not a firm conviction. He also emphasizes, however, that human groups often seem to demonstrate some of the characteristics of the primal horde:

> Human groups exhibit once again the familiar picture of an individual of superior strength among a troop of equal companions, a picture which is also contained in our idea of the primal horde. . . . Thus the group appears to us as a revival of the primal horde. Just as primitive man survives potentially in every individual, so the primal horde may arise once more out of any random collection. (pp. 69–70).

There can be no doubt that Freud harbored an at least partial phylogenetic assumption with regard to the causal basis of the primal horde phenomenon. He did not utilize merely the readily available ontogenetic hypothesis such as his conceptualizations of the oedipus complex, but rather took a huge speculative leap into the nebulous domain of phylogenetic theorizing. His later concept of the primal horde nature of groups seemed less tied to ontogenetic assumptions than did his earlier speculations, which were inferentially related to his notions of the dynamics of the oedipus complex. In his final statements on this matter, he had opted for the more complex (and certainly less empirically verifiable) phylogenetic explanation.

Appelbaum (1966), after exploring some of the group dynamics occurring in an unstructured laboratory group, came to a similarly strong phylogenetic conclusion:

> Further, the dramatic coalescing of members when the phallic struggle is at its height, with its requirement of unanimity if the attack is to be strong and concerted, seems to have little in common with the infantile experiences of most people. . . . If there is insufficient basis in past environmental experience to explain these events, it would seem justified to consider the hypothesis of the band of brothers, with its supporting evidence from anthropology and sociology. As Freud points out, it need not be an "either-or" problem. The emotional configurations may be activated not only because they are spurred by a person's early experience, but also as if they were a tropism from antiquity. (p. 402)

Thus, although he does not completely rule out ontogenetic possibilities, Appelbaum does not seem very convinced that they are the heart of the matter. He describes certain ways in which the typical group situation differs from both the preoedipal and oedipal historical experiences of the individual members, and he offers a number of sociological, historical, and psychological postulates that make the phylogenetic explanation of the primal horde phenomenon seem more tenable.

THE CENTRALITY OF THE LEADER IN THE PRIMAL HORDE THEORY

Freud's conception of group psychology was far from a democratic one. On the contrary, he envisioned a group of peers almost totally dependent upon and under the domination of a rather harsh and autocratic leader. His concretely pictorial image of the primal horde led by a domineering and controlling father figure had a strong impact on his group psychological theorizing. He states in *Group Psychology and an Analysis of the Ego* (1922/1965), "Many equals, who can identify themselves with one another, and a single person superior to them all—that is the situation that we find realized in groups which are capable of subsisting" (p. 68).

Freud held the notion that groups are at least partially welded together as a result of their strong and quasihypnotic attachment to a highly charismatic leader. The psychology of the leader is completely different from that of the members. The leader is a completely narcissistic figure whose real and fantasied physical and psychological attributes exert a powerful attraction and influence on the peer group members.

Despite charismatic tendencies, however, the leader is also viewed in more adaptive terms as an expert problem-solver who is potentially capable of resolving all the dilemmas that seem so frustratingly difficult for the group members. In discussing this aspect of group leadership, Appelbaum (1967) notes

> Leadership may be provided by a single person, a collection of persons, an idea, or under certain circumstances, a piece of work. The unifying attribute of leadership is that it provides a focus (goal, challenge, support, fear) common to all members. To Freud's (1921) comment, "It is impossible to grasp the nature of a group if its leader is disregarded", may be added the assumption that in all groups there is an impulse towards finding leadership. . . . The impulse towards leadership is fueled by the need to solve problems. Thus, it is no surprise that leaders come to the fore in time of stress; that is, when problems accumulate. A leader (letting the single word stand for all kinds of leadership) must have, or seem to have, power; that is, a leader emerges when the wish to have problems solved is joined by the belief that he is powerful enough to solve them. (p. 382)

Such an adaptive viewpoint softens Freud's rather harsh and autocratic description of the primal horde leader. It nevertheless does not depict a leader as a democratic figure whose influence and impact on group functioning is an only minimal one. The leader remains the central figure of the group, the one whose influence is always felt, even when she or he is behaving in an outwardly nondirective and passive manner.

The writings of Kurt Lewin (1943) emphasizing the powerfulness of "democratic" group processes have greatly influenced a number of modern contributions to the group psychological and therapeutic literature. Autocratic or excessively charismatic leadership techniques, according to the Lewinian theoretical position, are not as effective in influencing and changing group opinion as are more democratic leadership styles that allow the group itself to utilize peer discussion and consensual validation to come to a joint decision with regard to an important issue. Bion's notion of the "work group" (1959) would appear to stem at least partially from Lewin's field theoretical conceptualizations. One contemporary approach to group psychotherapy stresses the factor of peer interaction as being the most essential element in contributing to therapeutic gains by the group members (Goldberg, 1976). Such democratic approaches to group dynamics clearly stem from a theoretical base quite different than the Freudian one discussed here.

The marked contrast between the Freudian conception of group leadership, particularly as derived from the primal horde theory, and the Lewinian approach can best be described in terms of the difference between a leader-centered (Freudian) and a group-centered (Lewinian) approach to group management. But matters are not quite that simple. From a group dynamics standpoint the issue of leadership is quite complex. Leadership style is confounded with the issue of leadership itself in the process of most groups that have a designated leader. Thus, no matter how democratic a leader is in terms of basic personality style, the potential for a primal-horde-like atmosphere exists in many groups, whether structured or unstructured, therapeutic or nontherapeutic. Indeed, this chapter will develop the idea that the occurrence and ultimate working through of a primal horde group dynamic can facilitate a group's emotional growth and democratic problem-solving capacity. Therapeutic gains can also be derived from such a working-through process.

The first task, however, is to demonstrate the empirical face validity of the primal horde phenomenon in a variety of structured and unstructured group situations.

EXAMPLES OF PRIMAL-HORDE-LIKE GROUP REACTIONS

Bennis, in an important group dynamics paper (1961), described the reactions of unstructured laboratory group members to a number of sessions from which the leader had to be absent. Taped process recordings of sessions at which the leader was present were compared with those he did not attend.

The leader is described as an eminent group psychoanalyst in the Boston area, and his absence clearly had a solidly dynamic impact on the thematic content of group discussions. Bennis describes the heavily leader-oriented preoccupations of the members (evident in the symbolic content of group dreams and free associations) as well as a variety of defensive maneuvers they used in an attempt to camouflage latent feelings and concerns over the leader's absence.

Although Bennis focuses largely on certain defenses against depressive anxiety in an unstructured group, his study would appear to relate to the primal horde phenomenon. It can be inferred that the leader's absence partially contributed to the stirring up of the typical primal horde group rebellion with a number of members attempting to usurp the leader's role and replace him via their own clearly identificatory interpretive activities. The attempt by some of the members to establish an effective leaderless group (although partially understandable as a denial of depressive anxiety) probably involves a premature primal group rebellion against the authoritarian leader who is, in this instance, also viewed as an abandoner.

A similar reaction to a leader's absence in an unstructured laboratory group is described in chap. 4. The leader's impending absence in that instance led to a critical group decision-making session and ultimate polarization in which only half of the group agreed to meet for a leaderless session. The extreme polarization of the membership, however, was only temporary. Meetings after the group was reunited reflected a great deal of cohesiveness and generally more efficient forms of peer interaction between the members. In a certain sense, the splitting off of the total laboratory group into two subgroups due to the leader's impending absence can be viewed as a form of primal horde rebellion. The subgroup that decided not to attend the meetings was rebelling against the leader by diminishing the significance of the laboratory sessions, as if they were saying, "These meetings are not so vital that we cannot afford to miss a session." The attendees, on the other hand, were saying that the leader was not so important that a meeting could not be held without him. It is significant to note that the leader responded in a nondirective fashion and never expressed an opinion with regard to whether or not there should be a leaderless session during his absence.

Bennis's findings (1961), too, may involve a similar, though less spectacular, group polarization reaction to a leader's absence. He notes a significantly higher rate of absenteeism in those sessions from which the leader was absent than in those at which he was present. The members in that group therefore may have been expressing their rebellious feelings against the leader via absences from the meetings. That the content of the tape recordings reflect a strong preoccupation with the positive and supportive aspects of the peer interpersonal communication process during leader-absent sessions is strong corroboration of the hypothesis that the attendees were involved in a form of group rebellion against the leader. By idealizing and almost glorifying the quality of the leader-absent sessions, the members who attended may be disparaging the importance of the leader and elevating the significance of a unified peer group.

At any rate, it can be argued that heightened hostility toward the leader is implicit, although subtly so, in the peer group described by Bennis (1961) and the one described in chap. 4. A careful analysis of thematic content particularly reflecting anger toward the leader in leader-present sessions would be required to more thoroughly substantiate the inference that some form of primal-horde-like rebellion had occurred.

Appelbaum's paper on the reactions of an unstructured laboratory group to the John F. Kennedy assassination (1966) addresses itself more precisely to the issue of thematic aggression directed at the leader during the course of a leader-present session. Appelbaum describes a meeting held the day before Kennedy's assassination in which the group members deliberated over whether or not to meet for the next session, which was to fall on Thanksgiving day. Following an extended debate in which the members insisted upon a unanimous decision, an agreement was reached not to hold a meeting on that day. Appelbaum emphasizes that on the meeting just prior to this session, a certain amount of mild hostility had been expressed toward the leader by the group. The group rebellion was thus largely against what was imagined were the leader's feelings with regard to the group's decision not to meet for a scheduled session. Most members assumed that the leader strongly frowned on such a decision.

Appelbaum tends to underplay the degree of actual hostility that was evident in the group's reaction to the leader and goes on to note that, nevertheless, in the session following the Kennedy assassination (and the previous missed session) a tremendous degree of melancholy and guilt, almost "mourning," was implicit as a group theme. The fact that the members were extremely preoccupied with both the nature of Kennedy's death and the leader's health and well-being suggested the possible hypothesis that the members were overreacting guiltily and quite emotionally to the rebellion that had occurred during the previous session. The extremeness of this emotional reaction, given the fact that it had occurred at a fairly early point in the group's developmental history, further implied to Appelbaum a phylogenetic explanation (above and beyond any ontogenetic causes) of those highly emotional group events. Appelbaum thus feels that the fact of Kennedy's death may have stirred up some sort of collective group memory trace relating to the historical murder of the primal father by the horde of brothers. The latter highly emotion-laden memory retrieval is associated with a group psychological event that Appelbaum calls a "hurried cathexis of a phallic-oedipal organization" (p. 400). The group behaves as if it had truly rebelled against the leader in a fully phallic fashion when it actually had merely approximated such a hostile reaction.

Although Appelbaum argues for a phylogenetic mediating construct as having explanatory value in this instance, a more parsimonious hypothesis may be derived from an ego psychological theory of group development. Such an approach, taken together with the ontogenetic group psychological conceptualizations developed by Appelbaum in a number of articles (1963, 1966), would appear to be sufficiently explanatory, obviating the need for difficult-to-validate phylogenetic speculations.

Appelbaum's argument that the universality and depth of feeling in reaction to Kennedy's death cannot be explained simply by the traumatic and tragic nature of the event itself (i.e., simple group stress hypothesis)—hence implying some form of phylogenetic mediating construct—was not held up in a simple group experiment. As a group dynamics assignment, I invited a class to participate in a go-around in which each member was asked to describe his or her recollections of the events surrounding Kennedy's death. The descriptions were to center around personal memories and emotional reactions of the members. Given the fact that this experiment was attempted in the spring of 1975, more than 10 years after the catastrophic shooting of President Kennedy, it was surprising to discover the vivid and highly specific manner in which the class members recalled their own personal experiences of that event. In most cases, the members were able to recollect exactly what they had been doing when they first heard of Kennedy's assassination. A great deal of emotion was generated during the course of this experiment as well as a considerable degree of group cohesiveness.

The vivid emotionality arising from that discussion, clearly in response to memory traces more vague than the immediate emotional impact of the event itself, strongly suggests that in 1964 that event had a severely traumatic impact on the members of Appelbaum's group (as well as upon much of the world). Thus it is unlikely that a phylogenetic explanation is necessary to understand the strength of the group's highly emotional reaction at that time. An ontogenetic hypothesis, however, may still be valid when utilized in combination with certain ego psychological constructs.

The empirical reliability and validity of the primal horde phenomenon as an essential group dynamic are quite high, particularly in the minds of professionals who have been exposed to many unstructured laboratory groups. I have participated in five different two-day institutes, from 1970 through 1974, run under the auspices of the American Group Psychotherapy Association as part of their annual conference. Each institute consisted of an intensive laboratory experience (largely unstructured) in which approximately twelve group professionals interacted under the leadership of a highly trained consultant.

The focus of these groups was generally nontherapeutic (although therapeutic experiences occurred for most members in every group laboratory), and the primary interest was in learning about oneself by means of a thorough study of the group interactive processes that developed during each workshop. Typically, a didactic and more structurally formalized discussion led by the consultant occurred in a later stage of each institute experience. In most cases, the consultant restricted his or her communications during the unstructured portion to group-as-a-whole interpretations, although individual confrontations and interpretive interventions were made as well. Two institutes were focused on an intensive exploration of specialized theoretical approaches in the group field (i.e., Bion–Tavistock approach and General Systems Theory approach) via an intensive group experience of a largely unstructured nature.

My clear impression is that some form of primal horde rebellion of the peer group against the leader occurred during the course of each and every one of these intensive group experiences. Such an impression has been corroborated repeatedly both in the formal didactic discussions following the group laboratories and in informal discussions with colleagues who had been coparticipants in these experiences. The occurrence of primal-horde-like rebellions in such groups are so common that they have almost become institutionalized: At some point during the course of these unstructured laboratory experiences, the members take it for granted that a group rebellion against the leader will take place.

The primal horde group rebellion has also been demonstrated in relatively structured "work" groups. Grossman (1975) co-led an interview group screening five student applicants to Adelphi University's clinical psychology program. Her process recordings of the peer interactions taking place in one of these groups indicate the occurrence of a primal horde group rebellion directed against the co-leaders. Her notes capture the flavor of this rebellion quite well:

> ... The co-leaders attempted to intervene but were ignored. The members carried on their own discussion reviewing the group history and citing the incident at the beginning of the group when they introduced each other and discounted the leaders' introductions. They agreed that the tasks were "artificial" and that they preferred to relate to each other in their own way. One member expressed the group wish to have the group for themselves and eliminate the element of evaluation. (1975, pp. 5–6)

The task established for this group was to interact in a relatively structured work group so that the co-leaders could evaluate each group member as a potential clinical psychology candidate. The rebellion here is against both the co-leaders and the clearly avowed evaluative task.

A "GROUP DEVELOPMENTAL" CONCEPTUALIZATION OF THE PRIMAL HORDE PHENOMENON

Although the primal horde phenomenon tends to be expressed in both structured and unstructured groups in the form of outwardly rebellious behavior and hostility directed toward the leader by the peer members, it can have an adaptive and developmentally useful effect on group functioning. It may even be viewed as an essential group dynamic that must occur for a group to fully attain an advanced and sophisticated state of maturational growth. A number of authors (Appelbaum, 1963; Bennis & Shepard, 1956; Martin & Hill, 1957) have corroborated the existence of discrete stages during the course of a group's development. Appelbaum (1963), in particular, described these stages in ego psychological developmental terms as a shift in the group's capacity to accept the reality principle. In making such a developmental shift, the group yields its earlier proneness to relying almost solely on the pleasure principle.

In further elaborating on this hypothesis, Appelbaum relates the typical stages of group development to Freud's ontogenetic notions with regard to the oral, anal, and phallic stages of mental development. The group, too, is viewed by Appelbaum as proceeding through some form of approximation to an oral, anal, and finally phallic stage of development. It is in the later stage that the primal horde rebellion typically occurs, largely as a result of the oedipal dynamics valent in the group at that time.

The adaptive and ego-enhancing nature of the primal horde explosion can be most clearly appreciated in the group developmental stage that usually occurs following the rebellion's resolution. The group often shifts into a highly efficient peer interaction phase in which the members busy themselves with each other in much the same manner that they had earlier busied themselves with the leader. The symbolic killing of the leader allows for a more truly autonomous group interactive process between the peer members. In Bion's (1959) terms the group has shifted away from its "basic assumptions" and has become a "work" group. Appelbaum's description of developmental shifts through oral, anal, and phallic stages in many ways dovetails with Bion's description of group developmental shifts through dependency, fight–flight, and pairing phases.

The final work phase reached by the group as a result of its successful primal horde rebellion is a state of readiness for truly group therapeutic work. Most nontherapeutic laboratory groups end just prior to such a prolonged period of therapeutic peer interaction and interpersonal relatedness. Psychotherapy groups, however, would just be beginning at this point. Goldberg (1976) emphasizes the fact that the process of peer interaction is one of the most essential aspects of group psychotherapy. From a group psychoanalytic viewpoint, such a truly therapeutic stage of peer interaction cannot be reached until the group members successfully rebel against the leader and symbolically kill him or her off as an authoritative influence that restricts the group's capacity for relatively autonomous interpersonal functioning.

A phylogenetic hypothesis is certainly not necessary to explain this phenomenon. It can be fully understood in ego psychological terms without reference to such a highly speculative notion. As in individual psychotherapy, the concept of ego autonomy (White, 1963) has an important explicating value for the fields of group psychology and psychoanalysis. The group is propelled forward in its quest for autonomy via a primal horde rebellion against the leader. Such a rebellion can be viewed as a "group resistance" (Ormont, 1968), but a generally adaptive one for the group-as-a whole.

HYPOTHESES FOR FUTURE GROUP DYNAMIC RESEARCH

The rather intimate relationship between group dynamics and group psychotherapy has been studied by a number of authors, but particularly by Durkin (1964), who feels that the supposed differentiation between the two fields is an artificial one. In many instances, therapeutic experiences occur during the course of group dynamics laboratories. And in an approximately equal number of instances, the "group dynamics" aspects of psychotherapeutic groups offer an essential matrix of therapeutic gain for the members.

Group psychoanalysis, perhaps the most sophisticated extension of the group psychotherapeutic process, also offers many opportunities for testing out the therapeutic usefulness of hypotheses derived from group dynamics experiences. The following hypotheses are merely a sample of those that can be derived from this discussion of the primal horde phenomenon in groups, all of which can be empirically verified by the solid process recording of both unstructured group dynamics laboratories and group psychoanalytic therapeutic experiences.

Hypothesis One

Primal-horde-like peer rebellions against the leader can be empirically demonstrated to occur in both structured and unstructured laboratory groups and a broad variety of therapeutic groups. In general, they will facilitate and propel the group therapeutic process forward.

Hypothesis Two

The leader's personality will demonstrably effect and instigate such rebellions. "Charismatic" leaders may either tend to provoke such group reactions at earlier points in the group's developmental history or may delay them indefinitely.

Hypothesis Three

Nondirective styles of group leadership will produce earlier primal rebellions than will highly structured and reality-oriented leadership styles.

Hypothesis Four

Critical events occurring during the course of the group's history (i.e., leader's absence due to illness, vacation, etc.) will tend to precipitate premature primal rebellions against the leader.

Hypothesis Five

All things being equal, male group leaders will tend to produce earlier and more magnified primal rebellion reactions than will female leaders.

Hypothesis Six

Groups composed predominantly of male members will experience earlier and more visible primal rebellions than will groups consisting predominantly of female members.

The above hypotheses are being only tentatively presented as possible focal points for future group dynamics research. Since almost no solidly empirical research has been done in this area, the hypotheses must be considered of a preliminary nature. The possibility certainly exists that empirical findings will be in the opposite direction of the predictions in certain instances.

In summary, the primal horde phenomenon, a heretofore poorly understood and neglected aspect of group process, can be seen as an empirically verifiable and therapeutically important aspect of a broad variety of group experiences. A great deal of future research on its various ramifications will be required to fully understand its group psychological meaning and potential structural and dynamic import for therapeutic groups.

REFERENCES

Appelbaum, S. A. The pleasure and reality principles in group process teaching. *British Journal of Medical Psychology,* 1963, *36,* 1-7. (This book, chap. 12)

Appelbaum, S. A. The Kennedy assassination. *Psychoanalytic Review,* 1966, *53,* 393-404. (This book, chap. 13)

Appelbaum, S. A. The world in search of a leader: An application of group psychology to international relations. *British Journal of Medical Psychology,* 1967, *40,* 381-392.

Bennis, W. G. Defenses against depressive anxiety in groups: The case of the absent leader. *Merrill-Palmer Quarterly,* 1961, *7,* 3-30. (This book, chap. 7)

Bennis, W. G., & Shepard, H. A. A theory of group development. *Human Relations,* 1956, *9,* 415-437. (This book, chap. 10)

Bion, W. R. *Experiences in groups.* New York: Basic Books, 1959.

Durkin, H. *The group in depth.* New York: International Universities Press, 1964.

Freud, S. [*Totem and taboo*] (A. A. Brill, Ed. and trans.). New York: Vintage Books, 1946. (Originally published, 1918.)

Freud, S. [*Group psychology and the analysis of the ego*] (J. Strachey, Ed. and trans.). New York: Bantam Books, 1965. (Originally published, 1922.)

Goldberg, C. Peer influence in contemporary group psychotherapy. In L. R. Wolberg & M. L. Aronson (Eds.), *Group therapy 1975.* New York: Grune and Stratton, 1976.

Grossman, D. Two interview groups: Process and speculation. Unpublished manuscript, Institute of Advanced Psychological Studies, Adelphi University, 1975.

Kissen, M. The concept of identification: An evaluation of its current status and significance for group psychotherapy. *Group Process,* 1974, *6,* 83-97. (This book, chap. 16)

Lewin, K. Forces behind food habits and methods of change. *Bulletin of the National Research Council,* 1943, *108,* 35-65.

Martin, E. A., Jr., & Hill, W. F. Toward a theory of group development; six phases of therapy group development. *International Journal of Group Psychotherapy,* 1957, *7,* 20-30. (This book, chap. 11)

Ormont, L. Group resistance and the therapeutic contract. *International Journal of Group Psychotherapy,* 1968, *18,* 147-154. (This book, chap. 20)

Scheidlinger, S. The concept of regression in group psychotherapy. *International Journal of Group Psychotherapy,* 1968, *18,* 3-20. (This book, chap. 15)

White, R. W. Ego and reality in psychoanalytic theory. A proposal regarding independent ego energies. *Psychological Issues* (Vol. 3, No. 3). New York: International Universities Press, 1963.

15

The Concept of
Regression in
Group Psychotherapy

Saul Scheidlinger
Department of Psychiatry
Albert Einstein College of Medicine
Bronx, New York, New York

[Scheidlinger, one of the more important systematic theorists in the field of group psychology and psychotherapy, attempts in this chapter to clarify the very complex psychoanalytic concept of regression, particularly as it relates to groups. His use of an ego psychological conceptual model is particularly effective in that it allows for a distinction between the more structural and "cognitive" forms of ego regression and other related manifestations of that phenomenon (i.e., topographical regression, drive or instinctual regression, phylogenetic regression). His distinction between the *group-formative* type of regression and the more therapy-related *transferential* variety is a very useful one, as is his important clarification of the multiple simultaneous levels of group analysis (i.e., intrapersonal, interpersonal, group-as-a-whole). The treatment of the *group mind* issue in this paper is particularly illuminating and instructive.]

The special relevance of the psychoanalytic concept of regression to group psychotherapy is undisputed. And, yet, the utility of this concept has been much limited by its complexity and by the ambiguity of its usage in literature and clinical practice.

In group therapy theory, regression has served to explain *group psychological manifestations* characteristic of all human groups as well as the *therapeutic process* entailed in clinical work with disturbed people. In other words, there are regressive phenomena rooted in group psychology in addition to those which are a part of all reconstructive psychotherapy.

In the broader context of Freudian psychoanalysis the term regression was historically almost exclusively linked to individual psychopathology. Under the term were subsumed such varied behavioral manifestations as pathological defense mechanisms, symptom formation, unconscious content, a mental process, or even the end-product of a process. And it is this general view of regression which is still usually found in the dictionaries. English and English (1958) define regression as "... a return to earlier and less mature behavior; or, manifestation of more primitive behavior after having learned mature forms, whether or not the immature or primitive behavior had actually formed part of the person's earlier behavior." In the clinical literature, prior to the advent of ego psychology, regression—together with its sister concept, fixation—was couched in terms of the Freudian stages of psychosexual development, according to which psychological factors pertaining to any one phase are never entirely given up and the personality reverts under stress to earlier fixation points. Implicit is the notion that regression connotes maladaptation and that the further backward the move, such as to primary narcissism, the greater the psychopathology.

In a similar vein is Fenichel's (1945) assertion that regression, unlike the other pathogenic defenses, is not brought about by ego activity. Instead, "... the ego is much more passive ... regression happens to the ego; in general, regression seems to be set in motion by the instincts...."

Following a discussion of how the concept of regression has evolved in the group psychological as well as in the broader psychoanalytic literature, a broader view of it will be advanced in this paper which incorporates the most recent theoretical trends.

REGRESSION IN GROUP FORMATION

In his *Group Psychology and the Analysis of the Ego*, Freud (1921) advanced a number of new concepts depicting group formation as the reactivation of an earlier kind of libidinal relationship of the group members with a "father-leader," with ensuing "sibling" identifications among them. Following the first appearance of this little volume in its original German in 1921, the psychoanalytic literature largely ignored the subject of groups.

The first group therapists, such as Schilder (1940) and Wender (1945) whose papers appeared in the early forties, acknowledged the above-noted formulations of Freud's. Except for Redl (1942), however, no one at that time questioned these theories or explored their relevance to work with therapy groups. In the scanty references to analytic group psychology the implicit view of group emotionality as entailing each group member's regression to earlier stages of object ties, i.e., to identifications, prevailed. Even though, when Freud (1921) discussed mob phenomena, he had referred to behavior akin to *ego regression* (reversion to earlier modes of ego functioning), as well as to *topographical regression* (shifts from System Conscious to Unconscious), these distinctions were not mentioned in the subsequent literature. This was in keeping with the loose usage of terminology which characterized all early psychoanalytic writings. Similarly ignored but for different reasons were Freud's speculations about *phylogenetic regression* in which he viewed each group member's psyche as containing the archaic heritage of the drama of the "primal horde." In line with this now generally discarded speculation, group psychology was considered by him as being in a sense older as well as genetically more primitive than individual psychology.

As I noted in another context (1960), all of these Freudian postulates of group psychology were largely neglected in the American group therapy literature until the late fifties. Furthermore, with the latter being steeped in the precepts of individual psychopathology and of the therapeutic process, the concept of regression was rarely employed explicitly, except with reference to multiple transference manifestations.

The writings of some English group therapists, such as Ezriel (1950), Bion (1952), and Foulkes (1957), challenged this state of affairs. Bion, for instance, posited regressive phenomena in therapy groups which he viewed as being not only rooted in the dynamics of group life, but also as considerably more "primitive" than those assumed by Freud's group theories (1921). A proponent of Melanie Klein's (1950) ideas regarding the influence on personality of powerful fantasies from the infant's earliest months (prior to the onset of the classic Freudian neurosis), Bion suggested two analogous "depth" levels for therapy groups: Freud's level of "neurotic" family patterns with their associated conflicts, as well as his (Bion's) level of more primitive "paranoid-schizoid" and "depressive" anxieties.

In Bion's view, psychological group formation in a therapy group reactivates regressive levels of even greater depth than individual analysis. Thus, hand in hand with a work and reality orientation go patterns of functioning closely akin to primary process. Magical wish-fulfillment, splitting, and projection mechanisms, persecutory anxieties and condensation are part of this picture. As for the content of the fantasies, these pertain to perceptions of the leader as a positive, sustaining, and gratifying parent in the "Dependent Basic Assumption." He becomes a threatening parental image in what Bion terms the "Fight–Flight Basic Assumption"; and a Messianic symbol of the unborn genius in the sexually tinged "Pairing Basic Assumption." The fantasied perceptions of the group entity encompass notions of the mother's breast and at times even contents of her body. What is noteworthy, too, in Bion's theory, relates to his preference for such concepts as "projective" or "introjective" identifications over the concept of transference. In projective identification, for instance, there is a splitting off of parts of the self with a projection of them into another person. These defensive mechanisms are brought into play in response to the marked anxiety engendered by intrapsychic conflicts with what Kleinians term "internal objects" and "part objects," and by the threat of losing one's personal identity in the group.

One of the shortcomings of Bion's theory relates to his view of regression as primarily pathological and irrational. It fails to take into account modern ego psychology as discussed later in this paper. It is as though Bion refuses to give recognition to an individual's ego functions as intervening between impulse and actual behavior. Furthermore, he pays no attention to the individual differences in susceptibility to the regressive pull of the group. In his scheme, leader and group member alike are often powerless against the onslaught of unconscious stimuli, which propel them into acting out of impulsivity. Rationality and control are a function ascribed by him to the Work-Group, a *group* rather than an *individual* manifestation.

Despite their limitations, however, Bion's theories have undoubtedly served to focus the attention of group practitioners and theoreticians on the concept of regression, and on the broader issues of emotionality and of "depth" manifestations in group behavior.

SOME CURRENT VIEWS OF REGRESSION IN INDIVIDUAL PSYCHOANALYSIS

The concept of regression while basic to general psychoanalytic theory has been used in a variety of ways, frequently devoid of clear definition. Reference has already been made to four different kinds of regression: (1) *topographical regression*, wherein there is a shift of an individual's mental functioning from the System *Conscious* to *Unconscious*; (2) *drive or instinctual regression*, which is linked to the *libido theory* and involves a personality's reversion to partial drives characteristic of earlier developmental stages; (3) *ego or genetic regression*, referring to the emergence of earlier, usually infantile, modes of functioning; (4) *phylogenetic regression*, connoting a reactivation of assumed archaic and innate memories common to mankind. As ego psychological theory, with its emphasis on autonomous, nonconflictual and adaptive aspects of functioning gained in popularity, the ideas of regression changed accordingly. Not only did regression lose its earlier predominantly pathological taint, but, in addition, a new kind of "regression in the service of the ego" (Schafer, 1958) was postulated, with the promotion of healthy adaptation as its primary aim. Regression has furthermore been increasingly viewed as a broader, universal process characteristic of personality functioning. Closely linked to general *genetic* (when, why, and how) and *dynamic* (here and now) considerations, as well as to structural theory (id, ego, superego), its nature and significance at any one time call for a simultaneous assessment of all these elements. As Rapaport (1960) put it,

"Psychoanalysis as a genetic psychology deals with the genetic roots of behavior, with the degree of autonomy behaviors attain, and with the genetic roots of the subject's relation to the reality conditions which codetermine the appearance of a behavior at a given point in a person's life."

There is now increasing recognition that any or all of the three structures of the psyche—id, ego, and superego—may contain primary process phenomena. Thus, regression from *secondary process* functioning involving control, delay, or modification in drive discharge, to *primary process* functioning with its push for immediate drive (libido, aggression) gratification, no longer necessarily connotes pathology. The most recent definition of regression suggested by Arlow and Brenner (1964) is general enough to subsume the different major earlier meanings ascribed to this term. Their definition of regression speaks of a "... re-emergence of modes of mental functioning which were characteristic of the psychic activity of the individual during earlier periods of development."

If we were to accept this definition of regression for purposes of this discussion, we would have to assume that "modes of mental functioning" are meant to include ways of ego functioning as well as psychic content. Furthermore, we would conclude that the motivations for any regression can be varied, ranging from serving as a defense against intolerable threat from within the psyche (i.e., guilt) or fears of external objects to opening gateways for creative expression or freer communications with others. As Kris noted, control of regression is a part of the broader organizing function of the ego. Whether regression is pathological in a given instance depends less on its depth than on "... its persistent, irrevocable nature, the degree of conflict which it generates, and its effect on adaptation" (Arlow and Brenner, 1964). Ego strength relates in part to the ego's ability to resist pathological regression at points of stress, whether the stress is due to intrapsychic conflict or to external pressure.

Before returning to the more complex issue of group behavior, it should be noted that I utilize the concept of regression in this paper as referring to an individual personality's mode of functioning. It can be asked: since small groups and especially therapy groups abound in instances of regressive verbalizations or *acting out* of similar and perhaps even identical covert conflicts or fantasies on the part of many, if not all, members, are we not then dealing with a group regression? Or, can a mob scene or an incident of group hysteria be otherwise depicted? My answer would be that, despite the frequent use of such terminology, this is highly misleading. For, in the strictest sense, psychological processes such as regression or identification, or even fantasying or hating, operate in individuals only. Group members can maintain shared or common fantasies; they can even act in unison in response to group occurrences, such as the entry of a new member or the absence of the leader. And, yet, this need not mean that the group *as a group* now has a certain fantasy or acts in a certain manner. This view of mine, that shared fantasies are far from being the same in each individual, has found some support in the few instances in which training or therapy groups have been subjected to systematic observation. A group can possess observable characteristics, can be perceived and reacted to as a whole, but this makes it a social and psychological reality, not a physical reality; it does not indicate a "group mind."

FORCES FAVORING REGRESSION IN GROUPS

When Freud (1921) ascribed to group formation "the character of a regression," he was impressed by the degree to which the individual group member's internalized controls, including his superego, were subject to relaxation and change. In considering the elements which facilitate regressive manifestations in a therapy group, an entity unknown to Freud, we would today pay major attention to such factors as the degree of structure evolving both from the style of leadership (directive versus non-directive) and from the broader group situation (permissiveness, degree of role definition, task orientation), for there is now general agreement regarding the inevitable anxieties due to "presence and contact" (Semrad et al., 1963) which characterize group formation in all face-to-face groups. With a membership weighted by personal pathology, there is the added lowered tolerance for situational frustrations, for "object anxiety," as well as for instinctual pressures from within. Fried (1965) suggested, in this connection that the heightened climate of psychological stimulation enhances the regressive pull in therapy groups. Suggestibility and emotional contagion are undoubtedly a part of this picture. It would perhaps be no exaggeration to state that the therapeutic value, if not the very existence of a group, is predicated on maintaining an optimum regressive level. The same has often been said regarding the individual psychoanalytic situation.

THE ROLE OF REGRESSION IN SOME MODELS OF GROUP FORMATION: THE DEPENDENCY PHASE

Following Freud and Redl (1942), a number of writers have delineated the way emotional group processes evolve in analytic therapy groups with emphasis on the members' feelings toward the leader, toward the other group members, and toward the group entity. Some of these models center around hypothesized phases of development for the group, from its inception to its conclusion.[1]

My concern here will be limited to the question of how regression is handled in these models, with particular focus on the initial phase, where, theoretically at

---

[1] Similar theories have been advanced with respect to training groups which lie outside the scope of this paper. Kaplan (1967) has recently compared the salient emotional issues in therapy and training groups. See also Horwitz (1964) and Frank (1964).

least, in a developmental scheme, regression is at its height. I have already referred to Bion (1949) whose major criticism of the Freudian model of group formation was that the latter was not only incomplete but, above all, not "deep" enough. It might be of interest here to juxtapose Bion's view of the "Dependency Basic Assumption" with two parallel theoretical views of group formation. This is especially appropriate since almost all such models, beginning with Freud's, postulate an initial dependency phase: one connoting a regression of the group members to a dependent state in relation to a leader, followed by varied emotional manifestations in regard to the other group members and to the emerging group entity.

As already noted, in Bion's "Dependency Basic Assumption," hand in hand with the group's conscious work and task orientation, there is a shared unconscious group fantasy which springs into being spontaneously. This fantasy evolves around a leader, a magical superior being, who is there to feed, support, and protect. As part of the competition for the exclusive attention of this nurturing object, feelings of guilt for "being greedy in demanding more than one's fair turn in parental care" come to the fore. This fantasied relationship is an identification and could focus on the group therapist (the Work-Group leader) or on a symbolic idea, such as the group "bible." The "Dependency" phase also entails a defensive idealization of the group's history, which is accordingly utilized as a means of countering stimuli to individual growth and development. It is noteworthy that Bion does not allow here for relationships among the group members; the regressive tie to the leader is paramount. Except for stressing its greater "depth" when compared to the Freudian neurotic type of regression, Bion is not explicit on this point. One could assume, however, that the reactivated conflicts in this phase stem from the first six months of the infant's life, which in Melanie Klein's (1950) system are characterized by pregenital strivings and anxieties pertaining to part-object relationships. As noted earlier, Bion's fantasied group "culture" represents a defensive reaction against these infantile conflicts, symbolized, as they frequently are, by the group as a whole.

Foulkes (1957), another British group therapist, considers his orientation closer to Bion's than to that of the American group therapists. Nevertheless he gives far greater weight to the "here and now" interpersonal relationships and goals in therapy groups than does Bion. He has enumerated the following four depth levels for the group interactions: (1) the *current level*, which refers to reality perceptions of the leader and of the group; (2) the *transference level*, wherein the group represents a symbolic family with the leader as parent; (3) the *level of bodily and mental images*, which contains aspects analogous to Bion's "Basic Assumptions," including primitive "inner" object-relations and projective identifications; (4) a *primordial level* containing elements of the collective unconscious.

As for the earliest phase in group formation, which is my major concern here, Foulkes stresses its "leader-centered" character. There is a tendency at first to impute magical qualities to the therapist. In this infantile fantasy, he

"... is put in the position of the *primordial leader image*; he is omniscient and omnipotent. ..." In this phase, confessions, discussions of symptoms, and expressions of high hopes are intermingled. Again, not unlike Bion's "Basic Assumptions," "deep and primitive" group fantasies, symbols, and mental mechanisms emerge without apparent causality. The therapist encourages greater activity in the direction of self-awareness and independence in his effort to move the group toward maturation and away from the earlier dependence on irrational authority. As for the depth of the regressive phenomena, while Foulkes does refer to the occasional reactivation of Kleinian pregenital conflicts, his preponderant preoccupation is with group psychotherapy as a transference situation in which true transference neuroses can be elicited, with the patients being encouraged to move toward society and the community.

A more recent formulation of a comprehensive group developmental model for adult therapy groups was offered by Kaplan and Roman (1963). These authors' theoretical scheme, which includes a specific structure, theme, and interaction pattern, has markedly greater clarity than Bion's or Foulkes's discussions. According to Kaplan and Roman, at the group's beginning, the therapist constitutes the object of each group member's attention, and, on one plane, the members behave toward him in the traditional pattern of the patient–doctor relationship. The common covert concern, in contrast, is one of dependency on a magical leader. In their view, this general perception of the leader (a demigod in a shared mythology) fosters group formation to the point that the patients interact "as part of the group as a unit." Thus, an earlier desire for satisfaction of personal needs from the leader becomes reformulated in group terms. It is as if the magical therapist "... was withholding something precious which could magically cure them." The over-all tone is one of enthusiasm, almost adoration, with no hostility or disappointment coming to the fore. These developments are followed by beginning signs of attention to other group members.

Kaplan and Roman do not deal with the concept of regression in detail. Instead, they refer in general to the psychological group formation as a defensive regression wherein anxieties related to the need for intimate contact in a new situation promote primitive identifications, fantasied perceptions, and patterns of magical thinking. Except for parenthetical references to child-parent manifestations as part of the *dependency* theme and of adolescent concerns during this middle phase, they do not touch on the issue of depth or specific fixation points in the regression. Their overall observation that "... individual transference reactions could be experienced and verbalized" only after some maturation had occurred, as expressed by a partial dissolution of the psychological group (the 86th session in their illustration), is especially noteworthy. It stands in close agreement with several descriptions of developmental phases for training groups (Bennis and Shepard, 1956).

For purposes of this discussion, the similarity in the way the three theoretical models of Bion, Foulkes, and Kaplan and Roman portray the covert emotionality in the initial regressive phase in therapy groups is striking. All three emphasize the reactivation of early identification processes wherein group members in a shared fantasy appear to seek nurture and support from a magical parent-leader. In this dependency constellation, sexual or aggressive drive expression appears to be almost nonexistent, which is true as well for any concern with other group members. There are also, however, some differences in the way group formative processes are viewed by these authors. For instance, Bion, as well as Kaplan and Roman, place considerable emphasis on the marked degree of group cohesion, which is exemplified by the idealization of the group entity. This cohesion appears to serve defensive functions, standing in opposition to individual and group maturation. Foulkes, in contrast, does not deal with these issues in relation to the early phase in group formation.

As noted, in each of the above theoretical models regressive manifestations constitute a basic element. However, these are either not discussed explicitly or, if so, as with Bion, they are portrayed in a manner markedly removed from the traditional psychoanalytic formulations.

PERCEPTION OF THE LEADER IN GROUP FORMATION

In addition to the three models depicted above, most of the other theories which deal with the formation of a psychological group also evolve around the shared perception of a leader or, less frequently, of a common idea or characteristic. Since these perceptions inevitably involve regression, it would be useful to list some, albeit the writers presented them in a somewhat fragmentary manner.

To begin with, there is Redl's (1942) formulation which both encompasses the theory advanced by Freud and extends it considerably. Using the broader term of "central person" instead of leader, he lists three different kinds of relationships with the central person, each of which he deems capable of evoking group formation: (1) the central person as an object of identification on the basis of the group member's ego-ideal incorporation (as in Freud's model) or as a result of fear of the central person as an aggressor; (2) the central person as an object of the group member's libidinal or aggressive drives; (3) the central person as an object for the relief of similar inner conflicts.

While Freud and Redl referred to the perceptions of the leader as a father person, Money-Kyrle (1950) was the first writer to introduce the perception of a mother image in group formation. Extending the concept of a "good" and "bad" parent representation in a child's unconscious, he postulated the following three kinds of symbols: (1) the "good parents" (particularly the mother) representing the norms and ideals of the group; (2) the "bad parents" in the role of persecutors against whom the group values have to be defended; and (3) the "good parents," especially the father, who in his role as the mother's defender reappears as the group leader. Subsequently, Schindler (1951) advanced the view that transferences in every therapy group evolve on the pattern of a family. In this pattern, the therapist represents the father, the group members the siblings, while the group as a whole comes to represent the mother. In trying to conceptualize the group entity further, Schindler (1952) also refers to group formation as the development of a "group personality." He thought that this "common denominator" of the individual group member's characteristics can be divided into a group id, ego, and superego. The group *id* pertains to common needs such as security or pleasure. The *superego* refers to perceptions of the father–leader and mother–group, while the *ego* "registers" the id and superego functions and judges whether or not they serve the group's purposes.

It is noteworthy that Schindler (1966) followed Money-Kyrle in stressing the regressive unconscious perception of the group entity as a mother. Spanjaard (1959) observed that the regression in a therapy group composed of neurotic adults was less deep than that which he had noted in his practice of individual psychoanalysis. He thought that the group members perceived the leader both as a mother figure from the child's phallic–narcissistic phase and also in terms of a leader image from adolescence.

In a paper on group identification (1964), I suggested an outline for conceptualizing the individual group member's perceptions and attitudes toward the group as a whole. Viewed as an identification in the sense of an endopsychic process calling for a degree of individual involvement with a perceived object or its symbolic representation, it was distinct from transference. Such an identification with the group entity was believed to entail two related elements: (1) the ascribing to the group of an emotional meaning, as a conscious instrument of need satisfaction or, on the unconscious level, as the state of unconflicted well-being represented in the exclusive union with the pre-oedipal mother; and (2) the giving up of an element of "self" to the group.

Durkin (1964) has also advanced the idea of the group entity being perceived by patients in group formation as a pre-oedipal mother. Her formulation, however, is different from my hypothesis regarding the initial view of the nurturing, supportive mother-group. It also differs from the way the *dependency phase* was depicted in the above three theoretical models. According to Durkin, the suggestibility and submission of the individual noted by Freud when groups come into being is due to a regressive fear reaction. She postulates the following two separate steps as transference manifestations: (1) the idea of a group, i.e., a large totality of unknown power, conjures up the harsh, pre-oedipal mother image, reactivating the individual's narcissistic fear of her, and (2) the individual perceives the group accordingly in distorted fashion and behaves toward it in a way that resembles his mode of reacting to his mother but in "modern dress." While a member thus is afraid of the group as a whole, the therapist in turn is perceived "in the image of the good all-giving omnipotent mother."

These ideas of Durkin's, since they are clear and explicit, can be readily subjected to validation by comparing them with the clinical findings of other group therapists and, above all, by exposing the group therapy process to independent observation.[2] On another plane, however, Durkin's theoretical position, in my opinion, makes for possible misunderstanding and confusion. First of all, she fails to differentiate between Freud's incomplete discussion in 1921 of *group formative regression* based on identifications in large groups, with *therapeutic regression* centered on transference in today's therapy groups. She went so far as to criticize Freud's failure to be aware that, in a *therapy group*, "the individual is not inactive and does not just take over the leader in place of his own ego ideal: a complicated transference is set up through which this occurs." Had she kept in mind the historical factor, or had she addressed herself to Redl's contributions of 1942 which both include and extend Freud's formulations on group psychology in the light of more current psychoanalytic and group theory, this might have been avoided. This tendency to lump together latent group formative processes, individual personalities in interaction, and transference manifestations is also apparent in Schindler's earlier noted discussion.

SOME THOUGHTS FOR THE FUTURE

It is my hope that a systematic consideration of the concept of regression as attempted in this paper will help further the much-needed conceptual integration among intrapsychic, interpersonal, and group level phenomena in group psychotherapy.

The most recent psychoanalytic definition of this concept in ego psychological terms as the re-emergence of earlier modes of individual functioning could be readily adopted for theoretical and clinical purposes in group therapy. In viewing regression in this light, we must remember, as Bellak (1961) illustrated incisively, that the regressive process comprises two different, yet related, aspects: (1) the temporal regression of ego functions to modes which were characteristic in childhood, and (2) a topographical regression from primarily conscious to preconscious and unconscious levels of functioning, including the reactivation of primitive libidinal zones.

While not treated systematically, both of these aspects are included in the above-mentioned three models of group formation. The *dependency phase* comprises such infantile patterns of ego functioning as magical thinking, poor

---

[2] A promising method for such observations has been devised by Mann (1966) for training groups.

reality perception, or an anaclitic relationship to the object. In addition, in each model there is an unmistakable air of primary process coupled with oral-libidinal features.

There is no agreement in the literature regarding the exact causes for the regression induced in group formation. While Bion and Ezriel appear to hold intrapsychic anxieties responsible, American writers such as Semrad et al. (1963) or Stock and Lieberman (1964) stress the influence of interpersonal tensions. Following a similar observation of Redl's, Arsenian et al. (1962) believe that "regression from object choice to identification comes about because of the unavoidable frustration of the desire for exclusive union or fusion with the central figure."

Fenichel's assertion, quoted earlier, that regression generally "happens to the ego" and "seems to be set in motion by the instincts" exemplifies a historical tendency to ascribe pathology to this term. A new orientation is in order. In line with current concepts, including that of "regression in the service of the ego," preconscious and unconscious psychic contents as well as earlier modes of functioning can be precipitated in individuals for adaptive and growth-promoting purposes, as I discussed recently in relation to empathy in group psychotherapy (1966). Since there is general agreement that regressive elements are at work in all group formation, not only in therapy groups, it would follow that all group members are characterized by personal pathology unless we allow for nonpathological regression. To avoid such confusion, it is almost imperative to keep in mind the fact that the regression which accompanies group formation must be differentiated insofar as possible from the therapeutic regression which characterizes all analytic psychotherapy. Thus, all the major psychoanalytic hypotheses of group formation stress the preponderance of identification processes over transference manifestations in this initial phase. In line with the view of identification as a more primitive kind of involvement than object relationships, the group member is believed to perceive other people in the group in an undifferentiated way as representations of images rather than as complete objects. Furthermore, as part of this narcissistic orientation, objects are sought out primarily as instruments for the purpose of relieving inner tension. Insofar as transference reactions involve the unconscious reliving of powerful feelings of love and hate akin to more advanced stages of object relationships, these tend to emerge somewhat later, *after* group formation has taken hold.

In addition to analytic group psychotherapy's transference and resistance manifestations, a number of writers, including Foulkes and Anthony (1957) and Stock and Lieberman (1964), also assume that a kind of free association occurs in them. Not only is the manifest content believed to contain derivatives of the unconscious meanings but diverse individual comments also tend to cluster around shared group themes which encompass overt as well as latent levels.

Regarding the much-debated issue as to which is "deeper," individual or group analytic therapy, a perusal of the wide range of regressive behavioral manifestations encountered in groups suggests that perhaps this is really not the issue at all. Whether or not one would agree with Bion's extreme view that every group phenomenon *always* reflects the deepest layers of unconscious conflicts, the fact remains that clinicians have reported free associative productions and primary process manifestations such as dreams, from group members at least equal in "depth" to those encountered in individual psychoanalysis. Nevertheless, any comparison of the two treatment modalities, of individual and group analytic therapy, would have to address itself to a broader question: Does the totality of the therapeutic group experience, even if conducted along the classical Freudian lines of the "Fundamental Rule," and the "Mirror Image," permit the kind of detailed and continuous *working through in depth* which is called for when structural personality reorganization is the aim? The claim that analytic group psychotherapy entails phenomena akin to free association, that there can be "depth" interpretations with reliving of repressed conflicts together with analysis of transference and of resistance, still does not place it on the same plane as classical individual analysis. Unless presented with compelling evidence to the contrary, I agree with those who believe that the copresence of a number of patients in a reality-geared experience makes the group therapy process, and especially the nature of the therapeutic regression, basically different. For, theoretically at least, the crucial issue in utilizing *therapeutic regression* in psychoanalytic treatment is not whether phenomena of the greatest "depth" can be elicited, but, rather, the degree to which the observing, synthesizing, and control functions of the ego can be helped over layers of resistance to accept and to master them. This is a tedious, and with some patients who have disturbances in using free association an almost impossible, task (Bellak, 1961). The observation of Spanjaard's (1959), who is an individual and group analyst, is highly relevant: that though he could elicit a transference neurosis toward himself by maintaining the traditional analytic stance of detachment, the presence of others and, above all, his additional role as a source of suggestion and identification made it impossible for him to reach "the root problems of the personality and its structure." Group therapy's unique value for patients who either cannot utilize a dyadic, insight-geared treatment mode or who, in addition to insight, require the added dimension of a group's corrective emotional experience need not be repeated here.

I have already referred earlier to the theoretical dilemma created by the well-known fact that as part of the regressive group climate, shared fantasies, similar emotional expressions and behavioral manifestations abound. This has led some group therapists to speak in terms of a group regression (Bion, 1949), others in terms of a "group personality" or "group ego." Pending data from careful, independent observations of such group manifestations, I consider it sounder and less confusing to view a regressive group manifestation as the behavior of individuals. The fact that most, and perhaps on occasion all, group members appear to the clinician to share a fantasy or display an emotion as a result of identification processes does not, in the strictest sense of the word, make it a group manifestation. It is useful to remember here, in addition, that from a scientific standpoint, psychoanalytic concepts such as regression pertain to an inferred process which is utilized to explain certain kinds of behavior, not to an observable manifestation.

The three theoretical models of group formation which I have used for purposes of illustration allow for different depth levels in the group process. The phenomena described by these authors, as well as by others, could readily be subsumed under the two broader group process levels, a *contemporaneous-dynamic* and a *genetic-regressive*, which I have described elsewhere (1960). In this categorization, the *contemporaneous-dynamic* level pertains to "the more readily observed momentary expressions of conscious needs and ego-adaptive patterns, the group roles, the network of attractions and repulsions, as well as the group structure. The behavior here is primarily reactive to realistic group situational factors bringing into play the more external aspects of personality." The *genetic-regressive* level, in contrast, refers to unconscious and preconscious motivations, to defensive patterns and conflicts, to phenomena such as transference, countertransference, resistance, identification, and projection. The *genetic-regressive* type of phenomena is more apt to emerge in situations in which the personality restraints (ego defenses) have been loosened (regression), with consequent freer expression of repressed emotionality.

Faced with the challenge of differentiating among the plethora of therapeutic group approaches in mental health facilities, ranging from reality-geared and task-oriented groups to uncovering, analytic groups, I recently suggested a classification scheme (1967). In this scheme, the degree of regression promoted consciously by the therapist constitutes a major criterion for differentiation. The following are the five broad categories which encompass the major group influence attempts depicted in the literature: (1) Activity-Catharsis-Mastery Focus, (2) Cognitive-Informational Focus, (3) Interpersonal-Socialization Focus, (4) Relationship-Experiential Focus, and (5) Uncovering-Introspective Focus.

It is my hope that, if nothing else, this discussion demonstrates the crucial nature of the concept of regression in any attempt at evolving an integrated theoretical framework for group psychology, one which would take into account the complex interaction of individual personalities and of group dynamic manifestations on different depth levels. Only through further systematic considerations of regression and of other concepts in this new field—so rich in creative hypotheses, yet beset by loose and often confusing use of terms—can high-level clinical practice and research flourish.

REFERENCES

Arlow, J. A., and Brenner, C. (1964), *Psychoanalytic Concepts and the Structural Theory*. New York: International Universities Press.

Arsenian, J., Semrad, E. V., and Shapiro, D. (1962), An Analysis of Integral Functions in Small Groups. *This Journal*, 12:421–434.

Bellak, L. (1961), Free Association: Conceptual and Clinical Aspects. *Internat. J. Psychoanal.*, 42:9–20.

Bennis, W. G., and Shepard, H. A. (1956), A Theory of Group Development. *Human Relations*, 9:415–437.

Bion, W. R. (1949), Experiences in Groups. *Human Relations*, 2:13–22; 295–304.

—— (1952), Group Dynamics: A Review. *Internat. J. Psychoanal.*, 33:235–247.

Durkin, H. E. (1964), *The Group in Depth*. New York: International Universities Press.

English, H. B., and English, A. C. (1958), *A Comprehensive Dictionary of Psychological and Psychoanalytical Terms*. New York: Longmans, Green & Co.

Ezriel, H. (1950), A Psychoanalytic Approach to Group Treatment. *Brit. J. Med. Psychol.*, 23:59–74.

Fenichel, O. (1945), *The Psychoanalytic Theory of Neurosis*. New York: Norton.

Foulkes, S. H. (1957), Group Analytic Dynamics with Specific Reference to Psychoanalytic Concepts. *This Journal*, 7:42–51.

—— and Anthony, E. J. (1957), *Group Psychotherapy*. London: Penguin Books.

Frank, J. D. (1964), Training and Therapy. In Bradford, L. P. et al. (eds.), *Group Theory and Laboratory Method*. New York: John Wiley & Son.

Freud, S. (1921), *Group Psychology and the Analysis of the Ego. Standard Edition*, 18:69–143. London: Hogarth Press, 1948.

Fried, E. (1965), Some Aspects of Group Dynamics and the Analysis of Transference and Defenses. *This Journal*, 15:44–56.

Horwitz, L. (1954), Transference in Training Groups and Therapy Groups. *This Journal*, 14:202–213.

Kaplan, S. (1967), Therapy Groups and Training Groups: Similarities and Differences. *This Journal*, 16:473–504.

—— and Roman, M. (1963), Phases of Development in an Adult Therapy Group. *This Journal*, 13:10–26.

Klein, M. (1950), *Contributions to Psychoanalysis, 1921-1945*. London: Hogarth Press.

Mann, R. D. (1966), The Development of the Member-Trainer Relationship in Self-Analytic Groups. *Human Relations*, 19:85–115.

Money-Kyrle, R. (1950), Varieties of Group Formation. In Roheim, G. (ed.), *Psychoanalysis and the Social Sciences*. New York: International Universities Press.

Rapaport, D. (1960), The Structure of Psychoanalytic Theory. *Psychol. Issues*, Monogr. 14. International Universities Press.

Redl, F. (1942), Group Emotion and Leadership. *Psychiatry*, 5:573–596.

Schafer, R. (1958), Regression in the Service of the Ego: The Relevance of a Psychoanalytic Concept for Personality Assessment. In Lindzey, G. (ed.), *Assessment of Human Motives*. New York: Rinehart.

Scheidlinger, S. (1960), Group Process in Group Psychotherapy. *Amer. J. Psychother.*, 14:104–120; 346–363.

—— (1964), Identification, the Sense of Belonging and of Identity in Small Groups. *This Journal*, 14:291–306.

—— (1966), The Concept of Empathy in Group Psychotherapy. *This Journal*, 16:413–424.

—— (1967), Therapeutic Group Approaches in Community Mental Health. *Social Work*, 13:87–95 (April 1968).

Schilder, P. (1940), Introductory Remarks on Groups. *J. Soc. Psychol.*, 12:83–100.

Schindler, W. (1951), Family Pattern in Group Formation and Therapy. *This Journal*, 1:100–105.

—— (1952), The "Group Personality" Concept in Group Psychotherapy. *This Journal*, 2:311–315.

—— (1966), The Role of the Mother in Group Psychotherapy. *This Journal*, 16:198–200.

Semrad, E. V., et al. (1963), The Fields of Group Psychotherapy. *This Journal*, 13:452–464.

Spanjaard, J. (1959), Transference Neurosis and Psychoanalytic Group Psychotherapy. *This Journal*, 9:31–42.

Stock, D., and Lieberman, M. A. (1964), *Psychotherapy Through the Group Process*. New York: Athernon Press.

Wender, L. (1945), Group Psychotherapy. In Moreno, J. C. (ed.), *Group Psychotherapy—A Symposium*. Beacon, N.Y.: Beacon Press.

16

The Concept of Identification: An Evaluation of Its Current Status and Significance for Group Psychotherapy

Morton Kissen
Institute of Advanced Psychological Studies
Adelphi University
Garden City, Long Island, New York

[This chapter attempts to present a conceptualization of the process of identification as it occurs during the course of group psychotherapy. The positions of psychoanalytic theory, learning theory, social learning theory, and the psychology of cognition with regard to identification are explored and integrated into a unified conceptual framework.

The rather broad conception developed here highlights the importance of specific model attributes, particularly as they relate to characteristics of the group therapist that may enhance identificatory interactions. Four testable hypotheses with regard to the physical, physiognomic, psychological, and sociological characteristics of the group therapist are then presented as potentially important factors in determining whether or not the group members identify with the therapist.]

From "The Concept of Identification: An Evaluation of Its Current Status and Significance for Group Psychotherapy" by M. Kissen, *Group Process, Journal of the Association for Group Psychoanalysis and Process*, 1974, *6*, 83-97. Copyright 1974 by the Association for Group Psychoanalysis and Process. Reprinted by permission.

The concept of identification has always been a central one in the study of the psychotherapeutic process. It is widely agreed that, at some point during psychotherapy, the patient takes over for himself a number of the personality characteristics of his therapist. Patients are typically more similar to the therapist at the termination of therapy than they were at the outset. They have been found to internalize personality features such as the expressive and cognitive style, defensive structures, broad character patterns, and even a number of discrete personal traits and behavior patterns of their therapists. There is no reason to assume that such a process of internalization is restricted to individual psychotherapy. A similar process may be inferred as occurring during the group psychotherapy interaction. Individual group members, to varying degrees, presumably internalize personal characteristics of the group therapist.

The nature of the latter process of internalization is only vaguely understood at present. Attempts have been made to conceptualize the process from a variety of vantage points. Thus, psychoanalytic theory (Brody, 1964; Freud, 1960; Freud, 1933; Freud, 1953; Freud, 1953; Knight, 1940; Schafer, 1967; Singer, 1965), learning theory (Dollard, 1941; Lazowick, 1955; Mowrer, 1950), sociological and social learning theory (Bandura, 1963; Bandura, 1963; Bandura, 1961; Parsons, 1955; Sears, 1962; Whiting, 1962), and the psychology of cognition (Kagan, 1958), have all, at one point or another, served as the framework for an attempt at conceptualizing the process of identification. Although a great deal of overlap can be noted between each form of conceptualization, a unifying integration of all of them has not been attempted. In the present paper, the contribution of each of the previous approaches to the study of identification will be highlighted. A conceptual integration will subsequently be offered, as well as a number of hypotheses with regard to group psychotherapy interactions stemming from such an integration. The hypotheses will be focussed at the characteristics of the group therapist that are associated with heightened identificatory behavior.

THE PSYCHOANALYTIC CONCEPTION OF IDENTIFICATION

Freud placed the concept of identification within a *group* context in his volume entitled *Group Psychology and the Analysis of the Ego.* (1960). He referred therein to a process by which the individual members of a group tend to become an integrated unit via a common internalization of the leader. Thus, he defines a group as—". . . a number of individuals who have put one and the same object in the place of their ego ideal and have consequently identified themselves with one another in their ego" (Freud, p. 61, 1960). The members of a group, according to Freud, establish a regressive libidinal attachment to the leader, much as they had done to their parents at an earlier age. Under the spell of a strong leader, the group member becomes a dependent child.

While the members are bound by libidinous ties to their leader, the leader's psychology sharply differs from that of the members. He has no emotional attachments to anybody but himself and it is precisely this *narcissistic* quality which makes him a leader. Freud does not envision a leader whose political psychology is democratic in nature. He rather pictures a forceful, masterful, brutal, and highly narcissistic individual who uses his power to bend the members of the group to his will.

Identification, for Freud, at least within a group context, involves a regressive process of interaction that occurs when a group of individuals meet together with a strong and autocratic leader. The latter process of regression is coupled together with a loss of intellectual capacity, a heightened suggestibility, and a sort of overall state of *fascination*, not unlike the trance-like state induced by an effective hypnotist.

Freud elaborates upon essentially two different conceptions of identification in a series of writings (1960, 1933, 1953, 1953). In one conception, he speaks of identification as a form of restitution of lost love objects. Thus, the lost object is assumed to be introjected into the ego with the ego assuming the characteristics of that object. The latter introjected characteristics are further assumed to become the nucleus of the emerging superego. There is a regressive character to this conception of identification, the latter tending to resemble a primitive oral introjective process. Freud distinguishes between the more developmentally sophisticated *object* choice in which the child wishes to *possess* his parent and the more primitive state of identification in which the child wishes to *be like* his parent. Nevertheless, the latter involves a subtle process of ego alteration, in which the child takes over characteristics from his parents. Thus Freud, in speaking of character development, states—"The incorporation of the early parental function in the shape of the super-ego is no doubt the most important and decisive element; next come identifications with the parents of a later date and with other parents in authority, and the same identifications as precipitates of abandoned object-relations." (Freud, p. 126, 1933).

Freud propounds still another conception of identification. The latter is contained in the notion of *identification with the aggressor*, developed to explain the method by which the child resolves the oedipal crisis. In the narcissistic interest of protecting his penis, the child gives up his attachment to his mother, replacing the latter attachment by an identification with his father. Freud writes: "The authority of the father or the parents is introjected into the ego and there forms the kernel of the super-ego which takes its severity from the father, perpetuates his prohibition against incest, and so insures the ego against a recurrence of the libidinal object-cathexis." (Freud, p. 273, 1953). Thus, in males a civilizing process occurs as a result of the castration threat and consequent identification with the threatening father figure. Ego and superego development, for Freud, hence consists of a departure from primary narcissism brought about by libido being displaced to an externally-imposed ego-ideal. The renouncing of instinctual impulses proceeds precisely through an identification with the culture and its most potent transmittors. Singer, in a lucid but not altogether convincing article (1965), argues that such a notion of identification implies a form of externally-imposed social conformity and loss of identity—as opposed to a more spontaneous process of self-determination.

Brody and Mahoney, in a very important article (1964), make the critical distinction between processes of identification at early and late stages of ego development. They state that prior to the formation of the mature ego, perceptions are diffuse and there is no awareness of a self-object differentiation. Perceptions are, at that time, assimilated through primitive processes of *introjection*. Later on in development, when the ego is more sophisticated and capable of realizing that the object is external to itself, the process is referred to as *identification*. Thus, Brody and Mahoney place the concept of identification within a *developmental* context. They distinguish between a process of assimilation occurring at a developmental stage during which the ego is weak and only partially differentiated from the object world (introjection) and a more differentiated form of assimilation occurring at a later stage in which the ego-object differentiation has been firmly established (identification).

They make still another important distinction between identification as a *process* of ego development and as an *end result* of such development. Thus, they refer to identification, in one context, as the assimilative "process" by which the ego is gradually formed during the course of development. The process of additive ego alteration is caused, according to them by "... an integration of highly complex mental functioning, including memory, retention, conceptualization, degree of consciousness, and perception." (Brody, p. 61). In still another context, they refer to identification as the summated "content" of the afore-mentioned developmental process. Identification, in such a framework, involves the ego and superego as formed and organized structures, as well as their internalized contents (values, expressive styles, impulse–defense configurations, etc.)

Schafer (1967) enlarges the psychoanalytic conception of identification beyond the depiction of a process in which the child internalizes parental superego characteristics (instinctual renunciations, moral judgments) to one in which the child internalizes an integrated composite including ego and id attitudes as well. He states: "As in the case of ideals, this separation of identification is essentially a conceptual artifact. For what do we observe in our patients? We find that what they have identified with are complex id–ego–superego positions or mental organizations—particularly those of their parents. For example, in the identification with a parent given to outbursts of temper, it is not only discharge of id aggression that is involved; also included in the identification are ego positions on defense and control and superego positions on prohibition and renunciation" (Schafer, p. 142). Thus, in Schafer's conception, total structural constellations of the parental figures come to be duplicated in the child.

Knight (1940) adds still another dimension to the conception of identification, speaking of an interaction of introjective and projective processes. Thus, he argues that what exists in reality are complex introjective-projective processes, with one or the other predominating at a given moment of time. Knight thus thinks of identification as ". . . the result of various mechanisms, introjection being the principal one, but with projection, displacement, substitution and perhaps other mechanisms also in operation." (Knight, p. 336).

Psychoanalytic thinking has tended to be most incisive when describing the *end products* of identificatory processes such as ego ideals, impulse-defense configurations, and superego constellations. There has been slightly more fuzziness, however, in the analytic description of the *process* by which such structural contents come about. Psychoanalysts have largely restricted themselves to vague metaphorical analogies to oral incorporative processes such as biting and swallowing. The motivation for identification is, at times, assumed to be the threat posed by a potentially aggressive adult authority and, at other times, assumed to be an apprehension over the possible loss of love of a warm and supportive love object. Very little clarification of the exact mechanics of the process by which such motives lead to established identifications is offered, however.

LEARNING THEORY FORMULATION

The learning theory approach to the problem of identification has tended to focus upon an explication of the mechanism by which identification takes place.

Dollard and Miller (1941) propound a theory of imitation learning that, at least outwardly, appears relevant to the concept of identification. According to their theory, imitation learning consists of the positive reinforcement of a motivated subject for matching the correct responses of a model during a series of initially random, trial-and-error responses.

Although Dollard and Miller consider their illustrative experiments as demonstrations of imitation learning, Bandura (1963) has argued that they in fact represent only the special case of discrimination place learning, in which the behavior of others provides discriminative stimuli for responses that already exist in the subject's behavioral repertory. Such a theory, according to Bandura, cannot account for the occurrence of imitative behavior in which the observer does not perform the models' responses during the acquisition process and for which reinforcers are not delivered either to the models or the observers. At any rate, Dollard and Miller's theory must be viewed as relevant only to circumstances in which the observer is blind to the full nature of the stimulus circumstances and hence must depend upon a *matching* of the model's behavior in order to attain a rewarding outcome.

Mowrer's theory of imitative learning (1950) emphasizes the importance of the principle of *contiguity*. He describes a form of "vicarious learning" in which the response-correlated stimuli of the model arouses in the observer an expectation that he too will experience analogous response-correlated stimuli for acting in a manner similar to the model. Thus, when the observer sees a film model's verbal and behavioral expressions of satisfaction after emitting a particular response he is quite likely, according to Mowrer, to imitate that response. Mowrer argues that the learned imitative responses are sustained in the observer by a rewarding (motivational or emotional) proprioceptive feedback that has been associated through classical conditioning with that particular emitted response. Thus, imitation occurs only when the observer is directly or vicariously rewarded by the sensory consequences to himself of the model's instrumental responses.

Mowrer, in addition, describes a form of imitation learning in which the model directly rewards the observer while, at the same time, emitting a particular response. The model's response hence tends to take on a *secondary reward* value for the observer leading to attempts by the observer to approximate that response at times when it is not being made by the model.

The learning theory approach to the problem of identification has frequently been criticized for its *hyper-specificity* and elementaristic slant. Thus, there appears to be an emphasis upon the learning of specific S-R connections rather than upon the incorporation of total and complexly-organized behavior constellations. Lazowick (1955) describes a learning conception in which a subject matches the *mediating responses* or complexly-integrated "meaning systems" of the model rather than merely matching the discrete responses emitted by the model. In contrast to a mere *imitation* conception in which tiny and discrete behavioral responses are incorporated into the observer's response repertory, Lazowick proposes a concept emphasizing the incorporation of broad cognitive meaning systems. Such a conception, he feels, is much more relevant to the broad characterological, expressive, and moral structural changes that lie at the heart of the concept of identification.

SOCIOLOGICAL AND SOCIAL LEARNING THEORIES

The sociological conception of the identification process emphasizes that identifications occur within a social interaction matrix. Family interactions are seen as a crucial determinant of internalization processes. Thus, the total family is considered to be a complex interactional framework within which the child learns and hence takes over a variety of role identifications.

Sears (1962), studying the impact of particular child-rearing practices upon conscience development in children, concludes that the development of an adequate conscience requires an initial stage of dependence upon parents who are warm and affectionate within a family atmosphere of mutual trust and esteem in which love-oriented techniques of discipline are used. The child who is brought up in such a home adopts the parents' values and ideals as a part of his own charter of conduct in order to insure a continuation of his parents' love.

In the parent–child diad or interaction, the parent tends to have direct control over many *resources* which the child is capable of controlling only indirectly through the parent. The capacity of parents to mediate resources is an essential factor in Whiting's (1962) theory of identification. Whiting speaks of an initial *cognizance* stage in which the child develops the capacity to predict reciprocal adult behavior accurately. The child tends to envy the status of his parents whom he perceives as having more control over resources than he has. As soon as envy occurs of a given status, the child, according to Whiting, attempts to play the role associated with such a status. The child covertly practices the role, fantasizing himself as the envied person. He also practices the role overtly. The child during the series of processes depicted by Whiting, gradually takes over the disciplinary and moral roles of his parents.

Perhaps the most elaborate and empirically-validated conception of identification is contained in Bandura's writings (1963, 1963, 1961). Central to Bandura's approach is his emphasis upon the *modelling* process. Children, he feels, are capable of a form of observational learning in which they directly take over a number of traits, attitudes, and behavior patterns from adult models, without the mediation of reinforcements. Thus, neither the child nor the adult model need be rewarded for social learning to occur. The mere observation of an adult model's behavior sequence can, under certain circumstances, lead to an enhancement of that form of behavior in the child observer. To substantiate the existence of forms of social learning unmediated by reinforcement contingencies, Bandura presents a number of experimental demonstrations. In the demonstrations, children are shown to take over a variety of behavior patterns such as aggressive activities and patterns of self restraint.

Bandura does not, of course, deny the importance of reinforcement contingencies upon the modelling process. He feels, however, that rewards and punishments affect the *performance* of a given behavior pattern more than they do the initial *acquisition* of that pattern. Imitative responses are acquired, according to Bandura, primarily as a result of the contiguity of sensory events. Quite complex and totally novel behavioral sequences can be reproduced by children after merely a single observation of an adult model in action.

Bandura gives a number of examples of situations in which imitative social learning can run counter to standard social training practices. Thus, he describes the case of a parent who physically punishes a child for having struck a neighbor's child, and states: "Concurrently with the intentional training, however, the parent is providing a model of the very behavior he is attempting to inhibit in the child." (Bandura, page 1, 1963).

The primary contribution of Bandura's approach is his strong emphasis upon a form of social learning, directly *cognitive* in nature, and yet responsive to the standard learning principles of reinforcement. Identification, according to his conception, is thus a form of social learning in which the child imitates novel patterns of behavior that he has perceived in the adult models of his environment.

A COGNITIVE APPROACH

Kagan (1958) thinks of the identification process as involving an empathic cognitive bond between subject and model. The subject is motivated toward experiencing or obtaining positive goal states which he perceives that the model commands such as mastery of the environment and love and affection.

At some point during development, the subject is reinforced by the environment, according to Kagan, to believe that being similar to an esteemed model is equivalent to possessing his positive and desirable characteristics. Thus, the identification response is secondarily reinforced by perceptions of similarity between characteristics of the subject and model. An identification is maintained only so long as the subject perceives the model commanding desired goal states. The subject is hence constantly directed toward bringing his own self perceptions into congruence with those of an esteemed model with whom an empathic bond has been established. He attempts to establish behavioral similarities to the model, in some cases actively imitating activity patterns.

Kagan feels that identification tendencies should decrease with age as the subject begins to no longer need to gratify mastery and love needs through a "vicarious" mechanism. Behavioral tendencies that have been established as a result of identification can then function autonomously within the personality of the subject.

A CONCEPTUAL INTEGRATION

The theories of identification discussed above are all attempts at explaining the phenomenon by which one individual takes over attributes from another during the course of an interpersonal relationship. It is highly unlikely that any one of them is sufficient to deal with the phenomenon in and of itself. It is much more likely that an integration of all of them will be necessary, with an emphasis being placed upon both *process* and *content* aspects.

Identification, when viewed in terms of *process*, has structural, defensive, and cognitive characteristics, and is intrinsically related to social learning and character development.

The *structural* aspect of identification is clearly implied by its intimate involvement in the process of ego-formation. The very nature of the ego is shaped through identifications. The introjection of characteristics possessed by parental and other forms of authority figures helps to shore up the ego and give it substance. At moments of great object loss, introjection of certain characteristics of the lost love object typically occurs as a sort of restitution of that object. The developing individual thus takes on the personal characteristics of a number of persons with whom he has maintained an intimate object relationship. The ego is, to some extent, a structural composite derived from an individual's past object relationships.

Identification may also imply a *defensive* process. Thus, the concept of an *identification with the aggressor* involves a process by which an individual takes on the characteristics of a threatening and more powerful external figure. Identification, when viewed in such a light, involves a form of counter-phobic mechanism by which an individual comes to grips with a threatening passive experience, by taking on the role of the active aggressor. Although Freud tended to specifically relate such a defensive process to the resolution of the oedipal crisis, it may perhaps be generalized to a far broader series of identificatory coping maneuvers. Thus, throughout childhood and young adulthood, the individual is constantly faced with external authority figures who obviously are more powerful and effective copers than he is. Identifications, however, allow for an enrichment of the individual's coping capacity through an assimilation of mastery techniques. The initially weak and incompetent individual hence becomes more masterful by internalizing the characteristics of more powerful and aggressive authority figures.

The formation of a strong ego replete with a sense of mastery and a capacity for competent coping efforts is, of course, dependent upon the *social learning* history of the individual. If the individual has been lucky enough to have been confronted with masterful and competent models then he too will take on such attributes. If, however, he has been confronted with less competent models then he will not be capable of coping effectively. The process of modelling is directly cognitive in nature and occurs by means of perceptual imitation and a vicarious sharing of internal subjective states. The perceptual salience of the model hence is an essential factor in determining his social learning impact upon the perceiving subject. Particular attributes such as physical stature and expressive style and movements take on, therefore, extreme importance. Such a social learning process is, of course, also affected by standard principles of learning, such as reward and punishment, motivational variables, and degree of practice.

The *content* of identifications range from id factors such as anger and sexual dispositions to superego factors such as moral prohibitions and value judgments. Other forms of superego identifications may include types of self-restriction, impulse control, and disciplined work habits. Ego factors such as interests, characterological formations and expressive styles are also the product of identifications. The insight provided by Schafer's ego psychological approach (1967) must also, however, be kept in mind. Schafer noted that, beyond such part processes of identification, there can also exist complex composites of identifications. Some manifest forms of behavior that outwardly appear to be determined by superego processes thus may also be integrally connected to id and ego determinants.

Although such identificatory composites and part processes are initially formed on the basis of a *dependent* interaction in which a weaker and less potent subject is required to model himself after an outwardly stronger and more competent authority figure, such is not the case once the particular traits have been adequately internalized. At a later stage, the internalized traits become *autonomous* functions integrated within the fabric of the subject's total personality constellation, and can be maintained without modelling interaction.

THE IMPORTANCE OF MODEL ATTRIBUTES

The rather broad conception developed in the present paper implies the importance of model attributes in determining the nature and extent of identification processes. A number of specific hypotheses with regard to group psychotherapy interactions are suggested by such a conception.

Hypothesis One

Physical characteristics such as the height and build of the group therapist, since they effect his "perceptual salience," should tend to affect the degree to which he is identified with by the individual group members.

Hypothesis Two

Physiognomic characteristics conveyed through the therapist's habitual facial expression, bodily posture, and movement patterns should also be related to the degree of identification. Expressive styles conveying salient attitudes of confidence, activity, vibrancy, and involvement should, in general, lead to more identifications than more neutral nondescript expressive styles. No value judgment is implied by the particular expressive attributes listed above. The inference is merely being drawn that a more expressive therapist will be identified with more readily, all other things being equal, than a less expressive therapist.

Hypothesis Three

Psychological factors such as the apparent competence, powerfulness, narcissistic self assuredness, aggressiveness, and potential for assertive leadership, of the therapist will effect the degree to which he is identified with by the individual group members.

Hypothesis Four

Sociological characteristics such as the social status and powerfulness within a recognized social hierarchy of the group leader will effect the degree to which he is identified with.

The above four hypotheses, presented as they are in an oversimplified form are meant merely to be examples of the kind of inferences with regard to model characteristics that can be drawn from a broad conception of the identification process. They are not meant to be rigidly adhered to and are merely a series of tentative assumptions which need to be tested out through systematic observation of group interaction processes. A value judgment should not be implied with regard to the personal characteristics necessary for the *ideal* group therapist. On the other hand, it should be stressed that personal attributes of the therapist are quite relevant to whether or not identificatory interactions occur during the course of group therapy. Identification does not occur in a vacuum, nor is the therapist a mere *blank screen* upon whom the patient projects personal feelings and attitudes.

The personal characteristics of the subject are also, of course, important factors in determining whether or not an identification occurs. Thus, certain model attributes may be effective with one subject but not another. The interrelatedness between subject and model characteristics is thus also an important aspect of the identification process meriting serious systematic study.

In summary, a review of a number of different conceptions has led to an integrated formulation of the process of *identification*. The latter formulation incorporates principles derived from psychoanalysis, learning theory, social learning theory, sociology, and the psychology of cognition.

The formulation has been applied to the process of group psychotherapy, a number of hypotheses being suggested with regard to leader characteristics which should tend to enhance identificatory behavior.

REFERENCES

Bandura, A. and Walters, R. H. (1963): *Social Learning and Personality Development.* New York. Holt, Rinehart and Winston.

Bandura, A., Ross, D. and Ross, S. A. (1963): Imitation of Film-Mediated Aggressive Models. *J. Abnorm. Soc. Psychol.,* **66**, 3–11.

Bandura, A., Ross, D. and Ross, S. A. (1961): Transmission of Aggression through Imitations of Aggressive Models. *J. Abnorm. Soc. Psychol.,* **63**, 575–582.

Brody, M. W. and Mahoney, V. P. (1964): Introjection, Identification, and Incorporation. *Int'l J. Psychoanal.,* **45**, 57–63.

Dollard, J. and Miller, N. E. (1941): *Social Learning and Imitation.* New Haven. Yale Univer. Press.

Freud, S. (1960): *Group Psychology and the Analysis of the Ego.* New York. Bantam Books.

Freud, S. (1933): New Introductory Lectures on Psychoanalysis. New York. W. W. Norton and Co.

Freud, S. (1953): The Passing of the Oedipus Complex. In Freud, S. *Collected Papers.* Vol. II. London. Hogarth Press.

Freud, S. (1953): Mourning and Melancholia. In Freud, S. *Collected Papers.* Vol. IV. London. Hogarth Press.

Kagan, J. (1958): The Concept of Identification. *Psychol. Rev.,* 65, 296–305.

Knight, R. P. (1940): Introjection, Projection and Identification. *Psychoanal. Quarterly,* 9, 334–341.

Lazowick, L. M. (1955): On the Nature of Identification. *J. Abnorm. Soc. Psychol.,* 51, 175–183.

Mowrer, O. H. (1950): *Learning Theory and Personality Dynamics.* New York. Ronald Press.

Parsons, T. (1955): Family Structure and the Socialization of the Child. In Parsons, T. and Bales, R. F. *Family, Socialization and Interaction Process.* Glencoe, Illinois. Free Press.

Schafer, (1967): Ideals, Ego Ideal, and Ideal Self. In Holt, R. R. Edit. *Motives and Thought. Psychoanalytic Essays in Honor of David Rapaport.* New York. Int'l Univ. Press.

Sears, R. R. (1962): The Growth of Conscience. In Iscoe, I. and Stevenson, H. W. *Personality Development in Children.* Austin. Univ. of Texas Press.

Singer, E. (1965): Identity vs. Identification: A Thorny Psychological Issue. *Rev. of Existential Psychol. and Psychiat.,* 5, 160–175.

Whiting, J. M. (1962): Resource Mediation and Learning by Identification. In Isoe, I. and Stevenson, H. W. *Personality Development in Children.* Austin. Univ. of Texas Press.

V

GROUP PSYCHOTHERAPY AND PSYCHOANALYSIS

17

Notes on Psychoanalytic Group Therapy: Interpretation and Research

Henry Ezriel
Tavistock Clinic
London, England

["Here and now" aspects of the transference relationship are explored by Ezriel in terms of their therapeutic potential for both individual and group psychoanalysis. Such a contemporaneous (and clearly Lewinian field theoretical) orientation toward the process of transference interpretation—particularly in the group setting—allows, according to Ezriel, for a truly "experimental" and hence scientifically reliable and valid methodology within the framework of psychoanalytic inquiry. The group analyst's interpretive inferences with regard to the "common group tension" and its components (i.e., required, avoided, and calamitous object relationships) can thus truly be verified in a solidly empirical fashion.]

In this paper, I shall outline some suggestions for experimental research which have emerged from our experience in developing what we consider to be a strictly psychoanalytic approach to group therapy. These possible lines of research apply just as much to individual psychoanalytic treatment, but it will

From "Notes on Psychoanalytic Group Therapy: II. Interpretation and Research" by H. Ezriel, *Psychiatry*, 1952, *15*, 119–126. Copyright 1952 by The William Alanson White Psychiatric Foundation. Reprinted by special permission of The William Alanson White Psychiatric Foundation, Inc.

become apparent in what follows to what extent they have been stimulated by work with groups.

"HERE AND NOW" INTERPRETATIONS

My starting point is the development which has taken place in the use of transference interpretations in recent years. A comparison of the technique of interpretation as practiced by various psychoanalysts shows considerable differences. Almost all analysts, however, feel that it is necessary to link up *in their interpretations* the patient's present unconscious conflicts with his past, especially with his infantile experiences.

With regard to this point, the application of psychoanalytic therapy to groups presented to us a certain problem: When interpreting the unconscious common group tension, to what infantile experiences are we to refer? A therapeutic group is an artifact created by us which has, of course, no common infantile history with which we could link the unconscious common group tension.

If it is not the tracing back of present behavior patterns to the patient's past, especially to his infantile history, what is it then that forms the content of such "here and now" interpretations as those mentioned by Dr. Sutherland in his present paper? This issue may become clearer if I reproduce for you the train of thought I had when I started work with groups in 1945.

Freud's original view was that the patient's unconscious *memories* of conflicts concerning persons of his infantile environment acted as a dynamic source for his thoughts during a session, his so-called free associations. Further, Freud considered that psychoanalysis is a method which enables us to make use of these thoughts in order to reconstruct the historical genesis of the patient's symptoms and that the putting before the patient of such historical reconstructions removes these symptoms. Freud himself altered this hypothesis when he discovered two facts which he described as "psychical reality" and "transference." By psychical reality[1] he meant the fact that the so-called "memories" of forgotten events uncovered in psychoanalysis were not necessarily memories of *real* events, but were often phantasies. Nevertheless they were psychologically as effective as if they had been memories of real events. This meant, however, that what the analyst uncovered was not an objective reproduction of the patient's past but *unconscious structures active in the present*, though formed in the past out of phantasies and out of correct or distorted memories of past events.

The second discovery which led to the modification of the genetic theory of psychoanalytic therapy was the phenomenon of transference[2] —that is, the fact that patients who had set out with their analyst to study the genesis of

---

[1] Sigmund Freud, *Introductory Lectures on Psycho-Analysis* (Riviere, tr.), 2nd ed.; London, Allen and Unwin, 1949; pp. 307–309.

[2] Reference footnote 1; pp. 367–372.

their symptoms by unravelling the history of their past experiences, very soon reproduced, or as Freud called it, "transferred" the conflicts they had had with the persons of their early environment to their therapist in the here and now of his consulting room. While patient and analyst had started their work like two friendly archaeologists trying to dig up the patient's past, they had now become two human beings interacting with one another in the here and now, and the analyst represented to the patient—according to the latter's unconscious phantasies—something different in each session, friend or foe, victim or persecutor, and many other things.

However, once analysts focused their attention on the transference phenomenon, it became apparent that transference is not something that gradually appears in the course of an analysis, but that it is active from the patient's first meeting with his therapist.

Since then the vast majority of analysts have—from the first session on—used the material produced by a patient partly as transference material—that is, as the expression of the patient's *attempts to establish* in the here and now certain kinds of relationships with the analyst—and partly as extra-transference material—that is, as communications in which the patient *reports* to the analyst his presentday or past relations with others (openly or in a disguised form) and which the analyst then tries to interpret as expressions of the patient's unconscious conflicts with others, especially with persons of his infantile environment. Many analysts who employ a more rigorous transference technique still feel a need to combine, in their transference interpretations, explanations of the here and now with comments on the patients' past.

However, it seemed to me a logical step to extend the transference hypothesis—to treat *all* material as transference material and hence to use it for here and now interpretations. This means that everything the patient says or does during a session—movements, gestures, phantasies, dreams, correct memories, and even deliberate lies—is considered as the *idiom* used by the patient to give expression to his need in that session for a specific relationship with his therapist. In other words, even the patient's reports to the analyst about his relations with others, past and present, are taken as attempts to *involve* the analyst as an active participant in relations which the patient entertains with his unconscious objects as they seem to exist here and now and with their representatives in external reality. If this extension of the transference hypothesis were justified it would, of course, solve our difficulty with groups which have no infantile history to which we could refer.

Let us return to Dr. Sutherland's example to test this assumption. When I am listening to patients' discussions, I always put to myself the question, What makes these patients say and do these things in front of me at this moment? I make my interpretive comments as soon as I think that I can distinguish in the material *three kinds of object relations*: one, an object relationship which they try to establish within the group, and in particular with myself, and which I should like to call the *required* relationship; another, which they feel they have to *avoid* in external reality, however much they may desire it; and a third, which depicts a *calamity* which the patient seems convinced would follow inevitably if he allowed himself to give in to his secret desire of entering into the avoided object relationship. This conviction could be explained by making the hypothesis that the calamity *does* occur in the psychical reality of his unconscious phantasies, his inner world where he does establish the avoided relationship.

A detailed description of the operational rules which would enable us to recognize these three object relationships in the manifest material will have to form the subject of a separate paper. I do wish, however, to point out here that in *individual* sessions the most important of these rules consists in abstracting the common features of the total material verbalized or enacted by the patient in that session. For instance, if a patient enumerates various experiences in each of which a man appears who is either "disappointing" or "weak" or "not as good as I had thought" or "a rogue," the common dynamic feature may be a relationship with a man towards whom he feels critical. In the same way we try to abstract from the total manifest material three common denominators which correspond to the three object relationships already described—namely, the *required,* the *avoided*, and the *calamitous.*

In a group an additional analytic task is the finding of the common group tension. This is done in a similar way to that just described in regard to the unconscious tension in individual sessions. That is to say, the total material produced by *all* the members of the group is treated as if it had been produced by *one* patient in an individual session, and the object relationships that correspond to the common group tension are abstracted as the common denominators of this material.

For instance, in Dr. Sutherland's example, the calamity the group feared was their expectation of his rejecting them or even being angry with them. It was this fear which made them avoid giving in to their secret and largely unconscious wish to break up the supposedly intimate relationship between Dr. Sutherland and the two observers. You can recognize what they avoided if you consider, in conjunction, Mr. B's dream in which he injured the two men behind the counter and Mr. A's wish to establish an intimate nickname relationship with Dr. Sutherland's substitute, the officer Sutherland, to the exclusion of the two observers. The relationship they required in order to be able to suppress their desire for the avoided relationship was to comfort themselves with an intimate Christian-name relationship among themselves. This ostensibly excluded Dr. Sutherland and the observers, but in fact implied that they put up with the intimacies between the analyst and the observers—intimacies which, as their remarks after the interpretation show, represented to them sexual intimacy between a couple who excluded them and made them jealous. Another outlet which helped them to suppress the avoided relationship in external reality was to give expression to it in their dreams.

In previous papers[3] I quoted case material in an attempt to show that every interpretation, to be effective, must contain a "because" clause. Even if not actually couched in such words, an interpretation must—in my opinion—demonstrate to the patient that he is adopting one course of behavior and avoiding another *because* he fears the supposedly disastrous consequences of the latter. It is at this point that reality testing begins. Thus Dr. Sutherland's patients were able to compare their expectation of the officer Sutherland's becoming angry, with the behavior of the real Dr. Sutherland who showed to them, through his interpretation, that he knew about their wish to separate him from the observers but that he did not get angry.

It is this reality testing which enables patients to give less disguised expression in external reality to the hitherto avoided behavior pattern, and to integrate the experience gained in that session with experiences outside the analytic situation—experiences both in their present environment and in their past, especially also in their infantile past.

Dr. Sutherland's patients could suddenly recognize that the wishes expressed in their dreams were in fact directed towards him and the observers, and they could follow it up by thinking and speaking about past experiences concerning couples in sexual relationships of which they were jealous. As you can see, the analyst used only here and now interpretations in this session. Both this session and a number of group and individual sessions of which I have been able to make electrical recordings confirm the view that whatever effect interpretations referring to the past may have, the specific effects attributed to such interpretations can certainly be achieved by confining oneself to interpretations along the lines discussed by Dr. Sutherland and myself in these papers.

THE PSYCHOANALYTIC SESSION AS AN EXPERIMENTAL SITUATION

It is not, however, to consider the most effective kind of interpretation that I have raised the subject of a here and now approach in psychoanalysis. I have done so because I think that the recognition of transference as the driving force behind *everything* a patient does during his session has important implications for the use of the psychoanalytic method as a research tool. As long as analysts focus their attention on the patient's behavior *outside* the consulting room—for example, by trying to explain what made him behave in a certain way in his past—such conjectures, however near the mark they might be, cannot be tested within the psychoanalytic session and have to rely for scientific validation on other methods, such as confirmation by outsiders,

[3] Ezriel, "A Psycho-Analytic Approach to Group Treatment," *British J. Med. Psychol.* (1950) 23:59–74. Ezriel, "The Psycho-Analytic Session as an Experimental Situation," *British J. Med. Psychol.* (1951) 24:30–34.

behavioristic studies of children, statistical correlations between behavior in childhood and corresponding personality traits of adults, and so on.

If, however, the psychoanalytic method is one that permits the study of the dynamics underlying the interactions between patient and analyst as they take place in each session—that is, if this method examines events occurring in the here and now—then it ought to be possible to state the dynamics of these events in the form of hypotheses that can be tested, validated or falsified, through direct observation of the patient's behavior during his sessions. In other words, the psychoanalytic session thus becomes an experimental situation and we ought to be able to state the conditions, necessary and sufficient, to produce a predictable event during that session; in fact, we can formulate, as I have done elsewhere,[4] a law of behavior derived from such situations as were reported in Dr. Sutherland's group session.[5]

> If we set up a field by putting together a group of patients in need of treatment and a therapist presumably able to satisfy this need, and if the therapist assumes a passive nondirective role, then these patients will display in their words and actions a manifest form of behavior from which three kinds of object relationship can be inferred: (i) the avoided relationship, (ii) the calamity they fear, and (iii) the required relationship which they have to adopt because of this fear. If then the analyst gives an interpretation—that is, points out these three object relationships in the here and now—the subsequent material will contain the hitherto avoided object relationship in a less repressed form.

Such a law can even be expressed quantitatively if we use, like Lewin, a nonmetricized topological approach, for instance, by taking as one of our yardsticks the distance of an avoided object relationship from the here and now relationship with the analyst. Thus, as a result of Dr. Sutherland's interpretation, the officer Sutherland turned into the Dr. Sutherland; Mr. A's avoided object relationship had thus moved from the army unit in which he had served during the war into Dr. Sutherland's consulting room.

Analysts will, of course, realize that what is expressed in this law is nothing but the well-known fact which underlies all analytic theory and practice—namely, that analytic interpretations enable the patient to become conscious of his hitherto unconscious needs. A here and now approach has, however, made it possible to formulate this fact as a proposition which can be quantified and tested experimentally in the analytic situation.

The objection has been raised that psychoanalytic sessions cannot be regarded as experiments since the data collected cannot be examined by other observers. This is no longer true. Before analysts saw patients in groups they

[4] Henry Ezriel, "The Psycho-Analytic Session as an Experimental Situation," reference footnote 3; p. 33.

[5] The formulation given in this paper is, I think, more exact than the one given in the previous paper (reference footnote 4).

were convinced that the intrusion of a third person into this most intimate relationship would make analysis impossible. In the group, however, we soon discovered that by using here and now interpretations, which enable us to deal effectively with patients' persecutory fears stimulated by such intruders, analytic investigation and therapy *could* be carried out in the presence of seven or eight observers—namely, fellow patients. It was the utilization of this fact which led us to introduce colleagues as additional observers into such groups, and later on we openly suspended microphones as objective means of recording, both in groups and in individual sessions.

I have now collected electrically recorded sessions which provide a means of subsequent examination by other observers—naturally with due precautions to preserve the patients' anonymity—and which have confirmed in every case the law I have already stated.

Another objection is that phenomena observed in psychoanalytic sessions are unique and that only events which can be repeated can be made use of in experiments. I think this view is based on two misunderstandings. One is the clinging to the view that psychoanalysis is a method which reconstructs the unique history of an individual. I have in this paper tried to prove to you the opposite—that psychoanalysis is a method to study events in the here and now.

The second misunderstanding concerns what has and what has not to be observed repeatedly in order to form the basis of experiments or of scientific statements in general. Logicians will tell us that every event in the universe is unique if we take into account *all* its features—that is, if our observations are subtle enough. Every analyst knows that what we are wont to call the Oedipus complex, or any other analytic concept for that matter, manifests itself in a unique way in each session of the same or of different patients. In spite of that we can make scientifically valid statements if we abstract the common dynamically significant features from the dynamically insignificant historically unique differences of these sessions. We can thus—on a certain level of abstractions—arrive at the formulation of the dynamics of the Oedipus complex with as much justification as the physicist has to formulate the laws of gravitation from such manifestly different phenomena as the movements of planets, of a pendulum, or of a freely falling stone. The physicist is well aware that no two experiments he repeats with a pendulum, for instance, are identical in all their features. However, what matters is not that two experiments should be identical in every respect, but that they should have in common those properties which are dynamically significant for the particular kind of event we study. An individual's history is unique; whatever a patient reports in his session about his experiences, his remote or recent past, is always unique. However, the psychodynamically significant elements of this unique history are by no means unique, and it is these elements which allow the formulation of scientifically valid statements as well as the observation of phenomena under experimental conditions.

Perhaps you may feel by now that although this may be a legitimate experimental study of the effects of interpretations, it is of interest only to the psychoanalyst and to no one else. However, if we realize that hidden behind the desire for cure lie those most vital needs which an individual has not been able to satisfy, then we can see that the analyst's *comments* in the analytic situation, his correct as well as incorrect interpretations, represent to the patient *actions* of people who assume different kinds of attitudes towards the ways in which he can satisfy his basic needs. In other words, the analytic situation is a prototype of what underlies human behavior in general; it is a need situation, and the experimental study of an individual's behavior in this situation allows the formulation of laws underlying *all* human behavior.

THE THERAPEUTIC GROUP AS A MEDIUM OF STUDY

Our interpretive technique at present is very much more refined for individual therapy than for group psychoanalysis. I am therefore trying to study the main kinds of unconscious object relations and their role in the structure of personality from the records of individual sessions as well as of group sessions. Such studies should enable us to formulate basic laws of behavior. There are, however, specific problems which can only be investigated in groups.

Perhaps I may refer briefly to one recorded session. In the preceding sessions a man in this group, Mr. X, had tried to escape from various unconscious difficulties by making numerous attempts to oust me, the recognized leader of the group, and to gain the women's admiration. He had been rebuffed by the group on all those occasions. The group as a whole had become increasingly aware of their sexual jealousies and of the aggressive impulses aroused by them. They had also been able to give clearer expression to these impulses within the analytic sessions, but especially outside of the sessions, according to their own statements.

The session I wish to report started with a short silence followed by a few remarks which betrayed the uneasiness of the group at things to come. One woman then concluded this initial period by saying that they would probably go on dealing with the same problems as in previous sessions but on a more real level.

Another silence followed, this time broken by another woman who started putting relations in the group on a more real level by turning to a very practical problem. She asked me, "Do you think the fire could be switched off, Dr. E?" When I tried to turn this question back to the group with my usual remark, "What do you think?" an uproar started in the group. Several members expressed unconcealed anger with me, and one of them, a pregnant woman, looked so flushed and upset that I feared something might happen to her. I therefore gave in to the group's request by switching off the fire without seeing clearly what the upheaval was really about. Shortly after that the expression of hostility towards me fizzled out, and the group started speaking about teacher–pupil relations. In particular a teacher was ridiculed who kept on looking out of the window at the playgrounds while depriving his pupils of this pleasure.

Very soon a discussion developed on the benefits one might derive from attending the group and on the kind of discussion which would prove most helpful. At this time, a split occurred in the group. Up to now there had been a more or less cooperative discussion to which various members contributed; but suddenly Mr. X, the male patient mentioned before, became the center of critical remarks from the rest of the group who seemed to line up against him.

The issue under discussion seemed rather confused. Although Mr. X had stood up for the usefulness of psychoanalysis, against another group member's initial doubts that group treatment could help her beyond the point she had already reached, the other group members reacted towards Mr. X as if he had attacked psychoanalysis. The discussion then veered towards semantics. Here again the implication was that Mr. X was attacking and the rest were defending psychoanalytic therapy; yet this was in fact not true. While the rest of the group insisted that he was trying to avoid psychoanalysis by turning emotionally charged discussions into an intellectual semantic hair-splitting, he insisted that the separation between the intellectual content of a discussion and its emotional tone was an artificial one.

I must point out here that in previous sessions I had said much the same thing on those occasions when I tried to show the group that their ostensibly intellectual discussions were the expressions of emotional conflicts within the group. This time Mr. X had fully accepted the basis of here and now interpretations and was in fact standing up for what he had attacked on previous occasions, under the pressure of feelings of rivalry and jealousy towards me.

A significant point in this discussion was when Mr. Y, a most submissive patient who had consistently played in the group the part of a pacifying and soothing agent, suddenly became the spearhead of the attack against Mr. X and insisted on "having it out" with him with regard to the issue of intellectualizing the emotional content of psychoanalytic sessions. When this happened, the irony of the situation became obvious to the whole group; in fact this attempt to fight Mr. X on the issue of intellectualizing emotions led the group as a whole into the most intellectual hair-splitting discussion, for which, this time, not Mr. X but the rest of the group were responsible. Mr. X pointed this out to the group at the beginning of his contest with the others when he put the teasing remark to Mr. Y, "Are you starting an intellectual discussion?" and provoked laughter in the whole group. In spite of that, Mr. X and the rest of the group did not desist from engaging in what all group members pretended they were so much against—namely, a hair-splitting intellectual discussion.

If we ask again what were the underlying forces motivating the trend of the discussion in that session, it seems clear to me that from the moment I switched off the fire, the group started repeating the pattern which they had tried to enact before towards me. Apparently the reason for this repetition of pattern was that my giving in to their request to switch off the fire had resulted in their *not* being frustrated with regard to an issue which they would have liked to imagine was the cause of their frustration and of their wish to attack me. My behavior had therefore only shelved their problem. I had deprived them of the channel through which they tried to express their piled-up resentment towards a frustrating person. I had, however, not removed—by means of interpretation of the underlying motives—their need to adopt this kind of aggressive object relationship with me. The result was that they felt the same compulsion as before to attack some kind of leader on a displaced issue which allowed them to conceal the real cause of their anger—that is, their sexual frustration. By switching off the fire I had done what reassuring therapy usually does—namely, I had temporarily withdrawn myself from the patients' attempts to transfer their unconscious object relationships to the therapist. Thus, while this had established peace between us for the moment, it left the group with an undiminished need to find a leader whom they could attack.

What then developed between Mr. X and the rest of the group may serve as a good illustration of what is meant by unconscious collusion in interpersonal relations, one of the problems which can only be studied in groups. All members of this group seemed driven by forces beyond their control into what *they* considered to be a useless discussion. The group, for reasons they were not aware of, needed a leader whom they could attack, and they found such a scapegoat in Mr. X. Mr. X, on the other hand, by offering himself as a scapegoat for me achieved his equally unconsciously determined aim of becoming the central figure of the group round whom everything revolved. For this, he was prepared not only to waste a session, but even to become the most unpopular member of the group on that occasion.

This session shows how different unconscious needs of two or more individuals may interact and complement one another and lead to the kind of interpersonal relations which all of them deplore; further, how unconscious tensions may prevent a group from getting on with their job. (In this therapeutic group the apparent not-getting-on-with-the-job became, of course, the subject of interpretation.)

It may also serve as an example for the emergence of various group structures with different roles, such as leader, scapegoat, confronter, and so on, as an attempt to cope with unconscious tensions.

Another problem we can examine here is to consider what kind of personality will be pushed into what particular role which the group requires at that moment, in view of its need for a certain group structure. Further, we can study more lasting attitudes, likes and dislikes, which develop between certain group members who are persistently pushed into certain group roles and therefore become identified with these roles.

The advantage of the therapeutic group over the usual kind of task group in studying such problems is that in the therapeutic group, though it too has a certain preferred structure, this group structure is of comparatively small influence as compared with the unconscious forces within each group member. This therefore allows us to investigate the particular kind of interpersonal relations that develop under the influence of these unconscious factors. However, in principle these unsonscious factors are in no way different from similar forces within the conscious sphere; clashes of interest over real issues and the methods which individuals and groups adopt to solve them do not differ basically from the conflicts with unconscious objects which we can observe within an individual personality, or within a therapeutic group in which such *intra*-personal conflicts express themselves in *inter*personal relations.

In addition, a task group, as in a factory, office, or school, real clashes of interest within a group and such unconsciously determined conflicts as we study in our therapeutic groups are hopelessly intermingled and react upon one another. The therapeutic group therefore, seems an excellent opportunity for studying such problems in a comparatively simple field.

The detailed examination of every remark patient and analyst make by what might be called "microanalysis" of recorded sessions and, in addition, the development of a set of dynamic concepts seem promising approaches for the formulation and testing of hypotheses about the dynamics of human behavior.

18

Group-Analytic Dynamics with Specific Reference to Psychoanalytic Concepts

S. H. Foulkes
Group-Analytic Society
London, England

[Foulkes' goal is the translation of psychoanalytic principles from the sphere of individual to that of group psychotherapy. He specifically utilizes the term *group analysis* rather than *group psychoanalysis* to distinguish these two forms of therapy. Although he feels that basic structural concepts such as id, ego, and superego and a number of defense mechanisms such as identification, projection, and displacement can easily be translated from individual to group analysis, he also sees the need for a number of more specialized notions such as that of the group communicative "matrix," mirror reactions, and occupations. Such terms capture more fully for him the dynamic processes that occur in groups. Foulkes, like Ezriel, emphasizes the significance of the group-as-a-whole dynamic matrix in shaping the personality patterns of the individual group members and the nature of their interpersonal interactions with each other and with the leader.]

Group analysis is concerned with the total field of mental dynamics, whether these be better studied in an individual or group situation. In this paper a selection will be made and particular attention paid to psychoanalytic equivalents, in which connection some personal remarks may not be out of place.

From "Group-Analytic Dynamics with Specific Reference to Psychoanalytic Concepts" by S. H. Foulkes, *International Journal of Group Psychotherapy*, 1957, 7, 40–52. Copyright 1957 by the International Journal of Group Psychotherapy. Reprinted by permission.

In view of the fact that I am a practicing and teaching psychoanalyst of long standing, surprise has been expressed at my upholding the claim of group analysis to be considered as a therapeutic method valid in its own right and with its own specific theoretical concepts and contributions to make.[1] This does not imply that its practice and theory are at variance with psychoanalysis, indeed without psychoanalysis my particular approach could not have come into being. Incidentally, I would mention here that calling the method I use group analysis and not group psychoanalysis, I am in fundamental agreement with Miss Anna Freud, whose orientation I share closely in the psychoanalytic field. Psychoanalysis is in my view essentially confined to patient and therapist in the individual situation.

Why have I not taken Freud's own specific study of group psychology as the basis on which to form my concepts? Freud's contribution to group psychology was actually based on the findings of individual psychology, although he occasionally showed surprising insight in favor of the reverse procedure. He tended to see group processes merely as extensions of those activities going on in the individual mind which had led him to formulate the concepts of psychoanalysis. Moreover, in his book on this subject,[2] he studied groups of an entirely different nature to those investigated by the present writer. He used two large, highly organized groups—the army and the Catholic church—as models from which to illustrate such concepts as for instance the ego ideal and identification. He did not attempt to explain the dynamic processes taking place in these groups as germane to them, but rather to show how the internal forces characteristic of individual life sought their expression through the group medium.

Classical psychoanalytic concepts can be used with advantage in a group setting to facilitate the process of therapy, but the processes corresponding to them are equivalent to and not identical with those observed in the individual psychoanalytic situation. The wholesale transfer of psychoanalytic concepts to a new field would be particularly inadvisable at the present time when they have lost a good deal of original precision and meaning and are exciting controversy in their own field of origin. Even such vital concepts as transference and identification are in process of revision, or tending to become confused.

Our psychotherapeutic groups are in principle transference groups, in the sense that members can use each other and the therapist as transference figures, as it occurs in psychoanalysis between patient and analyst. However, the pattern of relationships develops with much more complexity in the group

[1] Slavson, S. R.: *Analytic Group Psychotherapy*. New York: Columbia University Press, 1950; Scheidlinger, S.: *Psychoanalysis and Group Behavior*. New York: Norton, 1952.

[2] Freud, S.: *Group Psychology and the Analysis of the Ego* (1921). London: Hogarth Press, 1947.

situation and cannot be explained by applying to it the term transference. On the contrary, the observation of classical transference processes within the group setting throws new light upon them as they are seen in the individual setting. In psychoanalytic literature, the term transference is increasingly used to cover all interactions between therapist and patient. This development applies equally well to the corresponding concept of countertransference. The group-analytic situation could of course be termed a transference situation in this sense, but it would be more correct to apply to it the symbol "t," meaning therapeutic.[3] Thus we can speak of a therapeutic, or "t" relationship, situation, etc., and reserve the term transference situation for its more specific and legitimate application.

Similar considerations obtain in the case of other terms, such as identification. Here again the group reaction seen as a whole cannot be understood simply on the basis of the psychoanalytic concept, whereas the understanding of the dynamics of the situation in which identifications germinate, precipitate or mature, helps us discern those aspects of the process which escape observation and explanation in the psychoanalytic situation.

Group analysis views man's social nature as basic to him and makes the group or community rather than the individual its primary basis for conducting therapy. Individuals emerge as the result of developments in the community, whether this phenomenon be viewed in historical perspective—a comparatively recent affair[4]—or in its current aspect of the individual personality emerging from and formed by his family, as is the case in psychoanalysis. Conceiving the social nature of man as basic does not deny or reduce the importance of the sexual instinct in the sense of psychoanalysis, nor of the aggressive instinct. The infant–mother relationship is the first social relationship in the same sense as it is the first sexual and love relationship.

In this way the psychoanalytic tendency, more specifically Freud's tendency, to look upon the social instinct as a deployment of the sexual or life instinct is quite acceptable, provided this is not held to be the explanation for the social nature of the species Man. The point we wish to make clear is that we hold man's social nature to be an irreducible basic fact. Therefore the group, originally the community, its cohesion and the currents moving in it are primary elements not to be *explained* in terms of the interactions of individuals. We conceive all illness as occurring and originating within a complex of interpersonal relationships. Group psychotherapy is an attempt to treat the total network of disturbance either at the point of origin in the root—or primary—group, or, through placing the disturbed individual under conditions of transference, in a group of strangers or proxy group.

[3] Foulkes, S. H. and Anthony, E. J.: *Group Psychotherapy—The Analytic Approach.* London: Pelican Books (in press).

[4] Elias, N. *Über den Process der Zivilization*, Vol. I: Prague: Academia Verlag, 1937; Vol. II: Basel: Verlag Haus zum Falken, 1939.

When people are brought together in a psychotherapeutic group, a struggle of conflicting tendencies asserts itself, but in spite of impulses to withdraw, the need of the individual to be understood by and related to the group finally and overwhelmingly prevails. This fundamental need to *relate* shows itself with particular clarity even in our groups. (I add "even," because our artificial groups are in effect conglomerations of isolated individuals.) The social basis at once asserts itself, and thus relatedness viewed within an all-penetrating group matrix is the cornerstone of our working theory. The idea of the group as the mental matrix, the common ground of an operational basis for relationships, comprising all the interactions of individual group members is central for the theory and process of therapy. Within this frame of reference all communications take place. A fund of unconscious understanding, wherein occur reactions and communications of great complexity, is always present.

A principle which can be illustrated and supported from observations in therapeutic groups is that every event, even though apparently confined to one or two participants, in fact involves the group as a whole. Such events are part of a gestalt, configuration, of which they constitute the "figures" (foreground), whereas the ground (background) is manifested in the rest of the group. We have described as *location* the process which brings to life this concealed configuration; it is, however, not always a simple matter to locate this pattern of the group's reactions. Other important concepts specific to group analysis and essential for understanding the group-analytic process are those termed *mirror reaction, occupation* and *translation*, which we can only describe briefly here.

Mirror reactions are characteristically brought out when a number of persons meet and interact.[5] A person sees himself, or part of himself—often a repressed part of himself—reflected in the interactions of other group members. He sees them reacting in the way he does himself, or in contrast to his own behavior. He also gets to know himself—and this is a fundamental process in ego development—by the effect he has upon others, and the picture they form of him.

By *occupation* is meant that which is the group's reason for coming together.[6] In everyday life this may be for the purpose of study or work, to play bridge or golf. Such a declared, manifest occupation is deliberately absent from a group-analytic group. In this it differs from a "free discussion" group. Observation of the group-analytic group makes it clear that such an "occupation" acts as a defensive screen to keep at bay intimate interpersonal reactions, thoughts and fantasies. This defensive or screen function makes the

[5] Foulkes, S. H. and Lewis, E.: Group Analysis. *Brit. J. Med. Psychol., 20*:175–184, 1944.

[6] Foulkes, S. H.: Group-Analytic Psychotherapy: A Short Account. *Acta Psychother., 3*:313–319, 1955.

concept of "occupation" important for the understanding of the dynamics both of the group-analytic group and, by implication, of any type of group. There is a tendency for analytic groups to behave as if they had an appointed *occupation*, such as "discussing our problems." An occupation can also be latent, and the group may not be conscious of it. This might be called its *preoccupation*.

Translation is the equivalent of the making conscious of the repressed unconscious in psychoanalysis. The whole group participates in this process, which ranges from inarticulate symptom to verbal expression, understanding and insight, from primary process to secondary process (in the psychoanalytic sense), from primitive to logical, rational expression. Interpretation, in psychoanalysis, refers by contrast only to a special contribution on the part of the psychoanalyst to this translation.

This concept of translation and that of the mental matrix of the group are closely allied to our ideas on *communication*. Group-analytic theory recognizes communication as a process of fundamental importance to the study of behavior and the practice of psychotherapy. In a group-analytic group, all observable data are held to be relevant communications, whether they take the form of conscious or unconscious, verbal or nonverbal communications.

Characteristic nonverbal communications are those made in the form of behavior, either on the part of individual members or by the group as a whole. Appearance and dress may be communications; an exuberant tie or conspicuous shoes, provocative disorder or meticulous neatness may excite comment and lead to insight in the same way as verbal exchange. One person will press for more light to be put on in the room where the group meets, while another will prefer to sit in near darkness, or mislay his spectacles in order not to see. The group as a whole may communicate tension in the shape of silences, or fitful, disjointed conversation. It may express a cheerful mood of relief, or group gloom in which everyone sits and glowers darkly, some on the point of tears.

At one end of the scale is the inarticulate symptom: it may be nail biting, excessive blushing, palpitation of the heart, or migrainous headache; at the other lies its representation in verbal imagery. Between these two must be cut an intricate sequence of steps leading to verbalization. Many complex processes have to play their part before the mute symptom of a fellow member can attain linguistic expression and its meaning be grasped by the others.

It is the *process of communication* rather than the information it conveys which is important to us. In a group-analytic group, communication moves from remote and primitive levels to articulate modes of conscious expression and is closely bound up with the therapeutic process. The therapeutic group establishes a common zone in which all members can participate and learn to understand one another. Within this process members of the group begin to understand the language of the symptom, symbols and dreams as well as verbal communications. They have to learn this through experience in order for it to be meaningful and therefore therapeutically efficient. The "conductor" strives to broaden and deepen the expressive range of all members, while at the same time increasing their understanding of the deeper, unconscious levels. The zone of communication must include the experience of every member in such a way that it can be shared and understood by the others, on whatever level it is first conveyed. This process of communication has much in common with making the unconscious conscious and altogether with the concepts of unconscious, preconscious and conscious in their topographical and dynamic sense. We will discuss these later.

EGO, ID AND SUPEREGO IN THE GROUP MODEL

Here we may pause to glance for a moment at the group-analytic group as a model of the mental apparatus. In what way do the psychoanalytic concepts of ego, id and superego reflect in the group? The group is like a model of the mental apparatus in which its dynamics are personified and dramatized. A process analogous to this may be seen in the theater where the characters not only represent themselves but also stand proxy for the audience both in their individual and community reactions. A very good illustration of the way in which this happens can be found in Friedman's and Gassel's study of the Sophoclean tragedy *Oedipus Tyrannus*.[7] Their paper is of no less interest to us because of the fact that it was not intentionally concerned with the dynamics of the group in relation to group psychotherapy.

Oedipus, having committed patricide and incest, had to be punished in order to assuage the guilt feelings aroused in the audience by the activating of their forbidden wishes. The tragedy is played out between Oedipus, representing one wish, and the Chorus representing the other. The authors write: "The chorus by remaining detached absolves itself from responsibility ... actually the chorus maintains a driving demand on the hero to fulfill what the community expects ... Oedipus accepts fully the responsibility which the community is so eager for him to assume ... The chorus is not unlike a helpless community in the habit of throwing responsibility to the leader." The hero, Oedipus, here represents the id, in that he stands for wishes and impulses inherent in everybody. He also embodies a kind of collective ego for the community (see Rank's description of the heroes of mythology as embodying "collective egos" who reflect the forces at work within the society which creates and projects them). Furthermore, he has to be punished for the crime he has committed in the name of the community and is thus in some sense a scapegoat. The

[7] Friedman, J. and Gassel, S.: The Chorus in Sophocles' *Oedipus Tyrannus. Psa. Quart., 19*:213-226, 1950.

conflict within the audience, within any given human being, is given expression by the conflict between Oedipus and the Chorus. The Chorus, which in present terms could delineate our group, plays the part of the superego; it remains detached and objective, but exerts a driving pressure on the hero to fulfill his destiny.

In another paper by the same authors, also of interest to us, on the Orestes drama,[8] the Chorus incites and drives on Orestes to murder his mother. Orestes is tried and acquitted by a jury which gives its verdict equally for and against him, thus expressing the ambivalence of the community toward its wish to be rid of the maternal tie through matricide.

We find in our own group similar configurations to those instanced above in the form of Sophoclean drama, notwithstanding the fact that very often the leader or conductor is felt to be in the role of the superego. Group members may also play the part of superego, ego and id in relation to each other. A good example of the latter role occurred in one of my groups, when an older, married woman registered considerable apprehension of a younger, single woman in the same group. Later it transpired that this younger member symbolized the maturer woman's fears of loss of control and impulses of an erotic nature. In other words, here was an incarnation of her own id functioning independently of her control and hence provoking anxiety. The group also manifests something in the nature of a collective ego.

I have repeatedly observed members functioning as scapegoats in place of the conductor. The group, angry with him but not daring to attack him directly or to show open hostility, will relieve and displace its emotion and fury onto one of themselves, usually a weak or absent member. The scapegoat thus chosen bears the brunt of a vicarious attack on the conductor. It therefore very often proves correct in the scapegoat formation for the conductor to look for latent and repressed hostility directed against his own person under guise of the scapegoat. Here is an interesting example of one variation of this process. One of my groups at various times repeatedly accuse me of bias against a certain member. In such instances, I assume in principle that the group must have its reasons, however dormant my own awareness. I did not succeed in this case in finding any evidence of bias either in my behavior or unconscious attitude. At a later stage, I had to defend the same patient against strong hostility on the part of the group. This made what had happened clear to me. The group, unconsciously wanting to make a scapegoat of the member in question, defended themselves against this tendency by first projecting it onto me and then accusing me of bias. This brief illustration of clinical importance is valuable for defining how personalization, displacement and location take place in our groups.

[8] Friedman, J. and Gassel, S.: Orestes. *Psa. Quart.,* 20:423–433, 1951.

MULTIPLE DIMENSIONS IN THE GROUP

I will now proceed to enlarge somewhat on concepts which may be helpful for orientation in studying the multiple dimensions operating in the group. In this connection I would like to draw attention to some old and very interesting concepts of Wernicke who thought the most important spheres in which psychosis could be placed were those of (1) the external world or allopsyche; (2) the *Körperlichkeit*, corporeality or somatopsyche; and (3) the *Persönlichkeit*, or autopsyche.[9]

A similar recent classification of interest in the present connection is that used by Erikson, who envisages three stages of childhood development which can be said to persist in some degree in adult life.[10] The first he called the "autocosmos," wherein the world is experienced and reacted to exclusively in terms of the child's own body. This stage is replaced by the "microsphere." Here object relations are formed, but the child endows the object with his own feelings and wishes, as for instance when the sofa becomes a boat, or the doll an angry mother. Eventually the stage of the "macrosphere" is arrived at, object relations being now experienced in a world genuinely shared with others. Among levels leading from surface to deeper and hidden aspects, four can be discerned in the group.

1. *The Current Level.* This is analogous to Erikson's "macrosphere." Here the group would be experienced as representing the community, public opinion, etc., and the conductor as a leader or authority.
2. *The Transference Level.* This second level corresponds to mature object relations experienced in the "macrosphere." It is the level most often envisaged by group psychotherapists of analytic orientation, on which the group represents the family, the conductor father or mother, and the other members siblings.
3. *The Level of Bodily and Mental Images (Projective Level).* This level corresponds to primitive, narcissistic "inner" object relations in psychoanalysis. Here other members reflect unconscious elements of the individual self. The group represents as outer what are in truth inner object relations. The closest analogy here is with the concept of play analysis and its resultant psychopathology much associated with the name of Melanie Klein. This is the level of the "microsphere" and also corresponds to Wernicke's allopsyche. Not only may individuals embody a part of the self, but the group as a whole may do so (autopsyche). The group often represents the mother image, as pointed out by Schindler.[11] The body

[9] Wernicke, C.: *Grundriss der Psychiatrie.* Leipzig: Thieme, 1906.

[10] Erikson, E. H.: *Childhood and Society.* New York: Norton, 1950.

[11] Schindler, W.: Family Pattern in Group Formation and Therapy. *Int. J. Group Psychother., 1*:101–105, 1951.

image is reflected and represented in the group and its members. This phenomenon would correspond with Wernicke's somatopsyche, although the concept of a body image, owed in the main to Schilder,[12] was in no way thought of or familiar to Wernicke's generation.

4. *The Primordial Level.* This fourth level is the one in which primordial images occur according to the concepts of Freud and those particularly formulated by Jung concerning the existence of a collective unconscious.

Further illustration of the functioning of all these levels is provided in the following table:

Levels and spheres in the group-analytic group

	(1) *Current level*
	Group = community, society, public opinion, etc.
Macrosphere	(2) *Transference level*
	Mature object relations. Group = family, father, mother, siblings
	(3) *Projective level*

	Primitive, narcissistic, "inner" object relations	allopsyche
Microsphere	Other members personify (a) part(s) of self	autopsyche
Autocosmos	(b) part(s) of body (-image)	somatopsyche
	(4) *Primordial level*	
	Collective images	

The conclusions arrived at by Schilder as to the close interrelationship between ego and outside world, the social nature of consciousness, and the relation between outer world and self as a fundamental human fact, come very close to our own. Schilder writes: "It is our contention that every experience not only refers to these fundamental spheres which form an inseparable unit. We may call the fact that experiences are experiences in the outside world, the body and the self, an a priori insight. I would prefer the more modest expression that here we deal simply with an experience which so far has been proved correct."[13]

Arriving now at even closer equivalents of psychoanalytic concepts in the group than those already shown, we will first of all examine the unconscious, conscious, and preconscious in a group setting.

UNCONSCIOUS, PRECONSCIOUS, AND CONSCIOUS

We have already spoken of the *systematic unconscious* as used in psychoanalysis. This primary language in symbolic or symptomatic form, the

[12] Schilder, P.: *The Image and Appearance of the Human Body.* New York: International Universalities Press, 1950.

[13] Schilder, P.: *Mind, Perception and Thought in Their Counteractive Aspects.* New York: Columbia University Press, 1967.

language of the dream, operates in the group context. We do not merely see the distinction between primary and secondary processes as in psychoanalysis, but also many transition stages, and our process of communication and translation is closely linked with the construction of an ever widening zone of mutual understanding within the group. The concept of unconscious understanding, familiar in psychoanalysis,[14] is one on which we build continuously. Every communication is understood unconsciously on some level and has to negotiate many levels before it can be grasped and shared in its full meaning.

Group Consciousness

Group equivalents of the *topographical* idea of consciousness, unconscious and preconscious, can also be clearly shown. To demonstrate this, we must recall Freud's metapsychological hypothesis that the process of becoming conscious is closely allied to or essentially characterized by the cathexis of word representation. This Freudian concept is of great importance for understanding the metapsychology of hysteria, schizophrenia and various neuroses. The group equivalent of consciousness in terms of the group entity thus consists in any one member's *saying something in so many words*. If the group is ready and able to understand and assimilate what he says, the particular matter at issue can be said to be fully in its consciousness. The word cathexis assumed by Freud would here exemplify in the act of verbal expression on the part of any one individual.

The *preconscious* could be defined as something that remains unspoken and the group is in no way conscious of it. But potentially anyone could give utterance to this particular matter at any time and it would meet with no dynamic resistance or lack of understanding on the part of the group. It is easy to see on these lines the group equivalent to the *unconscious* or *repressed*, but for this to be of use more detailed illustration is needed than can be given in this paper.

FREE GROUP ASSOCIATION

An equivalent of prime importance is that which corresponds to free association in individual psychoanalysis. "Free group association" evolved through my own approach, although it may possibly also have been used independently in the 1920's by Trigant Burrow and his circle.[15] An analytic approach to groups was made by Schilder and Wender, but my own differed from theirs in proceeding straightaway to a spontaneous handling of the group

[14] Fenichel, O.: Concerning Unconscious Communication. *Collected Papers, 1*, New York: Norton, 1953.
[15] Galt, W.: *Phyloanalysis*. Psyche Miniatures. London: Kegan Paul, 1933.

situation.[16] I instructed the patients who had had previous psychoanalysis to associate freely in the same way as in the individual situation. As expected, the associations which patients were able to produce were modified by the group situation. I then waited and observed developments over a number of years, eliciting the process to which I later gave the name of "free-floating discussion." Only at a much later date consequent on my studies in analytic groups did it become clear to me that the conversation of *any* group could be considered in its unconscious aspects as the equivalent of free association.

Today I am beginning to fathom what elements in the situation of any given group of people approximate their conversation to free group association. Naturally the group-analytic situation itself is devised to encourage an optimum degree of freedom from censorship. The group association here is therefore the nearest equivalent of free association in psychoanalysis and plays a similar part. More concisely this can be expressed as follows. The more the "occupation" of the group comes to the fore, the less freely can group association emerge; if the occupation is a pretext, or can be completely scrapped as in our own technique, group association can emerge freely. Social groups can stand further or nearer one or the other of these extremes. For example in a casually thrown together social group, such as is seen in a railway carriage, or on conducted motor tours, though there is nobody to interpret, the ongoing conversation approximates to "free group association," the unconscious meaning readily shows itself to my own observation in such contexts.

In the group-analytic group, the manifest content of communication, broadly speaking, relates to the latent meaning of this communication in a similar way as the manifest dream relates to the latent dream thoughts. This matter is so important and so bound up with our concept of a *group matrix* that I shall once more take occasion to stress the group matrix as the operational basis of all relationships and communications. Communications use this network, and the individual is conceived as a nodal point. An analogy can be made with the neuron in anatomy and physiology, the neuron being the nodal point in the total network of the nervous system which always reacts and responds as a whole. As in the case of the neuron in the nervous system, so is the individual suspended in the group matrix.

Looked at in this way it becomes easier to understand our claim that the group associates, responds and reacts as a whole. The group as it were avails itself now of one speaker, now of another, but it is always the transpersonal network which is sensitized and gives utterance, or responds. In this sense we can postulate the existence of a group "mind" in the same way as we postulate an individual "mind." Whereas it is difficult for us to abstract from the concept of an individual in a physical, bodily way, it should not be so

[16] Foulkes, S. H. and Lewis, E.: Group Analysis. *Brit. J. Med. Psychol.*, *20*:175–184, 1944; Foulkes, S. H.: On Group Analysis. *Int. J. Psa.*, *27*:46–51, 1946.

difficult to do so in the mental field, and to perceive that the matrix of response is indeed an interconnected whole. In the mental matrix individuals also emerge, but the boundaries of these (perhaps they should be called by some other name such as "psyche-individuals") do not run parallel with the boundaries of their physical person.

EQUIVALENTS OF MENTAL MECHANISMS

We have already exemplified *displacement* in a group. Suffice it to add here that the group equivalent is seen when repressed tendencies in individuals emerge in the roles of others. The process of displacement should be strictly viewed in this context as occurring between individuals inside the group, not simply as a function of the individual mind.

Isolation occurs when an individual within the group is assigned tendencies, forces or characteristics which are shunned in a phobic way by others. Isolation in the group is also manifested by punctuating silences, or by its abruptly turning from one theme to another at a certain point.

Splitting is another process clearly shown in the group. It takes the form in this context of subgroups, splitting into pairs, etc.

These few illustrations are given to underline the fact that even the processes akin to psychoanalytic ones should be seen as configurations in the group context. Clearly the processes of *personification* or *impersonation* and *dramatization* are particularly stressed in the group and play a much bigger part than in individual psychoanalysis. All the models of processes we have elaborated in this article incorporate this particular group feature, namely dramatization and personification, in this as in other instances reminiscent of the dream process itself.

In conclusion, I would like to stress the difference in emphasis between psychoanalysis and group-analytic psychotherapy.[17] Psychoanalysis, at any rate in its historical aspect, has laid great emphasis on the psychogenesis of illness. In group analysis we are more concerned with the outlook for change and the direction and means whereby to ensure it. We therefore work with operational concepts, formulated and applied in the therapeutic process itself and derived from immediate clinical observations. In our view a dynamic science of psychotherapy is needed which will incorporate and turn to good account the revolutionary idea that therapy is research and research in this field is therapy.

Group analysis as a method will then automatically fall into correct perspective as a powerful therapy, a stimulating theory and a fertile source of information and discovery in the psychosocial field.

[17] Foulkes, S. H.: Some Similarities and Differences between Psycho-Analytic Principles and Group-Analytic Principles. *Brit. J. Med. Psychol.*, 26:30–35, 1953.

VI

SPECIAL DYNAMICS OF THERAPY GROUPS

19

Observations on Transference and Object Relations in the Light of Group Dynamics

George R. Bach
Beverly Hills, California

[Bach captures certain unique aspects of the object relationships that typically occur in group psychotherapy sessions. The mode by which members influence each other both conjunctively and disjunctively is captured in Bach's use of the term *set-up operations* (a broader and more sophisticated concept than that of transference relationships). The "signal" function of certain member physical attributes, characterological orientations, and expressive patterns of behavioral interaction is seen as having a primary influence on the qualitative nature of interaction that characteristically takes place in a given group. The concept of *theragnosis* is developed to explicate the largely peer-rooted processes of psychotherapy and diagnosis that often take place in therapy groups. The fact that characterological development takes place during the course of group psychotherapy is noted in an exploration of the largely group-determined "role maturation" processes.]

When four female and four male, verbally fluid neurotic adults bombard each other with transference and other fantasies over several hundred group meetings, they create in the long run a unique micro-community. Observations

From "Observations on Transference and Object Relations in the Light of Group Dynamics" by G. R. Bach, *International Journal of Group Psychotherapy*, 1957, 7, 64–76. Copyright 1957 by the International Journal of Group Psychotherapy. Reprinted by permission.

of psychological and group-dynamic processes that are endogenous to such a therapeutic micro-community can be reported only with the use of new concepts. We deal with processes that cannot be observed in either individual therapy or in more conventional group settings such as family, work, social groups, etc.

It has already been ably demonstrated by Slavson, Wolf, and most recently by Helen Durkin that the dynamics of individual psychoanalysis such as identification and transference can be therapeutically worked through in group psychoanalysis.[1] In addition to psychoanalytic processes, certain group-dynamic forces of the kind first explored by the late Kurt Lewin can be clinically exploited to increase the effectiveness of analytically oriented psychotherapy in groups, as I have already described elsewhere.[2] It is, however, important to stress certain unique dynamics of therapeutic groups which so far have not been studied by either psychoanalysts or social-psychological researchers.

Our present task is to forge new, workable concepts that would aid in describing and evaluating the new group-dynamic, and the new interpersonal material observable in the new and historically unique phenomenon, the psychotherapeutic group.[3] A theory of group therapeutics requires new concepts because no theory of the healing function of the group is available. Psychoanalysis, so far, has depended on the healing functions of the doctor. Whatever loyalties may motivate current authors to "order" all the variety of interpersonal relations observable in therapeutic groups under Freud's principles of individual psychoanalysis, this respect for doctrine fails in its good intentions to advance our science, for Freud's concepts fail to draw attention to the healing functions of the group.

The many redefinitions of transference and countertransference currently offered in the psychoanalytic literature attempt to encompass all therapeutically significant events in groups. However, one can readily see that Freud's clear meaning of transference is being forced into a conceptual Procrustean bed in which the original definition is either stretched or cut down to fit the many new observations made in the new setting. This is not surprising since group psychotherapy in its contemporary form was unknown in Freud's days and remains unfamiliar to most contemporary psychoanalysts.

Our research is directed toward a *theory of group therapeutics*. We have found the use of a few new working concepts, e.g., Theragnosis, Set-Up Operation, Interpersonal Signaling, etc., stimulating for the development of our clinical techniques. These concepts fit new observations. They should be

[1] Slavson, S. R.: *Analytic Group Psychotherapy*. New York: Columbia University Press, 1952; Wolf, A.: The Psychoanalysis of Groups. *Am. J. Psychother., 3*:525–558, 1949; 4:16–50, 1950; Durkin, H. E.: *Group Therapy for Mothers of Disturbed Children.* Springfield, Ill.: Ch. Thomas, 1954.

[2] Bach, G. R.: *Intensive Group Psychotherapy*. New York: Ronald Press, 1954.

[3] Bach, G. R. and Illing, H.: Eine historische Perspektive zur Gruppen Psychotherapie. *Z. Psychosom. Med.*, 1955.

accepted as independent of the equally realistic need to preserve tested old concepts to fit the old universes of observations. This is not a question of validity but of scientific development and history.

EXTRA-ANALYTIC PROCESSES IN THERAPEUTIC GROUPS

When one looks beyond the trained healing functions of the official therapist, one can observe how individual patients and the group as a whole accomplish reconstructive changes in the personality of its members. This includes stimulating the maturational process within the official therapist. One can perceive that the group does *more* to and for its members than the therapist could do to or for his patients alone. In individual analysis the therapist exerts influence on his patient to become an active participant in a dyad devoted to free emotional expression, self-directedness, spontaneous association, dream analysis, gaining insight into transference distortions,[4] and working through resistances. In analytically oriented group psychotherapy, the therapist exerts the same influence on the group and thus creates an analytical "work group."[5] The analytic group therapist employs the same clinical strategy as in individual psychoanalysis which was his training background. He simply transfers his tactics from individual to group practice. A group of patients may appear to follow the therapist as easily as an individual or even more easily because of identification with him which is intensified by competition. Consequently all psychoanalytically oriented observers have been able to report honestly that psychoanalysis with some minor modifications can be done in groups.[6]

Is this all that occurs? Does the psychoanalysis of individuals in groups fully describe the group-therapeutic healing process? Are there other, extra-analytic processes generated by the group situation which are not due to the analytic leadership of the therapist but which are also of clinical importance?

Having been trained to observe group processes in the frame of reference of my former teacher, the late Kurt Lewin, I see the therapeutic group as a generator of pressures on its members which go beyond the kind of influence exerted by a psychoanalytic group therapist. When properly and fully understood these group-generated influences can be clinically utilized to effect a new type of psychotherapy which may reconstruct personalities in a different way than individual psychoanalysis. At present, the lack of sensitivity in observing extra-analytic phenomena occurring in therapeutic groups veils a clearer comprehension of this possibility. In order to "see"

[4] Wolstein, B.: *Transference: Its Meaning and Function in Psychoanalytic Therapy.* New York: Grune & Stratton, 1954.
[5] Bion, W. R.: Experiences in Groups I-VII. *Hum. Relat., 1-4*, 1948–1951.
[6] Wolf, *op. cit.*, see footnote 1.

group-generated healing forces one has to adjust the lenses of the psychoanalytic looking glass, or borrow some other frame of reference.

BEYOND TRANSFERENCE: SET-UP OPERATIONS

Transference has for me Freud's clear and specific meaning. In my frame of reference transference is a particular type of interpersonal contact in which individuals, while under the influence of unfulfilled regressive needs, seek to fulfill them with objects realistically unsuited for these now activated infantile motivations. Displacement is another type of set-up operation that is irrealistic but which, unlike transference, is not due to remote causes but more immediate ones, such as when our patients are frustrated by each other but displace their hostility on us. Unlike the official, disciplined, role-performing therapist, patients in contact with each other do *not* "hold still" when bombarded with transference demands. Instead they emotionally dovetail and actively countertransfer. In groups this exchange is so vivid that it is very difficult for the therapist alone to distinguish between unreal projections and justified reactions, between healthy self-assertions and the acting out of infantile wishes. The only obvious fact is that only a small portion of all interactions can be validly seen as manifestations of the repetition-compulsive transference neurosis.

Even severe neurotics relate to each other to fulfill other than regressive needs. They stimulate each other, as healthy personalities do, *in situ*; i.e., they create through their togetherness new motivations "here and now." Contact with each other activates *both* regressive (e.g., transference) *and* progressive (e.g., mutual aid) types of motivations. The group members try to satisfy both through further contact with one another. This effort of group members consciously and/or unconsciously to entice each other into behavior which will justify or fulfill their "here and now" acute needs, whether they be unrealistic or constructive, I have labeled *set-up operation*. This is a technical definition for interpersonal "relating." People in groups set each other up so as to activate and to release wishes and fantasies. The wishes thus instigated and reduced are not limited to the need to re-experience and to fulfill the kind of fantasies known under the concept of transferences. Transference tendencies are here viewed as only one specific kind of set-up operation occurring in groups.

With this broader concept we are now free to study other clinically significant object relationships without losing or isolating our valuable knowledge of transference phenomena. For example, one can clearly distinguish between defensive-disjunctive and therapeutic-conjunctive aspects of a given set-up operation. The broader concept of set-up operation allows the study of all types of contact phenomena such as *symbol assignment* and *role maturation* which will be described in this paper. A significant broadening of Freud's transference concept has already been necessitated to conceptualize the more active interpersonal exchange between analyst and analysand as practiced by the neo-analytic or "interpersonal" school of individual psychoanalysis. But even Wolstein's ingenious stretching, reinterpreting Freud's concepts[7] fails to encompass the great variety of experiences that are mediated by the patients' set-up operations. Through the catalytic process described by Slavson,[8] group therapy members activate very basic needs and affects within each other. Some of these are transference needs but others are maturational needs, and still others are needs to master group situational pressures.

Whatever the origin of affect instigation may be, the person whose emotional needs are mobilized has here and now to lower these aroused tensions. In order to reduce this tension, not created, but unleashed, by the stimulating group situation, the individual actively seeks *supporting figures* in the group whom he will try to entice to behave in a way that will help him to reduce the activated tension. In these attempts the patients learn, often by bitter experience, to discriminate between healthy and unhealthy, regressive and progressive aspects of their needs. In groups, patients, unlike even the most unorthodox Sullivanian analysts, frequently yield to and thus temporarily reinforce the unrealistic transference demands with which the peers in the group bombard each other. In constructive ways too, patients go beyond analytic therapists and actively challenge each other into realistically constructive behavior which they evaluate and reward. Patients show each other, for example, on numerous occasions, appreciation for the experience of "being understood." They can more freely reciprocate and show warmth toward each other while only the show of dependency seems to them appropriate in the relation to the therapist. Consequently much more than "transference distortions," an essentially regressive manifestation, takes place between patients, and this fact forces us to become sensitive to more than transference and to include in our interpretations other interpersonal, especially progressive occurrences.

BEYOND RESISTANCE AND TRANSFERENCE ANALYSIS: THERAGNOSIS

Neurotic adults have a broad view of human nature and of each other. Participants in fairly long-term group therapy feel each other out and react to each other as total personalities. They communicate to each other how it feels to be made a partner to the various set-up operations. Patients have what might be called a "heart-and-gut"-mediated rather than a brain-mediated diagnosis of each other. They tell each other how it feels to be made emotional use of and how it feels to use the other fellow for releasing tension. They let each know how good it feels to be conjunctive and how

[7] *Op. cit.*, see footnote 4.
[8] *Op. cit.*, see footnote 1.

anxiety-evoking it is to be parataxic. In this they are keen to sort out the disjunctive from the conjunctive, the helpful from the hurting, the archaic and anachronistic from the contemporary-realistic.

Through group-dynamically oriented leadership the "therapist–conductor" can help the patients to make their experiences with set-up operations most explicit and to share their insights into self–other, other–self, and self–group relationships. The pooling of these insights constitutes group-consensual perceptions or "diagnosis" which go amazingly deep and frequently have excellent reality sense. To the process of consensual diagnostic awareness of intrapsychic and interpersonal events on the part of the group of patients I have chosen the label *theragnosis*.

The therapeutic implication of this group-diagnostic process is that through theragnosis each patient learns to differentiate, first in others then in the self, appropriate from inappropriate wishes which he is trying to fulfill in his set-up operations. He then becomes genuinely motivated to develop further appropriate motivations and to track down the unconscious roots, inappropriate excitations and unrealistic cognitive fixations. Groups which have developed fine theragnostic sensitivity can be a great aid in the understanding and management of the countertransference and other parataxic tendencies on the part of the therapist.[9] The theragnostically active group can be likened to a complex set of differently polished mirrors which bring out sometimes fantastically distorted, sometimes clearly focused images.

From a psychodynamic standpoint, the group is a stage or projection screen onto which the total repertoire of conscious, preconscious and unconscious needs are externalized, projected, acted out, recognized and corrected through a group-centered therapeutic work process (theragnosis). The traditional dichotomy and antithesis of "the individual vs. the group" is resolved through the active participation of all members in the theragnostic process. Through this therapeutic work process all have the growth-furthering experiences of *receiving and of giving understanding*. This "understanding" which is the essence of theragnosis includes transference analysis but is broader as it encompasses the recognition of personality patterns (roles) and their conscious and unconscious (symbolic) "signaling" effects. Insight into both pathogenic-isolating as well as healthy-conjunctive tendencies is gained as automatic set-up operations come under conscious control. Resistance against "understanding," both of the self and of others, is overcome by the individual's needs to secure "understanding" and full group acceptance. Participation in theragnosis is the vehicle for undefensive exploration, self-correction, and eventually full *self-actualization*.[10]

    [9] Bach, G. R.: The Group as a Projection Screen in the Theragnostic Analysis and Control of the Therapist's Emotional Reactions. Presented at the Arrowhead Springs Conference, Los Angeles Society of Clinical Psychologists in Private Practice, Oct., 1954.
    [10] Maslow, A. H.: *Motivation and Personality*. New York: Harper, 1954.

The theragnostic process, as summarized above, depends on the freeing of the mutual aid and self-help tendency inherent in group life.[11] The therapist, and the *patient as therapist*, form a healing group which together has the courage fully to explore *all* aspects of the self, conscious and unconscious, past and present, real and fantastic.

Apart from the important therapeutic implications, elaborated in detail elsewhere,[12] the group process of theragnosis is of value in our research into the great variety of set-up operations of which only two can be described here: unconscious symbol assignments and role maturation.

UNCONSCIOUS SYMBOL ASSIGNMENTS AND "SIGNALING"

Studies of the projective doll play of boys and girls, 3 to 10 years old,[13] provide a clue for the significance of the projective aspects of set-up operations, because they show how and why children require, for their play, some extra ego externalization objects. Every child's nursery has a repertoire of toys and dolls used by the child as fantasy supports. To borrow a term from the ethologists, Lorenz and Tinbergen, the child assigns "signaling behavior" to the toys and dolls. It is true to say that the children "project" their needs onto the dolls, but this is not quite precise enough for our purpose. In order to overcome repression, the child sets up imaginary figures that first activate his unconscious need. Next, new signal assignments are made to find ways of catharsis. The dolls are "set up" to behave in such a way that the child experiences the reception of signals appropriate for experiencing not only all kinds of socially tabooed feelings such as murderous sibling rivalry or incorporation of the parents, but also exploration and mastery of new and unknown territories. Adult patients interact with their peers in the therapy group in ways that are somewhat analogous to the ways that children play with dolls, but the process is considerably more complex and has deep implications for therapy. In the group the various individuals serve each other as "fantasy supporters" on two levels. Both the prevailing group mood around which the members "rally"[14] as well as the expression of moods by individuals require certain *signal stimulation* to sustain them.

Human beings who live in close, semipermanent contact do not depend for signaling on brief specific response or behavior unit or single cues as do strangers or others who, when in contact, are ruled by communication conventions or social roles which by definition restrict their spontaneity.

[11] Montagu, M. F.: *The Direction of Human Development.* New York: Harper, 1955.
[12] Bach, *op. cit.*, see footnote 2.
[13] Bach, G. R.: *Young Children's Play Fantasies.* Psychol. Monograph, No. 272, 1945.
[14] Powdermaker, F., Frank J., et al.: *Group Psychotherapy Studies in Methodology of Research and Therapy.* Cambridge: Harvard University Press, 1953.

Signaling by people in long-term contact is mediated by certain molar aspects of their total life situation and their personality. These molar aspects trigger the activation of specific emotions. One such aspect is the "role" a person serves in the group. Most obvious is the example of the therapist. His role is that of a trigger for the creation and maintenance of that type of group atmosphere which allows the expression of "nurturing" and "understanding" attitudes.

In addition to group role our research has revealed the operation of other types of signals.[15] Body build, for example, contributes toward what use a person will be made of emotionally by the group. In all of our groups the physically strongest male is invariably utilized unconsciously to work out combative tendencies. This seems to be quite independent of whether or not the physically strong or "big man" feels or is actually aggressive or not. His physical "combat potential" triggers fighting moods. Another signaling factor is group-derived prestige position. The least defensive and most humanly understanding person in the group is a definite trigger for the full activation of dependency needs.

In contrast relatively consistent disjunctive acting-out patterns, i.e., fixated character armors, function as triggers for rejecting and isolating responses. For example, the violently aggressive combative character "draws" fearful submissive emotions. The person who has real sex appeal also has, as can be expected, an important signaling function in the group. The person to whom highest sex appeal is assigned, by spontaneous, usually covert consensus, primarily activates courting behavior in the opposite sex and possessive incorporative behavior on the part of the members ot tne same sex. The rigidly masochistic character defense, on the other hand, draws repressed sadism in all to the surface.

Observing these particular aspects of interpersonal relationships in group therapy, Leary and Coffey described in detail "interpersonal reflexes."[16] Our own research is beginning to isolate different types of molar manifestations, each of which serve specific signaling functions. We know that overt personality manifestations and neurotic defenses are only two classes of a great variety of cognitive triggers and cues which are indispensable for the human being as means of effecting emotional discharge. The human use of each other as signals for affect instigation and affect release shows clearly how the therapeutic exploration of the unconscious is effected by the absence or presence of the right kinds of trigger figures.

In this research I use a word–person-association test to force group members rapidly to assign random adjectives to each other. Patients in all the

[15] Bach, G. R.: Unconscious Assignment of Signals in Interpersonal Communication. Presented at the 36th Annual Meeting, West. Psychol. Assoc. Abstracted in *Am. Psychol.*, 9:558–565, 1954.

[16] Leary, T. and Coffey, H. S.: Interpersonal Diagnosis: Some Problems of Methodology and Validation. *J. Abn. & Soc. Psychol.*, 50:110–124, 1955.

groups we have so far tested tend to type each other unconsciously; i.e., they assign to each other symbolic roles. Each type personifies and externalizes some basic unconscious need or major defense. Group consensus, in various groups, covertly types the roster of members into a cast of basic symbols or types. For example, all groups will type one female and one male as the most desirable "sex object." The persons considered the most sexually desirable have a strong therapeutic influence on all other members in the group. Group prestige and respect is enhanced by the mere fact of being accepted as an ally by the male or female sex objects.

This research has made us sensitive to the existence of different levels of set-up operations. Social scientists do of course distinguish between defensive and self-accepting as well as between conscious and unconscious levels of personality dynamics. The interesting fact is that patients in group therapy learn to do this without any training in research observations. The therapeutic implications of this learning to understand others on increasingly deeper levels of motivation is obviously positive.

Therapeutic groups that were carefully selected on the basis of a personality structure criterion differed considerably from each other in *range* of symbolic trigger figures. In one group two or three persons were what we might call "loaded" trigger figures, whereas in another group the various qualities of signal behavior were more distributed among the members. The "loading" or concentration of signal significance on one or two patients is associated with a slower and less involved flow of communication from member to member. The centricity of the therapist is also greater in a group in which the repertoire of individuals does not allow a good spread of the assignment of signal behavior to all members. In a group in which *every* patient has some (usually more than one) specific signaling function, the general anxiety level is lower while the emotional interdependence is stronger. The free flow of transference and other set-up operations seem to be facilitated when the membership of a group is such that a variety of basic types can be assigned to all members. If the typing is concentrated only on the therapist or on one or two other members, a group cannot develop the same theragnostic sensitivity as a group with a broader cast of symbolic types.

Our research is beginning to isolate the repertoire of basic types that are apparently looked for by all patients in all groups. We are also beginning to understand the factors which earn typing labels. "Mother," "father," "errand boy," "tycoon," and "sex object" are assigned in part because of realistic perceptions of behavior patterns such as have been isolated by Frank and others.[17] These behavior patterns seem to us to function as triggers for the

---

[17] Frank, J. D.; Margolin, J.; Nash, H. T.; Stone, A. R.; Varon, E.; and Ascher, E.: Two Behavior Patterns in Therapeutic Groups and Their Apparent Motivation. *Hum. Rel., 5*:289–317, 1952; Rosental, D.; Frank, J. D.; Nash, E. H.: The Self-Righteous Moralist in Early Meetings of Therapeutic Groups. *Psychiatry, 17*:215–223, 1954.

externalization of specific unconscious motivations. While the therapist is sensitive to the fact that his patients are typed into particular symbolic roles, he can make clinical use of this knowledge and help each patient to understand what behavior patterns earn what type labels in the reality of social communications.

ROLE MATURATION AND THERAPEUTIC GROWTH PHASES

The total duration of therapy for each patient is relative to both the severity of the personality disorganization and the efficiency of clinical management. All patients "graduate" through four "roles," regardless of the time it takes them. It may be easiest for want of better terms to speak of these roles in terms of "novice," "sophomore," "junior," and "senior" levels.

Patients can be helped to become aware of and to differentiate these roles, thus providing them with a method for gauging their own progress. This is important for the maintenance of good morale while undergoing psychotherapy. Why do patients gradually improve their role? At the beginning novices have to survive the immediate shock of becoming part of a group that has established unique mores of free communications. After this the novices get quite excited over the opportunity to *set up the whole group as a supporting object* for all their unrealistic wishes and their neurotic anxieties. The novice typically tries to entice others into behavior that will justify or make appear realistic whatever unrealistic motivations he is conscious of. While defensively analyzing others, group consensus makes the novice aware of what his own needs are that he has to rationalize. After this phase his set-up use of others changes in quality.

As a sophomore he will utilize others as supporters for the catharsis of newly discovered emotional needs, the way young children make use of puppets as *fantasy supporters*. In my publication on the "Play Drama" I described how "adult" patients use paper puppets as "supporters" or "warmups" for the externalization of fantasies.[18] Often the acting out of fantasies looks and feels like creative spontaneity. Actually the sophomore is practicing counterphobic defenses. Nonetheless he will live through this rather turbulent period which is followed by a sobering-up process.

In their "junior" phase patients become self-analytic because gained insight develops the feeling of "having reached independence." In our program the successful patient moves on to participation in the final or "senior" phase. This requires the acceptance not only of the inner self and its needs, but also acceptance of the self's interdependence with others. For the senior in the therapy group this takes the form of practicing compassionate and conjunctive

[18] Bach, G. R.: Dramatic Play Therapy with Adult Groups. *J. Psychol., 29*:225–246, 1950.

understanding of the other, still less mature, group members. Acceptance of the psychological reality of the dynamic self as well as an appreciation of one's helpfulness to the others in the group makes the senior phase a prelude to "graduation" into the natural environment. The posttherapeutic role in real life is characterized by the ability to make use of the social field to support the drive to maturity in the self and in others throughout the life span.

Clinical experience with premature "drop-outs" shows that the picture is not always so neat. In fact any patient may "get stuck" in one of these four phases, and try not to move on. This has led some critics to believe that group therapy is inherently limited to creating acting-out sophomores.

A unique growth-inducing factor is the patients' experiencing himself as a "leader" of his peers. The patients' leadership of the group has many forms. The defensive authority-ridden patterns of the "misleaders" (described by Bion), the "doctor's assistants" (described by Frank), and the "monopolist" (described by Powdermaker and Frank) are leaders of the resistive or "acting-out" phases of group life. These resistive phases have worried many observers to the point where positive, growth-inducing aspects of the patients' tendency to lead one another have remained unobserved. While one approach will develop ingenious techniques to curb acting out, a rival approach has counterphobically elevated this sophomoric phase of undisciplined spontaneity into the final therapeutic goal.

Acting out is a necessary but *passing* phase in continuous, self-replenishing groups. Any session may be characterized by fluctuations of all four phases. Which phase becomes dominant depends on who initiates and/or who gives closure to the "rallying theme." The leader's functions of initiating and closing can be assumed by either the therapist or patient. The level of maturity of the theme-leader or phase-leader sets the quality of the then-and-there prevailing group atmosphere. Flexibility and spontaneity of "leading" presupposes the existence of a democratic-participative group culture where everyone can lead and where the therapist must *not* lead in the usual sense.

Freshmen must have the opportunity to lead in the expression of primary defensiveness. The sophomores must have freedom to see to it that everyone has a chance to "express their basic emotions anonymously," as Bion has put it. Juniors should have the chance to provide leadership in dream analysis and theragnosis, while the seniors actively support reality orientation. Because every patient has the opportunity to exercise leadership functions, he learns the responsibility inherent in leadership roles. Learning to lead the therapeutic group constructively has the same dynamic significance as growing from autistic-dependent to genital-creative sexuality. A therapist who always remains the central figure deprives the patients of this opportunity for overcoming pregenital defensiveness against responsible aggressiveness.

In groups in which every patient is at any given time at a different level of therapeutic growth the therapist *cannot* be identified as the leader of the senior or reality phase only. Just as in individual work the analyst does not allow himself to become identified with id, ego, or superego, or with any other single aspect of the individual personality structure. The group therapist must remain uncommitted as to his preference for one or the other of the four phases within which the group life continuously fluctuates. These observations indicate that the explanation of the patient's progress from novice to graduating senior requires more than the familiar idea of identification with the therapist. Since the therapist cannot be associated with one phase consistently (for he must reflect every level), identification with him is more complicated than in individual therapy.

It is possible to explain the fact that the patients do "grow up" as resulting from a need to maintain group cohesion, i.e., the need to make themselves as attractive as possible to each other. The therapeutic growth is not solely mediated by identification with the therapist; it is rather the group-dynamic force of cohesiveness that moves the patient forward. According to Kurt Lewin, groups tend to maintain their own existence by tension-reducing mechanisms. To maintain its life every group must have a minimum degree of cohesiveness. Seniors are the most attractive and therefore add to cohesion. The more attractive members help to keep group tensions within tolerable limits, while the immature create tensions, often detrimental to constructive communication. The preservation of the group gives centricity and attention to junior and senior behavior for such behavior is experienced as tension-releasing, while freshman and sophomore behavior threatens the existence of the group. Our patients improve their mental health through "role maturation" which goes *beyond insight into individual history* and pathogenesis. The process of gaining and holding the respect of their peers in the therapeutic group seems to stimulate the reconstruction of personalities.

20

Group Resistance and the Therapeutic Contract

Louis R. Ormont
Columbia University Teachers College
New York, New York

[Ormont utilizes a highly structured orientation device at the very beginning of his treatment groups in order to throw into bold relief the "group resistances" that so often sabotage the therapeutic effort and lead to premature dropouts. By establishing a therapeutic contract and continuously reinforcing it by pointing out divergences of individual members or subgroups from the previously agreed-upon criteria of that contract, the group leader tends to both encourage autonomous functioning in the members and expose for analytic study the latent group dynamics underlying any particular group resistance. The so-called paradigmatic interventions (i.e., "joining the resistance" of a given individual group member, mirroring of resistances, etc.) are seen to be quite effective in diminishing and ultimately allowing for the group analytic exploration of particularly rigid and intractable resistances.]

Some time ago, Spotnitz (1952) observed that group resistances were important factors in the psychoanalytic treatment of groups, and that an understanding of these reluctances could provide the analyst with maximum therapeutic leverage. To date, no writer has expanded Spotnitz's original observation with any detailed or rigorous efforts. Yet, if group resistances do operate, the ability to recognize them and cope with them would greatly enhance the therapist's effectiveness and allow him to deal more successfully with the ever-present problem of drop-outs.

From "Group Resistance and the Therapeutic Contract" by L. R. Ormont, *International Journal of Group Psychotherapy*, 1968, *18*, 147–154. Copyright 1968 by the International Journal of Group Psychotherapy. Reprinted by permission.

As in individual analysis, the patient in the group setting displays resistances to verbalizing unacceptable thoughts, feelings, fantasies, impulses, and memories, especially those relating to fellow patients or to the analyst. But beyond this, members of a group may, in subtle ways, share a common reluctance to verbalize rejected ideas and experiences; unconsciously, they may virtually make a pact with each other to hold back or impede such verbalizations.

Group resistance can be expressed as mutual hatred or love, generally directed toward the analyst. While comparatively rare, this is easy to recognize and will not be dealt with here. What is more common, subtle, and often unrecognized is a genre of shared but concealed attitudes which operate as a collective reluctance to fulfill the terms of the therapeutic contract. Such a resistance is at work whenever the group ignores, overlooks, encourages, or tolerates a violation of the analytic contract by one or more of its members. According to this contract, each member is to:

1. Tell the emotionally significant story of his life whenever it is pertinent, that is, his past, his present, and his plans for the future.
2. Make no decisions affecting any critical aspect of his life without discussing it beforehand with the group.
3. Understand the other group members and communicate this understanding in words.
4. Take a proportionate part of the total talking time.
5. Keep communications within the emotional current of the group.
6. Refrain from acting out.

In terms of the analytic contract, acting out may take such forms as: arriving late; smoking, eating, drinking, or engaging in other orally gratifying acts during the group sessions; allowing debts to build up; socializing or indulging in any other consistent extracurricular contacts; breaching the confidentiality of the group; hitting, kissing, or other forms of physical contact.

The analyst does not expect members to adhere to the contract; on the contrary, he expects deviations. But any deviation has to be analytically investigated. When the group collectively ignores, condones, or overlooks a deviation from the analytic contract, it is engaged in a group resistance. The deviant member expresses the resistance overtly, the condoning members, covertly. The deviant member is allowed to continue on his aberrant way unchallenged because he nakedly plays out the veiled attitudes of the rest of the members.

CASE 1

Lee, a bright and witty actor, had been the group's comic relief for some eight months. When a member approached a charged or uncomfortable topic, Lee could be counted on to drop a funny line to change the mood and subject. With some members, he gained considerable status and recognition; they reveled in his caustic comments, laughed at his jokes, and applauded his clownish antics.

One day, Lee opened the session in a mood of deep despair. He was discouraged about his career and his homosexual liaisons. He had reached a dead end, and he was thinking of leaving therapy. The analyst chose this moment to approach the role of the covertly resistant members by underlining how he had been used.

Analyst: Maybe you're right, Lee. Maybee you should have been paid for your work in the group. After all, the rest of us were using your time and your money, giving you nothing you couldn't get from any nightclub with your gifts.

Lee: [above the murmur of protest]: Wait a minute. I wouldn't go so far. . . .

Chuck: I would. I get the Doc's point. You got to admit it, Lee. You got nothing for your performance here.

Lee: What is this? You putting me on? Listen, I talked. That's what I'm supposed to do here.

Chuck: Sure, you talked. But, you know, I can't think of one emotionally loaded fact or incident in your life that has come from your mouth in the last two months. Yeah, two months.

Lee: Look, I've been here. . . .

Mark: You've been here, all right. Like a clown.

Hilde: He's a clown, and we're just angels, aren't we? Aren't we! Has any one of us taken it on himself to point out what Lee's been doing all this time?

Goldie [a new member]: Are we supposed to?

Mark: What do you think?

Goldie: I don't know what to think.

Mark: We're here to understand Lee like everyone else. He's no different.

Goldie: Oh, I understand him.

Mark: That's not enough. We're to put that understanding into words—spoken words.

Chuck: That's what the Doc means. We haven't been talking to Lee. We've been letting him hide behind his wise-cracking gimmicks.

Hilde: And what about us? We haven't been hiding? Hiding behind our laughs? Getting kicks out of him instead of getting to him? Getting him to talk about his work and sex life? First we use him, then we blame him.

The analyst's intervention had several effects. By joining Lee's resistance and focusing attention on his operation in the group, the analyst forestalled a drop-out. More important, the intervention started a chain reaction which uncovered the group's use of Lee's antics as a shield against talking about themselves. Two months previously, the analyst had spotted the prevailing resistance by noting that meaningful life communications were being replaced with increased joviality and jocularity, and that the majority of the members were egging on a deviant minority headed by Lee. The analyst had commented on this tendency, but at that time the members were caught up in unexpressed aggression toward him and were not ready to co-operate in facing this deviant behavior. The members knew that they were there to tell the emotionally significant stories of their lives and to demonstrate their understanding of each other. Each, for reasons of his own, chose to ignore this part of the analytic contract, but when they were reminded of the criteria for effective functioning in the group setting, they had no difficulty in locating the shared resistance: the misuse of Lee.

The analytic contract is a guide not only for patients in perceiving their own reluctances, but also for the analyst. Identifying a group resistance can be a bewildering task. Each patient may use any one or all of the five classic types of resistance—ego, id, superego, secondary gain, and transference—at once. Add to this the resistances of the other members—and sometimes even those of the analyst himself—and the result can be an elusive complex of communications. With the analytic contract clearly stated, a group resistance becomes a special divergence that is easily identifiable.

In any newly constituted group, the therapist must see to three developments, which are sometimes simultaneous but more often sequential: (1) preparation of the patients to become group members (Ormont, 1957), (2) initiation of the group meetings (Ormont, 1959), (3) establishment of the analytic contract (Ormont, 1962).

During this last step, the group members are educated in the ground rules of group analysis. The contract is established by making the group aware, again and again, of what is expected of them—the individual points being reiterated whenever the situation warrants it. When the analyst makes a remark about the contract, he studies the group activity, observing the attitude of the members toward the violation. A group resistance exists when the majority of the members permit a violation by a minority to persist unscrutinized.

CASE 2

When the analyst entered a session of a recently formed group, he noticed that a member, John, broke off what he was saying. After a moment of silence, another member volunteered the information that John was quitting his job. The analyst, underlining a point in the contract, indicated that critical decisions which materially affect one's life—such as work or marriage—might helpfully be discussed in the group before being acted upon. Again, there was a momentary silence. Another man started speaking anxiously about his sexual thoughts toward another man in the group, and the group's attention shifted. It did not return to John. Halfway through the meeting, Alice, another member, remarked that John had not said a word. The analyst suggested that Alice and others were ignoring John.

Discussion quickly led to the revelation that the group members were "fed up with him" and were expressing their anger indirectly by ignoring him.

John responded to this disclosure by declaring that they could feel any way they wanted because he was not going to be there much longer, he had applied for a job in California. This statement mobilized the members, and they proceeded to examine his tendency to stimulate interest with arresting statements and then sit back, expecting the members to come begging for further details.

In this episode, the analyst achieved two objectives. He helped the members focus on the group resistance, which in this case consisted of ignoring a member instead of talking about feelings toward him. The analyst also used the interchange to underline part of the contract. When a member announces a decision about a particular problem which he has not brought up or adequately discussed in the group setting, a drop-out is in the offing more often than not. The group must be taught to recognize this pattern early in the game, and the members must be willing to deal with it as soon as it appears. Failure to do so may result in a member's sudden withdrawal from treatment.

The novice group analyst may have difficulty grasping the importance of giving priority to a resistance expressed by the group's refusal to examine a member's behavior. Beginning therapists tend to focus on the more dramatic, but at the moment irrelevant, content rather than the more subtle but critical behavior. In supervision, they have to be reminded constantly that first things come first: no patients, no therapy. The language and activity of the group have to be measured frequently against the criteria of the analytic contract. For example, it is imperative to know why the members ignore one member's continual lateness, another member's reluctance to mention dreams or his remote past, and why a third member is given license to gobble down his lunch during the session. Why is that member breaking the contract, and why does no one mention it? It may be that the members are tolerating the deviant behavior because it reflects a hidden wish they all share. Or, it may be that they are protecting themselves against recognizing some unacceptable thought or feeling. Whatever the cause, it must be ferreted out as expeditiously as possible by describing the behavior and reminding the group of the contract.

Basic to the analytic contract is the explicit understanding that group analysis is a talking cure. Talking is the desired form of communication; acting out is not. The latter is more primitive, more frequently subject to misunderstanding, and often fraught with damaging potential. In fact, almost all of the resistances destructive to analysis involve acting out.

In a well-structured, co-operative group the members can be expected to explain to a wayward member that such behavior as an impulsive hug or slap is inappropriate and to withhold approval of such deviant behavior. Furthermore, they will tend actively to examine and explore the reason for the acting out on the part of a member. The members acquire this attitude from the analyst. They observe that a reluctance by any of them to just sitting and talking elicits an immediate intervention from him. They note that he identifies the activity as acting out and indicates a more appropriate form of behavior. He sometimes may go even further, training the members, by way of information and analysis, that it is well to inhibit impulses when they are on the verge of erupting into action, since the frustration that accompanies inhibition can lead to feelings, and the more feelings and thoughts that can be converted into words, the closer the members come to emotional maturity.

Physical contact is an obvious form of acting out. Where hostile impulses are involved, members are usually willing to deal with these outbreaks at once, but erotic impulses tend to get a more accepting reception; members may tolerate and even encourage them. The more the members engage in touching, kissing, or embracing, the greater is the danger of an interminable analysis. These acts give gratification; they also whet the emotional appetite for more gratification. The anticipation and desire makes patients reluctant to ventilate negative attitudes or abrasive feelings, and the result is frequently a stalemate or an erosive interaction that tends to produce drop-outs. The analyst must make the group aware of the fact that such acting out is a collective resistance rather than appropriate behavior.

CASE 3

An initially shy and withdrawn patient, Horace, fell into the habit of giving Amanda a farewell kiss at the end of each session. Alex, a psychology student, opened one session by congratulating Horace on his new-found freedom. When Alex was reminded by the analyst that this behavior was a form of socializing—a deviation from the accepted contract—he vehemently defended Horace's behavior as a "growth experience." Furthermore, he received support from Horace who enlarged on how grateful he was to the group for its acceptance of him. His life, he said, was expanding in many directions. With this glowing report of his progress, no one actively defended the contract.

The analyst directed the group's attention to this kissing for several sessions, and then, because of the meager response, dropped the matter. One day, Amanda called for an individual session. She blurted out with great anxiety that she and Horace had been to bed several times, and she was afraid she was pregnant. Although the pregnancy turned out to be a false alarm, Amanda no longer wanted to return to the group, and Horace was also on the point of breaking off treatment.

The analyst reported this event to his supervision group, the members of which pointed out his timidity as a group analyst and laid this to countertransference resistance. They also felt that the group had expressed its aggression by ingoring both the contract and his interventions. The analyst was urged to confront the members on their defiance and sedulously to pursue the reason for their lack of interest in scrutinizing the Amanda–Horace interaction. When the analyst did so and persisted, the members slowly revealed they had been receiving vicarious sensual gratifications from the budding relationship and that several members had been starting to grope toward similar liaisons.

In a group that has been analytically educated to deal with acting out, patients given to impulsive behavior are taught by the more therapeutically sophisticated to restrain their impulses and to tolerate their feelings. In such a group, the sophisticated members recognize that any behavior that interferes with verbal communication is a phenomenon to focus on. The analyst's intervention is scarcely required; for the group understands that this function is its responsibility.

The same is as true of silence as it is of acting out. The contract calls for each member to take a part of the total talking time; that is, in a group of eight, each member speaks approximately one-eighth of all the time over a period of weeks or months. Silence, when it does not contribute to group communication, is a form of resistance. The reason for it must be ascertained, particularly when the mute member is in a state of anxiety. The group needs to look not only into the question of why the member is suffering, why he is not talking, and why he is not discussing his discomfort in particular, but also what he needs to free him to speak. When the members fail to be interested in an agitated but mute member's state, they are displaying a group resistance. When a group is indifferent to a mute or withdrawn member, or indifferent to meeting a member's needs, it may be covertly suggesting to the member that it would like him to leave. In such instances, it is the task of the analyst to make the group aware of any shared resistant attitudes toward verbal participation. But, as with other aspects of the contract, although the members are expected to talk, the analyst does not urge or pressure them to do so. Rather, he focuses on removing the obstacles to easy participation in the on-going verbal give-and-take. He is always seeking the resolution of resistances against verbal communication.

SUMMARY

Group members are educated to point out to each other deviations from the therapeutic contract and to deal with individual resistances. When they fail to deal with a deviation from the contract, a group resistance may be operative. The analyst investigates and studies how to resolve this resistance. In this way, autonomy is encouraged and unexpected drop-outs are forestalled.

REFERENCES

Ormont, L. (1957), The Preparation of Patients for Group Psychoanalysis. *Amer. J. Psychother.*, 9:841–848.

—— (1959), The Opening Session in Group Psychoanalysis. *Acta Psychother.* (Suppl.), 7:288-294.

—— (1962), Establishing the Analytic Contract in a Newly Formed Therapeutic Group. *Brit. J. Med. Psychol.*, 35:333-337.

Spotnitz, H. (1952), A Psychoanalytical View of Resistance in Groups. *Int. J. Group Psychother.*, 2:3-10.

21

On the Concept of
the "Mother Group"

Saul Scheidlinger
Department of Psychiatry
Albert Einstein College of Medicine
Bronx, New York, New York

[It is significant that the group psychological discovery of the complex identification process by which group members relate to the group as a whole as though it were a sort of benign and potentially need-satisfying mother figure was historically late. In the earlier group dynamics and group psychoanalysis literature, the emphasis was more often on the paternal transference in which the members view the leader as a kind of father figure. Scheidlinger highlights a number of important dynamic aspects of the preoedipal identification with the group as mother. He also makes a plea for empirical group dynamic study of the mother group phenomenon as it occurs in unstructured laboratory groups and psychoanalytic therapy groups.]

There have been increasing references in the group process and group psychotherapy literature to observations that on the deepest levels group members perceive the group-as-a-whole as a maternal image. This paper scrutinizes the historical roots of what one might term the concept of a "mother-group" and the varied usages of the term by students of group behavior. An attempt is made to relate this concept to the better-known concepts of group identification and of transferences.

From "On the Concept of the 'Mother Group'" by S. Scheidlinger, *International Journal of Group Psychotherapy*, 1974, *24*, 417–428. Copyright 1974 by the International Journal of Group Psychotherapy. Reprinted by permission.

The earliest reference[1] to the group entity as a parental symbol appeared in a paper by R. Money-Kyrle (1950) in which he postulated three kinds of unconscious perceptions by members of groups:

(1) The "good parents," *particularly the mother*, representing the norms and ideals of the group; (2) the "bad parents" in the role of persecutors against whom the group values have to be defended; and (3) the "good parents," especially the father, who in his role as the mother's defender reappears as the group leader. While Money-Kyrle referred to larger societal groupings, Schindler (1951, 1952, and 1966) was the first group therapist to speak of the group as a mother symbol. He differentiated between transferences to the therapist as a father, to the group members as siblings, to the group entity as mother, on the one hand, and the "group personality" on the tripartite model of id, ego, and superego, on the other hand. W. R. Bion (1960) made repeated brief references in his writings to the group's being perceived unconsciously at times as a "part-object," such as the mother's breast or other body parts, in line with Melanie Klein's conceptualizations. Scheidlinger (1955 and 1964) hypothesized that the group members' identification with the group-as-a-whole represented a covert wish to restore an earlier state of unconflicted well-being inherent in the child's exclusive union with the mother.

Interestingly, S. R. Slavson's first and single mention of this theme occurred only 10 years ago, in 1964, when he briefly stated: "It has been shown that the group serves *in loco maternis*. The leader usually represents symbolically, the father figure, while the group represents the complementary figure of the mother" (p. 27). Similarly, Foulkes (1964) asserted at the same time that ". . . on different levels the group can symbolize a variety of objects or persons, e.g., the body . . . the inside of the mother, the womb. It frequently, possibly universally, represents the 'Image of the Mother' hence the term 'matrix' " (p. 115). In the same year, Durkin (1964) postulated two separate transference manifestations in therapy groups: "(1) The idea of a group—i.e., a large totality of unknown power—conjures up the harsh, pre-oedipal mother image reactivating the individual's narcissistic fear of her; and (2) the individual perceives the group accordingly in distorted fashion, and behaves toward it in a way that resembles his mode of reacting to his mother. While the group member thus is afraid of the group as a whole, the therapist, in turn, is perceived in the image of the good all-giving omnipotent mother" (p. 329). Basing his observations on T-groups and on self-analytic classroom groups, Slater (1966) discussed at some length the group members' perceptions of the group-as-a-whole in a maternal vein. According to him, this "mother-group" was at times perceived as ". . . a source of succorance and comfort, even a refuge." At other times, this mother image was a frightening

---

[1] I am not including here the much earlier appearance of such terms as "mother earth" or "mother country" in folklore and mythology.

one involving primitive fantasies ". . . of being swallowed and enveloped." The "group revolt" against the leader which was depicted as occurring in the early phase of T-groups Slater tied up, on the one hand, with the members' trying to get the loving indulgent "mother-group" away from the depriving paternal figure; on the other hand, this dethroning of the leader he also associated with a ". . . dramatic heightening of sexual interest" among the group members. Still more recently, Grotjahn (1972) asserted that "as a general rule, the group is a truly good and strong mother, not only in fantasies of transference but also in the reality of the group process" (p. 318). Ruiz (1972) described the early phase of a T-group in which the anxiety experienced by the participants appeared to be perceived as a threat to the idealized image of an unconflicted, nurturing "mother-group."

The most comprehensive discussion in the literature to date on this theme of the "mother-group" was that by Gibbard and Hartman (1973) who, following Slater (1966), asserted that the group members' ". . . affective response to the unconscious perception of the group-as-mother is profoundly ambivalent. The positive side of the ambivalence is the wellspring for what we [the authors] have called the utopian fantasy" (p. 127). This fantasy "offers some assurance that the more frightening, enveloping or destructive aspects of the group-as-mother will be held in check and that a host of oedipal feelings, libidinal and aggressive, will not become fully conscious and gain direct expression in the group. The essence of the utopian fantasy is that the good can be split off from the bad and that this separation can be maintained" (p. 126). (I shall return to some of the significant theoretical issues posed by Gibbard and Hartman at a later point in this paper.)

One might note here that, from the viewpoint of group therapy's history, the "mother-group" concept has begun to be discussed in the literature relatively late. The reasons for this are probably twofold: (1) the early psychoanalytic models of group formation, such as those postulated by Freud (1921) and Redl (1942), placed emphasis on the major role of a paternal "central person" in group psychology; and, (2) the recently growing stress on early object relations in psychoanalytic theory has affirmed the great significance of early mothering in personality development and in psycho-pathology. This stress has tended to focus the attention of individual and group therapists on the reactivation of early object relations in relation to the mother in the therapeutic process as well. An illustration of this trend is Stone's (1961) depiction of the classical psychoanalytic situation as representing on the unconscious level ". . . the superimposed series of basic separation experiences in the child's relation to his mother" (p. 35). More specifically, Stone viewed the analyst as representing what he termed "the mother of separation" as contrasted with the mother image associated with intimate bodily care.

In a previous publication of a decade ago (Scheidlinger, 1964) which dealt with the individual group members' identification with the group-as-a-whole, I defined identification (as distinct from transference and real object relations) as an endopsychic process calling for a degree of individual involvement with a perceived object or its symbolic representation. I hypothesized further that identification with the group entity entailed the following two related elements: (1) ascribing to the group an emotional meaning, i.e., as an instrument for need satisfaction or, on a genetically "deeper" level, as a mother symbol; (2) a self-involvement in the group, a "giving up" of an aspect of personal identity—from the *I* to the *We*—which can serve irrational purposes as well as those of adaptation or growth. I finally wondered whether, in a broader sense, the universal human need to belong, to establish a state of psychological unity with others, did not represent a covert wish to restore an earlier state of unconflicted well-being inherent in the infant's exclusive union with the mother to counteract a fundamental fear of abandonment and of aloneness in all of us. Continued observations of relevant aspects of group behavior since that time have strengthened my belief in the basic plausibility of the above hypotheses and have also led me to a search for additional data from current object-relations theory for their further elaboration.

Perhaps because of the impetus from the so-called "British School," recent psychoanalytic writings in America about early object relations have multiplied and have dwelled in considerably greater detail than did Freud on aspects of this crucial phase of development. Although Melanie Klein asserted that the infant's ego is capable in the first three months of life of perceiving and integrating parts of the first object, i.e., the mother's breast, serious questions have been raised by others whether an infant could conceivably be assumed to possess the perceptual capacity to accomplish this. Jacobson (1964) insists that for the baby to be able to relate psychologically to something external to himself which satisfies his bodily needs, he would have had to have passed through at least a rudimentary phase of ego development. This involves "... the laying down of memory traces, the organization of experiential states and the beginning ability perceptually to differentiate between the self and the object" (p. 34). Using Freud's better known terminology, the infant's transition from primary narcissism to secondary narcissism calls for some degree of reality-geared representations of self and of the maternal object and the perception of the latter as the source of tension relief and of need gratification. Only with this rudimentary recognition is the infant believed to experience anxiety in the absence of the mothering figure (Edgecumbe and Burgner, 1973). In this connection, Anna Freud (1965) postulated a separate stage of a *need-satisfying relationship* which falls developmentally between the phase of *primary narcissism* and that of *object-constancy*. This stage of a *need-satisfying relationship*, while still characterized by the baby's unique egocentricity, coupled with a symbiotic perception of the mother as a gratifier of needs, nevertheless represents an advance from primary narcissism in which a primitive state of experiential pleasure is assumed to prevail, devoid of any differentiation whatsoever between self and object-representations. According to Jacobson (1964), there is an ongoing conflict in the child between the wish to maintain this dependent, need-satisfying style of relating and opposing forces striving for independent ego-functioning. This conflict is believed to continue till the onset of the oedipal period.

In general, then, the term *need-satisfying relationship* refers to a specific mode of relating wherein the maternal object's need-satisfying functions are paramount. Furthermore, the maternal object is perceived as separate from the self only at moments of need; at other times, from the infant's subjective point of view, the object is believed to cease to exist as "somewhere out there." There is broad consensus in the literature that this phase of the need-satisfying relationship lasts from three months until the age of about 18 months. Gradually, this stage is believed to be supplanted by the psychologically more advanced stage of *object constancy*, in which concern for the mothering figure as an object takes precedence over her mere need-gratifying functions.

In returning to the earlier noted hypothesis regarding an aspect of identification with the group entity connoting a covert wish of group members to restore a state of unconflicted well-being characteristic of an earlier tie to the mother, I would like to be more specific. The group members' covert wish refers very likely to a yearning for a return to the need-gratifying relationship which I have just outlined. In this context I want to emphasize that the symbolic "mother-group" is accordingly perceived in purely positive, nonconflictual terms.

Guntrip (1961) related this phase of the child's positive early relationship to the mystic's experience of unity with the Deity, to Plato's "Idea of the Good," as well as to Freud's notion of an oceanic feeling, ". . . an indissoluble connection, of belonging inseparably to the external world as a whole" (p. 361). Guntrip felt, as I do, that this ". . . sense of identity or unity must be the basis of all kinds of feelings of oneness in both personal and communal living" (p. 362).

As I have noted elsewhere, the regressive emotional pulls which characterize the early group formative stages in unstructured groups tend to loosen the individual's self boundaries and to reactivate primitive wishes and modes of early objective relations, including identifications. Such regressive patterns are not necessarily pathological insofar as even in the most mature personalities the infantile, need-satisfying modes of relating persist and are subject to reactivation at moments of threat and of anxiety. Greenacre (1972) asserted in this connection that ". . . the introjective–projective reaction leading ultimately to the individuation, characteristic of the early stages of life, is never lost and may be revived with special strength in any situation of stress sufficient to cause a feeling of helplessness" (p. 147). Similarly, Schafer (1968) stated that in the realm of primary process emotionality (which, as I have noted, characterizes the anxiety-laden period of group formation)

"... the 'lost' object is not someone who will, it is hoped, return in the future: he is someone who still exists, though he is out of sight, touch, hearing, behind a wall, shattered, and so forth" (p. 222).

As mentioned, the most extensive discussion in the literature to date of the concept of the "mother-group" appeared in a recent paper by Gibbard and Hartman (1973) which is based on observations drawn from "self-analytic" classroom groups of college students. These authors not only found that the group entity was perceived by its members in a maternal vein but also that this shared unconscious fantasy comprised a splitting of the "good" mother image from the "bad." The "good" mother entailed nurturant and protective aspects; the "bad" mother, abandoning and destructive ones. The group members employed splitting "... to avoid both a state in which 'good' and 'bad' cannot be differentiated and a state in which both are experienced at the same time (genuine ambivalence)" (p. 127). These authors stressed, furthermore, that the utopian perception of the group as a benevolent maternal figure was a manifestation of defensiveness against dealing with painful intragroup conflicts. More specifically, according to Gibbard and Hartman "... the 'good' group functions as a defense both against the primitive, 'bad' engulfing and/or sadistic group (mother) and the fully heterosexual, oedipal group (which is no longer so clearly equated with the mother)" (p. 129).

I welcome Gibbard and Hartman's (1973) path of inquiry into the broader realm of group psychological regression and specifically into that of the relatively neglected concept of the "mother-group." While, as they have noted, there is much congruence between my earlier hypotheses regarding identification with the group-as-a-whole (1964) and their recent observations, I nevertheless would like to raise some questions here from the framework of group psychotherapy. To begin with, apart from Durkin's (1964) hypothesized split transference in which the group is perceived by the patients as a threatening pre-oedipal mother figure, with the therapist becoming the "good, all-giving omnipotent mother," I could find no reference in the group therapy literature to the kind of "bad" mother perception of the group entity which is stressed by Gibbard and Hartman (1973). Most other group therapists, as is evident from my earlier review of the relevant literature, refer to the group entity as being perceived in a benign maternal vein, on the one hand, with the *therapist* becoming the feared parental transference figure, on the other. Similarly, fears of abandonment by and of fusion with the group collectivity have been touched on only in rare instances in the American literature in connection with individual patients characterized by ego pathology in whom concern with self-object boundaries is marked. It should be noted in contrast that W. R. Bion (1960) and other British followers of Melanie Klein, such as Jaques (1970), have repeatedly written regarding group members' fears of engulfment by the group to the point of claiming that individual group belonging always entails a defense against loss of identity stemming from primitive, "psychotic" anxieties. (Jaques, to my knowledge, however, never referred to the group as a maternal image, while Bion made occasional references to the group entity's being perceived only as parts of the mother's body, in line with Kleinian postulates of part-objects.)

A number of possibilities suggest themselves as explanations here. It could be that the phenomena described by Gibbard and Hartman (1973) are in some way unique to short-term analytic classroom groups with their "normal" constituency, with assigned readings, an examination, and final grades. These groups are undoubtedly different in character from long-term psychotherapy groups with their composition of designated patients and their explicit goals of "repairing" identified personality pathology. (I was, in this connection, puzzled by the authors' occasional references in their paper to "working through" of conflicts or to "exploring in depth" the defensive nature of fantasies, which suggests, to me at least, a blurring of the aims of education and of therapy.)

There is also a question whether the verbal and nonverbal behavior noted in these classroom groups during their early periods of "manifest utopianism" might be subject to different theoretical explanations by others. Conversely, it is of course possible, too, that therapy groups would abound in the very same manifestations described by Gibbard and Hartman were it not for conscious or unconscious interferences with their open expression. For instance, in their understandable desire to prevent an unduly high anxiety level, especially in the groups' initial phase, group therapists might well be unwittingly discouraging the emergence of negative feelings toward the group entity. This would serve to reinforce the very mechanisms of repression and denial which Gibbard and Hartman postulated.

To answer such questions we obviously need carefully controlled observations of the relevant phases of group processes in therapy and other small groups, preferably by trained observers other than the therapists. These would not only serve to test the different hypotheses regarding the nature of the related individual and collective perceptions of the group entity in a maternal or perhaps other vein, but would also help to differentiate between the nature of these group manifestations in self-analytic and T-groups, on the one hand, and "true" therapy groups, on the other.

Pending such observations, I prefer to maintain the earlier stated, more parsimonious hypotheses regarding the perception of the group entity. In brief, according to these, the initial phase of unstructured therapy groups is characterized by nonpathological, regressive perceptions and relationships of all aspects of the group situation: of the leader, of the other group members, and of the group-as-a-whole. From a genetic, developmental viewpoint, these perceptions and relationships represent a reactivation, in the face of the individual and collective stresses and anxieties induced by group formation, of early patterns and especially of primitive identifications, including the search for the kind of nonconflictual, need-gratifying relationship to the mother which I discussed earlier in this paper. While the group entity is accordingly perceived in a positive and benign image, the group leader and the other members become almost immediately the objects of a gamut of partially ambivalent but largely hostile and fearful attitudes. As noted by Ruiz (1972) with reference to T-groups, and by Arsenian, Semrad, and Shapiro (1962) to therapy groups, when negative feelings thus aroused threaten the group's cohesiveness and basically positive climate, there is a tendency to displace negative feelings onto the leader, thus preserving the group's supportive character. While any perception or behavioral item can admittedly serve defensive purposes, I would like to await further evidence before accepting Gibbard and Hartman's conclusions regarding the regularity with which the members' perceptions of the benign "mother-group" represent an unwillingness "to come to grips with intragroup conflicts and other painful realities of group life." For it is also possible that this very perception is progressively utilized by both the members and by the therapist in the service of the "therapeutic alliance" or of group maintenance and cohesiveness so that the intragroup conflicts and personal problems can be subjected to analytic scrutiny in the context of an anxiety level which is not too threatening to the equilibrium of individual patients and of the group entity.

The complex theoretical issues posed by any attempt to scrutinize the conscious and unconscious aspects of concepts such as that of the "mother-group" tend to reaffirm the urgent need to try to differentiate descriptively in group psychology between individual and collective phenomena, as well as between identifications and transferences, on the one hand, and reality-geared perceptions, on the other. I would accordingly question the generally loose application of the term transference to either an individual or to a shared perception of the group entity in a maternal vein. For, in my view, transference as a concept pertains to an apperception in relation to a *person*, and moreoover to a repetition in the present of a relatively advanced past relationship where there has been some degree of differentiation between the self and the object. The perceptions and object relations in the earliest phase of group formation, including the perception of the "mother-group," are better connoted as various kinds of identifications which, in the psychoanalytic hierarchy of object relations, precede real object ties. This is congruent with Kaplan and Roman's (1963) views on group development in therapy groups. Interestingly, too, Abraham (1973) recently claimed to have *experimental* support for her contention that there are many more primitive kinds of object relations at work in therapy groups than transferences.

It should be noted here that, in the strictest sense of the word, "identification" or "transference" represents an explanatory construct. Each pertains to inferred processes which can be utilized to explain certain kinds of social behavior. Furthermore, in scrutinizing any item of an individual's behavior in a group, one must try to differentiate, as Couch (1961) has suggested, among (1) underlying needs, (2) concealment defenses,

(3) apperception of interpersonal forces, and (4) reaction to the behavioral press of overt acts of others. In this connection, group therapists must differentiate also between direct expressions of genuine needs, i.e., need for a mothering relationship, and defensive exaggerations or minimization of needs. There is also the issue of distinguishing such needs from shared fantasies which might be employed as a means of gratifying these needs.

What I termed in a previous publication the *early dependency phase* in a therapy group is characterized, in addition to the prevalence of multiple individual and group identifications, by poor reality perceptions and much magical thought, including oral fantasies. This phase is supplanted by a more advanced one in which transferences and real object ties predominate, with realistic perceptions including sexual and aggressive expressions.

I would concur with the many writers who have pointed to a probable link between our "age of anxiety" and the unprecedented recent popularity of varied experiential growth groups. The latter are sought out in people's search for intimacy, for enhanced self-esteem and sense of identity, and perhaps on a deeper level for support from a benign "mother-group." In this connection, in writing about our new human problems related to the unprecedented rate of societal change, Toffler (1970) envisioned "stability zones," "love networks," and time-limited supportive groups for people undergoing adaptational crises in order for them to experience, if only briefly, identification with others as well as the support of a benign group entity.

One might be justified in claiming, then, that when the small group is viewed as a helping system, not only do its members need the leader-worker and each other but also the group-as-a-group! Furthermore, in this context the crucial question is *not* how the leader-worker perceives the situation but how the group member does. These aspects have remained neglected for too long.

SUMMARY

In this paper the concept of the "mother-group" has been subjected to special scrutiny. A historical review of the literature reveals increasing references during the last decade to group members' perceptions of the group entity in a maternal vein.

A previously stated hypothesis of mine which related individual members' identification with the group-as-a-whole to an unconscious wish to restore an earlier state of unconflicted union with the mother has been developed in greater detail and tied more specifically to a yearning for a return to the child's purely positive "need-gratifying relationship," which Anna Freud has postulated as occurring developmentally between the phases of "primary narcissism" and that of "object constancy."

In contradistinction to some writers' views of the early phase of group development as regularly containing simultaneous perceptions of a threatening "mother-group" image, it is suggested that, pending further objective observations of therapy groups, it is more likely that the leader and the other group members, rather than the group-as-a-whole, are the objects of such early fearful and hostile feelings.

In order to attain the much-desired theoretical clarity in the group process field generally and in group psychotherapy specifically, the need for attempting to differentiate between individual and collective phenomena, on the one hand, and among identifications, transferences, and reality-geared perceptions, on the other hand, is reaffirmed.

A possible link between the recent mushrooming of various kinds of experiential "growth" groups and people's need for enhanced self-esteem and support from perhaps a benign "mother-group" in this age of anxiety is suggested.

REFERENCES

Abraham, A., (1973), A Model for Exploring Intra- and Interindividual Process in Groups. *Int. J. Group Psychother.*, 23:3–22.

Arsenian, J., Semrad, E. V., and Shapiro, D. (1962), An Analysis of Integral Functions in Small Groups. *Int. J. Group Psychother.*, 12:421–434.

Bion, W. R. (1960), *Experiences in Groups.* New York: Basic Books.

Couch, A. S. (1961), The Psychological Determinants of Interpersonal Behavior. In: Proceedings of the Fourteenth International Congress of Applied Psychology. Copenhagen: Munksgaard.

Durkin, H. E., (1964), *The Group in Depth.* New York: International Universities Press.

Edgecumbe, R., and Burgner, M. (1973), Some Problems in the Conceptualization of Early Object Relationships. *The Psychoanalytic Study of the Child*, 27:283–314. New York: Quadrangle Books.

Foulkes, S. H. (1964), *Therapeutic Group Analysis.* New York: International Universities Press.

Freud, A. (1965), *Normality and Pathology in Childhood.* New York: International Universities Press.

Freud, S. (1921), *Group Psychology and the Analysis of the Ego.* London: Hogarth Press, 1948.

Gibbard, G. S., and Hartman, J. J. (1973), The Significance of Utopian Fantasies in Small Groups. *Int. J. Group Psychother.*, 23:125–147.

Greenacre, P. (1972), Crowds and Crisis. Psychoanalytic Considerations. *The Psychoanalytic Study of the Child*, 27:136–154. New York: Quadrangle Books.

Grotjahn, M. (1972), Learning from Dropout Patients. *Int. J. Group Psychother.*, 22:287–305

Guntrip, H. (1961), *Personality Structure and Human Interaction.* New York: International Universities Press.

Jacobson, E. (1964), *The Self and the Object World.* New York: International Universities Press.

Jaques, E. (1970), *Work, Creativity and Social Justice.* New York: International Universities Press.

Kaplan, S. and Roman, M. S. (1963), Phases of Development in Adult Therapy Groups. *Int. J. Group Psychother.*, 13:10–26.

Money-Kyrle, R. (1950), Varieties of Group Formation. In: *Psychoanalysis and the Social Sciences*, ed. G. Róheim. New York: International Universities Press.

Redl, F. (1942), Group Emotion and Leadership. *Psychiatry*, 5:573–596.

Ruiz, P. (1972), On the Perception of the "Mother-Group" in T-Groups. *Int. J. Group Psychother.*, 22:488–491.

Schafer, R. (1968), *Aspects of Internalization.* New York: International Universities Press.

Scheidlinger, S. (1955), The Concept of Identification in Group Psychotherapy. *Amer. J. Psychother.*, 9:661–672.

—— (1964), Identification, The Sense of Belonging and of Identity in Small Groups. *This Journal*, 14:291–306.

Schindler, W. (1951), Family Pattern in Group Formation and Therapy. *Int. J. Group Psychother.*, 1:100–105.

—— (1952), The Group Personality Concept in Group Psychotherapy. *Int. J. Group Psychother.*, 2:311–315.

—— (1966), The Role of the Mother in Group Psychotherapy. *Int. J. Group Psychother.*, 16:198–200.

Slater, P. E. (1966), *Microcosm.* New York: John Wiley.

Slavson, S. R. (1964), *A Textbook in Analytic Group Psychotherapy.* New York: International Universities Press.

Stone, L. (1961), *The Psychoanalytic Situation.* New York: International Universities Press.

Toffler, A. (1970), *Future Shock.* New York: Bantam Books.

22

A Group Psychotherapy Approach to the Treatment of Separated Women

Morton Kissen
Institute of Advanced Psychological Studies
Adelphi University
Garden City, Long Island, New York

[Certain characteristic group dynamics that often occur during the course of treatment sessions with recently separated women are explored in this chapter. In particular, the often rigid and intractable "nesting" group resistance is descriptively elaborated as it relates to the severe dependency problems and acutely symbiotic characterological difficulties of such women. A number of realistic, psychosocial and psychodynamic difficulties typically seen in separated women are described as well as some therapeutic techniques for dealing with them. Certain structural aspects of group management such as the selection of members, group goals, and the issue of termination are dealt with.]

Recently separated women have been more frequently coming for treatment to mental health clinics across the country. Such women have very special adjustment problems unique to their contemporary life circumstances. Group psychotherapy is often the treatment modality of choice for the separated woman. In the present paper, an effort will be made to explore

From "A Group Psychotherapy Approach to the Treatment of Separated Women" by M. Kissen, *Group Process: Journal of the Association for Group Psychoanalysis and Process*, 1976, *6*, 195-209. Copyright 1976 by the Association for Group Psychoanalysis and Process. Reprinted by permission.

both the desirable aspects of the group therapy approach to the treatment of separated women and some of the specific difficulties often encountered during the course of such a therapeutic intervention.

The separated woman brings with her into therapy a variety of very special realistic and psychological difficulties. The initial part of this paper will focus upon an exploration of these difficulties. Next, the particularly useful aspects of the group therapy experience for separated women will be described. Since group psychotherapy can be envisioned along a continuum from supportive, directive and information-giving interventions, at the one end, to more depth explorative dynamically interpretive, and characterological restructuring interventions at the other end (Yalom 1970), the approximate placement of the separated woman's group along such a continuum (complex and ever-shifting as it may be) will be described as it relates to the desirable therapeutic derivatives of the group experience. The next portion of the paper will focus upon an elucidation of certain built-in group resistances inherent in the very dynamic fabric of the separated woman's group. The universal tendency toward exaggerated dependency and interdependency interactions in such groups will be described in terms of the "nesting" syndrome. Particular forms of acting-out resistances in such groups will also be explored. Finally, basic structural issues such as important group therapeutic goals, membership selection principles, and termination criteria, will be elaborated upon.

SPECIALIZED REALISTIC PROBLEMS OF THE SEPARATED WOMEN

A number of objective hardships and frustrations are essential aspects of the life of the separated woman.

Legal Difficulties

The separated woman must somehow wend her way through the maze of the court system seeking for herself a just and equitable financial settlement from her husband. She tends to become in the process an amateur lawyer who because of her life circumstances has been forced to master the complex technicalities of divorce law as it applies to her situation. She must learn which judge is relatively more sensitive to her own needs and which tends to overidentify with the plight of the separated husband. She needs to obtain an experienced lawyer who is willing to offer her continuous supportive legal advice whenever needed. She is often willing to offer her advice and counsel with regard to legal matters to a peer who is more recently separated and hence who may not be as well-versed as herself in the various details of divorce law. She often is forced to come upon the very painful discovery that, despite all of her legal knowledge and sophistication and all of the good will toward her in the courts, the obtaining of an adequate financial settlement from her husband hinges more upon his particular ethical code of conduct than upon any other factor. A narcissisically oriented, infantile, or psychopathic husband seldom respects or recognizes the legal mandate of the court system. Much of the discussion in separated women's groups is focussed upon common legal dilemmas that all of the women face. There is much sharing of information and mutual support as each woman in turn presents her particular plight and legal struggle with her husband.

Financial Hardships

Most separated women find themselves in an economically difficult situation. They are, at least, initially, almost totally dependent upon their husband for financial support. The husband's voluntary support payments allow for a temporary maintenance of the status quo but often introduce a number of economic deprivations. The recently separated woman must begin to carefully budget her financial assets and in general learn to run her household in as economically efficient a manner as possible. The contrast between her previous state of relative economic comfort and her present more limited state is ever-present on her mind. The extremes of such a contrast are particularly poignantly felt by women who have had successful professional husbands (i.e., doctors, lawyers, etc.) allowing them to maintain a comfortable upper middle-class existence. Many separated women have young children and are unable to seek out employment so that they can support their families in an independent fashion. The tragic and ironic situation of a once upper middle-class woman who must now go on welfare to keep her house and support her family because of her husband's failure to maintain his financial responsibilities is neither unusual nor infrequent. Many such women are forced into housing foreclosures and subsequent sub-standard apartments as a result of their financial plight.

Problems of Child Care

Many separated women are left with as many as three or four children to care for. Despite their own recent emotional hurt, they must somehow find the energy to cope with the physical and emotional needs of their children. Tremendous demands and strain are placed on most parents during the process of rearing children. The pressures of child-bearing are considerably exaggerated for the separated woman. She must attempt to explain the reason for the separation to her children and must somehow compensate for the father's absence. She must struggle with both her guilt feelings (and consequent need to over-compensate) and her rage and resentment toward the absent father (and consequent need to scape-goat or "victimize" one of the children). Visitation periods during which the father comes to the house to pick up the children are often periods of special stress and emotional ambivalence. The separated woman must constantly struggle against the natural tendency to involve the children in her conflict with her estranged husband. She often resents the positive feelings that the children display toward their father, and will often note in group therapy the fact that the husband has the best of both worlds with the children. Thus, he can be idolized by the children without having to have a continuous child care responsibility for them. Given the extreme stress that they are under, many separated women seek assistance and child guidance advice from mental health clinics.

SPECIALIZED PSYCHOLOGICAL PROBLEMS OF THE SEPARATED WOMEN

Certain psychological difficulties are repetitively seen in separated women's groups and are very much at the center of the therapeutic work.

Depressive Reactions

Almost every woman in such a group is experiencing some degree of depression and consequent reduction in her capacity to cope energetically with normal life stresses and pressures. Depression is often reflected in these women via mild psycho-motor retardation, loss of interest in the outer environment, social withdrawal tendencies, rapid mood swings, and in a preoccupation with morbid topics of conversation. The extent of the depressive reaction hinges very much on the ego strengths of the individual group members. Some manifest a far greater resiliency and ability to restore themselves to a relatively adequate level of adaptive functioning than do others. Very quickly, during the course of the group therapy sessions, the therapist gains a sense of hierarchy along an ego-strength continuum of the individual group members. Whereas some members have been deeply traumatized and made almost adaptively immobile by the separation experience, others are able to cope with the experience in a far more flexible and adequate fashion.

Exaggerated Dependency Feelings

A primary psychological reaction often noted in such groups is an exaggerated proneness to depend upon others for support, encouragement, and authoritative recommendations. The natural tendency to set up the leader as an idealized authority figure that occurs in all groups is a particularly strong and pervasive phenomenon in the separated women's group. It is somehow magically assumed that the leader is knowledgeable in all areas many of which are clearly beyond those of his actual professional experience. He is assumed to have an excellent understanding of the court system, the technicalities of divorce law, financial management, the welfare system, employment, and a host of other areas of specialization. It is seldom suspected, however, that the group leader is learning and making discoveries about these various problem areas together with the group members. The dependency upon the leader is particularly exaggerated with regard to difficulties that he can reasonably be assumed to know something about. Thus, questions with regard to child-rearing, current interpersonal relationships, and the choice of a subsequent mate are repeatedly brought up for his consideration. Given the inordinate nature of the dependency upon the leader, it is difficult for the group members to broach hostile or ambivalent feelings that they might feel toward him.

More so than upon the leader, however, the separated women's group members tend to establish strong dependency ties to each other. Much communication both within and outside the group centers about a sort of mutual helping process that will be more fully described later in this paper. The interdependency of the group members is very great during the course of the group's existence. The members communicate with each other a great deal outside of the group meetings. They often socialize together and assist each other on errands and with various transportation difficulties. Although some pairing and cliquing can occur in such groups, the primary force is toward an overall group cohesiveness largely due to the strong dependency relationships established between the members.

An air of helplessness often pervades the atmosphere of the group sessions. A pecking order tends to subtly be established during the course of the group meetings in which the most helpless and troubled member is somehow empathically chosen and allowed to dominate the initial portion of a group session with a description of her current plight. Stronger members are some times made to feel guilty by the group if they take up too much time or nudge out an obviously weaker or more contemporaneously burdened member. Dependency is the order of the day in such groups—with the most helpless and dependent member receiving prime time and attention.

Narcissistic and Psychopathic-like Reactions

Associated with the exaggerated dependency feelings frequently expressed in the separated women's group is the regressive and child-like reaction of certain of the group members. Such reactions resemble very much the personality constellation clinically found in individuals having infantile or psychopathic character structures. The deep hurt and sense of deprivation felt by such members are often used as a rationalization for a variety of narcissistic, self-indulgent, and socially aberrant behavior. Thus, one woman was prepared to take a vacation with her boy-friend, leaving her four children in the care of her ex-husband who was to reside in her home with them. Another felt it unnecessary to pay a plumbing bill since her financial situation was a very tight one as a result of her separation from her husband. The needs of many such women for time and attention from the therapist and other clinic staff (should the group therapy sessions take place in an out-patient clinic setting) are inordinate. Special favors and financial and other assistance are skillfully exacted by these women from the people in their outer environment.

The Recapitulation of Childhood Separation Trauma

The recent experience of separation apparently brings to the fore a variety of unresolved separation experiences from the patient's past. The loss of an idealized parent figure by illness or death or some form of rejection is frequently an important psycho-dynamic root of the separated woman's current depressive reaction. She reflects such earlier experiences of loss and abandonment in her transference relationships to both the leader and her group member peers. Her almost phobic attitude toward the possible establishment of another intimate relationship with a man of a permanent nature is probably also associated with her current re-experiencing of a separation trauma from the past. Her fear is that she will be hurt again as she has been very recently by her husband and in the more distant past by her parents.

Separation anxiety would appear to be at least one primary cause of the almost "frozen" and barren nature of the social and interpersonal life of a number of separated women. Their anxious constriction can be reflected via a variety of phobic reactions to such simple activities as driving a car, going shopping, as well as those involving possibly more intimate relationships to others (i.e., parents without partners meetings, dances, etc.).

THE USEFULNESS OF A GROUP EXPERIENCE

Group psychotherapy has a number of curative features which are particularly useful for the separated woman.

Peer Support and Information Sharing

Each woman in the group is given a great deal of support and encouragement by her peers. When specific personal problems are brought up for discussion, the group listens attentively and then comes up with constructive suggestions and recommendations. Each woman shares her knowledge and problem-solving techniques with the other members of the group.

The typical session consists of verbal presentations by members particularly in need of group attention to their current difficulties. Much positive reinforcement, moral support, and a number of concrete points of information and problem-solving approaches are then offered to them by the other members of the group. The women who have received the group's attention often leave the session in a better frame of mind and far more able to cope with their problems.

The Sense of Shared Experience

The fact that all of the women have suffered a recent object loss is another mutually supportive aspect of the group experience. Whereas she had originally felt alone and uniquely injured by her experience, the separated woman when placed in a group soon becomes aware that a number of people have had similar experiences. She also is made aware of the fact that others suffer as much and perhaps even more than she does. The sense of commonality and universality of experience implicit in the group interaction process is very reassuring to the separated woman.

Group Cohesiveness

It is because of this homogeneously shared experience that separated women's groups tend to become extraordinarily cohesive. A very intimate personal atmosphere pervades most group meetings. Feelings of warmth and concern are predominant aspects of the interaction between the members. Harsh feelings, jealousies, rivalries, and various other forms of interpersonal tension and conflict—although existing as latent group dynamics—are seldom directly expressed and consciously reflected upon by the group members. In order to maintain the interpersonal support and encouragement being derived from the group, the members attempt to avoid any expression of hostility or disharmony. Thus, a great deal of positive reinforcement and enhanced sense of self worth and personal security can be obtained as a result of the group interaction. The cohesion of the group is an extremely reassuring and anxiety-reducing aspect of the group experience for the separated woman.

The Opportunity for Interpersonal Learning

In addition to the positive feelings of cohesion, warmth and personal regard for one another inherent in the group interaction, the possibility for a more depth experience of personality feed-back, developmental growth, and characterological restructuring also exists as a potential resultant of the group experience. The leader makes it clear quite early and continuously during the course of the group's history that—although positive reinforcement, inter-member support and information-giving are essential aspects of the group process—they are not the only therapeutic activities to be involved in by the group.

The leader emphasizes his expectation that the members will explore as fully as possible their own personality dynamics as they are expressed in interpersonal interactions in the group itself, current outside relationships, and previous relationships to significant persons in the group member's past life. Of particular significance is an exploration of current interactional style as it might hinge upon the previous object choice and relationship with the member's husband. The previous relationship with the husband is microscopically analyzed and compared and contrasted with current relationships. Interpretations by the leader and other forms of confrontation both by himself and by the other group members are basic to the interpersonal learning process.

As a result of such interpersonal learning and personality feedback processes, the members are encouraged toward characterological shifts of functioning and developmental growth—much as they might be during the course of an individual psychotherapy experience.

GROUP RESISTANCES

Certain resistances are built into the very fabric of the separated women's group. Such resistances are typically expressed by the total group membership rather than by individual members and hence can be considered "group resistances" (Ormont, 1968).

Exaggerated Dependency Reactions

As previously mentioned, dependency feelings tend to be very strong in the separated women's group. Although such feelings are naturally inherent in the very difficult plight of the separated woman, they can be expressed in an exaggerated fashion during the course of the group sessions and hence can be viewed as a resistance to the therapeutic task. Extreme dependency reactions tend to interfere with the open and honest exploration of underlying feelings and personality tendencies. The members are far too concerned with the need to preserve group unity and to mutually support each other and thereby limit themselves to overly positive statements and observations of each other. Very little hostility, critical feed-back, or open competitiveness between the members can be expressed during the group session. The leader, too, is treated in an overly gentle fashion by the group. Hostile or ambivalent reactions toward him are submerged under the more prevalent tendencies to lean upon him and idealize him as an all-knowing and relatively benign authority figure.

To effectively deal with this form of group resistance, the leader must first be alert to its occurrence and second be prepared to focus upon it in an interpretive fashion at appropriate moments. The group members need to be encouraged to explore their underlying ambivalent feelings toward each other, the leader, and particularly toward their husbands. The difficult and tenuous process of working through such feelings is very much at the heart of the group's therapeutic task. The ultimate goal of attaining a firmly articulated "psychological" separation from the husband often comes long after the legal separation has been arranged. The group members must first, however, become acutely aware of the obstructive nature of their unresolved dependency attachments to their husbands which are often camouflaged via obsessive legal and financial ruminations.

The group dependency resistance must be thoroughly explored and worked through in order to assure for each member a relatively complete separation from the husband and ultimately from the group itself.

The "Nesting" Syndrome

The dependency feelings and positive inter-member support that occur in the group are often so pervasive that they lead to symbiotic-like attachments to the group. The strong attachment to the group by the members is reflected in the fact that there are very few absences from the group sessions, and in the difficulty that the leader often experiences in attempting to end each session at the appointed time. The members clearly enjoy the sessions, often continue them in clubby discussions after the meeting has formally ended, and look forward to the upcoming session with anticipation.

It is as if the group sessions afford a sort of womb-like and protective oasis away from the harsh and oppressive external world of reality. The tremendous cohesiveness and mutual support that is prevalent in the meetings contrasts markedly with the isolation and loneliness felt by the women in their everyday lives. The group has apparently become a sort of cozy little nest which is depended upon by the members for a bolstering up of their rather frail sense of security.

Although such a dependency phenomenon is an implicit component of all groups, it occurs much more rapidly and with greater pervasiveness in the separated women's group. In the traditional group, narcissistic defenses and individual personality structure are much more in the forefront as resistances to the incipient process of group formation and cohesion. Thus, Fried (1971) has described a particular individual defense against inclusion and involvement in the group interactional process as the maintenance of a "narcissistic cocoon." In the separated women's group, quite in contrast, the primary resistance is not against group involvement but rather against the eventual need for individualistic activity and separation from the group. The proneness of the members to make the group an all-protective enclosure against the harsh outside world must ultimately be interpreted by the leader as a form of group resistance to emotional and personality growth.

Acting-Out Tendencies

Certain forms of acting-out behavior are rather prevalent in such groups and can be viewed as a resistance to the therapeutic process of self-exploration and personality growth. One such form of acting-out can be found in the tendency to deal with important therapy-related issues in informal social meetings outside of the group. Since the members of such groups often fraternize a great deal outside of the group meetings, a number of important issues are explored without the leaders' presence. Frictions and tensions can be kept out of the group meeting proper and dealt with via sub-group encounters and telephone conversations. The group sessions are thereby deprived of a number of group dynamics (i.e.,–rivalries, competitive interactions, etc.) in that they are only dealt with outside of the group. The leader must be alert to the existence of such a form of acting-out and must consistently encourage the members to bring significant interaction from outside relationships into the formal group meetings.

Another form of acting out can be seen in the occasional tendency of the separated woman to resolve difficult internal conflicts or decision-making dilemmas via an attempt at manipulating either the leader or another member of the group. In one case, a member noted that her boyfriend seemed to have a number of severe emotional problems and hinted that she would like to have him evaluated by the group leader as a possible candidate for psychotherapy at the clinic. Her true wish, however, was clearly that the leader approve or disapprove of him as a suitable person for a more permanent relationship. In another case, two members went on a double-date and ended up very critically evaluating the personality characteristics of the men whom both had been seeing over an extended period. In both cases, the leader had to interpret quite firmly the underlying wish to escape the need for a mature and independent decision-making process. The dissonance and stressfulness of the difficult decision that needed to be made had led to an impulsive attempt at conflict-resolution by an active involvement of another person. An inner conflict had clearly been dealt with via the defense of externalization.

STRUCTURAL ASPECTS

A number of issues with regard to structure come up in working with a separated women's group.

Selection of Members

Although a certain degree of homogeneity is built into the group due to the fact that all of the members are women and are recently separated from their husbands, it is best to include a fairly broad variety of personality types and diagnostic categories of emotional disturbance. It is perhaps best to keep the number of severely disturbed individuals down to a minimum, if possible. A group of eight members should probably not contain more than one or two severely depressed or psychotic individuals.

Assuming that people can be rank ordered along a coping-collapse continuum in terms of the severity of their underlying disturbance and available ego resources, it is important to include in such a group at least two or three individuals possessing sufficient ego strength to offer a core of potential peer leadership to the group. The personality "resiliency" and potential for separation-individuation of such stronger group members are essential attitudes for later stages of the group's development, in that they can be utilized together with the leader as an identificatory model by the other weaker group members (Kissen). The leader will again and again rely upon such members to assist him in his interpretive effort to pull the group out of periods of despair, depressive inactivity, and group dependency resistances.

Goals for the Group Members

A number of specific goals can be mentioned as essential to the development of emotional growth and mental health in the group members. It should be expected that all of the members will seek out some form of employment in order to improve their financial status, offer themselves an experience of independent self-sustaining activity separate from their husbands, and to diminish via a form of work therapy the depressive potential of their current situation.

Social relationships should be encouraged for all members, particularly with members of the opposite sex. A number of recently separated women develop an almost phobic attitude toward socialization with men. Anxieties with regard to the pervasive sexual motives of men in social situations such as singles bars, dances, and Parents Without Partners meetings are frequently expressed during the course of the group sessions. The women need to develop the courage to risk the possibility of an intimate social relationship with a man—despite their past traumatic experience in this regard. A true psychological separation from the husband can seldom occur (despite the attainment of a legal divorce ruling), without some form of non-ambivalent involvement in a continuous relationship with another man.

Involvement in some form of consciousness raising women's group might also be considered a useful goal for the group members. Enhanced independence strivings and an increased sense of self-worth and pride might very well result from such an auxiliary group membership.

Termination of the Group

Despite some of the above mentioned group resistances, it is possible to successfully terminate the separated women's group in a reasonable amount of time—with a majority of the members having attained the goals just mentioned and an over-all improvement in their mental health and personality functioning. The leader must avoid, as much as possible, the development of a counter-transference reaction in which his own guilt feelings and need to be the indulgent all-giving parent allows the group to continue endlessly caught up in a cozy nesting type of resistance. The group should—if possible—have a finite period to perform its therapeutic work (perhaps one year), and should be terminated in a firm and decisive fashion at the end of that period. If the group is an "open" one, then the individual members should be terminated after a similar period or reasonable facsimile and replaced by new members.

REFERENCES

Fried, E. (Fall 1971): The narcissistic cocoon. How it curbs and can be curbed. *Group Process*, 4, 1, 87–95.

Kissen, M.: The concept of identification: An evaluation of its current status and significance for group psychotherapy. *Group Process*. In Preparation.

Ormont, L. (April 1968): Group resistance and the therapeutic contract. *International Journal of Group Psychotherapy*, 18, 147–154.

Yalom, I. (1970): *The Theory and Practice of Group Psychotherapy*. Basic Books, Inc., New York.

23

Group Dynamics of Acting Out in Analytic Group Psychotherapy

Isidore Ziferstein, M.D.
and
Martin Grotjahn, M.D.
Los Angeles, California

[The authors explicate the unique group dynamic aspects of the phenomenon of acting out as it occurs repetitively and pervasively during group psychotherapy meetings. They stress the therapeutic usefulness of a firm leadership style that relies heavily on psychodynamic understanding derived from solidly psychoanalytic inference process and interpretive methodology. They also describe a synthesis of "individual-within-the-group" methodology, within the broader framework of a rather sophisticated therapeutic awareness of group dynamic phenomena. They thus see clinical-case-study understanding of the latent psychodynamics underlying a given group member's acting-out behavior as being enriched by an appreciation of the fact that such behavior is enmeshed within a group-as-a-whole contextual matrix.]

The psychodynamics of acting out in analytic group psychotherapy are essentially the same as in individual psychotherapy. However, the group setting contributes several special characteristics:

From "Group Dynamics of Acting Out in Analytic Group Psychotherapy" by I. Ziferstein and M. Grotjahn, *International Journal of Group Psychotherapy*, 1957, 7, 77–85. Copyright 1957 by the International Journal of Group Psychotherapy. Reprinted by permission.

317

1. Group psychotherapy stimulates and invites acting out. Acting out in the group setting may frequently be a consequence of unconscious cues given by the "senior" or leading members of the group to the acting-out member.

2. Acting out may make group psychotherapy more active, more effective, but also more dangerous. The entire group may become involved in the acting out, so that the therapeutic function of the group is endangered. On the other hand, various group members can, if the situation is handled correctly by the therapist, play a crucial role in helping the acting-out patient achieve insight, and in the course of doing this gain insight into their own problems. In this way, the end result of the acting out, properly understood, interpreted, and worked through, is therapeutic progress for the entire group.

3. Acting out is used by patients as a resistance, as a substitute for remembering. However, acting out may also be a form of test-acting which, properly understood and interpreted, may lead to recollection and final integration.

These points will be demonstrated in the following clinical example.

Julia came as the newest addition to a well-established group. This reproduced in her the feelings she had had as the youngest child in a large family. She tried to gain recognition, as she had always done, through her superior intellect and ability to verbalize, of which she had always been proud. This attempt failed. The group quickly picked up her tendency to avoid emotional experiences by intellectualization, pointed it out to her, and interpreted her behavior. After a few months of fruitless effort to gain the spotlight, she broke out into a rash of acting out: she engaged in a series of promiscuous sexual affairs with older men. This was diametrically opposite to her previous pattern of behavior.

It appeared on the surface that the immediate cause of the acting out was that the patient despaired of ever establishing her position in the group by her accustomed technique of intellectual domination. She therefore began to engage in new, and to her, untried efforts to gain status. As will be seen later, her acting out was determined by much more fundamental, unconscious, deeply repressed oedipal and oral wishes, which were, however, not unrelated to her need for status and recognition. The patient's acting out became a serious resistance, not only to her therapy but also to the therapeutic progress of the group. Much of the group's time was taken up with her alternating triumphant and tearful recitals of her conquests and disappointments.

Julia received her cues for this behavior from other members of the group, who played an important part in stimulating her acting out and in encouraging her to continue it. There was the example of Rose, an older patient with psychopathic character traits, an acting-out character, who dominated the group with her intelligence and imaginativeness. To Julia, Rose now appeared to be the idealized, permissive mother figure—a person to be emulated, and whose approval and appreciation she sought. Julia was also subtly prodded by Barbara, the youngest patient in the group, who verbalized numerous fantasies of promiscuous sexual behavior, and always complained that she was too timid to do anything about them, while expressing admiration for Rose's "courage" and sexual "freedom." The precipitating cause, in retrospect, appeared to be a revelation by Hilda, who was about the same age as Julia, that she, Hilda, had some years back had intercourse with her older brother while they were visiting at their parents' home. This "confession" had a marked impact on the entire group, but was particularly disturbing (and stimulating) to Julia.

The immediate gain to Julia from her acting out was that, from being the rejected youngest daughter, she now became a focus of attention and of controversy. She now basked in the applause of Rose and Barbara, who hailed her "progress" in therapy, her breaking out of her intellectual defenses, her daring to "feel deeply and experience greatly." It was gratifying to Julia to get the approval of Rose, the permissive mother, and to have Barbara look up to her as an older sister, to be admired and emulated. On the other hand, Julia was viciously attacked by Mollie, a prudish, depressive older patient. Julia correctly interpreted Mollie's anxiety, her fear and guilt about her own repressed sexual feelings, which she then projected in the form of hostility against Julia. This insight helped to gain for Julia added prestige, particularly in the eyes of Rose and Barbara.

Another patient, Beulah, found herself quite disturbed by Julia's acting out, and attacked her bitterly. To her Julia's behavior recalled an earlier period in her own life, when she had had a series of sexual relationships with her employers. The men were strong and intelligent, and she admired and loved them. But all these relationships ended in rejection, grief and disaster. Beulah kept up a steady attack on Julia's behavior and kept warning her of dire consequences.

Throughout this period the therapist tried to focus attention on two characteristics of Julia's behavior. First, that the relationships were invariably with older men to whom she looked up and whom she admired. And secondly, that in spite of her show of bravado, these experiences were accompanied by severe guilt and little gratification. These observations by the therapist, which were reiterated and specifically pointed out as each new experience developed, were particularly disturbing to Beulah. They vividly recalled to her her own earlier sexual experiences with her employers. The oedipal nature of these relationships now became clear to Beulah. She could see now why she had reacted so violently to Julia's acting out, and why she had attacked her so bitterly. All of her own oedipal guilt had been expressed in her condemnation of Julia.

Julia now had an opportunity to see herself and her oedipal conflicts in Beulah as though in a mirror. She began to give up talking about her affairs, and instead began to verbalize sexual fantasies about the therapist. In this she was imitating the example of her admirer, Barbara, the youngest patient in the group, who had for some time been expressing similar fantasies without being censured even by the prudish Mollie.

This transition from acting out outside the group to verbalization within the group was facilitated by the therapist's consistent demonstration of her lack of satisfaction and her guilt in her promiscuous affairs. She finally responded to this demonstration with the following formula:

"I wouldn't need all these men if I could have you [the therapist]."

"You would be a satisfying lover, where these men are not."

"You would be all my lovers rolled into one."

"I would feel no guilt, because you're my therapist, and you would be giving me permission, as well as doing it for therapeutic purposes."

This formula was interpreted to the patient as a fantasy that the therapist was the omnipotent, all-giving, and permissive parent. Other patients produced material from their own dreams, fantasies, and memories, which reinforced this interpretation.

Finally, Julia began to produce associations concerning her father and an older brother. This brother visited her occasionally. He was a colorful person, a wanderer with whom she had stimulating discussions when he visited. He was much more exciting and stimulating to talk to than was her inarticulate husband. The next time this brother visited her, and stayed overnight, she became aware for the first time of strong sexual feelings about him. She spent a restless night, having vivid fantasies in which she re-enacted the scene of Hilda's seduction by her brother. Julia then realized that the intellectual stimulation she had experienced on her brother's previous visits had a strong sexual component. She recalled that, though her behavior throughout her marriage had been "correct and proper," she had engaged in many platonic friendships with "fascinating" intellectual men, culminating in a long friendship with a brother-in-law who was a university professor. The patient's husband finally stepped in and broke up this relationship because he suspected it was sexual. She now saw more clearly than ever that she had for many years intellectualized all her emotions, and that her sexual acting out during the therapy was a variation of her previous "intellectual" acting out.

With this insight came a flood of memories from early childhood: she recalled her seductive behavior as the "cute" youngest child toward her father, her brothers, and her grandfather. She had used her seductive behavior as a means of winning out over her older sisters, just as she was now attempting to use sexual seduction to triumph over her group "sisters" and win the therapist for herself. She had repressed all memory of this behavior as well as her guilt-laden incestuous wishes of that period. The repression was maintained with the aid of her character defense of intellectualization. However, this very defense was then employed to give expression to the repressed impulses. The patient now saw clearly that her verbalization, of which she had been so proud, was not used essentially for communication but as a concealed form of erotic interplay.

When the disapproval of the group deprived her of this tool, she employed a new tool: a plunge into promiscuous sexual activity. This was a less disguised derivative of her original incestuous wishes, and represented an acting out of her early seductive-youngest-daughter pattern. Interpretation of this acting-out resistance enabled the patient to recover and verbalize her early incestuous memories. The acting out was not only an expression of oedipal longings.

The sexual acting out served also and most importantly to rationalize and cover up, as well as give expression to, deeply repressed, oral-dependent longings for the preoedipal mother.

Julia was helped to gain emotional insight into this by identifying with one of the patients, Barbara. She had been particularly stirred and disturbed by Barbara's expressing fantasies of performing fellatio on the therapist. When she herself began to have fantasies about the therapist, the fellatio fantasy became quite prominent and deeply distressing. Here again, an interpretation of Barbara's fellatio fantasy helped show Julia the way to insight. Barbara, the "baby" of the group, had fantasies of nursing at the penis-breast of the therapist-mother. Julia had denied this vehemently. She had used her sexual acting out to demonstrate that she was not a baby, that she was a grown woman; that she did not have the deeply regressive longing for the love of the preoedipal mother but that she only wanted sex; that she wanted the father.

As Julia gained insight into her deeply repressed, oral-dependent longings, she began to realize that these longings were the basic cause of her acting out and found their expression in it. She realized, then, that she had related to the older men with whom she acted out as a hungry, dependent baby to a mother.

Before she came to group therapy, and in the first phase of therapy, her oral erotism found its expression in the relatively innocent and harmless pleasure in verbalization, which she also used as a tool for dominating her husband and her associates. Under the impact of the stimulation by other group members, her oral longings became intensified and threatened to break through into consciousness.

At this point, the patient escaped from the dangers of remembering into the pleasures of acting out, from the deeply repressed oral longings to the less deeply repressed and less objectionable oedipal wishes. *As long as this deep oral longing is not understood, interpreted, worked through, and integrated, it will lead to acting out.* It would appear, then, that not only in the case of acting-out characters, but also in the case of acting out in the course of therapy, *the basic cause of acting out is the patient's repressed orality,* and that acting out is essentially a defensive maneuver against orality.

Perhaps one reason for misunderstanding the role of acting out in group psychotherapy is the fact that the term is sometimes used loosely. Acting out is a form of activity whereby a patient unconsciously discharges repressed, warded-off impulses and relieves inner tension. Instead of remembering certain traumatic and therefore repressed experiences, the patient relives them. However, the patient is unaware of this fact, and to him his actions seem appropriate to the present situation. To him his actions appear ego-syntonic. We have here one of those rare situations in which id tendencies may find a direct motor outlet via ego activity. Acting out is constructed like sleepwalking: it is a dramatization of the unconscious.

There are people in whom the tendency to act out is prominent throughout life. These are the "acting-out" characters, who are frequently found to be oral individuals, with a low tolerance for frustration or postponement of gratification, and with defects in superego and ego formation.

In group psychotherapy we are concerned primarily not with the acting-out character, but with the problems presented by acting out which occur in the course of therapy. Many patients who are essentially not acting-out characters will act out at some time during the course of therapy. The group-therapeutic process itself stimulates acting out. The therapeutic process mobilizes repressed impulses at the same time that it loosens the patient's defenses. As a result, the patient is subjected to stronger pressures from impulses striving for discharge; and one form of discharge is acting out. This occurs when the patient experiences within the group a reactivation of repressed traumatic experiences, but does not wish to remember them. We can now see how group psychotherapy *invites* acting out, either within the framework of the group session or outside. Because so much of life consists of activity, our patients have to go through a period in which they change and wish to express the changes in their actions. On the other hand, in analytic group psychotherapy we do want to give them insight, and acting out is a form of resistance against insight into the unconscious. To keep acting out between therapeutic benefit and analytic resistance is a major technical problem in group psychotherapy. In the experience of many therapists, this becomes the central issue in the technique of group control.

The group-psychotherapeutic situation invites acting out to a much greater intensity than is the case in the setting of individual psychotherapy. But, since we want our patients to use their insight into their unconscious for proper conscious motivations of their actions, we cannot allow them to act on unconscious, uncontrolled, and therefore potentially dangerous motivations. This is the reason why we have to control acting out during analytic group psychotherapy. Acting out is only a temporary, and not a satisfactory, solution. The analytic handling of acting out, as of any resistance, is prompt interpretation. With the help of interpretation, "acting out" is changed to "working through."

Acting out may involve the patient in realistic troubles, sometimes of a serious nature. This may complicate the treatment if the therapist reacts with anxiety and tries to restrain the patient, by exercising his authority rather than by understanding and interpreting. The patient may then take advantage of the therapist's anxiety and punish him by further acting out, or he may react as to a forbidding parent with castration fear, or submissive compliance. The result may be a chaotic situation, aggravated in part by the countertransference of the therapist and the other group members. Most important: the therapist and the group may vicariously enjoy the patient's acting out and unconsciously encourage him, perhaps rationalizing it with the idea that it's good for the patient to develop the courage to gratify his impulses, test reality, learn in the school of life, etc., etc. In this situation the therapist and the group members are behaving like the parents of delinquent children who unwittingly encourage their children to act out the parents' own repressed impulses.[1]

This happens more readily in the situation of group psychotherapy than in individual psychotherapy. An encouraging remark by the therapist or any group member, even the question: "Why not?" asked of an inhibited member of the group may be unconsciously interpreted by another group member as an invitation or a command. The latter may then act out in order to gain status in the group or to set a shining example. This temptation is greater and more difficult to avoid in group psychotherapy than in the cautious setting and procedure of individual therapy. The patient often feels that he is under pressure from the therapist and the group to accept and express his unconscious trends before he can properly integrate them into his ego. This pressure then forms the basis for acting out.

It becomes clear now why acting out is partly responsible for the intense therapeutic impact of group psychotherapy and also for its dangers. The acting-out patient may discover that he becomes a center of attention and interest in the group. All the other patients are busy either condemning or defending him, being threatened by his behavior or being titillated by it. This secondary gain can be a factor in the patient's continuing his acting out. In individual therapy, on the other hand, the need to capture the spotlight is less, since the patient has the therapist to himself, at least during the therapeutic session, although the patient is, of course, still competing with the therapist's other patients, the therapist's friends and family.

Most actions of patients will contain elements both of healthy, realistic activity and of neurotic acting out. The healthy part is characterized by reality testing, emotional experiencing, and gratification of id strivings without conflict.

A clinical example will illustrate this complex situation. The patient had for a long time accepted, without conscious resentment, underpayment and humiliation on a job which was far below his real capacities. In the course of

---

[1] Johnson, A. M. and Szurek, S. A.: The Genesis of Antisocial Acting Out in Children and Adults. *Psa. Quart.*, *21*:323–343, 1952.

psychotherapy, he developed a mounting resentment of this situation. After one particular humiliation, he came to the therapeutic hour determined to quit his job forthwith. This was in many ways a healthy reaction. But it was also an acting-out resistance. He was dramatizing his identification with his father, who had always quit when the going got rough; who had deserted his domineering wife and his son, the patient; and who finally dramatically quit all of his problems by committing suicide. The patient had often been told by his mother: "You're just like your father. You have your father's temper."

His sudden decision to quit his job meant that instead of gaining insight into his unconscious identification with his father, he was dramatizing and playing the role of his father in real life. There were good reasons for the patient's need to repress all memory of wanting to be like his father, of wanting to act and live like him. To be his father meant not only to live like him but also to die like him, to die prematurely—a suicide.

This insight he tried at all costs to avoid. And he tried to block the road to remembering and to insight by acting out the identification instead: by living and behaving like his father. Without the conscious remembering and the insight, he would have been unconsciously fearful all of his life of having assumed an identity that was not his own. This might have led to disaster and possibly to eventual suicide. Interpretation of this identification, and his manner of acting it out, was instrumental in helping the patient hold on to his job, while taking positive steps to improve his status and obtain a salary increase. In the ensuing months, there was ample opportunity to work through this crucial identification. He eventually left this job when a better position became available. However, quitting when he originally intended to would have been another repetition of his pattern of self-defeat, another acting out of his identification with his defeated father; instead of an opportunity to work through and overcome this repetitive pattern.

This behavior illustrates both the healthy aspect of action, based on the wish to become strong and active, and the unhealthy aspect of dramatization whose aim was to avoid seeing the dangers of his father identification. The final analytic integration combines the healthy part of reality testing with the insight that his early identification with his father was only a beginning; that in the last analysis the patient had to form his own identity, which did not include the father's running away from problems and ultimate suicide.

As is always the case in psychotherapy, the acting out involved a major transference element: quitting his job was a displacement of his desire to quit therapy. Indeed, by quitting his job he would have been able to rationalize quitting therapy for financial reasons.

SUMMARY

1. The analytic-therapeutic process may stimulate acting out by mobilizing repressed impulses and loosening defenses.

2. Acting out is more common in group psychotherapy because the tendency to act out is stimulated by the unconscious impulses and anxieties of the other patients.
3. Acting out is, in and of itself, therapeutically useful only as a transition to understanding. Essentially it is a resistance, and should be handled as such.
4. Consistent interpretation of the acting-out resistance results in the recovery of therapeutically useful memories and associations and the development of insight. It also puts a stop to the acting out.
5. A clinical example is presented, which illustrates the above points. It demonstrates how a patient in group psychotherapy was pushed into acting out by her competitive drive for status in the group combined with stimulation of her repressed oedipal and oral wishes by the unconscious impulses and anxieties of the other group members. In order to help this patient, it was necessary to understand, interpret, work through and integrate not only her oedipal longings for the father but also her deeply regressive oral longing for the preoedipal mother.

VII

CONCLUSION
AND
INTEGRATION

24

From Group Dynamics to Group Psychoanalysis: Therapeutic Applications of Group Dynamic Understanding

Morton Kissen
Institute of Advanced Psychological Studies
Adelphi University
Garden City, New York

[The study of group dynamics as conceptually elaborated on in chaps. 1–3 and more concretely and descriptively delineated in chaps. 4–7 has a great deal of relevance for a group psychoanalytic model of psychotherapy (chaps. 17 and 18). This chapter summarizes the material covered and offers a conceptual integration of the issues raised in the group dynamic and group psychoanalytic literature surveyed in this volume.]

Traditionally, studies of group dynamics have been conducted by sociologists and social psychologists within a largely empirical and nontherapeutic frame of reference. Although a number of research-oriented laboratory approaches to group dynamic study have a quasitherapeutic intent, most of the social scientists leading these groups have sharply differentiated between the training, sensitivity, and empirical goals of such groups and their therapeutic aspects. Thus, Durkin (1964) notes, "In spite of the general impression to the contrary, there was almost no therapy actually being conducted on solely group dynamics principles by group dynamicists" (p. 4).

A truly group dynamic psychotherapy, according to Durkin, can be discerned only in the works of Ezriel (1950, 1951, 1959), Foulkes (1946, 1952, 1964), and Foulkes and Lewis (1944), British psychoanalysts who combined group dynamic principles within the framework of a solidly psychoanalytic therapeutic process. The group forces, Durkin further emphasizes, are viewed by these British group psychoanalysts as the primary source of group therapy. Thus, for Ezriel the primary therapeutic process can be facilitated via a largely contemporaneous analysis of the "common group tension" whereas for Foulkes such therapeutic results are derived from a sensitive and skillful attention by the group conductor to the "group specific factors."

A number of t-group approaches, particularly those included in this volume (chaps. 4–7), seem to fall within the vague middle ground between a clearly nontherapeutic, social psychological, and almost totally empirical approach to group dynamic study and the more directly therapeutic model of the British group psychoanalysts. The primary reason for the vagueness and lack of a clearcut differentiation here may stem from the fact that these particular laboratory groups were conducted by highly experienced clinicians whose basic theoretical orientations tend to approximate quite closely that of the British group analysts. The vague, but necessary, boundary line that must be maintained between an empirical, didactic, and largely "cognitive" t-group experience and a realistic, affect-laden, and approximately group psychoanalytic experience is fairly well captured in the occasional hairsplitting Horwitz resorts to in his treatise on the transferential differences between t-groups and therapy groups (chap. 6). The need to structure and control the degree of regression while nevertheless offering an emotionally realistic group experience is certainly a major dilemma confronting all serious psychoanalytically oriented group trainers.

The American Group Psychotherapy Association during the course of its annual institute and conference has often been confronted with a similar dilemma. The institute and a number of the subsequent small group workshops allow for the creation of highly time-limited (two days for the institute workshops and one day or a half-day for the conference workshops) laboratory groups in which the focus is alternatingly experiential–therapeutic and cognitive–didactic. The complex environmental press established by the interchange between the group leader's style and the therapeutic versus didactic needs and wishes of the members of a given group somehow leads to a differential and highly group-specific therapy/didactic ratio for each laboratory group. Given that the members of these short-term laboratory groups (whose purposes are at least outwardly educational rather than therapeutic) are almost all highly trained group therapists who possess a rather sophisticated awareness of group dynamic, individual psychodynamic, and interpersonal processes, it is not at all surprising that they often, in a very brief time, attain a level of intrapsychic, interpersonal, and group dynamic exploration that is almost never reached by more traditional psychotherapy groups composed of less sophisticated members.

Martin and Hill (chap. 11) describe this ideal and final phase of group development attained by only the most sophisticated groups as the stage in which the group itself can be utilized as an ". . . integrative–creative social instrument." The almost effortless and creatively fluid forms of interaction that occur in such groups are awe inspiring for both the group leader and the highly trained professional members. In such groups the leader is shifted increasingly into the role of educational consultant or resource person rather than transferentially distorted parental authority figure.

The symbolic father figure image represented by the leader is delivered a crushing blow during the very early developmental stages of these groups. The typical "primal horde rebellion" (chap. 14) occurs in a mercurial and almost effortless fashion and allows for the subsequent development, both in the group as a whole and intrapsychically within the individual members, of a heightened state of individuation and autonomous psychological functioning. Hence, the potential exists for an extended and highly concentrated period of productive and insight-producing group interaction. The short circuiting of the typical phases of group development taking place in these groups has been corroborated and replicated on numerous occasions by both the leaders and peer group members.

Thus, the fact that all groups go through a finite series of "developmental phases" (chaps. 8-11) must be viewed within the context of certain ego psychological variables such as ego strength, psychological mindedness, and capacity for autonomous ego functioning and for "regression in service of the ego," all of which are empirically observable aspects of the psychic functioning of the members of a given group. The "vertical" (intrapsychic) dimension is as important as the more commonly discussed "horizontal" (interpersonal) dimension in influencing the timing of the qualitative developmental shifts that take place during a particular group interaction experience.

In a certain sense, it is this very "ego psychological" dimension that is neglected in Bion's extremely influential and essentially Kleinian conceptualizations of the group process (chap. 8). The notion that all groups universally shift back and forth among various regressive basic assumptions (fight–flight, dependency, and pairing) does not fully take into account the factor of composite ego strength inherent in the membership of a given group and its impact on the group's ability to approximate rather quickly a relatively pure "work group" atmosphere.

In general, the group dynamic and group psychological literature has been rather heavily influenced by both Kleinian (Klein, 1946, 1948) and traditional Freudian (chaps. 12-16) conceptions with regard to the nature of group processes. The merging of these two theoretical orientations has contributed to a greater emphasis on the id as opposed to the ego psychological aspects of group behavior and functioning. The more modern conceptions of ego psychology have been generally overlooked in this area of study. The selection of Freudian concepts does, however, include a number of notions quite germane to ego psychology. Notions such as the pleasure and reality principles (chap. 12) and regression (chap. 15) clearly relate to the Freudian structural model subsequently elaborated by Hartmann (1950, 1961) and Rappaport (1951, 1958, 1959). The studies of the almost universal phenomenon of the primal horde rebellion against the leader (chaps. 13 and 14) also have substantial ego psychological significance, particularly when viewed in light of the conceptual framework developed in chap. 14.

Although the Freudian concept of identification (chap. 16) is very complex, with a number of both id and ego psychological ramifications, it is one of the central concepts in contemporary ego psychology. It has a number of synthetic and integrative possibilities that may one day allow for a conceptual clarification of some of the complex relationships between individual and group psychology. The therapeutic process in both individual and group psychoanalysis is facilitated by a shifting pattern of a patient–therapist identificatory interaction. What is initially a highly distorted and transferential form of identification relationship (projective identification) shifts toward a form of identification more consensually validatable, competence building, and social-learning enhancing. Identification can thus be viewed as an essential ego-formative process implicit in both individual and group psychotherapeutic transactions. It can be assumed to be a core aspect of the therapeutic "matrix" itself, an observable phenomenon in individual and group psychotherapy relationships as well as in a variety of seemingly nontherapeutic t-group interactions.

In a certain sense, the concept of identification involves an important dimension—perhaps as important as the concept of transference—that cuts across the intrapsychic, interpersonal, and group-as-a-whole spheres of psychological functioning. In its healthier and more ego autonomous forms, it occurs in the group process transactions of psychologically sophisticated normal individuals. It can also be observed in its more pathological forms in the projective-identificatory interactions of therapeutic groups consisting of neurotic or severely characterologically impaired individuals. This is not to say that healthy and more primitive types of identification do not occur both in therapy groups for disturbed individuals and in t-groups for highly sophisticated normals.

Thus the process of identification can be seen as one of the two basic ingredients of any therapeutic interaction. The exploration, analysis, and realistic correction of the more primitive forms of identification and the ego-building social-learning internalizations derivable from the more developmentally sophisticated forms of identification together form one of the major dimensions of the psychotherapy process. The second basic therapeutic ingredient is contained in the analysis and exploration of transference distortions that occur during the course of the psychotherapy relationship.

Some form of transferential therapeutic process can be assumed to occur in both t-groups and psychotherapy groups. A primary difference, however, is that in t-groups the leader's response to such transferential distortions is typically directed at group-as-a-whole (group dynamic) forms of interpretation whereas in therapy groups there is often an alternating pattern of both individual and group dynamic forms of intervention. The leader's interpretation of indiviudal psychodynamics, defensive maneuvers, or transference tendencies encourages a certain amount of passivity in the group members, which can temporarily retard group development, at least from an ego autonomy viewpoint. Such a regressive relationship, however, may be necessary to firm up a given group for a subsequently more autonomous form of therapeutic exploration.

The group psychoanalytic approach offers a far more sophisticated treatment model than does the more traditional individual-within-the-group approach (Wolf, 1949, 1950; Wolf & Schwartz, 1960), allowing for both regression-increasing intrapsychic forms of interpretations and autonomy-enhancing group dynamic interventions. The group psychoanalytic model is the only group treatment approach that allows an exploration of the special group dynamic patterns implicit in the very fabric of therapy groups (chaps. 19–23). Patterns such as group resistances, the experience of the group as mother, group "nesting" phenomena, and group-facilitated acting-out behavior all can be clearly observed in group psychoanalysis. The group-specific nature of such patterns, which are embedded within the very matrix of a given group's interactive process, are necessarily neglected in purely individual-within-the-group forms of group treatment.

Before a description is given of some very advantageous therapeutic possibilities inherent in a group dynamic approach to group treatment, a brief summary of two central controversies in the history of group psychotherapy will highlight some of the complexities inherent in a psychological analysis of group phenomena. The controversies under consideration are: field-theoretical (contemporaneous) versus genetic-historical approaches to the analysis of group process, and individual-within-the-group versus group-as-a-whole methods of group treatment.

THE FIELD-THEORETICAL VERSUS GENETIC-HISTORICAL CONTROVERSY

Although the genetic-historical model is only one of five basic psychoanalytic paradigms, according to Rappaport (1959), it has become the center of a significant controversy with regard to the proper mode of systematic study of group psychological phenomena. The other four theoretical models listed by Rappaport (structural, economic, dynamic, and adaptive) are all related to group psychology in varying degrees but have seldom been implicated in similarly controversial systematic discussions and debate.

Economic and adaptive models seem to have only tenuous connections to central issues of group metapsychology, while structural and dynamic models appear particularly relevant to the study of group phenomena. The structural model especially relates to the group field in that Bion, one of the most creative and influential group dynamic theorists, has tended to focus too much on id-related group processes and almost not at all on ego psychological factors. Compensating for this imbalance via extensive systematic and group psychological communication and theoretical debate would certainly be helpful. The dynamic model is also very basic to the group field in that it relates to the controversy, to be described, between the group dynamic (group-as-a-whole) and individual dynamic (individual-within-the-group) theoretical positions.

At any rate, the conflict around the genetic model has centered on its therapeutic potency when compared to a more contemporaneous "here-and-now" approach to group treatment. This issue has tended to be expressed in the form of a systematic debate between group dynamicists, largely influenced by Kurt Lewin's field theoretical orientation, and psychoanalytic group therapists, more heavily influenced by the theories of Sigmund Freud. Anthony (1975) alluded to this controversy in his review of the changes that have taken place in the field of group psychotherapy since 1951:

> It is always of interest when problems persist over decades of time. Even in 1951 it seemed that the central issue in group therapy concerned whether the therapeutic forcus should be on the individual or on the group, on the Freudian "there and then" or on the Lewinian "here and now." The "there and then" related to the individual since it belonged to past situations that were not sharable with the group; the "here and now" laid emphasis on the fact that the group was an ahistoric organism and that the common denominator for the membership was the interpersonal dynamics. (p. 165)

The division in the group movement between the analytic and group dynamic theorists has, at least to some degree, proved artificial. Peck (1975), in a review of the history of the group psychotherapy movement similar to Anthony's, notes:

> Few contemporary group therapists are prepared to exclude historical material from their sessions, but there is also a growing awareness of the unique opportunity afforded by the group to assist both the patient and the group to change their "here and now" as a means of altering the future. When a patient changes his characteristic mode of behavior in the group, it almost inevitably alters the group's shape and direction. When the group changes, it may in turn alter its impact on the patient and his fellow group members as well as on other groups with which he is engaged. (p. 156)

The modern psychoanalytic concept of the importance of the "here and now" and between the peer group members in group psychotherapy can be directly applied to this area of controversy and may well offer some possibilities for a synthesis of the two seemingly disparate theoretical positions.

It can thus be argued that although all therapeutic changes occur in the "here and now," a comprehensive understanding of the "there and then" factors existing in the individual members of a given group will further facilitate the movement toward ameliorative psychic changes. This may be one of the reasons for the inclusion by Ormont (a very modern group psychoanalyst) of a genetic-historical expectation in the "group contract" that he establishes with the members of his groups. He sets up such a contract expectation by requiring the group members to detail the stories of their lives at some point during the course of their group psychoanalytic experience (Ormont, 1964).

At any rate, it is fairly obvious that the seeming discrepancies between the "horizontal" (here and now, interpersonal) and "vertical" (there and then, genetic) forms of group interventions need not be of an either-or nature. It is quite possible (and perhaps even necessary) to meld these two forms of group intervention into a highly efficient and effective approach to group leadership and treatment.

Individual-within-the-Group versus Group-as-a-Whole Approaches to Group Treatment

One of the longest running and most intractable controversies in the history of group psychotherapy has been between group therapists who espouse a direct transposition of dyadic psychoanalytic techniques to the group situation (Wolf, 1949, 1950; Wolf & Schwartz, 1960) and those who believe that such a direct translation of principles and techniques from the classical dyadic situation to the group treatment situation is inadequate, due to the consequent neglect of the so-called group-specific factors (Foulkes, 1964). The theory supporting consideration of group-specific factors has been labeled "group dynamic psychotherapy" (Durkin, 1964) because it places a rather heavy emphasis on the potentially therapeutic nature of group dynamic factors.

Thus, whereas the individual-within-the-group approach focuses almost solely on the vertical dimension (genetic reconstructions and interpretations of intrapsychic dynamic patterns), the group-as-a-whole approach focuses the greatest amount of therapeutic time on the horizontal dimension (interpretation of broad interactive patterns existing within the overall matrix of a given group). The individual-within-the group theorists see group dynamic patterns as a distraction that often interferes with the more essential group therapeutic process of intrapsychic work, whereas the more group dynamically oriented theorists see the study of group-specific interactive patterns as the therapeutic heart of the matter.

Indeed, the most extreme group-as-a-whole theorists believe attention by the group leader to the vertical dimension via intrapsychic interpretive interventions may be completely unnecessary due to some form of dilution of therapeutic potential inherent in the very fabric of the group matrix. Borriello (1975) speaks of the possibility of directly applying to psychotherapy groups Bion's Tavistock approach, heretofore almost totally restricted to use as a training tool for sensitizing professional group therapists to group dynamics. Since the Tavistock model restricts interventions by the group consultant or leader to a very sparse number of group-as-a-whole interpretations, it is surprising to come across a recommendation for the use of such a paradigm in psychotherapeutic situations. An interesting example of the effective use of such an interpretive model in a nontherapeutic setting is provided by Bennis (chap. 7) who describes a group session in which the leader restricted himself to six brief group-as-a-whole interventions.

One way of phrasing the difference between these two group therapeutic positions is to note that in one position the leader devotes full attention to the individual members, allowing the group to take care of itself (individual-within-the-group), whereas in the other the leader concentrates on the group, allowing the individual members to take care of themselves (group-as-a-whole). The latter approach places a greater demand for ego autonomy on the individual members, and hence may not be suitable for relatively un-sophisticated groups whose members have only minimal ego strengths. Such an approach, however, may be an effective means of enhancing the ego autonomy capacities of group members and may well offer the purest example of a truly group psychoanalytic treatment methodology.

It is interesting, in this regard, to note how seldom such a methodology has been systematically utilized. Borriello (1975) states:

> The use of Bion's technique as a method of group psychotherapy is widespread among Kleinian analysts and those trained at Tavistock. In the U.S.A., this reviewer is aware of only two group psychotherapy training centers that teach and practice this group psychotherapy technique: Saint Elizabeths Hospital in Washington, D.C. and the Menninger Foundation in Topeka, Kansas. (p. 356)

The group psychoanalytic model that is most frequently used is that of Foulkes and Ezriel, the British analysts, in that it allows for more flexible interspersing of both individual-within-the-group and group-as-a-whole interventions.

Above and beyond the British group psychoanalytic model, which involves a random alternation of the two forms of intervention by one leader, it is also possible to imagine a coleadership model in which one leader systematically and consistently offers intrapsychic interpretations while the other leader equally systematically offers group dynamic interventions. The possibility for systematic shifts back and forth between the two basic paradigmatic approaches by coleaders can also be imagined. Thus, the leader who initially has adopted an individual-within-the-group approach can, after an extended period, shift to group-as-a-whole methodology while the other leader makes a systematic shift in the opposite direction. The impact of such complex but systematic coleadership arrangements on the group dynamics, transference manifestations, and therapeutic changes within a given group would, of course, need to be descriptively and empirically studied and thoroughly reported in the literature.

The individual-within-the-group approach, in its most extreme form, involves an assumption that group dynamics are essentially resistances and hence interfere with the basic therapeutic task, a thorough intrapsychic exploration of the dynamics and transference distortion tendencies of the individual group members. Leaders, according to such a model, need not have training in either group dynamics or specialized principles and methods of group psychoanalysis. They also need not necessarily have undergone a personal group psychoanalytic experience. This contrasts rather markedly with Foulkes' (1964) recommendations that the ideal group analyst undergo both specialized group psychoanalytic training and personal group psychoanalysis prior to independently assuming leadership of therapeutic groups.

The concept of "group resistance," creatively elaborated on by Ormont (chap. 20), most certainly differs in important respects from the concepts of group dynamics as resistances espoused by the most extreme form of the individual-within-the-group position. Ormont's formulation, developed in a number of articles (1964, 1969, 1974), places the concept of group resistance squarely within the group dynamic frame of reference and emphasizes that such resistances are not necessarily interferences with the therapeutic task at hand but rather are centrally related to that task. Thus, the group leader, according to Ormont, must often concentrate on the complex interactive processes of the group as a whole in order to discern these group resistances. The leader need not, however, interpret them in the group dynamic mode, but can instead work with a given group member who seems to most strongly represent the thematic preoccupation of the total group. Thus, an individual-within-the-group stylistic approach to leadership can be integrated within the framework of an essentially group psychoanalytic model.

Ormont's mode of handling group resistances is in many ways consonant with the concept of the "Figure-Ground" nature of group interactive process. Thus, a given individual's behavior as well as that of a subgroup may be representative of a far broader group-as-a-whole interactional tendency. The individual's behavior can therefore be considered the particular from which a dynamic pattern existing within the total group can be deduced. The concepts of "role suction" and projective identification are significantly related to this figure-ground phenomenon in groups. Individuals are assigned multiply shifting roles as well as stereotypical roles and often end up unconsciously expressing feelings and impulses that are valent within the overall matrix of a group at a given moment. For example, during the "fight–flight" phase the more aggressive members begin to act out common group feelings, and during the "pairing" stage the members who have noticeable symbiotic tendencies may come to the forefront.

Ormont, by focusing on the conflict or resistance being manifested by an individual group member, picks up on a common group tension. Since the other group members are empathically connected to the behavior of that member via the process of projective identification, they are also able to profit from the interpretive intervention the leader directs at the psychodynamics underlying the one member's behavior. The Ormont mode of handling group resistances falls midway along a continuum between individual-within-the-group and group-as-a-whole group psychotherapy. Despite the outwardly intrapsychic orientation of Ormont's style of leadership intervention, he appears to be involved in a largely group dynamic form of psychotherapy.

In summary, the basic issues in this controversy are highly complex and not always what they outwardly seem to be. Both individual-within-the-group and group-as-a-whole modes of leadership can focus on group dynamics, although it is possible to argue that the group-as-a-whole approach allows for a paradoxically greater degree of ego autonomy and individuality in the members of a given group. Most practicing group psychotherapists use a combination of these two approaches, with the primary emphasis on the individual within the group. It is safe to conclude that considerably more sensitivity to group dynamic processes on the part of therapists would contribute positively to therapeutic changes and maturational growth in the members of their groups.

DESIRABLE ASPECTS OF GROUP DYNAMIC PSYCHOTHERAPY

One important element in the desirability of a group-as-a-whole approach is the fact that the group dynamics elicited often represent partially camouflaged regressive fantasies and preoedipal experiences shared by all the group members. The Kleinian and Bion Tavistock concept of the group as part object or as representative of some form of malevolent or benign mother figure introject appear to have a certain degree of validity. Thus, the leader's group-as-a-whole interventions can contribute to releasing the members from preoedipal fixations and preverbal transferential distortions. Ormont (1974) recently argued that the group leader's use of "paradigmatic" forms of intervention (Nelson, 1962; Strean, 1964) can lead to freedom of affect and productive exploration of the largely preoedipal dynamics underlying a number of characteristic group resistances.

It may well be that the group-as-a-whole approach offers the closest approximation to a truly group psychoanalytic methodology and provides the best group method for treating psychologically sophisticated and highly motivated patients. Such a methodology assumes a certain degree of ego strength in the group members as well as the potential for an advanced state of ego autonomy and synthetic capacity.

Thus, a group dynamic therapeutic method provides an effective approach to the treatment of the most deeply repressed and preoedipally determined group resistances (perhaps more of a factor in patients manifesting severe character disorders or borderline states) and yet, at the same time, the most sophisticated method for treating highly motivated neurotic patients. The group-as-a-whole approach is certainly the most effective method in working with group laboratory workshops for professionals interested in enhancing their therapeutic skills and knowledge about group process. It allows for the occurrence of therapeutic experiences in the context of a group workshop whose outward format is largely of an educational nature, under circumstances of maximal ego autonomy and personal responsibility.

The authority, power, and influence of the leader—an ever-present factor in all groups—is somewhat diminished when the group-as-a-whole method is used. The leader whose role function is restricted to group dynamic interventions tends to talk less and to expose less of his own personality dynamics and expressive characterological functioning. His own needs are made secondary to the needs of the group. There is thus far less potential for narcissistic transference or countertransference distortions. The so-called charismatic leadership effect, often associated with encounter group casualties (Lieberman, Valom, & Miles, 1973), is much less likely to occur under these circumstances.

It can also be inferred that the "primal group rebellion" occurs earlier and with more force in such groups. The revolt against the leader and the ultimate minimization of the leader as an irrational power force within the group often allow for a cathartic expression of emotion and eventually for a more creative and peer-centered process of group interaction. Characteristic group therapeutic processes such as mirroring, feedback, and the working through of characterological difficulties and peer transference distortions often occur with great intensity and rapidity following the group rebellion. The degree of ego autonomy in the members will be considerably heightened.

When appropriately utilized, the use of a group dynamic leadership methodology can increase the depth of self-exploration by the members. The very "matrix" of the group itself becomes a central source of therapeutic understanding and gain for the members who became increasingly aware of their characteristic stances toward the group as a whole. Thus, some members tend to view the overall group as a nurturant mother, while others see it as a dangerous and malevolent mother. The leader, by "caring" for the group, enhances the capacities of individual members to autonomously confront difficult aspects of themselves.

Many therapists are reluctant to utilize a group-as-a-whole methodology because the impression of an uncaring attitude toward individual members can be created. That the leader cares, however, can be conveyed as well in group dynamic interventions as it can in intrapsychic comments and confrontations. In addition, under very special circumstances of individual need, the leader may flexibly shift to an intrapsychic working approach with a given member. The leader's attention can fluctuate between the group as a whole and the individual members, despite the primary focus being on the group.

As previously noted, the intrapsychic form of confrontation itself can be utilized as a group dynamic comment. Ormont (1964, 1969, 1974) has developed a methodology for therapeutic work with group resistances that demonstrates the potential for group dynamic use of individual-within-the-group interpretive interventions. This approach to group treatment reflects some of the desirable features of both group-as-a-whole and individual-within-the-group methodologies and can be considered a group dynamic form of psychotherapy.

Thus, in addition to some of the previously mentioned desirable aspects of group dynamic psychotherapy, one of its most important assets is the fact that it can be incorporated into a group psychoanalytic treatment approach that is flexibly adapted to the particular needs of individual members, the group as a whole, and the stylistic preferences of the psychoanalyst.

THE HIERARCHICAL ORDERING OF GROUP PSYCHOANALYTIC INTERVENTIONS: A GENERAL SYSTEMS THEORY FORMULATION

The concept of groups as open systems is not very modern or novel and can be traced to Kurt Lewin's (1935, 1936) field theoretical conceptions. Lewin introduced the notion that groups may be viewed as complex social psychological entities possessing certain distinctive "boundary" properties. One important feature of these group boundaries is the degree to which they are permeable or impermeable. Another is the degree of differentiation of the structural regions they enclose. Lewin's descriptive theoretical model has been translated into a more modern form and relabeled *general systems theory*.

A number of writers (Appelbaum, 1973; Durkin, 1974; Kernberg, 1975; Swogger, 1974) developed general systems formulations and attempted to apply them to the fields of group dynamics and group psychotherapy. A few more specifically attempted to relate general systems concepts to psycho-analysis (Appelbaum, 1973; Kernberg, 1975).

The very recent systems theoretical contribution of Kernberg, in particular, is extremely important and will probably have a significant influence on group psychotherapy for years to come. Given Kernberg's growing stature as psychoanalyst and expert on the so-called borderline states, his contribution must be given serious consideration and study. It particularly deserves such serious treatment because it attempts to present a model for conceptualizing the complex hierarchical nature of the treatment interventions open to the group psychoanalytic therapist.

Kernberg's essential point is that a serious and sophisticated group psychoanalyst must be completely aware of all the systemic factors concurrently influencing the group over the course of its life history. One must be aware of the potential simultaneous impact of a complex multitude of systemic influences such as the therapist's personality, the intrapsychic personality needs of the individual members, the group dynamic patterns implicit within the interactive fabric of the group as a whole, and the broader social psychological context and value system within which the particular group is enmeshed. Each of these specific systemic factors can be viewed along a hierarchical continuum whose discrete points can be labeled *subsystem, target system,* and *suprasystem.* The therapist's and the group members' individual personality systems can be structurally delineated as *id* (subsystem), *ego* (target system), and *superego* (suprasystem). Such basically intrapsychic systems can also be depicted in terms of their degrees of developmental differentiation and freedom from primitive preoedipal fixations.

The group as a whole, according to Kernberg, has a largely preoedipal connotative meaning. In this regard, he would appear to be strongly influenced by the theoretical group dynamic concepts of Bion. Group dynamic interventions are viewed by Kernberg as a response by the leader to the common preoedipal concerns of the group members, in contrast to the more intrapsychic and interpersonal forms of intervention that tend to clarify transferential distortions and hence have a more differentiated oedipal significance. The leader must be acutely aware of the impact of a particular style of intervention (i.e., intrapsychic, interpersonal, group dynamic, etc.) on the largely circular feedback and validation processes received in return from the group members.

The ideal group leader, according to Kernberg, utilizes a solid ego synthetic capacity and firm sense of ego identity both to select a particular constant (or even shifting) style of intervention and to tolerate the dissonance and conflict created by the complex variety of hierarchically structured intervention strategies available. The leader's ego strength should also be associated with a freedom from undue countertransference distortions such as the need to be a "charismatic" figure and to obtain narcissistic gratifications from interaction with the group members.

Since these various group intervention strategies are "nonconcentric," according to Kernberg, they cannot be reduced to a single hierarchical configuration. The leader is encouraged to direct his attention in a relatively flexible manner across each and every systemic area. The capacity for such a broad awareness and diversity of attentional shifts may be one of the more important "talents" of the effective group psychoanalyst.

Kernberg's general systems conceptualization does a great deal of justice to the enormity of the task confronting the group psychoanalyst. It is an interesting post-Lewinian systems theory approach to some of the complex "boundary" dilemmas observed on that broad interface connecting the intrapsychic, interpersonal, group dynamic, and group psychoanalytic fields of inquiry.

SUMMARY AND CONCLUSIONS

In summary, the collection of articles contained in this volume reflects some of the important developments in the history of psychoanalytic group psychotherapy. The shift from a primarily individual-within-the-group to a more group dynamic form of psychotherapy requires a rather sophisticated synthesis of group dynamics theory, t-group observational data, Freudian group psychology, the techniques of individual psychoanalysis, and more modern conceptions and techniques of group psychoanalysis.

The task confronting the serious group psychoanalyst is indeed mind boggling. One must attempt somehow to synthesize, through a variety of intervention strategies, many complex and partially overlapping data sources and therapeutic demands. One should not fall too easily into a stylistic interpretive format that neglects particular domains of therapeutic knowledge in favor of others. All levels of inquiry (i.e., intrapsychic, interpersonal, group dynamic, sociocultural, etc.) must somehow be incorporated into an overall intervention strategy during the course of the group psychoanalytic experience.

The future training of group psychoanalysts will have to involve an exposure to group dynamics and general systems theory principles above and beyond the more traditional training in psychoanalytic theory and techniques. In addition, some form of personal group psychoanalytic experience and frequent exposure to professional group workshops conducted under group-as-a-whole leadership formats are desirable.

Group dynamics need no longer be considered irrelevancies or distractions from the primary group therapeutic process. In many ways, they are central to a true group psychoanalytic treatment approach and should be repeatedly focused on by the group leader either directly, via group-as-a-whole interventions, or indirectly, via sophisticated individual-within-the-group interventions that address themselves to core aspects of the total group matrix.

REFERENCES

Anthony, E. J. There and then and here and now. *International Journal of Group Psychotherapy,* 1975, *25,* 163–167.

Appelbaum, S. A. An application of general systems concepts to psychoanalysis. *British Journal of Medical Psychology,* 1973, *46,* 115–122.

Borriello, J. F. Book review of *Experiences in groups and other papers* by W. R. Bion. *International Journal of Group Psychotherapy,* 1975, *25,* 348–357.

Durkin, H. *The group in depth.* New York: International Universities Press, 1964.

Durkin, J. E. *Group systems therapy: The structure of thinking and feeling.* Unpublished manuscript, Psychology Department, Lincoln University, 1974.

Ezriel, H. A psychoanalytic approach to group treatment. *British Journal of Medical Psychology,* 1950, *23,* 59–74.

Ezriel, H. The psychoanalytic session as an experimental situation. *British Journal of Medical Psychology,* 1951, *24,* 30–34.

Ezriel, H. Role of transference in psychoanalysis and other approaches to group treatment. *Acta Psychotherapeutica,* 1959, *7*(supplement), 101–116.

Foulkes, S. H. On group analysis. *International Journal of Psychoanalysis,* 1946, *27,* 46–51.

Foulkes, S. H. Some similarities and differences between psycho-analytic principles and group-analytic principles. *British Journal of Medical Psychology,* 1952, *25,* 229–234.

Foulkes, S. H. *Therapeutic group analysis.* New York: International Universities Press, 1964.

Foulkes, S. H., & Lewis, E. Group analysis. Studies in the treatment of groups on psycho-analytical lines. *British Journal of Medical Psychology,* 1944, *20,* 175–184.

Hartmann, H. Comments on the psychoanalytic theory of the ego. *Psychoanalytic Study of the Child* (Vol. 5). New York: International Universities Press, 1950.

Hartmann, H. *Ego psychology and the problem of adaptation.* New York: International Universities Press, 1961.

Kernberg, O. A systems approach to priority setting of interventions in groups. *International Journal of Group Psychotherapy,* 1975, *25,* 251–275.

Klein, M. Notes on some schizoid mechanisms. *International Journal of Psychoanalysis,* 1946, *27,* 99–110.

Klein, M. *Contributions to psychoanalysis 1921–1945.* London: Hogarth Press, 1948.

Lewin, K. *A dynamic theory of personality.* New York: McGraw-Hill, 1935.

Lewin, K. *The principles of topological psychology.* New York: McGraw-Hill, 1936.

Lieberman, M., Yalom, I., & Miles, M. *Encounter groups: First facts.* New York: Basic Books, 1973.

Nelson, M. C. Effect of paradigmatic technique on the psychic economy of borderline patients. *Psychiatry,* 1962, *25,* 119–134.

Ormont, L. R. Establishing the analytic contract in a newly formed therapeutic group. *British Journal of Medical Psychology,* 1964, *85,* 333–337.

Ormont, L. R. Acting in and the therapeutic contract. *International Journal of Group Psychotherapy,* 1969, *19,* 420–432.

Ormont, L. R. The treatment of pre-oedipal resistances in the group setting. *The Psychoanalytic Review,* 1974, *61,* 429–441.

Peck, H. B. Reflections on 25 years of the International Journal of Group Psychotherapy. *International Journal of Group Psychotherapy,* 1975, *25,* 153–157.

Rapaport, D. The autonomy of the ego. *Bulletin of the Menninger Clinic,* 1951, *15,* 113–123.

Rapaport, D. The theory of ego autonomy: A generalization. *Bulletin of the Menninger Clinic,* 1958, *22,* 13–35.

Rapaport, D. A historical survey of psychoanalytic ego psychology. *Psychological Issues* (Vol. 1, No. 1). New York: International Universities Press, 1959, 5–17.

Strean, H. The contribution of paradigmatic psychotherapy to psychoanalysis. *Psychoanalytic Review,* 1964, *51,* 365–381.

Swogger, G., Jr. *A systems approach to small groups—The group as a system.* Unpublished manuscript, Menninger Foundation, Topeka, Kansas, 1974.

Wolf, A. The psychoanalysis of groups. *American Journal of Psychotherapy,* 1949, *3,* 525–558.

Wolf, A. The psychoanalysis of groups. *American Journal of Psychotherapy,* 1950, *4,* 16–50.

Wolf, A., & Schwartz, E. K. The mystique of group dynamics. *Topical Problems Psychotherapy* (Vol. 2). New York: Korger, 1960.

Bibliography

Abraham, A. A model for exploring intra- and interindividual process in groups. *International Journal of Group Psychotherapy*, 1973, *23*, 3–22.

Appelbaum, S. A. The world in search of a leader: an application of group psychology to international relations. *British Journal of Medical Psychology*, 1967, *40*, 381–392.

Arsenian, J. An analysis of integral functions in small groups. *International Journal of Group Psychotherapy*, 1962, *12*, 421–434.

Asch, S. E. *Social psychology.* New York: Prentice-Hall, 1952.

Asch, S. E. Studies of independence and conformity. *Psychological Monographs*, 1956, *70*(9, Whole No. 416).

Bach, G. R. *Intensive group psychotherapy.* New York: Ronald Press, 1954.

Back, K. W. Influence through social communication. *Journal of Abnormal and Social Psychology*, 1951, *46*, 9–23.

Bales, R. F. *Interaction process analysis—a method of study of small groups.* Boston: Addison-Wesley, 1950.

Benne, K. D. Comments on training groups. In L. P. Bradford, J. R. Gibb, & K. D. Benne (Eds.), *T-group theory and laboratory method.* New York: Wiley, 1964.

Benne, K. D. History of the T-group in the laboratory setting. In L. P. Bradford, J. R. Gibb, & K. D. Benne (Eds.), *T-group theory and laboratory method.* New York: Wiley, 1964.

Bennis, W. G. Decision-making in groups. *Group Psychotherapy*, 1957, *10*, 287–298.

Bennis, W. G. Patterns and vicissitudes in T-group development. In L. P. Bradford, J. R. Gibb, & K. D. Benne (Eds.), *T-group theory and laboratory method.* New York: Wiley, 1964.

Bennis, W. G., Schein, E., Steele, F., & Berlew, D. (Eds.), *Interpersonal dynamics: essays and readings on human interaction* (Rev. ed.). Homewood, Ill: Dorsey, 1968.

Berger, I. Group psychotherapy training institutes: Group process, therapy, or resistance to learning? *International Journal of Group Psychotherapy*, 1967, *17*, 505–512.

Berman, L. Psychoanalysis and group psychotherapy. *Psychoanalytic Review,* 1950, *37,* 156–163.

Berman, L. A group psychotherapeutic technique for training in clinical psychology. *American Journal of Orthopsychiatry,* 1953, *22,* 322.

Bion, W. R. Group dynamics: A review. *International Journal of Psychoanalysis,* 1952, *33,* 235–247.

Bion, W. R. *Experiences in groups.* New York: Basic Books, 1959.

Bion, W. R. *Second thoughts: Selected papers in psychoanalysis.* London: Heinemann, 1967.

Blake, R. Studying group action. In L. P. Bradford, J. R. Gibb, & K. D. Benne (Eds.), *T-group theory and laboratory method.* New York: Wiley, 1964.

Bolman, L. *The effects of variations in educator behavior on the learning process in laboratory human relations education.* Unpublished doctoral dissertation, Yale University, 1968.

Bonner, H. *Group dynamics.* New York: Robert Press, 1959.

Borgatta, E., Bales, R., & Hare, P. *Small groups.* New York: Knopf, 1955.

Bradford, L. P. Membership and the learning process. In L. P. Bradford, J. R. Gibb, & K. D. Benne (Eds.), *T-group theory and laboratory method.* New York: Wiley, 1964.

Bradford, L. P., Gibb, J. R., & Benne, K. D. *T-group theory and laboratory method; Innovation in re-education.* New York: Wiley, 1964.

Bry, T. Acting out in group psychotherapy. *International Journal of Group Psychotherapy,* 1953, *3,* 42–48.

Bunker, D. R. Individual applications of laboratory training. *Journal of Applied Behavioral Science,* 1965, *1,* 131–148.

Burrow, T. The group method of analysis. *Psychoanalytical Review,* 1927, *14*(3), 268–280.

Campbell, J. P., & Dunette, M. D. Effectiveness of T-group experiences in managerial training and development. *Psychological Bulletin,* 1969, *70,* 73–103.

Cartwright, D. Emotional dimension of group life. In M. L. Reymert (Ed.), *International symposium on feelings and emotions.* New York: McGraw-Hill, 1950.

Cartwright, D., & Zander, A. (Eds.). *Group dynamics: Research and theory* (3rd ed.). New York: Harper, 1968.

Chapple, E. D., & Coon, C. G. The equilibrium of groups. In A. Hare, E. Borgatta, & R. Bales (Eds.), *Small groups: Studies in social interaction.* New York: Knopf, 1955.

Coch, L., & French, J. R. P. Overcoming resistance to change. *Human Relations,* 1948, *1,* 512–532.

Coffey, H. S. Socio- and psychological group process; Integrative concepts. *Journal of Social Issues,* 1952, *8,* 65–74.

Culbert, S. Trainer self-disclosure and member growth in two T groups. *Journal of Applied Behavioral Sciences,* 1968, *4,* 47–73.

Dreikurs, R. Group psychotherapy and the third revolution in psychiatry. *International Journal of Social Psychiatry,* 1955, *1,* (3), 23–32.

Durkin, H. E. *The group in depth.* New York: International Universities Press, 1964.

Durkin, H. E., & Glatzer, H. T. *Transference neurosis in group psychotherapy: The concept and the reality.* Unpublished manuscript, 1972.

Durkin, J. *Group Systems therapy: The structure of thinking and feeling.* Unpublished manuscript, Lincoln University, Pa., 1974.

Emerson, R. M. Deviation and rejection: An experimental replication. *American Sociological Review,* 1954, *19,* 688–693.

Ezriel, H. A psychoanalytical approach to group treatment. *British Journal of Medical Psychology,* 1950, *23,* 59–74.

Ezriel, H. The psycho-analytic session as an experimental situation. *British Journal of Medical Psychology,* 1951, *24,* 30–34.

Festinger, L. Informal social communication. *Psychological Review,* 1950, *57,* 271–292.

Festinger, L., Gerard, H. B., Hymovitch, B., Kelly, H. H., & Raven, B. The influence process in the presence of extreme deviants. *Human Relations,* 1952, *5,* 327–346.

Festinger, L., Schachter, S., & Back, K. *Social Pressures in Informal Groups.* New York: Harper, 1950.

Festinger, L., & Thibaut, J. Interpersonal communication in small groups. *Journal of Abnormal and Social Psychology,* 1951, *46,* 92–99.

Foulkes, S. H. *Therapeutic group analysis.* New York: International Universities Press, 1964.

Foulkes, S. H. On interpretation in group analysis. *International Journal of Group Psychotherapy,* 1968, *18,* 432–444.

French, J. R. P., Jr., Sherwood, J. J., & Bradford, D. L. Changes in self-identity in a management training conference. *Journal of Applied Behavioral Science,* 1966, *2,* 210–218.

Freud, S. [*Totem and taboo*] (A. A. Brill, Ed. and trans.). New York: Vintage Books, 1946. (Originally published, 1918.)

Freud, S. [*Group psychology and the analysis of the ego*] (J. Strachey, trans.). New York: Bantam, 1960. (Originally published, 1921.)

Fried, E. Some aspects of group dynamics and the analysis of transference and defenses. *International Journal of Group Psychotherapy,* 1965, *15,* 44–56.

Fried, E. The narcissistic cocoon: How it curbs and can be curbed. *Group Process,* 1971, *4*(1), 87–95.

Ganzarain, R. Group psychotherapy in the psychiatric training of medical students. *International Journal of Group Psychotherapy,* 1958, *8,* 137–153.

Ganzarain, R. Human relations and the teaching–learning process in medical school. *Journal of Medical Education,* 1966, *41,* 61–69.

Garwood, D. S. The significance and dynamics of sensitivity training programs. *International Journal of Group Psychotherapy,* 1967, *17,* 457–472.

Gassner, S., Gold, J., & Sandowsky, A. M. Changes in the phenomenal field as a result of human relations training. *Journal of Psychology,* 1964, *58,* 33–41.

Gerard, H. B. The effect of different dimensions of disagreement on the communication process in small groups. *Human Relations,* 1953, *6,* 249–271.

Gibb, J. Climate for trust formation. In L. P. Bradford, J. R. Gibb, & K. D. Benne (Eds.), *T-group theory and laboratory method.* New York: Wiley, 1964.

Gibbard, G. S., & Hartmann, J. J. The significance of utopian fantasies in small groups. *International Journal of Group Psychotherapy,* 1973, *23,* 125–147.

Gibbard, G. S., Hartman, J. J., & Mann, R. D. (Eds.). *Analysis of groups.* San Francisco: Jossey-Bass, 1974.

Glatzer, H. T. Working through in analytic group psychotherapy. *International Journal of Group Psychotherapy,* 1969, *19,* 292–306.

Goldberg, C. Peer influence in contemporary group psychotherapy. In L. R. Walberg & M. L. Aronson (Eds.), *Group therapy, 1975.* New York: Grune & Stratton, 1975.

Golombiowski, R. T., & Blumber, A. Sensitivity training in cousin groups. *Training and Development,* 1969, *23*(8), 18–22.

Grossman, D. *Two interview groups: Process and speculation.* Unpublished manuscript, Institute of Advanced Psychological Studies, Adelphi University, 1975.

Hare, A. P. *Handbook of small group research.* New York: Free Press, 1962.

Harris, G. T. Warren Bennis; A conversation. *Psychology Today,* Feb. 1970, 43–54; 63–71.

Harrison, R. Research on human relations training: Design and interpretation. *Journal of Applied Behavioral Sciences,* 1971, *7,* 71–85.

Harvey, O. J., & Consalvi, C. Status and conformity to pressures in informal groups. *Journal of Abnormal and Social Psychology,* 1960, *60,* 182–187.

Hempler-Turner, C. M. An existential learning "theory" and integration of T-group research. *Journal of Applied Behavioral Research,* 1966, *2,* 387–396.

Herbert, E. L., & Trist, E. L. The institution of an absent leader by a students' discussion group. *Human Relations,* 1953, *6,* 215–248.

Homans, G. C. *The human group.* New York: Harcourt, 1950.

Hulse, W. C. Applications and modifications of group psychotherapy in contemporary psychiatric and mental health practice. *International Journal of Group Psychotherapy,* 1963, *12,* 140–144.

Kadis, A. L. The alternate meeting in group psychotherapy. *American Journal of Psychotherapy,* 1956, *10,* 275–291.

Kadis, A. L., & Markowitz, M. Group psychotherapy. In L. E. Abt & B. F. Riess (Eds.), *Progress in clinical psychology* (Vol. 5). New York: Grune & Stratton, 1958.

Kadis, A. L., & Winick, C. (Eds.). *Group psychotherapy today,* New York: S. Karger, 1965.

Kaplan, H. I., & Sadock, B. J. (Eds.). *Comprehensive group psychotherapy.* Baltimore: Williams & Wilkins, 1971.

Kaplan, H. S., & Sager, C. J. (Eds.). *Progress in group and family therapy.* New York: Brunner/Mazel, 1972.

Kaplan, S. Therapy groups and training groups: Similarities and differences. *International Journal of Group Psychotherapy,* 1967, *16,* 473–504.

Kaplan, S., & Roman, M. S. Phases of development in adult therapy groups. *International Journal of Group Psychotherapy,* 1963, *13,* 10–26.

Kelley, H. H., & Shapiro, M. M. An experiment on conformity to group norms where conformity is detrimental to group achievement. *American Sociological Review,* 1954, *19,* 667–677.

Kelley, H. H., & Thibaut, J. Experimental studies of group problem solving and process. In G. Lindzey (Ed.), *Handbook of social psychology* (Vol. 2). Cambridge, Mass.: Addison-Wesley, 1954.

Kernberg, O. F. A systems approach to priority setting of interventions in groups. *International Journal of Group Psychotherapy*, 1975, *25*, 251–275.

Klein, M. Notes on some schizoid mechanisms. *International Journal of Psychoanalysis*, 1946, *27*, 99–110.

Koile, E., & Draeger, C. T-group member ratings of leader and self in a human relations laboratory. *The Journal of Psychology*, 1969, *72*, 11–20.

Kuehn, J. L., & Crinella, F. M. Sensitivity training: Interpersonal "overkill" and other problems. *American Journal of Psychiatry*, 1969, *126* (6), 840–844.

Lakin, M. Some ethical issues in sensitivity training. *American Psychologist*, 1969, *24*, 923–928.

Lewin, K. Forces behind food habits and methods of change. *Bulletin of the National Research Council*, 1943, *108*, 35–65.

Lewin, K. Frontiers in group dynamics: Concept, method and reality in social science; Social equilibrium and social change. *Human Relations*, 1947, *1*, 5–41.

Lewin, K. Group decision and social change. In T. M. Newcomb & E. L. Hartley (Eds.), *Readings in social psychology*. New York: Holt, 1947.

Lewin, K. *Resolving social conflicts*. New York: Harper, 1948.

Lewin, K. *Field theory in social science*. New York: Harper, 1951.

Lewin, K. Studies in group decision. In D. Cartwright & A. Zander (Eds.), *Group Dynamics: Research and Theory*, Evanston: Row, Peterson, 1953.

Lewin, K., Lippitt, R., & White, R. Patterns of aggressive behavior in experimentally created "social climates." *Journal of Social Psychology*, 1939, *10*, 271–299.

Lippitt, R. An experimental study of the effect of democratic and authoritarian group atmosphere. *University of Iowa Studies*, 1940, *16*(3), 43–108.

Lippitt, R., Polansky, N., & Rosen, S. The dynamics of power. *Human Relations*, 1952, *5*, 37–64.

Lohman, K., Zenger, J. H., & Weschler, I. R. Some perceptual changes during sensitivity training. *Journal of Educational Research*, 1959, *53*, 28–31.

Mann, R. D. The development of the member–trainer relationship in self-analytic groups. *Human Relations*, 1966, *19*, 85–115.

Money-Kyrle, R. Varieties of group formation. In G. Roheim (Ed.), *Psychoanalysis and the social sciences*. New York: International Universities Press, 1950.

Mullan, H., & Rosenbaum, M. *Group psychotherapy*. New York: Free Press, 1962.

Noy, P. Resistance to change in group psychotherapy. *International Journal of Group Psychotherapy*, 1967, *17*, 371–377.

Ormont, L. The preparation of patients for group psychoanalysis. *American Journal of Psychotherapy*, 1957, *9*, 841–848.

Ormont, L. The opening session in group psychoanalysis. *Acta Psychotherapy*, 1959, *7*, 288–294.

Ormont, L. Establishing the analytic contract in a newly formed therapeutic group. *British Journal of Medical Psychology*, 1962, *35*, 333–337.

Ormont, L. Acting in and the therapeutic contract. *International Journal of Group Psychotherapy*, 1969, *19*, 420–432.

Ormont, L. The use of the objective countertransference to resolve group resistance. *Group Process,* 1970-1971, *3*(2), 95-111.

Pino, C. *Interaction in sensitivity training groups.* Unpublished doctoral dissertation, Illinois Institute of Technology, 1969.

Psathas, G., & Hardert, R. Trainer interventions and normative patterns in the T-group. *Journal of Applied Behavioral Sciences,* 1966, *2,* 149-169.

Redl, F. Group emotion and leadership. *Psychiatry,* 1942, *5,* 573-596.

Redl, F. The phenomenon of contagion and "shock-effect" in group therapy. In K. R. Eissler (Ed.), *Searchlights on delinquency.* New York: International Universities Press, 1949.

Redl, F. Psychoanalysis and group therapy: A developmental point of view. *American Journal of Orthopsychiatry,* 1963, *35,* 135-147.

Rice, A. K. *Learning for leadership.* London: Tavistock, 1965.

Rioch, M. J. Group relations: Rationale and techniques. *International Journal of Group Psychotherapy,* 1970, *10,* 340-355.

Roseborough, M. E. Experimental studies of small groups. *Psychological Bulletin,* 1953, *50,* 275-303.

Rosenbaum, M., & Berger, M. M. (Eds.). *Group psychotherapy and group function: Selected readings.* New York: Basic Books, 1963.

Ruiz, P. On the perception of the "mother-group" in T-groups. *International Journal of Group Psychotherapy,* 1973, *22,* 488-491.

Saravay, S. M. Group psychology and the structural theory, a revised psychoanalytic model of group psychology. *Journal of the American Psychoanalytic Association,* 1975, *23,* 69-90.

Schachter, S. Deviation, rejection, and communication. *Journal of Abnormal and Social Psychology,* 1951, *46,* 190-207.

Scheidlinger, S. *Psychoanalysis and group behavior.* New York: Norton, 1952.

Scheidlinger, S. The concept of identification in group psychotherapy. *American Journal of Psychotherapy,* 1955, *9,* 661-672.

Scheidlinger, S. Group process in group psychotherapy. *American Journal of Psychotherapy,* 1960, *14,* 104-120; 346-363.

Scheidlinger, S. Identification, the sense of belonging and of identity in small groups. *International Journal of Group Psychotherapy,* 1964, *14,* 291-306.

Scheidlinger, S. The concept of empathy in group psychotherapy. *International Journal of Group Psychotherapy,* 1966, *16,* 413-424.

Schilder, P. Introductory remarks on groups. *Journal of Social Psychology,* 1940, *12,* 83-100.

Schindler, W. Family pattern in group formation and therapy. *International Journal of Group Psychotherapy,* 1951, *1,* 100-105.

Schindler, W. The "group personality" concept in group psychotherapy. *International Journal of Group Psychotherapy,* 1952, *2,* 311-315.

Schindler, W. The role of the mother in group psychotherapy. *International Journal of Group Psychotherapy,* 1966, *16,* 198-200.

Schutz, W. C. What makes groups productive? *Human Relations,* 1955, *8,* 429.

Schwartz, E. K., & Wolf, A. On countertransference in group therapy. In B. F. Riess (Ed.), *New directions in mental health* (Vol. 2). New York: Grune & Stratton, 1962.

Semrad, E., & Arsenian, J. The use of group process in teaching group dynamics. *American Journal of Psychiatry*, 1951, *108*, 358.

Semrad, E. V., & Arsenian, J. *On the concept of billets—the functioning of small groups*. Paper presented to Group Psychology Project, Harvard Medical School, 1958.

Semrad, E. V., Arsenian, J., & Standish, C. T. Experiences with small groups in teaching group psychology. *Group Psychotherapy*, 1957, *10*, 191–197.

Shapiro, D., & Zinberg, N. E. A group approach in the contexts of therapy and education. In N. E. Zinberg (Ed.), *Psychiatry and medical practice in a general hospital.* New York: International Universities Press, 1964.

Shepard, H. A. Explorations in observant participation. In L. P. Bradford, J. R. Gibb, & K. D. Benne (Eds.), *T-group theory and laboratory method.* New York: Wiley, 1964.

Shepard, H. A., & Bennis, W. G. A theory of training through the use of group methods. *Human Relations*, 1956, *9*, 403–414.

Sherif, M. *The psychology of social norms.* New York: Harper, 1936.

Sherif, M. Consistency in intergroup relations. *Journal of Social Issues*, 1941, *5*(3), 12–37.

Sherif, M. Formation of social norms: The experimental paradigm. In H. Proshansky, & B. Seidenberg (Eds.), *Basic studies in social psychology.* New York: Holt, 1965.

Slater, P. E. *Microcosm.* New York: Wiley, 1966.

Slavson, S. R. *An introduction to group therapy.* New York: Commonwealth Fund and Harvard University Press, 1943.

Slavson, S. R. (Ed.). *The practice of group therapy.* New York: International Universities Press, 1947.

Slavson, S. R. *Analytic group psychotherapy with children, adolescents, and adults.* New York: Columbia University Press, 1950.

Slavson, S. R. *Analytic group psychotherapy.* New York: Columbia University Press, 1952.

Slavson, S. R. *The fields of group psychotherapy.* New York: International Universities Press, 1956.

Slavson, S. R. The nature and treatment of acting out in group psychotherapy. *International Journal of Group Psychotherapy*, 1956, *6*, 3–26.

Slavson, S. R. *A textbook in analytic group psychotherapy.* New York: International Universities Press, 1964.

Slavson, S. The anatomy and clinical applications of group interaction. *International Journal of Group Psychotherapy*, 1969, *19*, 3–15.

Spanjaard, J. Transference neurosis and psychoanalytic group psychotherapy. *International Journal of Group Psychotherapy*, 1959, *9*, 31–42.

Spotnitz, H. A psychoanalytic view of resistance in groups. *International Journal of Group Psychotherapy*, 1952, *2*, 3–10.

Spotnitz, H. *The couch and the circle.* New York: Knopf, 1961.

Stein, A. The superego and group interaction in group psychotherapy. *International Journal of Group Psychotherapy*, 1956, *5*, 495–504.

Stein, A. Some aspects of the dynamics of group therapy with special reference to the function of patient leaders and spokesman. *International Journal of Group Psychotherapy*, 1961, *10*, 267–274.

Stock, D. A survey of research on T groups. In L. P. Bradford, J. R. Gibb, & K. D. Benne (Eds.), *T-group theory and laboratory method.* New York: Wiley, 1964.

Strodtbeck, F. L. The case for the study of small groups. *American Sociological Review,* 1954, *19,* 651–657.

Strodtbeck, F. L., & Hare, A. P. Bibliography of small group research (1906–1954). *Sociometry,* 1954, *17,* 107–178.

Sutherland, J. D. Notes on psychoanalytic group therapy. I. Therapy and training. *Psychiatry,* 1952, *15,* 111–117.

Swogger, G. A. *A systems approach to small groups—the group as system.* Unpublished manuscript, Menninger Foundation, Topeka, Kansas, 1974.

Thelen, H., & Dickerman, W. Stereotypes and the growth of groups. *Educational Leadership,* February 1949, 309–316.

Underwood, W. J. Evaluation of laboratory method training. *Training Directors Journal,* 1965, 19(5), 34–40.

Warringer, C. K. Groups are real: A reaffirmation. *American Sociological Review,* 1956, *21,* 549–554.

Wender, L. The dynamics of group psychotherapy and its application. *Journal of Nervous Mental Diseases,* 1936, *84,* 54–60.

Wender, L. Group psychotherapy. In J. C. Moreno (Ed.), *Group psychotherapy—a symposium.* Beacon, N.Y.: Beacon Press, 1945.

Wender, L. The psychodynamics of group psychotherapy. *International Journal of Group Psychotherapy,* 1963, *12,* 134–139.

Weschler, I. R., Massarik, F., & Tannenbaum, R. The self in process: A sensitivity training emphasis. In I. R. Weschler & E. H. Schein (Eds.), *Issues in training.* Washington: National Training Laboratories, 1962.

Whitaker, D. S., & Lieberman, M. A. *Psychotherapy through the group process.* New York: Atherton, 1964.

Whitman, R. M. Psychodynamic principles underlying T-group processes. In L. P. Bradford, J. R. Gibb, & K. D. Benne (Eds.), *T-group theory and laboratory method.* New York: Wiley, 1964.

Whitman, R. M., & Stock, D. The group focal conflict. *Psychiatry,* 1958, *21,* 269–276.

Wolf, A. The psychoanalysis of groups. *American Journal of Psychotherapy,* 1949, *3,* 525–558; 1950, *4,* 16–50.

Wolf, A. The psychoanalysis of groups. In M. Rosenbaum & M. Berger (Eds.), *Group psychotherapy and group function.* New York: Basic Books, 1963.

Wolf, A., & Schwartz, E. K. The psychoanalysis of groups: Implications for education. *International Journal of Social Psychiatry,* 1955, *1,* 17–24.

Wolf, A., & Schwartz, E. K. *Psychoanalysis in groups.* New York: Grune & Stratton, 1962.

Yalom, I. D. *Theory and practice of group psychotherapy.* New York: Basic Books, 1970.

Author Index

Subject Index

Transference (*continued*)
    248–251, 260, 261, 266, 274, 276,
      294, 295, 298, 300, 324, 332, 333
  and groups, 31, 40
Transference level, 266
Translation, 262, 263
Triad, 40, 41

Unconscious, language of, 28
Uniformity, group standards of, 12
Utopian fantasy, 295

Valency, 129–131
Values
  common, and groups, 8
  personal synthesis of, 14
  social support for, and groups, 8

Western electric study, 5
Women, separated, 305–316
Work group, 5, 123, 124, 212, 331